NEW DIRECTIONS IN GERMAN STUDIES
Vol. 21

I0593006

Volumes in the series:

Stereotype and Destiny in Arthur Schnitzler's Prose

Five Psycho-Sociological Readings

Marie Kolkenbrock

BLOOMSBURY ACADEMIC
LONDON • NEW YORK • OXFORD • NEW DELHI • SYDNEY

BLOOMSBURY ACADEMIC
Bloomsbury Publishing Plc
50 Bedford Square, London, WC1B 3DP, UK
1385 Broadway, New York, NY 10018, USA

BLOOMSBURY, BLOOMSBURY ACADEMIC and the Diana logo are
trademarks of Bloomsbury Publishing Plc

First published 2018
Paperback edition first published 2019

Cover design: Andrea Federle-Bucsi
Cover images © Wien Museum and © ÖNB/Wien

Bloomsbury Publishing Plc does not have any control over, or responsibility for,
any third-party websites referred to or in this book. All internet addresses given
in this book were correct at the time of going to press. The author and publisher
regret any inconvenience caused if addresses have changed or sites have ceased
to exist, but can accept no responsibility for any such changes.

A catalogue record for this book is available from the British Library.

A catalog record for this book is available from the Library of Congress.

ISBN: HB: 978-1-5013-3096-4
PB: 978-1-5013-5732-9
ePDF: 978-1-5013-3098-8
eBook: 978-1-5013-3097-1

Series: New Directions in German Studies

Typeset by Integra Software Services Pvt. Ltd.

To find out more about our authors and books visit
www.bloomsbury.com and sign up for our newsletters.

Contents

Acknowledgements

Andrew Webber has advised me during the research for this book with knowledge and insight, utmost generosity of time and support, and also with kindness. I am deeply thankful for his mentoring, which is always motivating and inspiring, but never restrictive or determining. Moreover, I would like to thank Michael Minden and Robert Vilain for their critical reading, insightful comments, and support, as well as Peter-André Alt, Dagmar Lorenz, Eric L. Santner, and Norbert Christian Wolf for their stimulating input and advice. Two anonymous reviewers gave extremely nuanced and productive feedback, for which I am grateful. The series editor Imke Meyer has provided invaluable guidance throughout the publication process. I would like to thank her, as well as publisher for literary studies Haaris Naqvi, editorial assistant Katherine de Chant, copy-editor Anna Carroll, and everyone else at Bloomsbury Academic, who all have been an absolute pleasure to work with.

The full-cost scholarship from Gates Cambridge Scholarships allowed me to undertake the main research for this book. I revised the final version of the manuscript while being supported by the Ludwig Boltzmann Institute for the History and Theory of Biography, Vienna, and the Schröder Fund Cambridge. Some passages in Chapters Three and Five draw on my article 'Gothic Infections', published in *Modern Language Review* 113.1 (2018), 150–170. I would like to thank *MLR* for the permission to reuse this material. I also would like to thank the Syndics of Cambridge University Library for the permission to cite from their archival sources.

More warm thanks go to the following people, who also had an immense (direct and indirect) influence on the progress of this book: Mirjam Berg, Andreas Gehrlach, Lukas Held, Charlotte Lee, Ina Linge, Annja Neumann, Annie Ring, Astrid Schmidt, Lizzie Stewart, Andrea Wald, and Erica Wickerson for helpful comments and encouragement. Alphia Klingenstein for a regular supply of German bread and home-made jam. Karoline Kuchenbäcker and Nadja Tschentscher for sharp debates and unwavering care. Steve Ruiz for letting me talk through my ideas and for making me feel at home wherever we are.

I would like to dedicate this book to the memory of my three parents: Jutta Kolkenbrock-Netz, Maria Klingenstein, and Hansjörg Kolkenbrock.

List of Abbreviations

Full bibliographical references to the texts can be found in the Bibliography at the end of this book.

AT   *Andreas Thameyers letzter Brief* (Andreas Thameyer's Last Letter)
CUL   Cambridge University Library, Schnitzler's manuscripts
E   *Fräulein Else* (Miss Else)
F   *Die Fremde* (The Stranger)
FiF   *Flucht in die Finsternis* (Flight into Darkness)
NL   *Das neue Lied* (The New Song)
SL   *Das Schicksal des Freiherrn von Leisenbohg* (Baron Leisenbohg's Destiny)
T   *Traumnovelle* (Dream Story)
W   *Die Weissagung* (The Prophecy)
WiF   *Der Weg ins Freie* (Road into the Open)

Introduction

Viennese Types and Habsburg Nostalgia

Iconographical representations of so-called 'Viennese types' were immensely popular in *fin de siècle* Vienna. Serial photographs of street vendors, laundry girls, knife grinders, and other characters deemed typical for the Viennese cityscape appeared in journalistic feuilletons, on postcards, and commercial advertisements.[1] The two images on the cover of this book, *Polnischer Jude* (Polish Jew, 1887) and *Wäschermädel* (Laundry Girl, 1886), are taken from one of the most prominent representatives of this visual trend: Otto Schmidt's commercial photography series *Wiener Typen* (Viennese Types, 1873–*c.*1878). The photographs by Schmidt and others referred back to an older iconographical tradition of 'Viennese types' that emerged in the second half of the eighteenth century in the form of so-called *Kaufrufe* (vendors' calls): little porcelain figurines and graphical etchings depicting street vendors in their traditional attire and with their typical attributes. The modern medium of photography appears to sit in tension with the anti-modern nostalgia these images evoked in the late nineteenth century. In a time of rather radical social change, brought about through processes of urbanization, industrialization, and migration, these 'Viennese types' were meant to embody an idealized urban legend of 'Alt-Wien' (old Vienna) – something that was already almost completely lost in modernization, but still palpable enough to be remembered and cherished.[2] This corresponds to the idealized image of the Habsburg Empire that Claudio Magris famously dubbed the 'Habsburg myth' in 1963.[3]

Many of his contemporaries saw Schnitzler's writings as the literary pendant to this form of Viennese nostalgia: he was known for his

---

1   See Kos, Wolfgang (2013), 'Einleitung,' *Wiener Typen: Klischees und Wirklichkeit*, ed. by Wolfgang Kos, Vienna: Christian Brandstätter (= Exhibition Catalogue of *Wiener Typen: Klischees und Wirklichkeit – 387. Sonderausstellung des Wien Museums*, Wien Museum Karlsplatz, 25 April – 6 October 2013), 14–23, 14.
2   See Ponstingl, Michael (2013), 'Otto Schmidts Spektakel der Wiener Typen,' *Wiener Typen*, 192–201, 192.
3   See Magris, Claudio (2000), *Der Habsburgische Mythos in der österreichischen Literatur*, Vienna: Zsolnay.

literary depiction of Viennese social types, most notoriously for that of his 'süße Mädels' (sweet girls), and sentimentality and backwardness were the most common verdicts uttered by literary critics at the beginning of the twentieth century. The German literary critic Alfred Biese for example described Schnitzler's literature in his *Deutsche Literaturgeschichte* as an 'Anhauch von Sentimentalität und Mystik, endlich aber einer Mischung von parfümierter Erotik, Frivolität und altwienerischer Behaglichkeit' (a breath of sentimentality and mysticism, but finally a mix of fragrant eroticism, frivolity and old-Viennese cosiness).[4] This reputation of Schnitzler as the author of a 'versunkene Welt' (sunken world)[5] would become even more prominent during the years of the First World War and, much to his dismay, would not cease to pursue him until the end of his life.

Although Schnitzler indeed remains well known for his notorious representation of such Viennese social types as the *süße Mädel* (sweet girl), scholarship has long since exonerated him from his reputation of backwardness. He has been established as the key critical observer of Viennese bourgeois society.[6] Scholars have convincingly argued that, rather than participating in the perpetuation of the Habsburg myth, Schnitzler 'pitilessly dissected its corpse'.[7] My suggestion is, accordingly, that rather than indulging the longing for old-Viennese cosiness through the representation of typecast figures, Schnitzler's prose reveals the psycho-sociological mechanisms behind this form of nostalgia.

---

4   Biese, Alfred (1913), *Deutsche Literaturgeschichte: Dritter Band: Von Hebbel bis zur Gegenwart*, Munich: Becksche Verlagsbuchhandlung Oskar Beck.

5   Schnitzler, Arthur and Georg Brandes (1956), *Ein Briefwechsel*, ed. by Kurt Bergel, Bern: Francke, 146.

6   See Swales, Martin (1971), *Arthur Schnitzler: A Critical Study*, Oxford: Oxford University Press, 280; Janz, Rolf-Peter and Klaus Laermann (1977), *Arthur Schnitzler: Zur Diagnose des Wiener Bürgertums im Fin de siècle*, Stuttgart: Metzler; Fliedl, Konstanze (2005), *Arthur Schnitzler*, Stuttgart: Reclam, 70–72; Gay, Peter (2001), *Schnitzler's Century: The Making of Middle-Class Culture, 1815–1914*, New York: Norton; Lorenz, Dagmar (2003), 'The Self as Process in an Era of Transition: Competing Paradigms of Personality and Character in Schnitzler's Works,' *A Companion to the Works of Arthur Schnitzler*, ed. by Dagmar C. G. Lorenz, Rochester, NY: Camden House, 129.

7   Le Rider, Jacques (1993), *Modernity and the Crises of Identity: Culture and Society in Fin-de-siècle Vienna*, New York: Continuum, 17. Schnitzler's precise analytical gaze has been plausibly linked to his professional medical background. See e.g. Boetticher, Dirk von (1999), '*Meine Werke sind lauter Diagnosen': Über die ärztliche Dimension im Werk Arthur Schnitzlers*, Heidelberg: Winter; Herzog, Hillary Hope (2003), '"Medizin ist eine Weltanschauung": On Schnitzler's Medical Writings,' *A Companion to the Works of Arthur Schnitzler*, ed. by Dagmar C. G. Lorenz, Rochester, NY: Camden House, 227–241; Müller-Seidel, Walter (1997), *Arztbilder im Wandel. Zum literarischen Werk Arthur Schnitzlers*, Munich: Verlag der Bayerischen Akademie der Wissenschaften). Through the example of

If the sentimentalism of the 'Viennese types' photographs reso-
nated with large parts of the Viennese bourgeoisie, it is because they
addressed a need for individualization through the de-individualizing
typecasting of 'otherness'. In this way, they contributed to the romantic myth of the Habsburg monarchy as a stable social order, in which
everyone had a legitimate place within a pluralistic society. Particularly
in their seriality, these photographs create a vision of social harmony.
The types depicted in them are almost exclusively representatives of
the lower social classes, who had to live under often extremely precarious conditions. This precarity, however, is not addressed in the images.
The implied spectator's gaze of these photographs was therefore
directed 'von oben nach unten' (downwards).[8] While bourgeois portrait photography focused on the individual self, these 'Viennese types'
remained – as the title indicates – de-individualized in their typological
representation. Representing a social 'otherness', they were thus meant
to produce a feeling of difference to the bourgeois individual, which in
turn provided a reassuring sense of individuality for the latter.[9] In this
way, the 'Viennese types' worked to stabilize the power structures of a
social order, which was increasingly under pressure.

By the time of Jacques Le Rider's (1993, French original 1990) fundamental study *Modernity and the Crises of Identity: Culture and Society in
Fin-de-siècle Vienna*, the terms 'Vienna' and '1900' had become unthink-
able without the immediate association of 'crisis'.[10] That this is also the
tone of the key themes of Schnitzler, one of the key figures of the *Jung
Wien* (Young Vienna) group, is not very surprising: from 'epochale Lebenskrisen' (epoch-making life crises),[11] to the 'Krise des Gedächtnisses'
(crisis of memory),[12] or the 'Krise des männlichen Blicks' (crisis of the

---

Schnitzler's play *Professor Bernhardi* (1912), Annja Neumann has recently shown
that Schnitzler's 'dissecting practices' go beyond his analytical observation of
Viennese society, but inform his writing practice on several levels. On the one
hand, Neumann identifies medical topographies through which the dramatic
space is negotiated in the play; on the other, Schnitzler's unpublished early drafts
reveal the author's anatomical approach to his own process of writing, editing,
and re-writing. See Neumann, Annja (2016), 'Schnitzler's Anatomy Lesson:
Medical Topographies in Professor Bernhardi,' *Jahrbuch Literatur und Medizin*,
Bd. 8, ed. by Christa Janson and Florian Steger, Heidelberg: Winter, 31–60.

8   Kos, 'Einleitung,' 15.
9   Ponstingl, 'Otto Schmidts Spektakel der Wiener Typen'.
10 Le Rider, *Modernity and the Crises of Identity*.
11 Lukas, Wolfgang (1996), *Das Selbst und das Fremde: Epochale Lebenskrisen und ihre
    Lösung im Werk Arthur Schnitzlers*, Munich: Fink.
12 Fliedl, Konstanze (1997), *Arthur Schnitzler: Poetik der Erinnerung*, Vienna,
    Cologne, Weimar: Böhlau.

male gaze),[13] to name just a few examples, the crisis of modernity at the beginning of the twentieth century proves to be inextricably linked to Schnitzler and his literature. Rather than giving yet another account of the well-researched subject of crisis in Vienna 1900 and Schnitzler's writings, this study focuses on the way in which Schnitzler's prose engages with the presence of forces that deny the existence of crisis and that aim to contain its subversive potential. These forces find their expression in the 'Viennese types': by dint of the de-individualizing typologization of the 'other', these photographs provided the bourgeois subject with a reassurance of their own legitimacy in a harmonious social order. In this way, they offered comfort in the face of one of '[d]ie tiefsten Probleme des modernen Lebens' (the deepest problems of modern life), as identified by Georg Simmel,[14] in his essay *Die Großstädte und das Geistesleben* (The Metropolis and Mental Life, 1903): 'dem Anspruch des Individuums, die Selbständigkeit und Eigenart seines Daseins gegen die Übermächte der Gesellschaft [...] zu bewahren' (the demand of the individual to maintain the independence and individuality of his existence against the sovereign powers of society).

My claim in this book is that the coping mechanism of 'stereotype and destiny' in Schnitzler's prose addresses precisely this difficult relationship between individual and society in the age of modernity. Schnitzler's characters often display a striving for a somewhat paradoxical reassurance: while they long to be assured of their position within the social order, they also want to be certain of what one could call their individual 'essence'. I call this paradoxical, because it implies the desire to be considered both as normal *and* special – thus to belong to the norm and to exceed it at the same time. The interrelation between stereotypes and destiny is closely linked to this paradoxical conflict: in short, stereotypes are ordering tools,[15] which stabilize the position of the self within the norm by manifesting the difference of the stereotyped 'other'.[16] The belief in the higher power of destiny promises an individually laid out path of life, thus reassuring the subject of his or her singular identity. My readings in this study will show that the way in which Schnitzler's characters invoke their own metaphysical destiny

---

13 Meyer, Imke (2010), *Männlichkeit und Melodram: Arthur Schnitzlers erzählende Schriften*, Würzburg: Königshausen & Neumann, 11.
14 Simmel, Georg (1995), 'Die Großstädte und das Geistesleben,' *Gesamtausgabe*, ed. by Otthein Rammstedt, vol. 7: *Aufsätze und Abhandlungen 1901–1908*, vol. 1, ed. by Rüdiger Kramme, Angela Rammstedt, and Otthein Rammstedt, Frankfurt a. M.: Suhrkamp, 116–131, 6.
15 Dyer, Richard (2002), *The Matter of Images: Essays on Representation*, London: Routledge, 12.
16 Gilman, Sander L. (1985), *Difference and Pathology: Stereotypes of Sexuality, Race, and Madness*, Ithaca, London: Cornell University Press, 17.

intersects with the formation of their perception through stereotypical representations of 'otherness'. 'Stereotype' and 'destiny' are forces that are counter-critical in both senses of the word: the invocation of destiny as well as the practice of stereotyping work to contain the destabilizing effects of crisis by reassuring the protagonists of their privileged social position. And, in this way, they are prevented from developing a critical consciousness of the social and cultural conditions that surround and determine them. In an often almost tragic-comical way, they remain loyal to a system that has begun to disintegrate, while they are incapable of showing solidarity with those whom this system rejects, excludes and dominates. Therefore, the recognition of this coping mechanism is not only crucial when one tries to understand the concept of destiny in Schnitzler's prose texts, but also when situating these texts in the context of modernism and its central questions concerning identity, subjectivity, and power. In order to make this clear, however, it is first necessary to contextualize Simmel's remark in the broader theoretical context of modernity and modernism.

The Ambivalent Problem of Modernity

Le Rider makes an interesting distinction between 'modernism' and 'modernity':[17] he understands 'modernism' as a dogmatic trust in 'modern ideas' such as in the idea of inevitable scientific, technological, and cultural progress, the triumph of reason, and the sovereignty and autonomy of the modern Enlightened subject. 'Modernity', in turn, is for him 'a way of living, thinking and creating which was not afraid of change and innovation, but still kept a critical awareness of modernization; it expressed itself in aesthetic and theoretical language and kept its distance from "modernism"'. This differentiation is extremely useful when discussing the way in which writers and artists engaged with the social, political, economic, and cultural processes of modernization. It allows us to draw a demarcating line between anti-modern (i.e. conservative, traditionalist, nostalgic etc.) tendencies on the one hand, and a more critical questioning of the fundamental ideas of modernization (progress, autonomy, reason etc. – or what Le Rider defines as 'modernism') on the other. The latter, rather than being 'anti-modern', resonates more with a form of thinking that would later be known as 'post-modernist'. And indeed, Le Rider argues that post-modernism, with its critical questioning of Enlightenment ideas and doubts regarding reason and reasonable individuals, 'renewed and radicalized the activities of modernity'.[18]

---

17 Le Rider, *Modernity and the Crises of Identity*, 27.
18 Le Rider, *Modernity and the Crises of Identity*, 28.

I will refrain from using 'modernism' and 'modernity' in the way Le Rider suggests, as I find that most critics refer to the critical engagement with modernization, particularly through aesthetic devices, as 'modernism'.[19] Thus, when I refer to Schnitzler as a modernist writer, I am following this convention and am not suggesting that his works display a dogmatic belief in progress and reason. However, the link that Le Rider identifies between post-modernist thought and the critical problematization of modern trust in the Enlightened subject will prove helpful to my analysis of Schnitzler's prose. Le Rider argues that more than other European centres of modernism, Vienna 1900 can be understood as a phenomenon of post-modernism *avant la lettre*, because its socio-economical, political, and cultural processes of modernization were accompanied by a particularly critical awareness of the problematic insecurities engendered by these processes.[20] The trust in inevitable progress and the triumph of reason and in the sovereignty of the enlightened subject was unsettled by feelings of alienation, estrangement, and objectification in all areas of life. On the one hand, the modernization of society was pushed forward in the name of reason and was thus based on the idea of the rational subject. On the other, this very modernization led to disciplining practices being applied to the individual, which undermined the sense of individual reason and autonomy. This sheds light on Simmel's diagnosis of the individual's struggle for independence from the sovereign powers of society, and has indeed been established as the 'ambivalente Grundproblem der Moderne' (ambivalent central problem of modernity).[21]

This ambivalence is also a central concern in the work of Eric L. Santner, who has described it in his study *My Own Private Germany* as 'the central paradox of modernity: that the subject is solicited by a will to autonomy in the name of the very community that is thereby undermined, whose very substance thereby passes over into the subject'.[22] Santner refers here to the way secular societies of the post-Enlightenment era are based on the idea of the autonomous subject, while the functioning of the same societies depends on the submission of individuals to societal norms and regulated performances. Therefore, too radical an understanding of autonomy threatens the social order. In order to maintain the idea of the enlightened and autonomous subject, the

19 See Gay, *Schnitzler's Century*; Santner, Eric L. (2011), *The Royal Remains: The People's Two Bodies and the Endgames of Sovereignty*, Chicago: University of Chicago Press, xi.
20 Le Rider, *Modernity and the Crises of Identity*, 37.
21 Goltschnigg, Dietmar (2009), '*Fröhliche Apokalypse' und nostalgische Utopie: 'Österreich als besonderer Fall der modernen Welt*,' ed. by Charlotte Grolleg-Edler Vienna, Berlin: Lit Verlag, 1.
22 Santner, Eric L. (1996), *My Own Private Germany*, Princeton, NJ: Princeton University Press, 145.

community, i.e. the social order, has to 'pass over into the subject', thus to be fully internalized and accepted as natural essence on the one hand or appear freely chosen on the other. Seen in this light, we can recognize how this central problem of modernity does indeed extend to the concerns of post-modernist thought. The difficult question of what it means to be a subject, which has been at the heart of post-modernist thinking, seems to be already addressed in Simmel's remark. As Judith Butler writes, the subject 'is a figure of autonomy',[23] thus based on the very assumption that it acts independently, but at the same time becoming a subject means being subjected to a social order, which in turn is produced and reproduced through its subjects: 'This is not simply to act according to a set of rules, but to embody those rules in the course of action and reproduce those rules in embodied rituals of action'.[24] If subjectivity is, then, the 'lived and imaginary experience of the subject',[25] the originality and autonomy of this experience is called into question.

This resonates intimately with Schnitzler's conception of subjectivity in both his literary and non-fiction writings. 'Es ist immer wieder beschämend', he writes in one of his aphorisms, 'in einem eigenen Erlebnis, dessen Einzigartigkeit man eben zu empfinden glaubte, das hundertmal Dagewesene, den typischen Kern zu erkennen' (It is, time and time again, embarrassing to recognize in your own experience a typical core, to recognize it as something that has happened a hundred times before, even though it felt unique and original just a moment ago).[26] The iterative notion of 'immer wieder' (time and time again) enhances and multiplies the typicality of that which has happened a hundred times before and evokes an endless spiral of the repetition and recognition of experience, reminiscent of Butler's repetitive embodied rituals of action. In an accordingly repetitive manner, Schnitzler's literary writings, too, reveal this insecurity concerning the possibility of original experiences and their individual expression and communication. This raises the question of the subject's room for agency in the process of subjection.

Butler's theorization of power that is reproduced through the re-iterative performances of the subject correlates with the concept that the French sociologist Pierre Bourdieu has called 'social destinies'.[27] I will

---

23 Butler, Judith (1997), *The Psychic Life of Power: Theories in Subjection*, Stanford: Stanford University Press.
24 Butler, *The Psychic Life of Power*, 119.
25 Butler, *The Psychic Life of Power*, 122.
26 Schnitzler, Arthur (1985), *Aphorismen und Notate: Gedanken über Leben und Kunst*, Leipzig and Weimar: Gustav Kiepenheuer, 33–34.
27 Bourdieu, Pierre (1992), *Language and Symbolic Power: The Economy of Linguistic Exchanges*, ed. by John B. Thompson, Cambridge: Polity Press, 122.

argue in the following five readings that this Bourdieusian concept is significant for the understanding of the function of invocation of the higher power of destiny in Schnitzler's prose. Bourdieu describes how social rites and institutions carry out a 'performative magic',[28] which assigns individuals their social statuses and roles, and in this way take on a fate-like character:

> 'Become what you are': that is the principle behind the performative magic of all acts of institution. The essence assigned through naming and investiture is, literally, a fatum. [...] All social destinies, positive or negative, by consecration or stigma, are equally fatal – by which I mean mortal – because they enclose those whom they characterize within the limits that are assigned to them and that they are made to recognize.[29]

Bourdieu speaks here of the institution of identity that creates a certain kind of social essence, which imposes on a person not only a name, but also certain rules of behaviour: 'It is to *signify* to someone what he is and how he should conduct himself as a consequence'.[30] This is obviously the case in more or less openly constructed social roles and symbolic functions, as for example when one is assigned a title of nobility or appointed to an academic position, but also at much earlier points in life, for example, as Butler has analyzed, when one is assigned one's gender.[31]

In order to work, all these assignments of social essence require the reiteration of certain social performances through which they become realized and create the social facts that they describe: 'Social essence is the set of those social attributes and attributions produced by the act of institution as a solemn act of categorization which tends to produce what it designates'.[32] When the social order is perceived as natural and legitimate and thus unquestionable, these performances will feel either naturally given or freely chosen. However, when the social order is threatened by a state of crisis, the ordering tools which make that order appear self-evident become 'visible', and as such weakened in their power to naturalize given social facts. In this case, the compulsion to repeat the performances linked to one's social role or symbolic function becomes palpable and can be perceived as coercive. Santner argues

---

28 Bourdieu, *Language and Symbolic Power*, 122.
29 Bourdieu, *Language and Symbolic Power*, 122.
30 Bourdieu, *Language and Symbolic Power*, 120.
31 See Butler, Judith (1993), *Bodies That Matter: On the Discursive Limits of 'Sex,'* London, New York: Routledge, xii.
32 Bourdieu, *Language and Symbolic Power*, 121.

that the consciousness of critical upheaval at the end of the nineteenth century is such a crisis of 'investiture': the normative pressures of social destiny create a 'loss of distance to some obscene and malevolent presence that appears to have a direct hold on one's inner parts'.[33] In other words, the fatal character of one's social destiny begins to feel like a heteronomous force. Such a crisis of investiture is therefore ultimately a threat to the perceived legitimacy of the social order and its power structures. I will show in my readings that the invocation of a metaphysical destiny in Schnitzler's prose can be seen as a coping mechanism for this feeling of being coerced by social destiny. The invocation of the higher power of destiny therefore works to contain a threatening loss of legitimacy of the social order.

As Santner argues in *The Royal Remains*, the modern shift from royal sovereignty to popular sovereignty opens up a 'symbolic space' at the foundation of the social order.[34] Building on Ernst Kantorowicz's notion of the king's two bodies, Santner suggests that the king's second body, 'seen to embody a "vertical" link to transcendence – to divine authorization – comes to be dispersed "horizontally" among the "people"'.[35] The central question of modernity is then how the sense of legitimacy of social orders can be maintained when this foundational authorization is missing. The risk of 'exposure to the radical contingency of the forms of life that constitute the space of meaning within which human life unfolds' creates an *'ontological vulnerability'* (italics in original).[36] In order to minimize this vulnerability, cultures apply 'defence mechanisms'[37] against the risk of this exposure. In the readings in this study, I argue that the practice of stereotyping and the invocation of the higher power of destiny emerge as precisely such a defence mechanism in Schnitzler's prose.

Destiny as Defence Mechanism

As the invocation of a higher power of destiny engenders a structure of pre-determined inevitability, it may be well suited to fend off any exposure to the 'radical contingency' of the social order. Of course, it sits in tension with the post-Enlightenment conceptions of autonomy and individual responsibility. In the increasingly secularized era of turn-of-the-century Vienna, speaking of destiny may therefore appear almost like an anachronism, and yet, it proves to be a returning concept in Schnitzler's prose. However, while the characters invoke their des-

---

33 Santner, *My Own Private Germany*, xii.
34 Santner, *The Royal Remains*, xxi.
35 Santner, *The Royal Remains*, xii.
36 Santner, *The Royal Remains*, 5–6.
37 Santner, *The Royal Remains*, 6.

tiny as some form of higher power, there is a striking lack of reference to any religious framework: the belief in destiny appears to have become generally detached from the belief in a divine will. This resonates with Hermann Broch's by now canonical dictum of Vienna 1900 as a 'Wert-vakuum'[38] (vacuum of values) – a sensation which peaked in both Germany and Austria by the end of the First World War and the collapse of both empires. Simmel observes in 1918 that many of his contemporaries seem to have lost their religion without losing their religiosity: one could say 'sie hätten den Glauben abgetan, um die Gläubigkeit zu behalten' (they had disposed of their faith in order to keep their piety), he writes.[39] Simmel seems to suggest that for these individuals, getting rid of religion was in fact a necessary condition for their moral codes to remain intact. He clarifies further that they understand religiosity no longer as necessarily linked to an external belief system but as 'ein schlechthin von innen bestimmtes Verhalten' (a form of conduct, which is plainly determined from within). Simmel's description seems to resonate with the 'obscene and malevolent presence that appears to have a direct hold on one's inner parts' that Santner speaks of.[40]

As has been well documented, other than in Germany, the sense of decline of the Empire – or of the incipient decomposition of the emperor's second body, to use Santner's image – had set in already in the decades before the First World War. By 1900, democratic advances made by the liberalist movement in the nineteenth century had come to a halt. Emperor Franz Josef's own pointed anti-modern attitude seemed to underline the beckoning expiration date of his rule and the hierarchical structures below him: 'With political institutions paralyzed, the emperor and its court locked behind an unyielding façade, and a despotic (though avowedly neutral and impartial) bureaucracy, Austria was in what Hermann Broch called a "political vacuum"'.[41] In his canonical novel *Radetz-kymarsch* (Radetzky March, 1931) the writer Joseph Roth describes the decline of the Habsburg era as a process of physical decay: 'Natürlich [...] wörtlich genommen, besteht sie [the monarchy, M.K.] noch. Wir haben eine Armee [...] und Beamte [...]. Aber sie zerfällt bei lebendigem Leibe' (Of course [...] literally, the monarchy still exists. We have an

38   Broch, Hermann (1975), *Schriften zur Literatur 1: Kommentierte Werkausgabe*. Vol. 9/1, ed. by Paul Michael Lützeler, Frankfurt a.M.: Suhrkamp, 153.
39   Simmel, Georg (1999), 'Lebensanschauung: IV Das individuelle Gesetz,' *Gesamtausgabe*, ed. by Ottheim Rammstedt, vol. 16: *Der Krieg und die geistigen Entscheidungen, Grundfragen der Soziologie, Vom Wesen des historischen Verstehens, Der Konflikt der modernen Kultur, Lebensanschauung*, ed. by Gregor Fitzi and Ottheim Rammstedt, Frankfurt a. M.: Suhrkamp, 346–425, 359.
40   Santner, *My Own Private Germany*, xii.
41   Le Rider, *Modernity and the Crises of Identity*, 22.

army [...] and civil servants [...]. But its living body is falling apart).[42] The shift from royal to popular sovereignty in Austria thus appears as a drawn-out transition period, caught up in a declining order that is no longer apt to reassure its subjects of its own legitimacy and therefore also calls the secured position of these subjects into question. Moreover, Le Rider stresses that the very idea of the Habsburg order was 'founded not on rights but on duties':[43] individual responsibility weighed heavily, but the hierarchical structures of the monarchy were meant to offer protection. The bureaucratic structure relied on the 'performative magic' of investiture.[44] Individual legitimacy of bourgeois subjects invested in this structure was therefore intimately dependent on the legitimacy of the hierarchical power investments of the social order. We will see in the individual chapters of this study that the civil servant who no longer feels fully addressed – and hence legitimized – by his social destiny is a recurring character in Schnitzler's prose. I will show that the characters invoke their individual metaphysical destiny precisely when the legitimacy of their social destiny is called into question and the contingency of the social order threatens to be exposed.

The wavering protection through hierarchical structures therefore puts 'a new political weight on every citizen'.[45] The shift of political authority is notably accompanied by the modern processes of secularization and the devaluation of holistic interpretative systems. Ostensibly, this reinforces the need for the autonomous reasonable subject, as it makes necessary the individual search for meaning and orientation. As Martina King puts it, 'In einem pluralen Gemenge von Sinnverarbeitungsangeboten wird [dem Subjekt] die Konstitution von Identität, die jeweilige Selbstbeschreibung, ausschließlich eigenverantwortlich zugemutet' (with the diverse range of interpretative systems offered [in the modern age, M.K.], constitution of identity and self-definition become entirely the subject's individual responsibility).[46]

By the same token, the invocation of personal destiny in Schnitzler's prose may be understood as an individually laid-out path which originates within the self. Recalling Simmel's remark about the deepest problem of modern life, destiny therefore appears to defend the individual's independence from the sovereign powers of the social order. In a social and political moment in which the coercive quality of social destinies threatens to become palpable, the idea of destiny may therefore be a comforting reassurance of the subject's individualized existence. In his

---

42 Roth, Joseph (1932), *Radetzkymarsch*, Berlin: G. Kiepenheuer, 281.
43 Le Rider, *Modernity and the Crises of Identity*, 16.
44 Bourdieu, *Language and Symbolic Power*, 122.
45 Santner, *The Royal Remains*, 5.
46 King, Martina (2009), *Pilger und Prophet: Heilige Autorschaft bei Rainer Maria Rilke*, Göttingen: Vandenhoeck & Ruprecht, 24.

article on Schnitzler's *Traumnovelle* (Dream Story, 1925/26), Hans Joachim Schrimpf offers a definition of destiny in Schnitzler's writings which seems to support this interpretation. According to him, 'besagt Schicksal bei Schnitzler das unverwechselbar Zugemessene, das was das Leben im Ganzen und im Besonderen individuell auszeichnend zugewogen ist' (destiny refers in Schnitzler's texts to that which has been unmistakably tailored to the individual, or in other words to that which has been individually assigned to a person and which therefore distinguishes this person's life in its entirety and uniqueness).[47] In this way, the concept of destiny may at least superficially relieve the pressures of self-description and self-identification mentioned by King: finding one's true inner self to fulfil one's destiny becomes a moral obligation when holistic belief systems and their corresponding codes of conduct have been suspended.

Accordingly, destiny appears in Schnitzler's prose as a force of individualization, or, in Schrimpf's words, 'aus dem Alltäglich-Festgelegten ein Durchbruch zum Eigenen' (a breakthrough from the pre-assigned quotidian to a realm of one's own).[48] In this way, destiny seems to stand in opposition to – religious or secular – social norms (the 'pre-assigned quotidian'), a re-enforcement of the position of the individual within the normative pressures of society. It may appear counter-intuitive that this separation of the individual from the social order leads to an affirmation of the latter. That this is nevertheless the case becomes clear when one recalls what Bourdieu writes about the concept of the self: the 'individual, the person, the self', he remarks, 'is also the seemingly most real of realities'.[49] Bourdieu speaks here of the way the concept of a unified self seems so immediately evident that it is almost impossible to be challenged. It is the idea of a self that exists, as it were, *a priori*. This conception of self gives human life an 'origin (both in the sense of a starting point and of a principle, a *raison d'être*, a primal force), and a termination, which is also a goal'.[50] Destiny appears like an expression of this primal force, and following one's destiny is then the realization of its goal. In a historical moment where the legitimacy of the social order and its power structures appear to be called into question, recourse to the 'seemingly most real of realities' will feel reassuring. In this way, this 'breakthrough to a realm of one's own' is

---

47 Schrimpf, Hans Joachim (1963), 'Arthur Schnitzlers *Traumnovelle*,' *Zeitschrift für deutsche Philologie* 82: 172–192, 175.
48 Schrimpf, 'Arthur Schnitzlers *Traumnovelle*,' 175.
49 Bourdieu, Pierre (2017), 'The Biographical Illusion (1986),' *Biography in Theory: Key Texts and Commentaries*, ed. by Wilhelm Hemecker and Edward Saunders, Berlin: de Gruyter, 210–216, 217.
50 Bourdieu, 'The Biographical Illusion (1986),' 210.

as much a symptom of crisis as it is a coping mechanism: particularly when the social order demands a heightened individualization, but at the same time the established interpretative patterns are increasingly weakened, the need to assure oneself of one's own individual, but secured and legitimate, position becomes prominent. Recurring to the notion of one's own individual destiny provides a sense of independent legitimacy when the social order fails to provide a source of security about one's own place within it.

With his interpretation of destiny in Schnitzler's texts, Schrimpf remains caught up in the perspective of the characters, for whom the belief in destiny indeed promises a way to individuation. As I wish to show in this study, however, this promise is a dead end and the protagonists' attempts at self-realization qua destiny are doomed to fail. The focus on the self as a surrogate for divine authorization displaces the problem of a lack of a legitimizing origin without solving it. This also emerges in Schrimpf's interpretation: his use of passive constructions ('das was das Leben im Ganzen und im Besonderen individuell auszeichnend zugewogen ist' – that which has been unmistakably tailored to the individual, it refers to that which has been individually assigned to a person) carefully avoids the question of this destiny's source. One cannot help but wonder, who (or what) is responsible for the uniquely tailored assignments which unmistakably mark and delineate a life as an individual destiny. This question is also tightly linked to the debates about the relationship between individual and society: the beginning of the twentieth century saw a vivid emergence of philosophical and psychological explorations of what determines human character and personality. These discussions often focused on the question of a personal essence as opposed to an acquired social role. The idea of destiny, at least as Schrimpf introduces it, seems to be concerned with this essence, again in Bourdieu's words, 'the seemingly most real of realities, the *ens realissimum*, immediately freed to our fascinated intuition, *intuitus personae*'.[51] For Bourdieu, this search for individual essence, however, is carried by a '*socially reinforced* narcissistic drive' (my emphasis, M.K.).[52]

If Bourdieu is correct in his assumption that the search for the self is socially reinforced, then the social order reinforces something that, on the face of it, seems to stand in opposition to it. This can be explained by the fact that Bourdieu's conception of the subject does not allow for a clearly distinguishable demarcation between individual and social essence – or in fact individual and social destiny. His thinking intersects here with other (post-modernist) theorists like Butler and Santner.

---

51 Bourdieu, 'The Biographical Illusion (1986),' 216.
52 Bourdieu, 'The Biographical Illusion (1986),' 216.

Moreover, three of these thinkers stress that, nevertheless, the idea of such an individual essence that is somewhat independent from the social order is necessary so that the coerciveness and at the same time contingency of the latter remains hidden.

It is the claim of this book that when Schnitzler's characters invoke their personal destiny, they are moved by this 'socially reinforced narcissistic drive'. Not only does the idea of a metaphysical destiny serve as interpretative frame, it can also provide one with a certain kind of individual trajectory and can even contain the fantasy of being 'chosen'. In this way, the invocation of destiny can be understood as an attempt at re-establishing one's sense of singularity, while the coercive power of social destinies may be seen as a kind of 'stereotypy' – not only in the pathological sense of the word as behavioural repetition compulsion, a coercive 'immer wieder' (time and time again), but also in the way that these social destinies have a typecasting effect on individuals.[53] The conventionalized modes of conduct that the social destinies require can be seen as a threat to the possibility of original experience: if one's actions, behavioural patterns and ways of perceiving begin to appear imposed by pre-formed, external structures, the longing for alternative, individualized ways of existence becomes stronger.

Stereotypes as Defence Mechanism and Destiny

Anton Zijderveld has defined stereotypes as a sub-category of clichés, which, by the same token, have a simplifying perceptual ordering function.[54] With their repetitive quality, which avoids the reflection on meaning, clichés 'provide us, in an unobtrusive manner, with some degree of clarity, stability and certainty, while they do exert a social control which we will in no way experience as being oppressive or repressive, because we are hardly aware of them'.[55] Thus, clichés can be seen as a part of the repetitive performances that stabilize (and re-produce) the power structures of the social order. Furthermore, Zijderfeld suggests that by virtue of their reassuring repetitiveness, recognizability, and easy application, they may satisfy 'some deep-seated, residually magic needs which we have otherwise covered with heavy layers of modern civilization'.[56] If

---

53 In modern psychology, such compulsive repetitive behaviour in both animals and humans is called 'stereotypy'. See the section V, F98.4, on 'Stereotyped movement disorders' in the *International Catalogue of Diseases* of the WHO: http://apps.who.int/classifications/icd10/browse/2016/en#/F90-F98.
54 Zijderveld, Anton C. (1987), 'On the Nature and Function of Clichés,' *Erstarrtes Denken: Studien zu Klischee, Stereotyp und Vorurteil in englischsprachiger Literatur*, ed. by Günther Blaicher, Tübingen: G. Narr, 26–40, 28.
55 Zijderveld, 'On the Nature and Function of Clichés,' 39.
56 Zijderveld, 'On the Nature and Function of Clichés,' 35.

clichés (and by implication stereotypes) have to be understood as secularized interpretative patterns, which replace those of metaphysics and religious cults in modern times, the functional relation between stereotypes and the belief in destiny becomes plausible. At the same time, the emphatic invocation of destiny must then be seen as a symptom of a threatening crisis, as it seems to indicate that the secular ordering tools of the dominant order have lost their capacity for satisfying those magic needs.

While the political, social, economic, and cultural processes of modernization at the end of the nineteenth century led in some parts of Europe to successful unifications (e.g. the building of nation states like Germany and Italy), within the Habsburg monarchy they highlighted massive heterogeneities engendered by a social, cultural, ethnic, religious, and even linguistic pluralism. Rather than a multi-cultural melting pot, Vienna 1900 appeared more like a 'battleground for different nationalities'.[57] The bourgeoisie in the urban centres experienced this complex diversity increasingly as threatening to their own existence and identity.[58] In contrast to the idealized idea of the Habsburg Empire as a harmonious culturally pluralistic society, Vienna, and Austria at large, became the site of increasing social and cultural tension. Against the backdrop of the threatening crisis of investiture and rising insecurities about the legitimacy of the social order, this increased the need for stable demarcation lines that would provide reassurance about the secured and legitimized position of the bourgeois subject.

The fascination with typologies and classification, which I have already discussed briefly with regard to the 'Viennese types' photo series, tends to be a common phenomenon in times of social insecurity. In the words of Helmuth Lethen: 'When the external moorings of convention relax, when the blurring of familiar boundaries and roles and ideological constellations stimulate fear, elements of ideological stabilization and schematicism come more forcefully into play. In a classification mania, contemporary observers of the social field categorize phenomena ranging from body type to moral character, from handwriting to race'.[59] This 'classification mania' seeps into everyday practices of perception and experience. It is striking that the way Schnitzler's characters perceive the world around them relies heavily on stereotypes,

---

57 Le Rider, *Modernity and the Crises of Identity*, 22.
58 Goltschnigg, *'Fröhliche Apokalypse' und nostalgische Utopie*, 2.
59 Lethen, Helmut (2002), *Cool Conduct: The Culture of Distance in Weimar Germany*, Berkeley: University of California Press, 23.

particularly those of 'otherness'.[60] Stereotypes function as an ordering process to confirm and reproduce the norm. While the activity of ordering is necessary for societies to define and reproduce themselves,[61] stereotypes are key ordering tools, 'part of our way of dealing with the instabilities of our perception of the world',[62] and thus equally necessary. While there is no way of avoiding stereotyping altogether, it is important to note that stereotypes almost always help to naturalize and legitimize the given dominant order: what stereotypes do is to identify one or more features of a social group's situation, place a (generally) negative evaluation on them, and then establish them as innate characteristics so they become cause rather than effect.[63] Thus, they 'present interpretations of groups, which conceal the "real" cause of the group's attributes and confirm the legitimacy of the group's oppressed position'.[64] This is, for example, the case when biologistic explanations are used to account for social inequalities, such as ethnic or sexual differences.

In this way, stereotypes can be understood as a specific form of social destiny: in their negative sense, particularly when they designate the position of 'otherness', they enclose the typecast person within the limits of the social position defined and legitimized by them. Stereotypes of 'otherness', then, are used to put individuals in 'their place', which can take on a form similar to an act of institution, as they are both enactments of communication with an immediate effect, i.e. performative speech acts:

> The act of institution is thus an act of communication, but of a particular kind: it signifies to someone what his identity is, but in a way that both expresses it to him and imposes it on him by

---

60 Imke Meyer's study *Männlichkeit und Melodram* provides a thorough analysis of the construction and deconstruction of bourgeois masculinity in Schnitzler's narrative works and also touches on the topic of stereotypical representations of gender. Her analysis shows that Schnitzler's male protagonists are caught up in a melodramatic mode of perception and self-fashioning, which reveals that the rigid structures of a monolithic ideal of masculinity are no longer able to contain the crisis-like experiences of the male bourgeois subjects. Meyer provides convincing exemplary readings that demonstrate how the male protagonists rely on conceptions of 'otherness' in order at once to project their own transgressive tendencies and to preserve their self-image as representatives of the bourgeois norm. My approach incorporates these insights in a broader analysis of the function of the conceptual link between stereotype and destiny.
61 See Dyer, *The Matter of Images*, 12; Gilman, *Difference and Pathology*, 16.
62 See Gilman, *Difference and Pathology*, 15.
63 Perkins, T. E. (1979), 'Rethinking Stereotypes,' *Ideology and Cultural Production*, ed. by Michèle Barrett, Philip Corrigan, Annette Kuhn, and Janet Wolf, London: Croom Helm, 133–159, 154.
64 Perkins, 'Rethinking Stereotypes,' 55.

expressing it in front of everyone [...] and thus informing him in an authoritative manner of what he is and must be. This is clearly evident in the insult, a kind of curse [...] which attempts to imprison its victim in an accusation which also depicts his identity.[65]

There is, however, a decisive difference between the imposing and restricting effect of an act of institution and the typecasting of a person as 'other': while both impose a form of identity with prescriptive modes of existence onto the person, the first is, even though restrictive and determining, a confirmation of a position within the norm, whereas the second refers the individual to a place outside of it. Stereotypes tend to represent societal outsiders as opposed to social types, which are defined as 'representations of those who "belong" to society'.[66] While constructed iconographically in a similar way, social types are not reduced to a fixed function within a fictional plot as is the case for stereotypes. Social types can take over a variety of roles and positions, 'whereas stereotypes always carry within their very representation an implicit narrative'.[67] This narrative inherent in stereotypes is crucial, as it not only applies to the fictional representation of literary characters, but to typecast social groupings, for which it in fact can take on the quality of an unchangeable destiny: stereotypes deny the typecast person an individual development and restrict them within the boundaries of the stereotype's narrative. A stereotype of 'otherness' is thus above all a stigma, and to be called into it through a speech act almost always takes on the form of an insult and hence does injury. As Judith Butler writes of such injurious speech acts:

To be injured by speech is to suffer a loss of context, that is, not to know where you are. [...] Exposed at the moment of such a shattering is precisely the volatility of one's 'place' within the community of speakers; one can be 'put in one's place' by such speech, but such a place may be no place.[68]

A stereotype of 'otherness', then, has an, as it were, negative fate-like quality: for members of the typecast group, it has an exclusionary and restrictive effect, and it denies them an individual development: the idea of a destiny in the sense of achieved 'chosen-ness' seems to be

---

65   Bourdieu, *Language and Symbolic Power*, 121.
66   Dyer, *The Matter of Images*, 14.
67   Dyer, *The Matter of Images*, 15.
68   Butler, Judith (1997a), *Excitable Speech: A Politics of the Performative*, New York, London: Routledge, 4.

reserved for representatives of the norm. If stereotypes of 'otherness' define the norm through their own exclusion, they create a sense of security and legitimacy for positions within the norm, but also provide them with the possibility of an individual development (or 'destiny'), while denying it to the typecast 'other'.

However, when the contingency of the social order (which constitutes the positions within the norm) becomes exposed, the fatal quality of social destinies emerges. This can have unsettling effects on the stability of the social order and the reproduction of its power structures. It can create a moment in which 'elites cease to believe in themselves', which will ultimately lead to a wasting away of these elites. Stereotypes of 'otherness' and the invocation of an individual destiny thus work to reassure the elites of their legitimate and privileged position within the norm and in this way prevent any attempts 'to cross the line, to transgress, desert, or quit' this position.[69]

Stereotype and Destiny and the Risk of Failure

While Schnitzler's characters strive for the fulfilment of their individual destiny, their efforts are ironically undermined by the repetitive and mirroring structures of the texts. It becomes clear that the conventionalized modes of conduct are not restricted to the symbolic function, i.e. the performances required by social status (e.g. as nobleman or ministerial official), but also to 'private selves'. The most stabilizing effect of destiny may be yielded when one's destiny appears to be found within the realm of the norm: for example when the arguably highest individualizing destiny – the experience of romantic love – becomes institutionalized in the form of marriage. Schnitzler's narratives point up the pre-formed cultural narratives that influence the protagonists' perception of the social reality around them and also their own actions: besides stereotypes of 'otherness', clichéd representations of the norm, for example conventionalized expressions of love or concepts of masculinity, also determine the protagonists' behaviour and undermine their proclamations of originality.

Schnitzler's texts also reveal the weakness of the defence strategies like stereotype and destiny by showing how easily they fail to really keep the subjects 'on the right site of the line', to 'stop those who are inside, on the right side of the line, from leaving, demeaning or down-grading themselves'.[70] When the threatening lack of legitimacy of the social order produces the heightened desire for an individual, metaphysical destiny independent of one's status and role within the dominant order,

69 Bourdieu, *Language and Symbolic Power*, 122.
70 Bourdieu, *Language and Symbolic Power*, 122.

the excluded position of the 'other' may come to appear desirable in an idealized way. Particularly because it is not firmly secured within the realm of the norm, it seems to promise, despite the often highly restricting quality of the narrative within the stereotype, a certain paradoxical kind of freedom. It is precisely what Butler calls the 'volatility of one's place' that can lead to such mystifications of the 'other'.[71] The perception of the 'other' is thus always highly ambivalent, contradictory even, and makes the 'other' appear at once abjected, demonized, and idealized. It is crucial that Schnitzler's characters do not develop alternative identity constructions, but their failures and crises point up the inadequacy of existing ones. It becomes clear that the idealizing mystification of 'otherness' is also a cultural narrative inherent to the stereotype. The mystification of the formerly abjected 'other' often becomes linked with the idea of destiny: the desire to be chosen for something 'special', and thus to overcome the restrictions of the norm, cannot be thought positively, but needs to be associated with a position only known outside of the boundaries of the norm. Since the position of the 'other' is not developed independently, but only in relation to the norm, it does not provide the possibility of any new concept for rethinking the existing normative structures. This ambivalence, in which the stereotyped 'other' is used to define the self and still secure its position within the norm, but also becomes idealized as an 'alternative' mode of existence and a way to escape the restrictive structures of the dominant order, is a central topic in Schnitzler's writings.[72]

When, in states of crisis, the fascination with the position of the 'other' as an alternative existence becomes stronger, this obviously does have a destabilizing effect on the dominant order in its entirety: it is precisely a moment when those who 'are on the right side of the line' are beginning to leave, demean, or downgrade themselves. Thus, when

---

71 Butler, *Excitable Speech*, 4.
72 Wolfgang Lukas recognizes a 'Basisopposition' (central opposition) between bourgeois norm and deviance. On the level of the literary characters, this is expressed through a binary opposition between 'A-Figuren' (A-characters), representatives of the norm or 'A-Welt' (A-world) and 'B-Figuren' (B-characters), representatives of deviance or 'B-Welt' (B-world). See Lukas, *Das Selbst und das Fremde*, 21–22. This classification is compatible with my approach in the way that it already introduces the desire of the protagonists to transgress the bourgeois norm and the fatal idealization of the 'other'. However, Lukas does not take into account the stereotypical cultural narratives that lead to the ambivalent perception of the 'other'. His classification of the B-characters seems to imply deviance mainly by choice: 'Künstler,' 'Magier-Psychotherapeuten,' 'Abenteurer' (artists, magician-psychotherapists, adventurers) attributing a particularly privileged social position to the B-world. See Lukas, *Das Selbst und das Fremde*, 24. My focus rather lies on stereotyped social groups that are *considered* as deviant and excluded from the norm.

representatives of the norm begin to cross that line, the social order and its norms are endangered. However, as Bourdieu points out, while a crisis is a necessary condition for the questioning of the dominant order, it is not a sufficient condition for the production of a critical discourse.[73] As long as there is still a sufficient number of subjects securely located within the realm of the norm, it makes a difference for the stability of the dominant order whether those who are crossing the line are united by a shared critical discourse or whether they are individualized 'cases' that can be re-integrated as exceptional transgressions that can be perceived to prove the rule. It is this not-(yet)-critical, in-between state that Schnitzler's texts describe. My claim in this book is that Schnitzler's characters demonstrate that the belief in destiny brings about such individualization and prevents the development of critical awareness of the social structures around them. This also becomes reinforced on a stylistic level, where Schnitzler's prose often features self-referential effects of Romantic and Gothic literature. I will show in my readings how the texts feature Romantic and particularly Gothic elements, which often seem to be of an almost 'Hoffmannesque' quality.[74] In this, the texts inscribe themselves into a literary tradition particularly known for its critical questioning of dogmatic trust in reason and progress.[75]

The Gothic Horror of Stereotype and Destiny

Peter von Matt has pointed out E. T. A. Hoffmann's influence on Modernist authors, albeit without mentioning Schnitzler explicitly:[76]

> Vom Erzähler E.T.A. Hoffmann laufen mehrfache Linien über ein Jahrhundert zu den modernen Autoren. Zu ihnen gehört die Kultur des Nachdenkens über das Erzählen während des

---

73   Bourdieu, Pierre (1977), *Outline of a Theory of Practice*, Cambridge: Cambridge University Press, 69.

74   I follow here the suggestion of Andrew Cusack to describe the genre of the German *Schauerroman* as 'German Gothic,' a 'species of border-crossing popular fictions referred to in Germany as *Ritter-, Räuber- und Schauerromantik*, and in Britain as the Gothic'. The advantage of using the term 'Gothic' to describe elements of *Schauerromantik* in works of Modernism is also that it brings out the comparability to other modern forms of Gothic fiction, such as the Victorian. See Cusack, Andrew (2012), 'Introduction,' in *Popular Revenants: The German Gothic and Its International Reception, 1800–2000*, ed. by Andrew Cusack and Barry Murnane, Rochester, New York: Camden House, 1–9.

75   On Schnitzler's knowledge and appreciation of Hoffmann's work, see Aurnhammer, Achim (2013), *Arthur Schnitzlers intertextuelles Erzählen*, Berlin; Boston, MA: De Gruyter, 150.

76   Matt, Peter von (1989), *...fertig ist das Angesicht: Zur Literaturgeschichte des menschlichen Gesichts*, Frankfurt a. M.: Suhrkamp, 236f.

Erzählens, des Redens über die poetische Arbeit in deren Vollzug
selbst. [...] Damit entdeckt und definiert sich die berichtete Welt
als eine konstruierte. Das Erzählen wird von einem Medium,
das gesicherte Welt vermittelt, zu einer Tätigkeit, in der
eingestandenermaßen etwas aufgebaut und angefertigt wird.
There are several threads connecting the narrator E. T. A.
Hoffman to the modern writers a century later. They include a
cultivation of thinking about narration while narrating, of talking
about the poetic work while doing it. In this way, the narrated
world explores and defines itself as something that has been
constructed. Narration, which used to be a medium representing
a secured world, becomes a practice, which makes transparent its
processes of construction.

Schnitzler's texts also display this reflection about the narrative process and its constructed quality and, in this way, destabilize the cultural narratives that build the foundation for the normative system
of social reality. Thus, the concept of destiny in Schnitzler's writings
at once covers up *and* reveals a much more uncomfortable threat for
autonomy than its only ostensibly metaphysical determinism: if one
cannot help but repeat the 'assignments' of one's social destiny, one is
not only restricted in one's agency, but also endangered in one's individuality and capacity for an original experience. Moments in which
the compulsive quality of these repetitions threatens to become conscious are highly uncanny in the classically Freudian sense, as something familiar which should remain hidden begins to emerge.[77] What
comes to the surface is the constructed quality of the cultural narratives
that constitute social reality, of the acts of performative magic which
delineate the boundaries around the norm. In Schnitzler's texts, these
moments of exposure are marked by the recurring sensation of *Grauen*
(horror), which appears to be an allusion to the *Schauerroman* (Gothic,
or 'shudder', novel) of German Romanticism. 'Das Grauen empfing
überhaupt seinen ästhetischen Adel erst von der Romantik' (*Grauen*, or
horror, first received its aesthetic nobility from Romanticism), writes
Manfred Schneider, who defines it as a 'Verlust an Unterscheidungs-
fähigkeit' (loss of the ability to differentiate).[78] According to Schneider,

77 See Freud, Sigmund (1947b), 'Das Unheimliche,' *Gesammelte Werke*, vol. 12:
    Werke aus den Jahren 1917–1920, ed. by Anna Freud, Edward Bibring, Willi Hof-
    fer, Ernst Kris, and Otto Isakower, London: Imago, 227–268, 251.
78 Schneider, Manfred (1999), 'Das Grauen der Beobachter: Schriften und Bilder
    des Wahnsinns,' *Bild und Schrift in der Romantik*, ed. by Gerhard Neumann and
    Günter Oesterle, Würzburg: Königshausen und Neumann, 237–253, 247.

Grauen (horror) occurs when a subject is confronted with a fading of differences, which had been taken as given and secure before. In my reading of the Schnitzler texts selected in this study, I will show that the recurring sensation of *Grauen* (horror) corresponds to this definition and can thus be understood as relaying a Romantic disposition. This Romantic *Grauen* (horror) is in turn tightly linked to the complex of 'stereotype and destiny' in Schnitzler's texts: as it occurs when formerly established differences appear to fade, it is connected to the blurring of the demarcating line between norm and 'other' provided by stereotypes. Thus, when stereotypes of 'otherness' become subtly twisted in Schnitzler's texts, and the 'other' appears suddenly much closer to the self than can be comfortable, the protagonists experience a sensation of *Grauen* (horror). This resonates with Santner's analysis of another German word for horror:

> *Entsetzen*, which literally means to de-pose or de-posit, did indeed at one time signify the act of removing someone from a position of authority, the undoing of their *Einsetzung* or investiture. [...] *Horror* thus places us in a semantic field of violent actions pertaining to the constitution and de-constitution of political and social realities; it can be understood as the experience of being violently thrown, removed, torn from one's position or place, of an undoing – a *flaying* – of one's symbolic skin.[79]

Although often to a less dramatic degree, horror (most eminently expressed through *Grauen*, but at times also through *Schauer* and *Entsetzen*) in Schnitzler's prose texts marks precisely moments in which the symbolic status of the protagonist and their legitimate position within the social order (or the legitimacy of the order itself) appear called into question.

The invocation of destiny as a reaction to this horror also can be read further in this context of Romanticism: one of the symptoms of the Romantic concept of madness is the suspension of contingency,[80] which is one of the main effects of the belief in the higher power of destiny, particularly when arbitrary events are interpreted as prophetic signs. As a symptom of Romantic madness, this elision of contingency appears as a kind of coping mechanism to keep the *Grauen* (horror) of fading differences at bay.[81] This underlines my claim that the invocation of destiny in Schnitzler's texts has a compensatory function in the face

---

79   Santner, *The Royal Remains*, 49.
80   Schneider, 'Das Grauen der Beobachter,' 249.
81   Schneider, 'Das Grauen der Beobachter,' 249.

of a weakened identification with the social order and its power invest-ments. It completely denies any form of contingency and therefore pro-tects against the ontological vulnerability, the missing authorizing link at the foundation of the law.

Through the subtle allusions to the literature of *Schauerromantik* (Dark Romanticism), the texts draw on the aspect of Romanticism that, as Andrew J. Webber has analyzed, can 'be said to serve to unsettle new orders that are in danger of becoming fixed in damaging ways, making claims for subjectivity and mystery against the false security of a cul-ture under the hegemony of positivism'.[82] However, it will become clear that, while Schnitzler's texts do have the potential to unsettle rigid, 'naturalized' boundaries, they do not endorse any mysticist tendencies. While the protagonists are prone to this kind of thinking, their often tragic failures demonstrate that the suspension of contingency through the invocation of destiny does not provide an escape, but a dead end. Schnitzler's narratives are thus not necessarily to be understood as an 'alternatives Erkenntnismedium' (alternative cognitive medium)[83] to knowledge systems such as medicine or psychoanalysis, as is so often suggested, but as an alternative to stereotypical cultural narratives, serving to undermine their fate-like character.

A Psycho-Sociological Reading

While my analysis is informed by the psycho-sociological theories of thinkers like Butler, Bourdieu, and Santner, I want to stress that the way stereotype and destiny function together as a counter-critical coping mechanism has emerged from my readings of Schnitzler's prose. My interpretation of destiny, in its conjunction with the practice of stereo-typing, is concerned with the insights into psycho-social structures that are offered by his narratives. Taking my cue from Le Rider's sugges-tion that Viennese modernism can be understood as a post-modernism *avant la lettre*, I find that Schnitzler's prose seems to take into account how power structures are being produced and reproduced through the subject. While other scholars have noted the importance of the ten-sion between social order (in the form of social roles) and individual in Schnitzler's writing, I am suggesting that Schnitzler texts can be read in a way that not only makes the separation between social and individual 'essence' practicably impossible, but reveals the very pursuit of such an individual essence as a reinforcement of social power structures.

---

82   Webber, Andrew J. (2005) 'The Afterlife of Romanticism,' *German Literature of the Nineteenth Century 1832–1899*, ed. by Clayton Koelb and Eric Downing, Roches-ter, NY: Camden House, 23–43, 40.
83   Perlmann, Michaela L. (1987b), *Arthur Schnitzler*, Stuttgart: Metzler, 183.

Compared with previous interpretations, this approach therefore leads to a different evaluation of the topic of destiny in Schnitzler's work. So far, the topic of destiny in Schnitzler's writings has been regarded mainly in this context of individual responsibility. The tension between free will and determinism is generally regarded as one of the most central themes in Schnitzler's writings.[84] As the main goal tends to be (more or less explicitly) to determine Schnitzler's own position on the topic, critics have tried to evaluate his understanding of destiny and free will by taking into account not only his literary writings, but also his aphorisms and journal entries.[85] However, as Schnitzler never developed anything comparable to a philosophical or scientific theory about free will (or anything else), Horst Thomé has rightly pointed out that an exhaustive determination and definition of his position on the subject is probably impossible.[86] Critics generally struggle to pin Schnitzler

---

84 See Imboden, Michael (1971), *Die surreale Komponente im erzählenden Werk Arthur Schnitzlers*, Bern: H. Lang, 50; Swales, *Arthur Schnitzler*, 118–180; Segar, Kenneth (1973), 'Determinism and Character: Arthur Schnitzler's *Traumnovelle* and his Unpublished Critique of Psychoanalyis,' *Oxford German Studies* 8: 114–127, 117ff; Scheible, Hartmut (1977), *Arthur Schnitzler und die Aufklärung*, Munich: W. Fink, 102; Dangel, Elsbeth (1985), *Wiederholung als Schicksal: Arthur Schnitzlers Roman 'Therese: Chronik eines Frauenlebens,'* Munich: Fink, 76; Thomé, Horst (1984), 'Kernlosigkeit und Pose: Zur Rekonstruktion von Schnitzlers Psychologie,' *Fin de Siècle. Zur Naturwissenschaft und Literatur der Jahrhundertwende im deutsch-skandinavischen Kontext*, ed. by Klaus Bohnen, Uffe Hansen, and Friedrich Schmöe, Kopenhagen and Munich: Fink, 62–87; Thomé, Horst (1993), *Autonomes Ich und 'Inneres Ausland': Studien über Realismus, Tiefenpsychologie und Psychiatrie in deutschen Erzähltexten (1848–1914)*, Tübingen: Niemeyer, 598–722; Haberich, Max (2013), '"daß ich ja nicht im entferntesten daran gedacht habe, irgendeine Frage lösen zu wollen": The Development of Arthur Schnitzler's Position on the "Jewish Question" from *Der Weg ins Freie* to *Professor Bernhardi*,' *Journal of Austrian Studies* 46 (2): 81–102, 91. See also Thomé's literature overview on individual responsibility in Schnitzler (*Autonomes Ich und 'Inneres Ausland*,' 600, fn. 9). In the Schnitzler scholarship of the 1970s and 1980s, destiny is practically exclusively discussed in this context. See Just, Gottfried (1968), *Ironie und Sentimentalität in den erzählenden Dichtungen Arthur Schnitzlers*, Berlin: E. Schmidt; Imboden, *Die surreale Komponente im erzählenden Werk Arthur Schnitzlers*; Segar, 'Determinism and Character'; Allerdissen, Rolf (1985), *Arthur Schnitzler: Impressionistisches Rollenspiel und skeptischer Moralismus in seinen Erzählungen*, Bonn: Bouvier; Dangel, *Wiederholung als Schicksal*; Luprecht, Mark (1991), *What People Call Pessimism: Sigmund Freud, Arthur Schnitzler, and the Nineteenth Century Controversy at the University of Vienna Medical School*, Riverside, CA: Ariadne Press. See also the literature overview in Lukas, *Das Selbst und das Fremde*, 264.

85 See above all Imboden, *Die surreale Komponente im erzählenden Werk Arthur Schnitzlers*; Allerdissen, *Arthur Schnitzler*; Luprecht, *What People Call Pessimism*.

86 See Thomé, 'Kernlosigkeit und Pose,' 86, fn.72.

down on either side, as determinist on the one hand or as defender of free will on the other. Accordingly, most critics come to the conclusion that, also in his literary writings, he did not aim for an unequivocal position.[87]

Consensus seems to have been reached about Schnitzler's emphasis on the necessity of a concept of free will, no matter to what extent the human psyche may be determined by internal or external forces: only the assumption of a free will allows the subject to address individual and ethical responsibility. Thus, critics have focused on the ethical implications of Schnitzler's writings, particularly on the ethical deficiency of most of his protagonists, who seem to serve as negative examples of responsible conduct.[88] Thomé, in particular, insists on the high importance of a concept of autonomy in Schnitzler's literary writings, which is necessary for his 'moralkritische Erzählung' (ethically critical narrative).[89] This leads to an argument that Schnitzler's characters avoid individual responsibility by escaping into conventionalized codes of social norms and roles. He also mentions in passing the de-individualizing and typologizing effect of those pre-formed social roles.[90] However, Thomé focuses more on the individual 'moralische Versagen' (ethical failure) of the characters, while my readings are concerned with the social power structures and cultural narratives that

---

87 See Allerdissen, *Arthur Schnitzler*, 128.
88 Often this is taken as an opportunity to highlight Schnitzler's differences to his alleged *Doppelgänger*, Sigmund Freud, emphasizing Schnitzler's focus on half-conscious states rather than unconscious ones, which would mitigate an ethical evaluation of the protagonist's actions. See for example Swales, *Arthur Schnitzler*, 118–149; Segar, 'Determinism and Character,' 114–127, 120; Scheible, *Arthur Schnitzler und die Aufklärung*, 102–105). This frequently leads to an implicit critique of Freud and psychoanalysis, in which Schnitzler's writings appear to provide an alternative (implicitly almost always superior) anthropological/psychological approach. The most extensive and thoroughly researched example of this kind of Schnitzler interpretation has been provided by Thomé, who takes into account not only Schnitzler's literary texts, aphorisms, journal and medical writings, but also contemporary scientific and philosophical sources beyond Freud. See Thomé, 'Kernlosigkeit und Pose'; Thomé, *Autonomes Ich und 'Inneres Ausland,'* 608–670. The way in which Schnitzler serves literary scholars as an agent for their own implied rejection of psychoanalysis would be a research project in itself, and cannot be pursued further in this book. Thomé concedes that literature occupies its own space (according to him, that of ethics) and that it is not its task 'Seelenforschung praktisch in "Parallelaktion" zur Psychoanalyse zu betreiben' (to undertake psychical research as an alternative to psychoanalysis). See Thomé, *Autonomes Ich und 'Inneres Ausland,'* 606.
89 Thomé, *Autonomes Ich und 'Inneres Ausland,'* 630.
90 Thomé, 'Kernlosigkeit und Pose,' 73.

determine the perception and actions of the protagonists.[91] In a similar vein, my conclusion differs from that of Wolfgang Lukas, who also proposes a reconstruction of the concept of destiny in Schnitzler's writings.[92] He shows that Schnitzler's characters tend to appropriate other people's destinies as their own, which creates a repetitive structure in the texts. While this seems to confirm my claim that Schnitzler's texts undermine the originality and individuality of experience, Lukas states that for Schnitzler the subject is 'für sein Schicksal in letzter Instanz immer selbst verantwortlich' (after all always responsible for his or her destiny). In my readings of the texts selected in this study, I understand these appropriations less as autonomous acts than as internalizations of stereotypical cultural narratives.[93]

I certainly do not want to deny that the ethical question of individual responsibility is a relevant topic for Schnitzler and that this is reflected in his literary writings. The characters' behaviour often appears ethically more than questionable – particularly when it comes to their interactions with those who are socially inferior to them. However, we should be cautious with the judgement of the individual characters, as it allows the reader to take on an ethically superior position, which is not encouraged by the texts. I suggest that it is more productive to focus less on the autonomy of the characters, and therefore on their ethical failure to make the right choices, than on the constructed cultural narratives of normativity through which they perceive the world and which emerge in the texts as prompting those failures. What makes Schnitzler's texts still relevant and interesting today is that, read in this perspective, they bring to awareness the constructed quality of the norms and conventions that form the social reality of the protagonists. By doing this, the

---

91 See Thomé, *Autonomes Ich und 'Inneres Ausland,'* 608. Dangel seems to suggest a similar approach, when she states that, although Schnitzler stressed the importance of individual responsibility in his work, the small realm of agency is time and again interrupted by unknown powers. See Dangel, *Wiederholung als Schicksal,* 76. Already the title of Dangel's book, *Wiederholung als Schicksal* (Repetition as Destiny), indicates interesting points of contact to the approach proposed here. Her focus lies solely on Schnitzler's novel *Therese,* thus on a protagonist who could be considered as representative of 'otherness'. While Dangel does not spell out the connection between social determinants and the notion of metaphysical destiny in the text, her reading implicitly brings out the negative, fate-like quality of the position of the 'other': 'Ohne wirklich ein Schicksal zu haben, schicksalslos gleichsam, reproduziert Therese schicksalhaftes Leben' (Without really having a destiny, practically fate-less as it were, Therese produces fateful life). See Dangel, *Wiederholung als Schicksal,* 91.

92 See Lukas, *Das Selbst und das Fremde,* 277.

93 However, Lukas's argument that Schnitzler's characters tend to appropriate other people's destinies as their own, which creates a repetitive structure in the texts, confirms my claim that Schnitzler's texts undermine the originality and individuality of experiences.

texts evoke the effect of Romantic irony and ask readers to reflect in turn on the constructedness of the cultural narratives that influence their own perception of the world.

The corpus of this study consists of a representative selection of narrative works from the first three decades of the twentieth century, spanning most of Schnitzler's writing career: all five narratives compiled in the volume *Dämmerseelen* (Dozing Souls) of 1907 (*Das Schicksal des Freiherrn von Leisenbohg* (Baron Leinsenbohg's Destiny), *Die Weissagung* (The Prophecy), *Das neue Lied* (The New Song), *Die Fremde* (The Stranger) and *Andreas Thameyers letzter Brief* (Andreas Thameyer's Last Letter) as well as the more substantial texts *Der Weg ins Freie* (Road into the Open, 1908), *Traumnovelle* (Dream Story, 1925/26) and *Flucht in die Finsternis* (Flight into Darkness, completed 1913, published 1931). This selection allows a paradigmatic analysis of the complex of stereotype and destiny in Schnitzler's narrative writing: first, the texts provide rich material in terms of the representation of stereotypes of 'otherness' (race, gender, class, and madness). Second, they display the invocation of destiny in a differentiated range from more subtle 'every-day superstitions' in realistic settings to the extreme forms of psychotic delusions or the play with fantastic elements and supernatural higher powers.

It is not the aim of this book to trace a chronological development of the thematic complex of stereotype and destiny in Schnitzler's work, as this would have posed a methodological problem: the work process of the two texts published later, *Traumnovelle* and *Flucht in die Finsternis* in both cases spans almost two decades between first drafts and publication.[94] A reconstruction of the chronological development would thus have required a project of textual genealogy, which would have exceeded the frame of this study. Correspondingly, the chapters do not follow the chronological order of the publication of the texts, but are structured in a way that allows me to establish the framework for my argument from the beginning and develop it incrementally in the following chapters.

The first chapter on Schnitzler's novel *Der Weg ins Freie* (Road into the Open, 1908) analyzes the practice of stereotyping as an essential part of the protagonist's perception of the social reality around him. It will be argued that Georg's function as a reflector figure allows the novel to explore the intersectionality of anti-Semitic and misogynistic stereotyping. The focus lies on physiognomy as a central aspect of stereotyping and on the specular function of the non-Jewish male protagonist

---

94 Neymeyr, Barbara (2006), 'Nachwort,' Arthur Schnitzler, *Flucht in die Finsternis*, ed. by Barbara Neymeyr, Stuttgart: Reclam; Heinzmann, Bertold (2006), *Arthur Schnitzler: Traumnovelle: Erläuterungen und Dokumente*, Stuttgart: Reclam.

Georg in his relationships to Jewish acquaintances and to his lover Anna. The close reading of the novel shows how the text toys with stereotypes and how it reveals their fate-like quality in a highly aesthetic manner: featuring different forms of representation such as the motif of modern photography on the one hand and Romantic imagery on the other, the novel refers as much to its own constructed quality as to that of the social reality it represents.

In the second chapter, on *Flucht in die Finsternis* (Flight into Darkness), the connection between social destinies and the invocation of a metaphysical destiny is developed in more detail. The reading suggests that the psycho-pathological crisis of the protagonist has to be understood as a crisis of investiture. A close intersection emerges between the protagonist's weakened symbolic function (the subject's secured and legitimized position in society), stereotypes of madness, and the development of his symptoms. This is supported by the motif of Romantic *Grauen* (horror), which occurs repeatedly in moments when the protagonist feels increasingly detached from his position within the norm of the bourgeois order. The invocation of the higher power of destiny then appears as coping mechanism that contains this anxiety. However, as the protagonist's idea of his individualized destiny is fundamentally informed by stereotypical idealizations of madness, he is unable to develop a critical consciousness with regard to the bourgeois order.

The readings of *Die Weissagung* (Prophecy, 1905) and *Andreas Thameyers letzter Brief* (Andreas Thameyer's Last Letter, 1903) in the third chapter address the function of destiny in relation to the representation of stereotypes of race (Jewishness and Blackness) in the texts. The ironic play with fantastic elements in *Die Weissagung* (The Prophecy), which toys with the presence of the higher power of destiny, is linked to both the protagonist's social destiny and his use of anti-Semitic stereotypes. In *Thameyer*, the protagonist is unable to reconcile his experiences either with his stereotypical perceptions of Blackness and femininity or with his own position as representative of the bourgeois male norm. The text reveals how scientific and non-scientific discourses of sexual and racial difference reinforce the rigidity of the stereotypes that inform the protagonist's perception. The inability to maintain the stereotypical boundary between self and 'other' is then experienced as a form of 'infection with otherness'. This leads to an overwhelming sensation of Gothic *Grauen* (horror), which the protagonist can only escape through suicide. In this way, the novella underlines the fatal quality of social destinies.

The fourth chapter focuses in particular on *Die Fremde* (The Stranger, 1902), but also refers to *Das Schicksal des Freiherrn von Leisenbohg* (Baron Leisenbohg's Destiny, 1903) and *Das neue Lied* (The New Song, 1905). The concept of romantic love is analyzed in its function as cosmic destiny. In the form of love, the individualizing function of destiny becomes most evident. My reading of *Die Fremde* (The Stranger) shows that the protagonist tries to replace his social destiny by his individualized cosmic destiny, which he claims to have found in the love for a woman. With regard to the ambivalent function of the stereotyped 'other', this chapter gives further substance to observations made in the previous chapters. All three texts undermine the protagonists' striving for individualization by bringing to the fore their stereotypical perception of femininity as well as the clichéd quality of their love affairs. The analysis in this chapter reveals how the texts toy with literary quotations and stereotypes, and by doing so effectively create a polar tension between the protagonists' claim to originality and the serial and stereotypical quality of their experience. With intertextual references to the motif of courtly love and masochism in *Die Fremde* (The Stranger) and *Leisenbohg*, and the play with idealized stereotypes of poverty in *Das neue Lied* (The New Song), this chapter also addresses the intersection of destiny and stereotypes of class.

Schnitzler's perhaps most popular narrative, *Traumnovelle* (Dream Story, 1925/26), is analyzed in the concluding, fifth chapter. While the concept of love as destiny is explored in the previous chapter as a mode of transgression, it appears here in the institutionalized form of marriage. Love has thus become social destiny, from which both the protagonist and his wife – at least temporarily – seek to escape. Particularly the male protagonist seems to fight an 'infection' with 'otherness', which undermines his performances of habitus as a sovereign bourgeois subject. The chapter thus focuses on the aesthetics of infection through which the text negotiates the tension between normative social destiny and the seductive transgression that falsely promises an individualized destiny. Moreover, we will see that the text displays in paradigmatic fashion how stereotype and destiny occur as a composite coping mechanism in the face of an acute state of crisis.

One Stereotypes and Physiognomy in *Der Weg ins Freie* (Road into the Open)

The question of the main theme in Schnitzler's first novel *Der Weg ins Freie* (Road into the Open, 1908) has been raised by various literary critics.[1] Two storylines seem to be developed rather independently of each other – the so-called love story between the young gentile composer Georg and the bourgeois Anna and a complex picture of the Viennese Jewish bourgeoisie and its controversial discussions of anti-Semitism and Zionism. As the reader sees the other characters and the events of action mainly through Georg's eyes, the novel displays crucial mechanisms of the social practice of typecasting with regard to the relation between norm and the so-called 'other'. Georg's function in the novel is not as a moral lead but rather, as we will see later on, as a specular lens.[2] He has access to various cultural and social spaces, an asset which he puts to good use. Georg's *flânerie* through the streets of Vienna can be understood symbolically as his idle roaming through a distinct selection of social fields: the exclusive club for the Viennese male nobility where his brother Felician passes his spare time is one of Georg's sanctuaries but not a place he is restricted to. As a composer he finds himself also welcome in the intellectual circles that meet in coffee houses, he is invited to the salons and holiday resorts of rich

---

1 See Swales, Martin (1971), *Arthur Schnitzler: A Critical Study*, Oxford: Oxford University Press, 29; Low, D. S. (1986), 'Questions of Form in Schnitzler's *Der Weg ins Freie,' Modern Austrian Literature* 19 (3/4): 22–27; Segar, Kenneth (1992), 'Aesthetic Coherence in Arthur Schnitzler's Novel *Der Weg ins Freie,' Modern Austrian Literature* 25 (3/4): 95–111; Gidion, Heidi (1998), 'Haupt- und Nebensache in "Der Weg ins Freie",' *Text + Kritik, Zeitschrift für Literatur* 138/139: 47–60.
2 See Neubauer, John (2003), 'The Overaged Adolescents of Schnitzler's *Der Weg ins Freie,' A Companion to the Works of Arthur Schnitzler*, ed. by Dagmar C. G. Lorenz, Rochester, NY: Camden House, 270.

families of the Jewish bourgeoisie such as the Ehrenbergs, and he enjoys his visits to the middle-class family home of his lover Anna Rosner. While the title of the novel suggests a form of progress and development towards freedom, evoking the genres of *Bildungs-* or *Entwicklungsroman* (novel of personal development),[3] Georg is already in the beginning freer than most of the other characters of the novel – as a non-Jewish male of the Viennese upper class he really is at liberty to go where he pleases (one could say, literally a *Freiherr* (free gentleman)).[4] As Wolfgang Müller-Funk has described in some detail, the social milieus are realistically reflected in the localization of the houses and apartments of the characters.[5] Georg lives, unsurprisingly, in the first district of Vienna, and thus in the very centre of urban life. Despite his objective freedom and privileges, however, Georg finds himself floating between the position of the insider, bringing with it the feeling of being locked in and the longing to escape, and that of the outsider who seeks entrance to exclusive circles. In what follows, this back-and-forth-movement will be mapped out in relation to the serving of contemporary stereotypes that seem to be worked into the narrative structure of the novel. However, in connection with the psychological embodiment of the characters, they appear subtly twisted in such a way that a gap between the signifier (stereotype) and the signified (the individual represented by the stereotype) becomes perceptible. Moreover, this gap is not a static incongruence but more likely caused by a shifting of signifiers; more than once the categories that define the boundaries between 'self' and 'other' seem to become unstable.

---

3   On the failed *Bildung* (education/personal development) in the novel see Abigail Gillman's 2004 article, 'Failed Bildung and the Aesthetics of Detachment: Schnitzler's *Der Weg ins Freie*,' *Confrontations/Accommodations: German-Jewish Literary and Cultural History from Heine to Wassermann*, ed. by Mark Gelber, Tübingen: Niemeyer, 209–236. Detlev Arens claims that the novel blurs the distinction between *Bildungsroman* (novel showing an individual development) and *Zeitroman* (novel depicting social types of the time), which will become significant later on. See Arens, Detlev (1981), *Untersuchungen zu Arthur Schnitzlers Roman 'Der Weg ins Freie,'* Frankfurt a. M.: Peter Lang, 106.

4   Hawes, J. M. (1995a), 'The Secret Life of Georg von Wergenthin: Nietzschean Analysis and Narrative Authority in Arthur Schnitzler's *Der Weg ins Freie,'* *Modern Language Review* 90 (2): 377–387, 378.

5   See Müller-Funk, Wolfgang (2006), 'Der gewohnte Bezirk seines Daseins: Räumlichkeit und Topografie Wiens in Schnitzlers *Der Weg ins Freie*: Mit einem Vergleich der Filmversion von Karin Brandauer,' *Die Tatsachen der Seele: Arthur Schnitzler und der Film*, ed. by Thomas Ballhausen, Barbara Eichinger, Karin Moser, and Frank Stern, Wien: Filmarchiv Austria, 211.

Stereotypes and Images of 'Normality'

'Nun ja, ein schöner, schlanker, blonder junger Mann; Freiherr, Germane, Christ – welcher Jude könnte diesem Zauber widerstehen?' (WiF908) (Oh well, a slim handsome blond young man, a baron, a German, a Christian – what Jew could withstand the magic?)[6] It is only in the last chapter that the reader encounters this condensed description of the protagonist Georg von Wergenthin. These words, sarcastically uttered by the young doctor Bertold Stauber, do not say anything about Georg as an individual character but refer to him as a type. The charm that Bertold mentions can only be understood as the charm of the norm, of the privileged position that Georg holds. According to Bertold's characterization, Georg fulfils the contemporary criteria of the masculine norm to the extent that he seems to represent what Sander Gilman calls a 'positive stereotype',[7] which appears to be something close to an idealized version of the self, the good other 'which we fear we cannot achieve'. This is curious, however, in the way that the representative of the norm is usually not the one who is stereotyped but belongs rather to the grouping that does not need any labelling because it has the power to label different types of others in order to define itself. When one thinks of stereotypes, one generally rather means negative stereotypes, 'which we fear to become',[8] and which imply a pejorative aspect.[9] Bertold refers sarcastically to the way the privileged holder of the normative position functions as an idealized icon even for the marginalized group of the stereotyped other, in this case, the Jews. However, his comment also points out that this idealized image of the non-Jew is stereotypical in itself, as it fundamentally depends on the stereotypization of 'the' Jew (the non-Jew as everything the Jew is not). This dependency is, of course, a source of unease for representatives of the norm and needs to be repressed. The selection of terms that Bertold

---

6   Schnitzler, Arthur (1913b), *Road into the Open*, translated by Horace Samuel, London: Howard Latimer, 350. All translations for the novel *Der Weg ins Freie* (Road into the Open) are taken from Horrace Samuel's translation from 1913. All other translations from the German are my own.

7   Gilman, Sander L. (1985), *Difference and Pathology: Stereotypes of Sexuality, Race, and Madness*, Ithaca, NY, London: Cornell University Press, 20.

8   Gilman, *Difference and Pathology*, 20.

9   Perkins, T. E. (1979), 'Rethinking Stereotypes,' *Ideology and Cultural Production*, ed. by Michèle Barrett, Philip Corrigan, Annette Kuhn, and Janet Wolf, London: Croom Helm, 133–159, 144. There are certainly also so-called 'positive' stereotypes of 'otherness' that do not refer to the norm. While not pejorative on the surface, these stereotypes are nevertheless harmful and offensive, because they reduce the stereotyped individual to the narrative inherent to the stereotype and deny him or her an individual development. This will be discussed in more detail in Chapter Three of this book.

uses to describe Georg sheds light on this dependency that binds the self to the other, the norm to the stereotyped deviance, and therefore undermines the ordering function of stereotypes.

Unsettling the ordering function of stereotypes disrupts reassuringly rigid ideas of society and social roles and in the process 'make[s] normality strange, that is, visible and specific'.[10] Towards the end of the novel, Heinrich, who has often been considered as an alter ego not only of Georg but also of Schnitzler himself,[11] compares his writing self-dismissively with the work of a mad photographer: 'Am Ende [...] wird es ein Portät sein, aufgenommen von einem irrsinnigen Photographen durch einen verdorbenen Apparat, während eines Erdbebens und bei Sonnenfinsternis' (WiF930) (The result [...] will be a portrait taken by a mad photographer with a spoilt camera during an earthquake and an eclipse of the sun).[12] The use of photography as a metaphor refers to the topic of legitimate representation. Heinrich responds here to his fellow writer Nürnberger, who accuses him of rendering only distorted images of the people he seeks to describe. What Heinrich seems to admit with his response is that his writing does indeed make the world represented appear rather strange and abnormal. We may here assume an implicit articulation of the aesthetic goal of Schnitzler's novel itself: a distortion not of *reality* but of *normality* to bring out the gap between social representations and the subjects repesented.[13]

This interpretation becomes more plausible when contrasted with another passage in the novel that also brings up the medium of photography. In the first weeks of their relationship, Georg and Anna spend much time wandering around Vienna together, exploring the city almost like tourists, enjoying floating through the streets without an actual destination:

Sie blieben vor verschiedenen Auslagen stehen, entdeckten unter einem Haustor den Glaskasten eines Photographen und waren

---

10   Dyer, Richard (2002), *The Matter of Images. Essays on Representation*, London: Routledge, 4.
11   See Fliedl, Konstanze (1997), *Arthur Schnitzler. Poetik der Erinnerung*, Vienna, Cologne, Weimar: Böhlau, 218; Gidion, 'Haupt- und Nebensache in "Der Weg ins Freie",' 48; Haberich, Max (2013), '"daß ich ja nicht im entferntesten daran gedacht habe, irgendeine Frage lösen zu wollen": The Development of Arthur Schnitzler's Position on the "Jewish Question" from *Der Weg ins Freie* to *Professor Bernhardi*,' *Journal of Austrian Studies* 46 (2): 81–102, 93.
12   Schnitzler, *Road into the Open*, 377.
13   John Neubauer also uses the photography metaphor to describe Georg's narrative function as 'filter' or 'lens' that renders an image of Viennese society that is rather unfocused and blurred as it is 'continually changing according to the situations and his mood'. See Neubauer, 'The Overaged Adolescents of Schnitzler's *Der Weg ins Freie*, 270.

sehr belustigt von der mühselig-ungezwungenen Haltung, in der hier Jubelpaare, Kadettenoffiziersstellvertreter, Köchinnen im Sonntagsstaat und für den Maskenball kostümierte Damen aufgenommen waren. (WiF702)
They remained standing in front of various shops. They discovered a photographer's show-case by a housedoor and were much amused by the laboriously-natural poses in which golden and silver wedding couples, [representatives of, M.K.] cadets, cooks in their Sunday best and ladies in masked fancy dress were taken.[14]

Recalling the *Wiener Typen* (Viennese types) photo series discussed in the introduction of this book, the vitrine exhibits pictures of people in their social roles, and not as individuals (as underlined by the inclusion of 'Stellvertreter' (representatives) in the list). Anna and Georg are amused about the lack of authenticity which becomes obvious not only because of the clothes that are worn for the special occasion of the photo but also ironically because of the models' attempts to look casual. Moreover, the fact that the cooks are apparently nevertheless recognizable as such even though they are depicted in their Sunday best underlines the failure of the photo to resemble the individualized portraits of bourgeois family members. Even though they were taken under normal conditions (probably not by a mad photographer, and with a working camera and not during any environmental catastrophe), these photographic representations fail to convince as individuals. They lack what Bourdieu has called a 'belief effect' that brings social types to 'life' in literature by virtue of psychological individuation.[15] Together with Heinrich's metaphor of photography for his own writing, this almost unremarkable passage might be read as a meta-fictional hint at the insufficiency of popular social and cultural representations, especially stereotypes.

The case for this is strengthened when one takes into account the fact that Heinrich at an earlier point in the novel points out what he considers to be his only true strength of both character and talent:

Das einzige, was mir eine gewisse Sicherheit gibt, ist eigentlich nur das Bewußtsein, in menschliche Seelen hineinschauen zu können ... tief hinein, in alle, in die von Schurken und ehrlichen Leuten, in die von Frauen und Männern und Kindern, in die

---

14 Schnitzler, *Road into the Open*, 85.
15 Bourdieu, Pierre (1996), *The Rules of Art: Genesis and Structure of the Literary Field*, Stanford, CA: Stanford UP, 32.

von Heiden, Juden, Protestanten, ja selbst in die von Katholiken, Adeligen und Deutschen, obwohl ich gehört habe, daß gerade das für unsereinen so unendlich schwer, oder sogar unmöglich sein soll. (WiF670)
The only thing that gives me a certain amount of confidence is simply consciousness of being able to see right into people's souls … right deep down, every one, rogues and honest people, men, women and children, heathens, Jews and Protestants, yes, even Catholics, aristocrats and Germans, although I have heard that that is supposed to be infinitely difficult, not to say impossible, for people like myself.[16]

This again describes quite precisely Schnitzler's own narrative technique, namely the psychological personalization of social types.[17] Obviously, there is another meta-fictional twist implied here, when Heinrich refers to the prejudice that Jews are unable to understand the Catholic, noble, and German psyches. With Georg as main character and reflector figure, Schnitzler gives an evident example and proof of the falsity of this stereotype. It is the text's play with stereotypes and how this 'makes normality strange' that will be the focus of what follows.

Physiognomy and Destiny

Physiognomic thought, one of the most obvious fields of stereotyping, is subtly but nevertheless persistently present throughout the novel. Already on the first pages, one of Georg's Jewish acquaintances, Willy Eisler, casually refers to the Swiss physiognomist Johann Kaspar Lavater. Willy explains here that he feels rather sentimental about his time in the military, which for him seems to have meant predominantly a play with social identity: 'So sehr ich mich dem Greisenalter nähere, es hat mir doch noch immer Spaß gemacht, so mit den gelben Aufschlägen umherzuwandeln, Sporen klirrend, Säbel schäppernd, eine Ahnung drohender Gefahr verbreitend, um von mangelhaften Lavaters für einen

---

16 Schnitzler, *Road into the Open*, 45.
17 See Gillman, 'Failed Bildung and the Aesthetics of Detachment,' 223. Gillman goes on to suggest that we therefore have to access Georg's character 'through psychology rather than typology' and offers an insightful psychological reading of Georg's character, also considering the information the text gives on his family background. See Gillman, 'Failed Bildung and the Aesthetics of Detachment,' 224. In contrast, Arens argues that 'der Protagonist [gerät] gleichsam hinter dem Rücken der Intention zum Typus' (the protagonist turns out as a type in spite of the opposite authorial intention. See Arens, *Untersuchungen zu Arthur Schnitzlers Roman 'Der Weg ins Freie*, 106. *Untersuchungen zu Arthur Schnitzlers Roman 'Der Weg ins Freie,'* 106). Here, I propose to focus more on the specific *tension* between the typological and the psychological, between the individual and the general.

bessern Grafen gehalten zu werden?' (WiF641) (Though I'm nearly an old man, I've always found it a joke to trot about with my yellow epaulettes, clanking my spurs, dragging my sabre along, spreading an atmosphere of impeding peril, and being taken by incompetent Lavaters for a noble count).[18] This remark on the physiognomist Lavater is particularly interesting for our context of stereotype and destiny. Lavater's main work, *Physiognomische Fragmente zur Beförderung der Menschenkenntnis und Menschenliebe* (1775–1778), gave instructions to analyze facial features as signs of talent and character. Arguing that the human body was an expression of personality and ability, Lavater was ostensibly concerned with defending human individuality: 'Jeder Mensch soll an sich selbst gemessen werden' (Every man should be measured against himself).[19] However, his exuberant work of four thick volumes, which are richly illustrated with portraits and silhouettes of distinctive profile pictures, invites the reader to classify and typecast individuals against a clearly Euro-centric, Aryan ideal. For Lavater, as for his successors in the physiognomic tradition, nature is destiny: the body delineates the boundaries of any individual's abilities. In his study *About Face*, Richard T. Gray shows that 'Lavater's physiognomic theories display a hybrid character that attempts, in an uncanny manner, to fuse a scientific methodology with metaphysical speculation'.[20] By employing seemingly objective and positivistic strategies of empirical science (e.g. observation and classification), Lavater's physiognomics were ultimately concerned with the metaphysical, internal characteristics of an individual. This practice led to the naturalization of cultural stereotypes, particularly with regard to race: Lavater's judgements, derived from his interpretations of allegedly typical racial facial features, often anticipate the stereotypes associated with Blackness and Jewishness in Schnitzler's times – some of which remain active and harmful in Western culture even today.[21] Arguing that bone structure and facial features were an expression of pure pre-destination,[22] Lavater's text already paves the way for the legitimization of stereotypes as destiny.

Willy's remark on Lavater reveals an awareness of the way these stereotypes serve as cognitive ordering tools in the Viennese society. The

---

18 Schnitzler, *Road into the Open*, 8.
19 Lavater, Johann Caspar (1968–69), *Physiognomische Fragmente zur Beförderung der Menschnekenntnis und Menschenliebe: Eine Auswahl mit 101 Abbildungen* I, Zurich: Orell Fussli, 167.
20 See Gray, Richard T. (2004), *About Face: German Physiognomic Thought from Lavater to Auschwitz*, Detroit: Wayne State UP, 111.
21 Gray, *About Face*, 107.
22 Lavater, *Physiognomische Fragmente zur Beförderung der Menschnekenntnis und Menschenliebe* I, 46.

pleasure Willy draws from the fact that at least in his military uniform, he 'passes' as a Gentile noble man, is clearly a reaction to the experience of anti-Semitic stereotyping. On the face of it, his comment appears to self-ironically mock the aspiration to 'pass' as non-Jewish – a reflection on the seductive effect of the idealized non-Jewish norm, also addressed in Bertold's characterization of Georg mentioned above.[23] However, Willy seems to enjoy his 'passing' mainly for the unsettling effect it has on the people who fail to successfully typecast him, the 'mangelhaften Lavaters' (incompetent Lavaters). This becomes clear two pages later, when the subject of physiognomy and stereotypes is raised again by Georg – although without a conscious link to Willy's comment:

Er [Georg] fühlte, daß Willy ein Mensch war, der ununterbrochen eine Stellung verteidigte, wenn auch ohne dringende Notwendigkeit. [...] Er empfand es, wie schon öfter, sonderbar, daß Willy Jude war. Schon der alte Eisler, Willys Vater, der anmutige Wiener Walzer und Lieder komponierte, und sich kunst- und altertumsverständig mit dem Sammeln, zuweilen auch mit dem Verkauf von Antiquitäten befaßte und seinerzeit als der berühmteste Boxer von Wien gegolten hatte, mit seiner Riesengestalt, dem langen, grauen Vollbart und dem Monokel, sah eher einem ungarischen Magnaten ähnlich, als einem jüdischen Patriarchen; aus Willy aber hatten Anlage, Liebhaberei und eiserner Wille das täuschende Ebenbild eines geborenen Kavaliers gebildet. Was ihn jedoch vor anderen jungen Leuten seines Stammes und seines Strebens auszeichnete, war der Umstand, daß er gewohnt war, seine Abstammung nie zu verleugnen, für jedes zweideutige Lächeln Aufklärung oder Rechenschaft zu fordern und sich über alle Vorurteile und Eitelkeiten, in denen er oft befangen schien, selber lustig zu machen. (WiF643)
He felt that Willy was a man who was continually defending a position though there was no pressing necessity for him to do so. [...] He felt now as he had done before, that it was almost extraordinary that Willy would be a Jew. Why, old Eissler, Willy's

23 This aspiration to 'pass' as non-Jewish is also addressed in Schnitzler's *Fräulein Else* (1924). Else internally sneers at her extortioner, the art dealer von Dorsday, whom she suspects of having changed his name to hide his Jewishness: 'Was hilft Ihnen Ihr erster Schneider, Herr von Dorsday? Dorsday! Sie haben sicher einmal anders geheißen' (E8) (Your individually tailored clothes do not help you, Herr von Dorsday! Dorsday! You certainly used go by a different name). Moreover, Else takes pride in her own ability to 'pass': 'O ich kann mir das erlauben [referring to using anti-Semitic stereotypes]. Mir sieht's niemand an' (E17) (Oh, I'm allowed to. In my case, no one can tell). On the subversive potential of 'passing' see Ginsberg, Elaine (1996), *Passing and the Fictions of Identity*, Durham and London: Duke UP, 4–5.

father, who composed charming Viennese waltzes and songs, was a connoisseur and collector, and sometimes a seller of antiques, and objets d'art, and had passed in his day for the most celebrated boxer in Vienna, was, what with his long grey beard and his monocle, far more like a Hungarian magnate than a Jewish patriarch. Besides, Willy's own temperament, his deliberate cultivation of it and his iron will had made him into the deceptive counterpart of a feudal gentleman bred and born. What, however, distinguished him from other young people of similar race and ambition was the fact that he was accustomed to admit his origin, to demand explanation or satisfaction for every ambiguous smile, and to make merry himself over all the prejudices and vanities of which he was so often the victim.[24]

Georg's characterization of Willy shows various different aspects at once. First of all, it demonstrates how apt Willy's ironic remark was, because Georg indeed seems to struggle with the incongruence of Willy's performative and physical appearance and the stereotypical image of the Jew. On the contrary, both Willy and his father seem to embody 'prototypes' of acculturation. More than that, Willy seems to enjoy the confusion about his identity and to deliberately enforce it not only through his physical appearance but also through the usage of his voice, which is, much like physiognomy, also a central category of stereotypes and further highlights their performative aspect as social roles: 'Willy sprach äußerst rasch, wie mit einer absichtlichen leisen Heiserkeit, scharf, salopp, mit ungarischen, französischen, wienerischen, jüdischen Akzenten' (WiF641) (Willy spoke extremely quickly, with a deliberate though slight hoarseness, briskly and yet nonchalantly with a combination of the Hungarian, French, Viennese and Jewish accents).[25] However, according to Georg's estimation, what makes Willy stand out from other acculturated Jews is the fact that he nevertheless does not deny his Jewishness. Thus, while Willy enjoys his performative game with identity, he does not allow his 'passing' to be complete and therefore uses it effectively to challenge rigid stereotypes and normative boundaries.

This leads back to the first sentence of the quoted passage: Georg sees in Willy someone who is always in a defensive position. If one takes into account Willy's paradoxical situation of being a non-religious,

---

24 Schnitzler, *Road into the Open*, 11.
25 Schnitzler, *Road into the Open*, 8.

'acculturated' Jew in an increasingly anti-Semitic society, one has to be sceptical about Georg's dismissive addition that 'there was no pressing necessity'. Willy's position is indeed in danger of being attacked from different directions: not only from anti-Semitic aggression, but also from the Jewish community which, in the face of such racist aggression, might call its members to return to their Jewish roots. This aspect is addressed in the novel, when the old Ehrenberg criticizes the writer Nürnberger. Because of his lack of faith, Nürnberger does not consider himself as Jewish. Ehrenberg confronts him: 'Wenn man Ihnen einmal den Zylinder einschlagt auf der Ringstraße, weil Sie, mit Verlaub, eine etwas jüdische Nase haben, werden Sie sich schon als Jude getroffen fühlen, verlassen Sie sich drauf' (WiF689) (If someone were to bash in your top hat in the Ringstrasse because, if you allow me to say so, you have a somewhat Jewish nose, you'd realise pretty quick that you were insulted because you were a Yiddisher fellow. You can take my word for it).[26] Here, again, the linking between physiognomy and stereotype is striking. The Jewish nose might after all be the most widespread Jewish stereotype. The mentioning of the Ringstraße is certainly not coinciden-tal. As the street with the most important buildings of Vienna, encircling the central district of the city, it can be understood as a representative, mobile 'stage' for the entire Viennese society. If racist harassment is possible on the Ringstraße, it means it has become broadly respecta-ble. What Ehrenberg implies with his comment is the experience that once the anti-Semitic tendencies have gained a certain degree of social acceptance, people who are considered as members of the stereotyped social grouping 'Jews' cannot escape their Jewishness as it is no longer a question of individual self-articulation or choice.[27]

In this way, the appellation 'Jew' is not only more than the neutral description of someone's confessional membership, it is also more than 'just' an insult: it turns into the enunciation of an unchangeable destiny. Georg almost becomes aware of this fate-like implication of the posi-tion of Jews, when he actually tries to understand what the term 'Jew' implies for those addressed with it. This – for Georg very exceptional – moment of acknowledgement and recognition happens during a cycling tour with his friends Leo and Heinrich, where he spends almost the entire day listening to the heated discussion between the two others about Jewish identity and Zionism.

---

26 Schnitzler, *Road into the Open*, 68.
27 See also Swales, *Arthur Schnitzler*, 41, who already mentions in passing the 'pro-cess of mutual image making' in the novel, and also points out that this process is 'even more fatal if there is a store of collective images which can drive the process of dehumanization to its ultimate conclusion'.

Zum erstenmal begann ihm die Bezeichnung Jude, die er selbst so oft leichtfertig, spöttisch und verächtlich im Mund geführt hatte, in einer ganz neuen gleichsam düstern Beleuchtung aufzugehen. Eine Ahnung von dieses Volkes geheimnisvollem Los dämmerte in ihm auf, das sich irgendwie in jedem aussprach, der ihm entsprossen war; nicht minder in jenen, die diesem Ursprung zu entfliehen trachteten wie einer Schmach, einem Leid oder einem Märchen, das sie nichts kümmerte, – als in jenen, die mit Hartnäckigkeit auf ihn hinwiesen, wie auf ein Schicksal, eine Ehre oder eine Tatsache der Geschichte, die unverrückbar festsstand. (WiF722)

He saw for the first time the designation of the Jew, which he himself had often used flippantly, jestingly and contemptuously, in a quite new and at the same time melancholy light. There dawned within him some idea of this people's mysterious destiny, which always expressed itself in every one who sprang from the race, not less in those who tried to escape from that origin of theirs, as though it were a disgrace, a pain or a fairy tale that did not concern them at all, than in those who obstinately pointed back to it as though to a piece of destiny, an honour or an [sic] historical fact based on an immovable foundation.[28]

The oxymoronic formulation 'düstern Beleuchtung' (gloomy/melancholy light) not only expresses Georg's realization of the inescapability of Jewish heritage and its implications but also the cloudiness of the said realization. Other terms like 'dämmerte' (dawned), 'geheimnisvoll' (mysterious), and 'Ahnung' (idea/premonition) insist that the subject is still utterly obscure for Georg. At the same time, they bring across a certain tendency of a metaphysical mystification of Jewishness, which is here explicitly referred to as a form of destiny.

This corresponds, in fact, to the contemporary discussions around the 'Jewish question' and does not have only metaphysical implications: central for the development of anti-Semitism at the beginning of the twentieth century was the debate about the 'biology of the Jews', thus genetic predispositions associated with Jewishness as a 'race'.[29] The way Jewishness had become a biological marker of difference is comparable to the idea of an unchangeable destiny, very much in line with Lavater's idea of physiognomy as fate: a biological predisposition is inescapable and cannot be shed like a religious confession or

---

28 Schnitzler, *Road into the Open*, 111.
29 See Lipphardt, Veronika (2008), *Biologie der Juden: Jüdische Wissenschaftler über 'Rasse' und Vererbung 1900–1935*, Göttingen: Vandenhoeck & Ruprecht, 188.

lost like the membership of a nation state. The idea behind it is that no matter what a Jewish person does, no matter how far their striving for 'assimilation' or 'acculturation' goes – they will stay different from the non-Jewish norm and never reach a fully accepted and recognized position in society. At the same time, the formulation 'aussprach' (expressed itself/spoke) brings to mind a performative speech act of interpellation which generates the subject by calling it.[30] It also seems to hint at how identity has to be constantly reproduced through the repeated performances of the subject. The destiny of the Jew would thus have less to do with any natural (or even divine) preconditions than with the label 'Jew' and the complex web of social functions and meanings it entails. While this is obviously not part of Georg's conscious reflections, the moment nevertheless marks a potential for understanding, for breaking rigid stereotypical patterns. This is demonstrated by Georg's immediate reaction, which refers again to the relation between stereotypes and physiognomy and can be understood as a reminiscence of his conversation with Willy:

> Und als er sich in den Anblick der beiden Sprechenden verlor und ihre Gestalten betrachtete, die sich mit scharf gezogenen Linien von dem rötlich-violetten Himmel abzeichneten, fiel es ihm nicht zum ersten Male auf, daß Heinrich, der darauf bestand, hier daheim zu sein, in Figur und Geste einem fanatischen, jüdischen Priester glich, während Leo, der mit seinem Volk nach Palästina ziehen wollte, in Gesichtsschnitt und Haltung ihn an die Bildsäule eines griechischen Jünglings erinnerte, die er einmal im Vatikan oder im Museum gesehen hatte. (WiF723)
>
> And as he lost himself in the contemplation of the two speakers, and looked at their figures, which stood out in relief against the reddish-violet sky in sharply-drawn, violently-moving lines, it occurred to him, and not for the first time, that Heinrich who insisted in being at home here, resembled both in figure and in gesture some fanatical Jewish preacher, while Leo, who wanted to go back to Palestine with his people, reminded him in feature and in bearing of the statue of a Greek youth which he had once seen in the Vatican or the Naples museum.[31]

In Georg's perception, his friends appear like silhouettes against the evening sky, which subtly hints again at the physiognomist Lavater.

---

30 See Althusser, Louis (1971), 'Ideology and Ideological State Apparatuses,' *Lenin and Philosophy and Other Essays*, London: New Left Books, 127–188, 174.
31 Schnitzler, *Road into the Open*, 111.

This implication demonstrates both Georg's automatic attempt to inte-
grate his new insights within the ordering patterns he has internalized
and his failure. As with Willy, and here again 'nicht zum ersten Mal'
(not for the first time), Georg has to acknowledge that the stereotypes
do not exactly fit the individual: while Heinrich's stereotypical Jewish appearance is betrayed by his refusal to be identified through his
Jewishness, Leo's classical beauty (the young Greek being a positive
stereotype – albeit one co-opted by other cultures for their museum
collections) contradicts his radical views on Jewish identity. For Abigail E. Gillman, this demonstrates that after the short moment where
he broadens his usual perception, Georg immediately narrows his gaze
again by 'shrink[ing] Jewish characters into type-figures'.[32] While this is
certainly true, it is also a moment of confusion where the incongruence
of stereotype and individual appears and the relativity and constructedness of stereotypes emerge.

Moreover, the passage demonstrates that the physiognomic interpretation tells always at least as much about the observing and describing
subject as it does about the subject described.[33] Indeed, through Georg's
descriptions of Heinrich and Leo, we learn more about Georg himself
than about the other two. The passage renders evident how strongly
the cultural narratives inherent to stereotypes influence his perception
of his Jewish friends. In fact, we learn less about him individually than
about his 'cognitive ordering tools'. As Peter von Matt writes, 'Was im
fremden Gesicht den Betrachter gegenwärtig macht, sind […] die mor-
alisch-gesellschaftlichen Normen, *seine* Normen, welche sich mit der
Gesichtsbeschreibung automatisch verbinden' (The observer is made
present in the description of the other's face through the moral and
social norms, *the observer's own* norms, which are automatically connected with the description of a face).[34] The description of the cycling
trip with Leo and Heinrich contains the entire range of Georg's ambivalent positions towards Jews in general and his Jewish friends in particular; it encapsulates Georg's ignorance and indifference as well as
his potential to overcome internalized stereotypes. Even if only for a
short time, he too feels affected by the urgency and determination both
Leo and Heinrich display in their conflict. He finds himself for once in
an outsider position and does not participate in the discussion. Only
at the very end does he feel the need to intervene, when Leo utters
an only seemingly improbable apprehension: 'Aber wenn die Schei-
terhaufen wieder angezündet werden …?' (WiF724) (but supposing

---

32 Gillman, 'Failed Bildung and the Aesthetics of Detachment,' 222.
33 See Matt, Peter von (1989), *… fertig ist das Angesicht: Zur Literaturgeschichte des
     menschlichen Gesichts*, Frankfurt a. M.: Suhrkamp, 113.
34 Matt, *… fertig ist das Angesicht*, 113.

the mediaeval stake were to be lighted again?).[35] During the previous
discussion, Georg has felt too unfamiliar with the topic of discussion
to have an opinion of his own. However, at this point he claims with
certainty: 'O [...] diese Zeiten kommen doch nicht wieder' (WiF724)
(Oh [...] those times will certainly not come again).[36] His friends find
his aplomb amusing: 'Die anderen mußten lachen, daß Georg sie durch
diese Worte, wie Heinrich bemerkte, im Namen der gesamten Christen-
heit über ihre Zukunft zu beruhigen so liebenswürdig wäre' (WiF724)
(Both the others were unable to help laughing at George [sic] being kind
enough to reassure them in that way about their future, in the name, as
Heinrich observed, of the whole of Christendom).[37]

It becomes clear that such a statement cannot be made independently of the social position of the speaker. The entire discussion
is based on the function of the Jew as the other that is excluded and
deviant from the norm. So when Georg enters the debate, the others
cannot just take his statements as his individual opinion but perceive
him as representative of the privileged norm. Obviously, Heinrich's
remark is meant to be humorous but it still reminds Georg of his outside position in this particular constellation of people and subject of
discussion. Leo implicitly mentions this as well when he assumes that
Georg might have been bored by the long discussion of his friends.
However, when Georg reacts defensively, he stresses that he does not
think of Georg as ignorant: 'Leo hielt Georgs Hand fest. "Ich halte Sie
für einen sehr klugen und auch für einen sehr guten Menschen [...]".
[...] "Sie sind mir wirklich sympathisch, Georg." Er sah ihm tief in die
Augen' (WiF724) (Leo held George's hand in a firm grip. 'I take you
for a very shrewd man and also for a very good sort [...]'. [...] I really
feel a sympathy between us, George'. He looked him straight into
his eyes).[38] It is hard to say what drives this unexpected praise but it
gives a rare glimpse of an outside perspective on Georg. Since the text
remains focalized through Georg's perspective, it is impossible for the
reader to know whether this is an authentic expression of Leo's feelings for Georg in general or of a more spontaneous affect.[39] The sudden

---

35   Schnitzler, *Road into the Open*, 113.
36   Schnitzler, *Road into the Open*, 113.
37   Schnitzler, *Road into the Open*, 113.
38   Schnitzler, *Road into the Open*, 113.
39   There is an almost erotic aspect to the sudden mutual attraction between Georg
     and Leo, which is underlined by Georg's associative memory that Anna had once
     had a crush on Leo a few years ago: 'Georg kam es manchmal so vor, als stünde
     seine eigene Sympathie für Leo mit jener längst verflossenen Neigung Annas
     für ihn in einem tieferen Zusammenhang. Denn nicht zum ersten Male fühlte
     er sich in ganz sonderbarer Weise zu einem Manne hingezogen, dem früher
     eine Seele zugeflogen war, die jetzt ihm gehörte' (WiF726) (It always seemed

cordiality between the men is peculiar in this passage: 'Sein [Leo's] Ton bekam etwas wahrhaft Herzliches' (WiF724) (His voice assumed a tone of genuine sincerity);[40] and later, '"Glückliche Reise", sagte Georg, reichte ihm [Heinrich] die Hand und drückte sie mit besonderer Herzlichkeit' (WiF729) ('*Bon voyage*', said George, and shook hands with him with unusual affection).[41] One may wonder whether this sudden feeling of connectedness emerges due to a better mutual understanding and acceptance or rather to a compensation for the articulation of difference that has evidently and inevitably been implicit in the conversation. Georg's thoughts when he is finally alone demonstrate ambivalence between these two directions:

In diesem Augenblick wußte er, daß er mit keinem von beiden bei aller Sympathie jemals zu einer unbefangenen Vertrautheit gelangen werde, wie sie ihn noch im vorigen Jahre mit Guido Schönstein [...] verbunden hatte. Er dachte darüber nach, ob das vielleicht wirklich in dem Rassenunterschied zwischen ihm und jenen begründet sein mochte, und fragte sich, ob er, ohne das Gespräch der beiden, durch das eigene Gefühl dieser Fremdheit sich so deutlich bewußt geworden wäre. Er zweifelte daran. Fühlte er sich nicht gerade diesen beiden und manchen anderen ihres Volkes näher, ja verwandter als vielen Menschen, die mit ihm vom gleichen Stamme waren? Ja spürte er nicht ganz deutlich, daß manchmal irgendwo in der Tiefe zwischen ihm und diesen beiden stärkere Fäden liefen als von ihm zu Guido, ja vielleicht zu seinem eigenen Bruder? (WiF730)
[A]nd he realised at this moment that in spite of all the sympathy he felt for both of them he would never attain with either that unrestrained sense of intimacy which had united him

---

to George as though his own sympathy for Leo were fundamentally connected with Anna's long-past fancy for him. He felt, and not for the first time, curiously attracted to a man to whom a soul which now belonged to him, had flown in years gone by). See Schnitzler, *Road into the Open*, 115. This recalls Freud's description of jealousy as a form of 'detour' for repressed homoeroticism when a man's own attraction for another man is projected onto the woman ('Nicht *ich* liebe den Mann – *sie liebt ihn ja*' (It is not I who is in love with the other man, *she* is). See Freud, Sigmund (1943), 'Über einen autobiographisch beschriebenen Fall von Paranoia (Dementia Paranoides),' in *Gesammelte Werke*, vol. 8: *Werke aus den Jahren 1909–1913*, ed. by Anna Freud, Edward Bibring, Willi Hoffer, Ernst Kris, and Otto Isakower, London: Imago, 239–320, 301 [emphasis in the original]. Even if Georg is not jealous of Leo, his associative thought of his lover Anna obviously brings an erotic dimension to his attraction towards Leo.
40 Schnitzler, *Road into the Open*, 113.
41 Schnitzler, *Road into the Open*, 120.

last year with Guido Schönstein and previously poor Labinsky. He reflected whether perhaps the fundamental reason for this was not perhaps [sic] the difference of race between him and them, and he asked himself whether leaving out of account the conversation between the two of them, he would of his own initiative have realised so clearly this feeling of aloofness. He doubted it. Did he not as a matter of fact feel himself nearer, yes even more akin, to these two and to many others of their race than to many men who came from the same stock as his own? Why, did he not feel quite distinctly that deep down somewhere there were stronger threads of sympathy running between him and those two men, than between him and Guido or perhaps even his own brother?[42]

Georg struggles here to understand and define his relationship with Leo and Heinrich. His contradictory pondering about the possible intimacy between himself and his Jewish friends in comparison to his bond with his non-Jewish friend Guido or his own brother demonstrates how deeply the afternoon with Leo and Heinrich has affected him. The expression 'innere Fäden' (inner threads) seems to imply an almost fate-like relationship between himself and his Jewish friends, which refers back to Georg's 'Ahnung' (idea) about the 'geheimnisvolle Los' (mysterious destiny) of the Jews and the consolidation of Jewishness as destiny.[43] Strikingly, Georg feels like his own destiny is intertwined with that of his Jewish friends. Thus, he seems to some extent to identify with them, which might at first seem curious, considering his privileged position. However, as Georg's character has been identified as 'impressionist',[44] this feeling of connection is less surprising: the character traits of the impressionist type – 'Nervosität, Reizabhängigkeit, Verantwortungsscheu und "Wurzellosigkeit"'[45] (nervousness, dependence on external stimuli, lack of a sense of responsibility, and rootlessness) – were said to stem from the Jewish influence on Viennese culture: 'Zur Identifikation mit dem Juden lud die Fungibilität des "impressionistischen Menschen" geradezu ein'[46] (The fungibility of the 'impressionist character' lent itself perfectly to an identification with the Jew). In

---

42 Schnitzler, *Road into the Open*, 120.
43 The Greek mythology of the *Moirai*, who spin, measure and cut the 'thread' of humans' life, is more explicitly used by the writer Nürnberger later in the novel: 'Weder Sie noch ich wissen es, wo in diesem Augenblick ein Faden zu unserm Schicksal gesponnen wird' (WiF933) (Neither you nor I know the place where a strand of our fate is being spun at this very moment, Schnitzler, *Road into the Open*, 381).
44 Fliedl, *Arthur Schnitzler*, 219.
45 Fliedl, *Arthur Schnitzler*, 217.
46 Fliedl, *Arthur Schnitzler*, 217.

this way, Georg's identification with his Jewish friends ironically has
anti-Semitic foundations: it might well be his restlessness and unsteadi-
ness which make him relate to those of this 'people', and with Heinrich
in particular he shares the tendency of procrastination and the lack of
discipline.[47] An anti-Semitic reading of the book could thus understand
Georg's sensation of connectedness with the Jews as proof of the latter's
devastating influence: 'Die "pathologischen" Züge des Jungen Wien
führte man auf den jüdischen Einfluß zurück und erklärte Dekadenz
zu einem "semitischen" Phänomen' (The 'pathological' traits of Young
Vienna were explained with the Jewish influence and the feelings of
decadence were declared a 'semitic' phenomenon).[48]

From the first page on, the lack of productivity is a recurring topic
in the text: 'Er hatte wieder ein halbes Jahr oder länger nichts Rech-
tes gearbeitet' (WiF635) (He had done no real work for six months or
more).[49] While he shares this tendency of procrastination with Heinrich,
the inner bonds he feels between himself and his Jewish friends are
less likely to have their origin in this shared struggle with productivity,
but rather in Georg's self-image as an artist, which also explains his
general fascination with Jewish circles. It is not only the unequivocally
negative stereotype of Jewishness that seems to play a part in Georg's
fascination and identification with the Jews as a group, but also the positive mystification of the Jew as 'quintessential outsider',[50] which for
him, as an aspiring artist, holds a certain promise. Georg's status as a
nobleman-artist makes him a suspect of potential dilettantism, which is
one of his sorest spots: 'Georg [...] erinnerte sich jetzt, daß ein Kritiker
ihn nach dem Konzert [...] als "dilettierenden Aristokraten" bezeichnet
hatte' (WiF743) (George [...] now remembered that after the concert [...]
a critic had described him as an aristocratic dilettante).[51] The connection
he feels has less to do with himself, Leo, and Heinrich as individuals,
than with the respective stereotypes of their social roles. At another
point, Georg almost realizes this with regard to Heinrich: 'Er für seinen

---

47   Tiziane Schön's reading focuses on the motif of 'Nervenschwäche' (weakness of
     the nerves) as generational symptom that fostered anti-Semitic prejudices. See
     Schön, Tiziane (2004), 'Nervenschwache Generation – begabte Neurastheniker:
     Georg Hermanns *Der kleine Gast* als Berliner Pendant zu Arthur Schnitzlers,'
     *Der Weg ins Freie, Georg Hermann: Deutsch-jüdischer Schriftsteller und Journalist,
     1871–1943*, ed. by Godela Weiss-Sussex, Tübingen: Niemeyer. On the aspect
     of 'sentimentality' in the novel, see also Angela H. Lin, 'Resisting "Bad Taste":
     Sentimentality, "Jewishness", and Modernity in Arthur Schnitzler's *Der Weg ins
     Freie*,' *The German Quarterly* 79 (3): 366–380.
48   Fliedl, *Arthur Schnitzler*, 217.
49   Schnitzler, *Road into the Open*, 2.
50   Gilman, *Difference and Pathology*, 232.
51   Schnitzler, *Road into the Open*, 138.

Teil wußte, daß es weniger Freundschaft war, die ihn zu dem jungen Schriftsteller hinzog, als Neugier, einen seltsamen Menschen näher kennenzulernen; vielleicht auch das Interesse, in eine Welt hineinzuschauen, die ihm bisher ziemlich fremd geblieben war' (WiF708) (He for his part knew that it was not so much friendship that attracted him to the young author, as the curiosity to get to know a strange man more intimately. Perhaps also the interest of looking into a world which had been more or less foreign to him).[52]

Heinrich's world of Jewish intellectuals is not only interesting because it is somewhat foreign to Georg, it is of particular interest to Georg because it is emblematically intertwined with the world of art: not only because Jews were perceived as dominating the artistic and literary avant-gardes,[53] but also because of the outsider position of the Jew. Not only is this outsider position itself practically a prerequisite to be taken seriously as an artist, the stereotype of the artist and the stereotype of the Jew share the label of a predisposition to mental illness. Through its idealized stereotype, insanity is linked to higher creativity and genius. If the Jews are said to be more prone to 'madness', the mystification of the Jew as mad creative genius seems a short step away.

This complexity of the stereotype of the Jew with its contradictorily pejorative and idealizing connotations also explains the constant ambivalence Georg feels toward his Jewish friends: while his perception is highly influenced by the negative stereotypes of the Jew, other stereotypical images of the Jew also give reason for his fascination – and for something which in fact could be described as the envy of the norm. The verdict 'aristocratic dilettante' suggests that due to his privileged position, Georg's art can only be an idle and entertaining pastime. Implicitly, we also recognize here the mystification of suffering as creative potential. This is why there might be a hidden form of jealousy lying in Georg's ambivalent feelings towards the Jews around him and particularly towards Heinrich: their ascription to Judaism, even though it is not necessarily practised or even actively declared by them, seems to give them a kind of open credit as artists, which is assigned to them by birth in the same way as the suspicion of dilettantism is assigned to him as an aristocrat. Looking closely at Georg's repeated feelings of resentment towards Heinrich, his own sense of being excluded from the Jewish community becomes clear:

---

52 Schnitzler, *Road into the Open*, 92.
53 See Gilman, *Difference and Pathology*, 233.

Er ist in seiner Art genau so krank, wie sein Vater es war.
Dabei kann man doch nicht sagen, daß er persönlich schlimme
Erfahrungen gemacht hat. Und er hat mal behauptet, daß er sich
mit niemandem zusammengehörig fühle! Es ist ja nicht wahr. Mit
allen Juden fühlt er sich zusammengehörig, und mit dem letzten
von ihnen noch immer enger als mit mir. (WiF833)
He is quite as morbid [ill, M.K.] as his father was. And at the same
time one can't say that he has been personally through bad times.
And he has asserted on one occasion that he felt there was no one
with whom he had anything in common. It is not a bit true. He
feels he has something in common with all the Jews and he stands
nearer to the meanest of them than he does to me.[54]

'Schlimme Erfahrungen' refers here to experiences of anti-Semitism, which in Heinrich's father's case destroyed his political career
and caused a lapse into mental illness. Georg's remark that Heinrich
himself has not had any experience of this kind is crucial: while it is
here a rather dismissive comment about Heinrich's – in Georg's view
– neurotic fear of anti-Semitism,[55] it also suggests that Heinrich has not
'earned' his suffering through experience, but that is has been 'given'
to him by his Jewish birth. This is obviously foremost a negative perception of Heinrich which reproduces the equally negative stereotype
of the 'mad Jew'. However, through the fact that Georg immediately
moves on to Heinrich's ties to other Jews to whom he will always feel
closer than to Georg himself, we can detect the feeling of rejection and
jealousy. This makes the passage quoted earlier, which speaks of the
'innere Fäden' between Georg and his Jewish friends, appear more like
a wish than a description of their actual relationship.

In fact, this moment of putative connection to his Jewish friends
is followed by one of the very few times where Georg actually comes
close to consciously analyzing his relationships to other people as well
as the internal and external factors by which these are determined. He
goes on wondering about the intimacy with Heinrich and Leo that was
just expressed:

Aber wenn es so war, hätte er das nicht diesen beiden Menschen
heute nachmittag [sic] in irgendeinem Augenblick sagen müssen?

---

54 Schnitzler, *Road into the Open*, 252.
55 The fact that the young Jewish physician Bertold Stauber experiences the reality
    of anti-Semitism in politics in the Viennese parliament, which mirrors the expe-
    riences of Heinrich's father, can be understood as a latent authorial distancing
    from the perspective of Georg, who wishes to dismiss Heinrich's concerns as
    neurotic.

Ihnen zurufen: vertraut mir doch, schließt mich nicht aus. Versucht es doch, mich für einen Freund zu halten!.... Und als er sich fragte, warum er das nicht getan und an ihrem Gespräch teilgenommen hatte, da ward er mit Verwunderung inne, daß er während dessen ganzer Dauer eine Art von Schuldbewußtsein nicht los geworden war, gerade so, als wäre auch er sein Leben lang von einer gewissen leichtfertigen und durch persönliche Erfahrung gar nicht gerechtfertigten Feindseligkeit gegen die 'Fremden', wie Leo sie selbst nannte, nicht frei gewesen und hätte so sein Teil zu dem Mißtrauen und dem Trotz beigetragen, mit dem so manche sich vor ihm verschlossen, denen entgegenzukommen er selbst Anlaß und Neigung fühlen mochte. (WiF730)

But if that was so, would he not have been bound to have taken some opportunity this afternoon to have said as much to those two men? to have appealed to them? 'Just trust me, don't shut me out. Just try to treat me as a friend ...' And as he asked himself why he had not done it, and why he had scarcely taken any part in the conversation, he realised with astonishment that during the whole time he had not been able to shake a kind of guilty consciousness of having not been free during his whole life from a certain hostility towards the foreigners, as Leo called them himself, a kind of wanton hostility which was certainly not justified by his own personal experience, and had thus contributed his own share to that distrust and defiance with which so many persons, whom he himself might have been glad to take an opportunity to approach, had shut themselves off from him.[56]

This is a neat description of the functioning of stereotypes. Georg realizes his internalized hostility against the Jews has nothing to do with his real contacts with Jewish individuals. The fact that he had not been conscious of that internalized hostility before also explains his incomprehension of Willy's allegedly defensive position discussed earlier: he had not been aware of the implicit hostility and discrimination Jews have to face on an everyday basis in an increasingly anti-Semitic society. This recognition might of course have been a turning point in Georg's personal development, but this is not the case. His inner turmoil comes to an end with the 'dumpfen Einsicht, daß reine Beziehungen auch zwischen einzelnen und reinen Menschen in einer Atmosphäre von Torheit, Unrecht und Unaufrichtigkeit nicht gedeihen können' (WiF730) (dull realisation that clean relations could not flourish even between clean men in an atmosphere of folly, injustice and

---

56 Schnitzler, *Road into the Open*, 121.

disingenuousness).[57] Critics have discussed the authorial voice behind this statement and wondered whether it can be understood as some sort of key message of the novel or if it represents only Georg's individual perspective.[58] Obviously, it is characteristic for the entire narrative structure of the novel that the authorial narrative voice blends in with the characters' perspective (mostly Georg's) to an extent that it becomes almost completely indistinguishable. Georg's insight can certainly be seen as a true acknowledgement of the power of stereotyping and the power structures represented by it; and as has already been shown here and will be discussed in more detail later on, this is demonstrated by the interactions between the characters in the novel. What makes this recognition so 'dull' is the resignation attached to it for Georg. He realizes that the 'atmosphere' in Vienna is stupid and unjust but all he longs for is 'diesem Unbehagen zu entfliehen' (WiF730) (to escape this feeling of depression), and so he seeks comfort by meeting his lover Anna. On this note, he immediately represses the new threatening view he has gained on the society he lives in – because acting on his new insight would mean a deeper engagement with his own position and the newly discovered feeling of guilt. The novel here highlights clearly the privilege of the protagonist to let his newly gained insight into the workings of unjust power structures simply slip away. This fits well with the way Georg often reacts exasperatedly when Jewish characters confront him with anti-Semitic stereotypes and discrimination. One may interpret this reaction as a disguised form of the guilt he discovers after the day with Leo and Heinrich. This guilt shows itself nevertheless in various encounters with Jewish acquaintances but is immediately transformed into a general feeling of renunciation and hostility, as demonstrated in the examples discussed in the next section.

Stereotypes and Performative Speech Acts

Let us return once more to Bertold Stauber's sarcastic characterization of Georg as the positive stereotype of the norm. Of course, Bertold's hostility derives from the fact that he himself has shown some interest in Georg's lover Anna, but certainly also from his personal experience of being discriminated against and stereotyped as a Jew. One of the first things the reader learns about Bertold is the fact that he has resigned from his mandated position in the Viennese parliament because of anti-Semitic insults against him.

---

57 Schnitzler, *Road into the Open*, 121.
58 See Segar, 'Aesthetic Coherence in Arthur Schnitzler's Novel *Der Weg ins Freie*,' 107.

'[...] Und was das kräftigste Argument einer gewissen Sorte von Staatserhaltern gegen meine Ausführungen war, können sie sich ja denken, Herr Baron.'
'Nun?' fragte Georg.
'Jud, halt's Maul', erwiderte Bertold mit schmal gewordenen Lippen. (WiF657)

'And of course you can imagine what the strongest argument was, which a certain type of conservatives used against my points.'
'Well?' queried George.
'Hold your jaw, Jew', answered Berthold with tightly compressed lips.[59]

The passage is dominated by the theme of speech and performance. Bertold's own outrage shows in his tightly shut lips, which, in the context of the insulting order to 'shut up', appears like an aggressive mimicry of the harassment itself. The incident took place in the parliament after Bertold had made a critical public speech that outraged the nationalist-conservative members, who demonstrated their disapproval not by engaging in the actual argument but by insulting Bertold and reducing him to the stereotyped role of 'the' Jew. As Butler writes, '[t]o be injured by speech is to suffer a loss of context, that is, not to know where you are'.[60] This is precisely what Bertold experiences: the insults take him out of the context of the parliamentary discussion because they are not at all related to the content of his own speech but deny him his right to be heard out and taken seriously as a politician in the arena of political speech: 'Exposed at the moment of such shattering is precisely the volatility of one's "place" within the community of speakers; one can be "put in one's place" by such speech, but such a speech may be no place'.[61] The anti-Semitic insult sends Bertold off the political stage to an uncertain non-place outside of the community of speakers, assigning him the position of the 'other'.

Despite the obvious humiliation, Bertold stresses, however, that the main reason for his resignation is not the insults but the sheer inauthenticity of the whole farce. After the debacle he met one of his strongest opponents, the paper salesman Jalaudek, who 'innocently' greeted him with the words: 'Habe die Ehre, Herr Doktor, auch eine

---

59 Schnitzler, *Road into the Open*, 28.
60 Butler, Judith (1997a), *Excitable Speech: A Politics of the Performative*, New York, London: Routledge, 40.
61 Butler, *Excitable Speech*, 4.

kleine Erfrischung gefällig?' (WiF657) (Hallo, Doctor, won't you have a drink with me?).[62] The reality of politics appears as pure theatrical performance, as 'Komödienspiel' (WiF659) (comedy),[63] as Bertold puts it, where the contents of the debates do not matter. This implies the idea that the public and political performance does not bear upon the real everyday life of the members of society whom the members of parliament are supposed to represent. Jalaudek's comment at the buffet is meant to be 'off stage' and indeed shows his indifference to the debated matters. He has played his part and feels no need to stay in character during his break at the buffet. This, however, exemplifies the gap between the insulting and insulted position. The injury caused by the insulting speech 'on stage' is real and therefore Bertold cannot shrug off his role in the same way as Jalaudek. Analogously to Ehrenberg's example of the anti-Semitic insult on the Ringstraße as representative stage for society, the parliament is exactly this: the place of social representation, and if anti-Semitism is acceptable here it might just as well be so in everyday life.

The text addresses here the fate-like function of stereotypes: the insult 'Jud, halt's Maul!' turns out to be performative not only in the sense of the theatrical quality it seems to have for the speakers, but also in the way it becomes a performative speech act that assigns a certain social 'destiny' to the one who has been typecast by the insult. The performative aspect is underlined when Bertold shows his outrage by imitating his aggressors: '"Ruhig, Jud! Halt's Maul! Jud! Jud! Kusch!" fuhr Bertold fort und schien in Erinnerung zu schwelgen. Anna sah vor sich hin. Georg fand innerlich, es wäre nun genug. Ein kurzes, peinliches Schweigen entstand' (WiF657) ('Be quiet, Jew! Hold your jaw! Jew! Jew! Shut up!' continued Berthold, who seemed to somewhat revel in the recollection. Anna looked straight in front of her. George thought that this was quite enough. There was a short, painful silence).[64] Bertold's outburst is almost reminiscent of a compulsive repetition or acting out in which he re-lives the offending incident. Also his 'schmal gewordene Lippen' (tightly compressed lips) mentioned earlier, while they are certainly mainly a sign of his anger, appear as a form of mimicry, not to say a performative *realization* of the insulting demand, which culminates in Bertold's final decision to give up his political career. What appeared to be mainly theatrics in the parliament thus turns out to have a real effect, which, interestingly and significantly, seems to be denied not only by the harassers like Jalaudek, but also by Georg and Anna.

---

62 Schnitzler, *Road into the Open*, 28.
63 Schnitzler, *Road into the Open*, 30.
64 Schnitzler, *Road into the Open*, 28.

The formulation 'in Erinnerung zu schwelgen' (revel in the recollection) is striking, of course, as it suggests a pleasant memory and
appears misplaced in the context of the experience of discrimination.
The narrative perspective seems here totally congruent with that of
Georg: in his perception, Bertold must find a distorted pleasure by
being singled out and insulted or at least by being able to tell the story
of his discrimination. For both Georg and Anna, Bertold's way of talking about his experience is uncomfortable because while they do not
consider themselves as anti-Semites they still do not seem to be able to
identify with him or to show him their solidarity. It is clear that they
would prefer if he did not take the incident so seriously and at least
did not dwell on the details. This is an evident reaction of the disguised
feeling of guilt of which Georg will become aware after the discussion between Leo and Heinrich analyzed above. The embarrassing or
embarrassed silence in the room appears like an ironic completion of
Bertold's re-enactment as it follows after the order to 'shut up' quoted
earlier. In this way, they reinforce not only Bertold's humiliation but
also the negation of the reality of anti-Semitism that comes along with
Jalaudek's behaviour.

Anna's and Georg's reaction proves that the manner in which stereotypes are transported and dealt with in the political field is closely
connected to social reality. The question is also for whom the silence
is meant to be embarrassing: for Bertold, because he made Anna and
Georg uncomfortable, or for the latter because they do not know how
to react? Evidently, Anna and Georg do not take the situation as seriously as Bertold and in this way implicitly accept Jalaudek's separation of public and private speech and the resulting performative aspect
of the former. This of course doubles the shame of the discriminating
experience and makes the moment embarrassing for him. However,
the embarrassment might well be on the side of Georg and Anna, who
silence their latent feeling of guilt with their refusal to take the incident
seriously. When, after his day with Leo and Heinrich, Georg comes
to the realization that he himself might be guilty of a certain *Leicht-
fertigkeit* (levity) towards anti-Semitic tendencies, it is surely because
of situations like this one, when the insulted and marginalized Jew
is confronted by indifference and mockery rather than sympathy and
solidarity.

Bertold realizes their incongruent points of view when he notices
Anna's *leiser Spott* (gentle derision) (WiF657):

'Sie haben ja wahrscheinlich recht, Fräulein Anna', sagt er, 'wenn
Sie darüber lächeln, daß ich wegen dieses läppischen Abenteuers
mein Mandat niedergelegt habe. Ein parlamentarisches Leben
ohne Komödienspiel ist ja überhaupt nicht möglich. Ich hätte es

bedenken und selber mitagieren, dem Kerl womöglich zutrinken sollen, der mich öffentlich beschimpft hat. Das wäre bequem, österreichisch – und vielleicht sogar das richtigste gewesen.' (WiF659)

'You are probably quite right, Fräulein Anna', he said, 'if you smile at my resigning my seat on account of that silly incident. A parliamentary life without its share of comedy is an absolute impossibility. I should have realised it, played up to it and taken the opportunity of drinking with the fellow who had publicly insulted me. It would have been convenient, Austrian – and possibly even the most correct course taken.'[65]

The reason why for Bertold the incident is indeed not as 'läppisch' (silly) as it might seem to Anna and Georg, and therefore why he has much more trouble in accepting the 'script' of the putative comedy, is quite obvious: the part he has to play as 'the Jew' is not only far more uncomfortable than theirs, it also hinders him from playing others such as that of member of parliament. That it is indeed the mechanisms of stereotype that are at work here is shown precisely in the gap between public and private speech. Stereotypes are related to social roles and social status: 'Status refers to a position in society which entails a certain set of rights and duties. Role refers to the performance of those rights and duties, it is relational. Stereotype refers to both role and status at the same time, and the reference is perhaps always predominantly evaluative'.[66] The evaluative aspect of the stereotype of the Jew in the Vienna of Der Weg ins Freie (Road into the Open) is certainly pejorative. The insult 'Jud, halt's Maul' (Hold your jaw, Jew) belongs to this stereotype and is, in a way, stereotypical in itself. The parliament is a symbolic space of representation and it is no coincidence that Bertold's discrimination is to be experienced here. The verbal abuse reduces him to the status and social role of a Jew, does not allow him to be perceived as a complex individual and member of society who is not only Jewish but also a doctor, a member of parliament etc. This is why Jalaudek is able to address him in an innocently friendly way at the buffet: at this point, the representative function has been replaced by the individual encounter where the stereotypical reduction is, if not eliminated, at least weakened.

Stereotypes do not necessarily cease to function in people's minds when they are proven wrong by personal experience. This can be explained through the function of stereotypes within the social order.

---

65   Schnitzler, Road into the Open, 30.
66   Perkins, 'Rethinking Stereotypes,' 142.

A stereotype is, first of all, a cultural representation of a specific social grouping which in cultural analysis is often addressed and scrutinized in so-called 'image of' works. As Richard Dyer points out, these works usually have a political impulse as they spring 'from the feeling that how social groups are treated in cultural representation is part and parcel of how they are treated in real life, that poverty, harassment, self-hate and discrimination [...] are shored up and instituted by representation'.[67] This is what the passage about Bertold's harassment at the parliament discussion demonstrates: the appellation 'Jud' puts members of the group in question in an inferior position as the term 'Jew', at least in the context above, is already an insult in itself that is enough to silence the addressed person. The words 'halt's Maul', which would be expected to be infelicitous on the representative stage of parliament, therefore belong to the stereotype 'Jew', an explicit articulation of what the term connotes: a Jew is someone who should not have the right to speak in public. If we consider the parliament as space of representation and speech in the most literal sense, as it is the place where the *represent-atives* of society get together to debate, we get back to Dyer's remark on the link between cultural representations and their corresponding reality in everyday life. As we have seen, this link is being denied or at least blurred by and for the non-Jewish characters in the novel, while Bertold sees himself forced to draw the consequences.

It seems obvious that there is both a gap and link between the 'image' or stereotype on the representational level and the individual supposed to be represented by the image. The public speech act, in this case, the public insult, reinforces the cultural image, while the private speech act seeks to soften or qualify it. This qualification, however, works only for the subject outside the stereotyped grouping. For the latter, the gap can only be perceived as further insult because it not only takes away the possibility of a real argument and examination of the structures within parliament and society but also any option of defence for the insulted individual and his social grouping. For Gilman, there is a difference between a normal form of stereotyping 'which all of us need to do to pre-serve our illusion of control over the world' and a pathological form.[68] The latter is incapable of distinguishing the individual from the stere-otyped class, while the former still realizes that there is such a distinc-tion. One can easily see how here the two different forms of stereotyping defined by Gilman melt into each other: the insults against Bertold are already a real aggression against an individual, so the incident is obvi-ously to be considered as the second, pathological form of stereotyping.

---

67 Dyer, *The Matter of Images*, 1.
68 Gilman, *Difference and Pathology*, 18.

Nevertheless, the aggressors still distinguish between the role the individual represents (the Jew in parliament) and the individual person (Dr Stauber). Georg is even more on the borderline as he, unlike Jalaudek, is not part of any anti-Semitic movement and foregathers with various Jews on a regular basis but still cannot help but apply internalized stereotypes onto his Jewish acquaintances. As this happens on an at best half-conscious level, it rarely affects his interactions with Jews directly and thus appears to remain unnoticed by the latter.

We, thus, have here again in some way a distinction between public (what Georg actually says or does) and private speech (what he thinks and feels). After the passage with Bertold, his father, old doctor Stauber, arrives as well. As it turns out that the three Jewish families most present in the novel, the Ehrenbergs, the Golowskis, and the Staubers, are all somehow related, Dr Stauber casually drops another Jewish stereotype: 'Und übrigens [...] weiß der Herr Baron gewiß, daß alle Juden miteinander verwandt sind' (WiF661) (Anyway [...] the Baron is bound to know that all Jews are related to each other).[69] This remark hints at the stereotype of Jewish inbreeding that was held as one explanation for another stereotype, that is, the assumption of the Jewish precondition for diseases and impurity.[70] Georg's initial reaction is annoyance, covered by a polite smile towards the older man:

Seiner Empfindung nach bestand durchaus keine Notwendigkeit, daß auch der alte Doktor Stauber ihm offizielle Mitteilung von seiner Zugehörigkeit zum Judentum machte. Er wußte es ja, und er nahm es ihm nicht übel. Er nahm es überhaupt keinem übel; aber warum fingen sie denn immer selbst davon zu reden an? Wo er auch hinkam, er begegnete nur Juden, die sich schämten, daß sie Juden waren, oder solchen, die darauf stolz waren und Angst hatten, man könnte glauben, sie schämten sich. (WiF661)
There was no necessity at all, in his view, for Doctor Stauber as well officially to communicate to him his membership of the Jewish community. He already knew it and bore him no grudge for it. He bore him no grudge at all for it [German original reads: he did not bear anybody any grudge for it, M.K.]; but why do they always begin to talk about it themselves? Wherever he went, he only met Jews who were ashamed of being Jews, or the type who were proud of it and were frightened of people thinking they were ashamed of it.[71]

69 Schnitzler, *Road into the Open*, 33.
70 See Gilman, Sander L. (1995), *Freud, Race, and Gender*, Princeton, NJ: Princeton University Press.
71 Schnitzler, *Road into the Open*, 33.

Gillman has noted that here Georg moves on smoothly from the individual remark to its type and from there to the 'logical next step, by
typecasting not the remark but the individual who uttered it – hence
the move from singular to plural [...]'.[72] Moreover, one has to stress that
Stauber's remark really is already a stereotype itself, an ironic quotation
of an opinion commonly held by the increasingly anti-Semitic Viennese
society. The effect is, however, lost on Georg, who, just like in the earlier
passage with Bertold, reacts with defensive withdrawal. In both passages, there seems to be an underlying misunderstanding between the
Jewish person and Georg, the non-Jew with the non-anti-Semitic (self-)
image.[73] Both Staubers seem to trust Georg to be 'on their side' and
thus include him in their outrage against or ironic dismissal of anti-Semitic stereotypes. Yet Georg does not feel included but rather the opposite: for him, as he is not directly affected by anti-Semitism himself,
the repeated mentioning of it is annoying. From Georg's point of view,
Stauber's mentioning of his Jewishness is as unnecessary (lacking in
Notwendigkeit (necessity)) as Willy Eisler's constant defensive position.
This shows Georg's at least initial unwillingness to empathize with his
Jewish acquaintances. Not being an anti-Semite for him means above
all an indifference towards the Jewish question. Thus, the ironic remark
of old doctor Stauber triggers the exact opposite reaction in Georg to
that intended: while he obviously wanted to build a common ground of
discussion by signalling that he believed Georg to be unaffected by stereotypical thinking about Jews, Georg's inner response is to stereotype
him.[74] So while Georg does not show any explicit aggression towards
Jews, his inner stereotyping does have a real effect because it allows
him to stay detached from their problematic position within society. In
this way, he does not have to think about a possible responsibility to
position himself against anti-Semitic forces or to openly demonstrate
his solidarity with the Jews. This again shows the floating distinction
between Gilman's two types of stereotyping and the ever-present danger of slipping into the so-called pathological form. The character of
Georg as protagonist and reflector figure plays an important role in this
context. His reactions to Bertold's experience as well as to Dr Stauber's remark seem to demonstrate an unclear position between Gilman's

---

72 Gillman, 'Failed Bildung and the Aesthetics of Detachment,' 221.
73 In the manuscripts, Georg's own active anti-Semitic thinking is made more
    explicit than in the final, published version. In one of the drafts (CUL A132,16),
    he compares Anna and Else and thinks of the latter dismissively as 'freilich ver-
    judet' (jewified, of course).
74 Gillman writes, '[t]he response as a whole exemplifies how the racist gaze
    reduces the Jews, no matter how different, to a single stereotype'. See Gilman,
    'Failed Bildung and the Aesthetics of Detachment,' 221.

two categories of stereotyping: since he does not consider himself an anti-Semite, he would never consciously agree to the insults uttered at the parliament, nor to the stereotype mentioned by Dr Stauber. However, in his renunciation of Bertold's outrage and in his unspoken thoughts towards Dr Stauber lies a latent acceptance of anti-Semitism as an ordering structure of society. Throughout the novel, he continually slips into an internalized application of stereotypes towards Jews and shows more than once this inner acquiescence in anti-Semitic tendencies.

This also becomes clear when Leo, who is a military officer, kills a former superior, who used to harass him because of his Jewishness, in a duel. Georg feels sympathy for the dead man and finds excuses for his behaviour: '[Georg] nickte nur und dachte an den armen jungen Menschen, den Leo erschossen und der eigentlich gar nichts anderes gegen die Juden gehabt hatte, als daß sie ihm so zuwider gewesen waren, wie schließlich den meisten Menschen – und dessen Schuld im Grunde nur darin bestanden hatte, daß er an den Unrechten gekommen war' (WiF936) ([Georg] nodded and thought of the poor young man whom Leo had shot, who as a matter of fact had had nothing else against the Jews except that he disliked [rather: felt repulsed by, M.K.] them just as much as most people did after all – and whose real fault had only been that he had tried the wrong man).[75]

One cannot but notice the unusual notion of guilt that Georg's musing implies. This passage can count as a representative example of the functioning of the narrative perspective in the novel. While the narrator indeed renders only Georg's thoughts without any comment, there still seems to be a latent gap between Georg's point of view and the narrative perspective which can be understood as a hint for the reader not to just accept the former as authorized. It seems striking that Georg should find it so natural to perceive Jews as repulsive while he himself appears extremely attracted by the company of his Jewish friends, particularly Leo. The choice of the word 'zuwider' (repulsive) again mocks the statement of the first subordinate clause, that Leo's antagonist 'had nothing more against the Jews but', after which one would expect rather a minor annoyance than revulsion. These discontinuities are warnings for the reader not to take over Georg's perspective without questioning.

Recognitions and Repetitions

The male gender of the Jew seems to be essential for the functioning of the stereotype 'Jew'.[76] This is the case because the norm, which is

---

75 Schnitzler, *Road into the Open*, 384.
76 See Gilman, *Freud, Race, and Gender*, 8–10.

stabilized by the stereotype of the Jew, is a norm of masculinity. The position of the Jew seems thus to be similar to that of Woman. In *Der Weg ins Freie* (Road into the Open), the two supposedly isolated storylines, Georg's relationship to Anna and the descriptions of Jewish life, reflect upon this similar function through being connected by the non-Jewish male subject, Georg. After decades of discussions in Schnitzler scholarship about the coherence in the novel, more recent critics seem to tend to abandon earlier verdicts of 'formlessness' and incoherence. A convincing example is the interpretation by John Neubauer who argues that 'the novel presents both gender and Jewishness as problems of identity for characters who are well into the third decade of their lives'.[77] Through the protagonist, the novel creates a field of tension between the heterosexual and the homosocial and the latter is evidently dominated by Georg's relationship to Jewish men.[78] Georg's interaction with both topics, Jewishness (through his Jewish friends) and femininity (his relationship to Anna), seems to have a similar function: 'Indeed, one of the key elements linking the love story to the Jewish Question is that Georg is simultaneously but differently attracted to Anna Rosner on the one hand and to the Jewish intellectuals and writers Bermann, Nürnberger and Golowski on the other'.[79]

Anna's storyline represents in exemplary form how stereotypes as cultural narratives take on the form of destiny in the sense that they elicit and engender a repetitive structure of performances which then create social realities. At the same time the text demonstrates that the fate-like character of these cultural narratives does not necessarily mean the fulfillment of the 'promise' some of them entail. It is striking how often the notion 'bestimmt' is used in combination with Anna. While Leo's prophecy is that Anna is 'bestimmt, im Bürgerlichen zu enden' (WiF718) (destined to end her days in respectable middle-class life),[80] Heinrich stresses that she is 'zur Mutterschaft bestimmt' (WiF888) (She really seems to be one of the few women who are made to be mothers).[81] No character in the novel draws more comments about her alleged 'destiny' than Anna, which is significantly explained by virtue of her physiognomy that apparently corresponds to the stereotypical image of motherly femininity: '[e]s gibt Frauen, die sehr häßlich werden in diesem Zustand [i.e. pregnancy] ... Sie nicht, nein, sie nicht ... Immer hatte sie so etwas Mütterliches in ihrem Aussehen' (WiF752) (There are women who grow very ugly in that condition ... but not she, no, not she

---

77 Neubauer, 'The Overaged Adolescents of Schnitzler's *Der Weg ins Freie*,' 269.
78 See Neubauer, 'The Overaged Adolescents of Schnitzler's *Der Weg ins Freie*,' 270.
79 Neubauer, 'The Overaged Adolescents of Schnitzler's *Der Weg ins Freie*,' 269.
80 Schnitzler, *Road into the Open*, 131.
81 Schnitzler, *Road into the Open*, 323.

... There was always a certain touch of the mother in her appearance).[82] The strong impact of this link between stereotypical image, physiognomic trait, and the perception of a person becomes clear when the cultural narratives attached to the stereotype take on an almost magical quality that denies the possibility of deviance from them. When Georg is confronted with Anna's not yet fully confirmed pregnancy, he finds it hard to believe: 'Wie eine Beruhigung fiel ihm jene Äußerung Leo Golowskis ein, daß Anna bestimmt wäre im Bürgerlichen zu enden. Wahrhaftig es konnte nicht in der "Linie ihres Schicksals" liegen, von einem Liebhaber ein Kind zu bekommen' (WiF738) (He felt almost reassured as there came into his mind that remark of Leo Goowski's that Anna was destined to end her days in respectable middle-class life. Having a child by a lover really could not be part of her fate line).[83] Anna herself also seems to be convinced by the necessary completion of her 'narrative' and is willing to accept her 'fate' on the basis of the outlook of a 'happy ending' attached to it: 'mit dem untrüglichen Gefühl, daß es einen Menschen auf der Welt gab, der aus ihr machen konnte, was ihm beliebte; mit dem festen Entschluß, alle Seligkeit und alles Leid hinzunehmen, das ihr bevorstehen mochte; und mit einer leisen Hoffnung, schöner als alle, die ihr je erschienen waren, auf ein beständiges und ruhevolles Glück' (WiF711) (She had for the first time in her life the infallible feeling that there was a man in the world who could do anything he liked with her. Her mind was firmly made up to take all the happiness or all the sorrow that might lie in front of her, and she had a gentle hope, more beautiful than all her dreams of the past, of a serene and abiding happiness).[84]

Her willingness to sacrifice herself for Georg not only corresponds to her Catholic background,[85] but is also an expression of her acceptance and internalization of her social 'destiny' as woman and mother in the bourgeois order. At the same time, a strong stereotypical narrative is at work here: the 'Hoffnung, schöner als alle, die ihr je erschienen waren' (hope, more beautiful than all her dreams of the past) stems from the fairytale of the prince, who marries the girl who has proven her ethical impeccability by enduring various strokes of fate. The danger of this narrative and its possible impact on women's lives are in fact mentioned by Bertold Stauber with regard to the young socialist Therese Golowski: while he thinks her capable of doing great things for the Socialist Party, he fears she could go off course: 'wenn sie nicht aus ihrer Bahn gerissen wird' (WiF954) (if she isn't torn away from her career

---

82 Schnitzler, *Road into the Open*, 148.
83 Schnitzler, *Road into the Open*, 131.
84 Schnitzler, *Road into the Open*, 96.
85 See Gillman, 'Failed Bildung and the Aesthetics of Detachment,' 236.

[rather: path, track, M.K.]).[86] Interestingly, this formulation evokes also the idea of a predestined path, but admits the possibility of going awry and losing it. When asked what could make Therese lose her path, Bertold replies: 'entweder sie redet sich einmal um den Kopf [...] [o]der sie heiratet einen Baron' (WiF656) (she will either talk her head off one fine day [...] [o]r she'll marry a Baron),[87] and appeases the easily offended Georg: 'Daß ich Baron sagte, war natürlich ein Spaß. Setzen wir statt Baron Prinz, so wird die Sache klarer' (WiF656) (I only said 'Baron' for a joke, of course. Substitute Prince for Baron and I make my meaning clearer).[88] And indeed, when Georg's and Anna's relationship comes to an end, he wonders, 'Wer weiß, ob ich sie nicht aus ihrer Bahn gerissen habe' (WiF954) (Who knows, if I have not spoilt her life [rather: thrown her off her track, M.K.]),[89] thus repeating the very same formulation Bertold used. In this way, what will happen between Anna and Georg is already prefigured in Bertold's comment, which also points to the serial quality of their experience. Moreover, the choice of expression 'Bahn' implies the assumption of a predetermined individual destiny. The use of train metaphors of destiny is a recurring element in Schnitzler's text to which I will return in the next chapters.

Anna's hope of becoming a singer has been replaced by this other, most beautiful hope, which of course means a possible marriage with Georg. This might be understood as confirmation of Leo's characterization of Anna, that she is 'dazu bestimmt, im Bürgerlichen zu enden', but only if 'bestimmt' means here rather 'determined' than 'destined'. It is the promising narrative that any suffering will be rewarded with a prize (the prince), which makes it possible for her to conceal the fact that her love affair with Georg is condemned in the moral standards of the Catholic and bourgeois setting of which she considers herself part. She plays the role of the bourgeois house-wife and mother so convincingly even to herself ('Anna bedankte sich, als wäre sie nicht nur hier in der Villa Hausfrau, sondern innerhalb dieser ganzen, abendlich-stillen Welt' (WiF849) (Anna thanked him with an air which indicated that she was not merely the hostess of the country house but of the whole world itself within the evening calm)[90] that she does not recognize the irony when she acts dismissively towards the lovers of Georg's friends, Guido Schönstein and Heinrich. 'Ich bin keine Rattenmamsell' (WiF733) (I am not a Rattenmamsell),[91] stresses Anna, referring to

---

86 Schnitzler, *Road into the Open*, 26.
87 Schnitzler, *Road into the Open*, 27.
88 Schnitzler, *Road into the Open*, 27.
89 Schnitzler, *Road into the Open*, 407.
90 Schnitzler, *Road into the Open*, 273.
91 Schnitzler, *Road into the Open*, 124.

Guido's lover who is said to be intellectually superior to the latter and makes him read literature and philosophy, which, however, seems to have no effect on him other than using Ibsen's characters as nicknames for her. Georg's reply is as deflecting as it is empty: 'Das trifft mich nicht, liebes Kind, ich unterscheide mich auch in mancher Beziehung von Guido' (WiF733) (That doesn't apply to me, my dear child. There are many points of difference between Guido and me).[92] The question is, however, in what ways are Georg and Anna different from Guido and his lover? Both couples consist of a young noble man and a socially inferior woman and neither man has so far shown any intention to marry his mistress. The same can be said for Heinrich's actress who kills herself in the end and for whom Anna feels no sympathy at all: 'Georg fühlte, daß ihre Güte hier völlig versagte. Er sah Widerwillen aus ihrer Seele fließen, nicht lau wie von einem Wesen zum andern hin, sondern stark und tief, wie ein Strom des Hasses von Welt zu Welt' (WiF899) (George felt that her kindness completely failed here. He saw a loathing flowing out of her soul, not tepidly, as though from one person to another, but strong and deep like a stream of hate from world to world).[93] Considering that Anna has just lost her baby at this point, it may not be surprising that she has not much compassion left for other people's suffering, but her renunciation seems to stem from more fundamental roots. Georg's perception is unusually attentive here, which might be interpreted as the narrator's voice behind Georg's inner musing. Either way, the formulation 'von Welt zu Welt' describes the social chasm between the two women: Anna's Catholic middle-class background forbids her from identifying and sympathizing with Heinrich's lover from the lower artistic milieu.

Instead of solidarity, Anna thus feels the need to distance herself from the women who actually have a lot in common with her in terms of being utterly dependent on their male, socially superior lovers. By highlighting the parallels between Anna and Heinrich's lover, the text both re-invokes and undermines the stereotypical dichotomy of the female as sinner and saint, mother and prostitute. It is no coincidence that these labels are assigned to the two women above all by the male friends of their lovers. While Georg's friends feel entitled to make judgements on Anna's 'destined path' particularly on the basis of her motherly appearance, Georg thinks himself able to see at first sight that Heinrich's actress is a 'fallen woman': 'So sehen Wesen nicht aus […], die dazu bestimmt sind, nur *einem* zu gehören' (WiF836) (This is not how persons [rather: creatures, M.K.] look […] who are fated to belong only to *one* man,

---

92   Schnitzler, *Road into the Open*, 125.
93   Schnitzler, *Road into the Open*, 388.

[italics in original]).[94] Again, physiognomy is used to draw conclusions about a person's character and with that about their destiny.

The parallelism between Heinrich's and Georg's 'love stories' reveals both women as the two sides of the same coin – the sinner and the saint, the split imagery of the feminine par excellence. In contrast to Heinrich's 'sinner', Georg feels the need to present Anna as a flawless angel after her miscarriage ('Er hatte das Bedürfnis, sie als vollkomme-nen Engel darzustellen' (WiF888) (He felt the need of describing her as a perfect angel.[95] *Darstellen* (describing/representing) is here a cru-cial term: the text demonstrates how the cultural narrative of sinner and saint not only determines the male perception of the female char-acters, but also how much this typecasting perception functions as an assignment of social roles: Heinrich's lover is already an actress, Anna is not (although her attempted singing career might put her also in the periphery of the artistic milieu), but both play the parts that are laid out for them with a tragic consistency and perfection. Stereotypes, as Dyer remarks, 'always carry within their very representation an implicit nar-rative'.[96] The early death of the fallen woman is certainly one of those narratives. The death of Heinrich's actress can be understood as the logical result of her role in the story, which de-individualizes her sui-cide considerably. This coincides with Nürnberger's suspicion about the woman's suicidal motives: 'Warum sie sich umgebracht hat, können wir alle nicht wissen, und vielleicht hat die Arme es selbst auch nicht gewußt' (WiF931f.) (None of us can know why she killed herself, and perhaps the poor girl herself didn't know either).[97] This suggests the possibility that the actress did not make the independent and rational decision to kill herself but rather acted out of a spontaneous feeling, perhaps caused by the influence of cultural representations – stereo-types – that determined her self-perception.

The fictional quality of her death is underscored by another mirror-ing effect in the novel: the story of Nürnberger's sister, which Georg keeps mixing up with that of Heinrich's lover (see WiF834). Nürnberg-er's sister used to be an actress who deluded herself about her career, getting lost in an imaginary world of glamour, while in reality she was too lacking in talent and looks to be really successful. It is only when she became really sick that, according to Nürnberger's memories, she unleashed a hitherto hidden talent:[98] 'Und das allersonderbarste war,

---

94 Schnitzler, *Road into the Open*, 256.
95 Schnitzler, *Road into the Open*, 323.
96 Dyer, *The Matter of Images*, 15.
97 Schnitzler, *Road into the Open*, 379.
98 The connection between illness (particularly tuberculosis) and artistic refinement is another stereotype, which I will discuss in more detail in the next chapter.

wie in den letzten Wochen ihres Lebens das Talent, dem sie ihre ganze Existenz hingeopfert, ohne es wirklich zu besitzen, geheimnisvoll dämonisch zum Vorschein kam' (WiF772) (And the strangest touch of all was the way in which, in the last weeks of her life, that talent to which she had sacrificed her whole existence without ever really possessing it manifested itself with diabolic uncanniness).[99] While Nürnberger concedes that his memory might play a trick on him here, Georg insists on the truthfulness of his perception, because he likes the ending of the story: '"Warum denn?" fragte Georg, dem dieser Abschluss so gut gefiel, daß er sich ihn nicht verderben lassen wollte' (WiF772) ('But why', asked George, who was so pleased with this *finale* that he did not want to have it spoilt).[100] The fictional quality of the story derives from the stereotype within: the fallen woman who regains some of her dignity and perhaps atonement through a tragic death. That Georg mixes up the fates of Nürnberger's sister and Heinrich's mistress even *before* the latter commits suicide points up the typological quality of their characters and Georg's expectations and perceptions that are determined by the cultural narrative inherent to stereotypes.[101] Thus, the actress's suicide could be understood as one last performance with which she completes the role she is expected to play.

While Anna does not have to redeem herself in death, as she is Georg's motherly angel, her death would be the last logical step in her sacrificial function. Significantly, Georg imagines her death twice. The first time is during the later stages of her pregnancy: 'Plötzlich, er wußte nicht, woher der Gedanke ihm kam, fuhr es ihm durch den Sinn: Wenn Anna stirbt!....Wenn das Kind ihr Tod wäre! Er erschrak aufs tiefste, als hätte er mit dem Gedanken eine Schuld auf sich geladen' (WiF846) (Suddenly, he did not know where the thought came from, the idea ran through his mind: 'Supposing Anna dies … Supposing the child were her death …' He felt deeply shocked, as though he had committed a crime by the very thought).[102] Georg's feeling of guilt derives from the wishful quality of his imagination of Anna's death. This wish is obviously not articulated on a conscious level but corresponds to the role of the 'saintly, self-sacrificing […] vessel'[103] he unconsciously expects her to play. Her death would free him from the modicum of accountability

---

99 Schnitzler, *Road into the Open*, 173.
100 Schnitzler, *Road into the Open*, 174.
101 It also highlights the fictional and constructed quality of the novel itself by prefiguring the actress's death and in this way revealing it as a narrative 'move'. I will elaborate on the function of self-referentiality at the end of this chapter.
102 Schnitzler, *Road into the Open*, 269.
103 Bronfen, Elisabeth (1992), *Over Her Dead Body: Death, Femininity and the Aesthetic*, Manchester: Manchester University Press, 218.

he might feel towards her, it would save him from the guilt of abandoning her but guarantee him the freedom and lack of commitment he
seeks.[104] He would have been able to benefit from her complementary
effect on him without binding himself to her and without being responsible for her misery. The second time Georg imagines Anna's death –
once more marked by the extremity of *Erschrecken* (fright) – is when
she suffers from the painful hours of labour, with the unborn child's
life hanging in the balance: 'Und jetzt liegt sie da unten und stirbt ... Er
erschrak heftig. Er hatte denken wollen ... sie liegt in den Wehen, und
auf die Lippen hatte sich gleichsam gestohlen: sie stirbt' (WiF872) (and
now she lies down there dying ... He gave a violent start. He had meant
to say mentally ... 'She is lying in labour', and the words 'lies dying' had
as it were stolen their way on to his lips).[105] Schnitzler's novel breaks the
stereotypical pattern, however, by not letting Anna die but having her
lose the child. Georg therefore does not escape his responsibility for
leaving her on his own account. Georg even explicitly comments on
this incongruence with the unconsciously expected pattern: 'Und wenn
Anna heute dahingegangen wäre, in der Stunde, da sie einem neuen
Wesen das Leben gab, sie hätte gleichsam ihr Los erfüllt und ihr Ende
hätte seinen grauenvollen, aber tiefen Sinn gehabt' (WiF877) (And even
if Anna had passed away to-day [sic], in the hour when she gave life
to a new being, she would as it were have fulfilled her lot and her end
would have had its terrible but none the less deep significance).[106] Here,
the function of the stereotype as destiny is made explicit.[107] Losing the
baby seems equivalent to losing her maternal function for Georg, and it
certainly erases the absolute necessity for Anna to get married, which of
course may ease some of Georg's feeling of responsibility towards her.
The still-birth can thus be seen as Anna's last – even if unintentional –
sacrifice for Georg that leads him to his *Weg ins Freie*. Like Heinrich's
actress and Nürnberger's sister, she completes the part that has been
laid out for her.

---

104 Hawes' analysis also shows how Schnitzler's text exposes the 'Ideologie der
   Freiheit' (ideology of freedom) as 'bloße Bezugslosigkeit' (lack of interpersonal
   connectedness). See Hawes (1995b), '"Als käme er von einer weiten Reise heim."
   Fremderfahrung als Erfahrung des eigenen entfremdeten Ichs in Arthur Schnitzlers Roman *Der Weg ins Freie*,' *Reisen im Diskurs: Modelle der Fremderfahrung von
   den Pilgerberichten bis zur Postmoderne; Tagunsgakten des internationalen Symposiums zur Reiseliteratur University College Dublin vom 10. – 12. März 1994*, ed. by
   Anne Fuchs and Theo Harden, Heidelberg: Universitätsverlag C. Winter, 516.
105 Schnitzler, *Road into the Open*, 303.
106 Schnitzler, *Road into the Open*, 309.
107 Also the link between destiny and the sensation of *Grauen* (horror) seems prefigured here, which I will elaborate on in more detail in the next chapters.

These parallels between Anna, Heinrich's mistress, and Nürnberger's sister are part of the iterative structure in the narrative, which brings about an almost uncanny effect of repetition compulsion. While basically all characters in the novel are striving in one form or another for a certain kind of self-realization and originality of experience, the text undermines this quest for individuality through various mirroring structures, inter-textual references, and stereotypical images which render the characters' hope to fulfil their 'destiny' both ironic and uncanny: uncanny, because the structure of repetition has the effect of the return of the 'Altbekannte, Längstvertraute' (that which has been known and familiar for a long time)[108] which had been repressed. Indeed, in order to maintain their idea of individuality and originality, the characters have to deny their *Doppelgänger*-like relationships to others (as with Anna, when she stresses 'Ich bin keine Rattenmamsell') and the influence that cultural narratives have on their perception.

While trying to secure their own sense of selfhood, the characters, and first of all Georg, become lost in an endless series of repetitions and mirror images. This is exemplarily exposed in a very short passage in the last chapter. After saying goodbye to Heinrich and Nürnberger, Georg is struck by an imaginary picture as if from one of his dreams:

Vor Georg erschien ein Bild, das er so oder so ähnlich irgendeinmal in einem Traum gesehen zu haben glaubte. Die zwei [Heinrich and Nürnberger] saßen sich gegenüber; jeder hielt dem anderen einen Spiegel vor, darin sah der andere sich selbst mit einem Spiegel in der Hand und so fort in die Unendlichkeit. Kannte da einer noch den anderen, kannte einer noch sich selbst? Georg wurde schwindelig zumute. Dann dachte er an Anna. (WiF934)

A scene which he thought he had seen some time or other in a dream came into George's mind. The two sat opposite each other, each held a mirror in front of the other. The other saw himself in it with the mirror in his hands, and so on to infinity; but did either of them really know the other, did either of them really know himself? George's mind became dizzy. Then he thought of Anna.[109]

The image obviously refers to the figure of speech, 'jemandem den Spiegel vorhalten' (to hold up a mirror to someone). Nürnberger and Heinrich hold a mirror up to each other but since they do it simultaneously the

---

108 Freud, Sigmund (1947b), 'Das Unheimliche,' *Gesammelte Werke*, vol. 12: *Werke aus den Jahren 1917–1920*, ed. by Anna Freud, Edward Bibring, Willi Hoffer, Ernst Kris, and Otto Isakower, London: Imago, 227–268, 231.
109 Schnitzler, *Road into the Open*, 381.

effect of self-recognition becomes lost in a dizzying line of infinite reflection images. The fact that Georg thinks he has seen the twin image of Heinrich and Nürnberger in a dream may allow us to suspect the possibility of displacement. While Nürnberger and Heinrich certainly share a few similarities – they are both Jewish writers who do not consider themselves as mainly Jewish but above all Austrian – the thematic and narrative structure of the novel suggests a stronger parallelism between Heinrich and Georg himself. With the mirror motif, Georg's own position as the novel's 'reflector figure' comes into view. Gillman has pointed out that in contrast to the opinion of other critics,[110] Georg is not merely an indifferent filter but rather 'circulates within the Jewish world, observes the Jews, and for a time, becomes a cipher or figure for the Jewish experience'.[111] While Gillman does not use the term reflector figure, she refers nevertheless to Georg's specular function when she quotes Heinrich's comment on Georg's feeling of guilt towards Anna and their stillborn child: 'Nie in Ihrem Leben wäre Ihnen etwas derartiges eingefallen, wenn Sie nicht mit einem Subjekt meiner Art verkehrten und es nicht zuweilen Ihre Art wäre, nicht Ihre Gedanken zu denken, sondern die von Menschen, die stärker – oder auch schwächer sind als Sie' (WiF957) (An idea of that kind [i.e. feeling of guilt] would never have occurred to you your whole life long if you hadn't been intimate with a person of my type, and if it hadn't been your way sometimes not to think your own thoughts but those of men who were stronger – or even weaker than you are).[112] According to Gillman, the notion of *Verkehr* (interaction) 'creates the desire to emulate the other', which 'represents an enlightened reversal of the one-sided mimicry that is Jewish acculturation'.[113]

It seems hard to decide whether Heinrich's evaluation is accurate and Georg's feeling of guilt is indeed a mimicry of the behaviour and thinking patterns he has observed in his Jewish friends, or whether it belongs to the characteristic properties *assigned* to Jewishness, which makes Georg feel connected to his Jewish acquaintances, particularly Heinrich. Both are confronted with a case of death they feel indirectly responsible for – Heinrich for the suicide of his mistress and Georg for the death of his stillborn son – but they both are and were nevertheless unwilling to draw any consequences from this feeling of guilt except for the occasional touch of melancholia. Thus, after all, it is not only the

---

110 Cf. Krobb, Florian (2000), *Selbstdarstellungen: Untersuchungen zur deutsch-jüdischen Erzählliteratur im neunzehnten Jahrhundert*, Würzburg: Königshausen und Neumann, 158, but also Neubauer, 'The Overaged Adolescents of Schnitzler's *Der Weg ins Freie*,' 270.
111 Gillman, 'Failed Bildung and the Aesthetics of Detachment,' 220.
112 Schnitzler, *Road into the Open*, 410.
113 Gillman, 'Failed Bildung and the Aesthetics of Detachment,' 220.

feeling of guilt that Heinrich and Georg both share,[114] but rather also the absolute refusal to take over responsibility, which is – under the label *Verantwortungsscheu* (avoidance of responsibility) – one of the 'symptoms' of both the so-called 'impressionist character' and of stereotypical Jewishness 217).[115] When Heinrich then refuses to accept Georg's feeling of guilt as genuine and ascribes it to the influence imposed by 'einem Subjekt meiner Art' (WiF957) (a person of my type),[116] he in turn replicates the anti-Semitic stereotype of the decadent *Jung Wien* (Young Vienna) as an indicatively Jewish phenomenon. At the same time, with regard to Georg's possible envy of the idealized Jewish outsider position as a prerequisite of artistic seriousness, Heinrich's comment might be accurate in the sense that Georg 'performs' the feeling of guilt, maybe half-consciously to gain more artistic 'depth'. This aspect of 'Seelenschmerz' as 'creative accelerator' is mentioned by Nürnberger, when he refers to Heinrich's suffering after the death of his mistress:

> Es rührt wohl daher, daß jeder Seelenschmerz irgendwie unserer Eitelkeit schmeichelt, was man von einem Typhus oder einem Magenkatarrh nicht behaupten kann. Und beim Künstler kommt vielleicht dazu, daß aus einem Magenkatarrh absolut nichts zu holen ist […] aus Seelenschmerzen hingegen alles, was man nur will, vom lyrischen Gedichte bis zu philosophischen Werken. (WiF931)
> It comes no doubt from the fact that every emotional pain flatters our vanity somehow or other, and that you can't say the same thing about an attack of typhoid or a catarrh in the stomach. Then there is this additional point about artistic people, for while a catarrh of the stomach provides positively no copy at all […] you can get anything you jolly well like out of your emotional pains, from lyric poems down to works on philosophy.[117]

Heinrich's assumption that Georg's feeling of guilt derives from his own influence on Georg might thus be an apt description in the sense that Georg is unconsciously trying to 'exploit' the inner turmoil he experiences due to the stillbirth of his child as a mode of self-fashioning which would give him more artistic credibility.

---

114 Although Heinrich claims that he does not even feel guilty about it and gives long explanations as to why he does not have to, this appears to be an attempt at negating his own feelings of guilt.
115 Fliedl, *Arthur Schnitzler*, 217.
116 Schnitzler, *Road into the Open*, 410.
117 Schnitzler, *Road into the Open*, 377–378.

Heinrich's habit of speaking his mind quite bluntly reveals a kind of selfishness that Georg must recognize in himself. When Heinrich tells him openly about his hostile feelings towards the mother of his deceased lover, for example ('Man haßt doch niemanden mehr als jemand Gleichgültigen, der einem Mitleid abfordert' (WiF943) (There is no one one hates more than someone who is quite indifferent to you and requires your sympathy),[118] and his other experiences linked to the funeral of his lover, Georg shudders: 'Georg empfand ein leises Grauen' (WiF943) (George felt a slight horror).[119] Akin to the *Erschrecken* (fright) in self-encounter noted before, this *Grauen* (horror), which appears with great frequency in Schnitzler's writings to describe a feeling of horror and uncanniness, marks a moment in which Georg is reminded of the 'längst Bekannte' (what has been known for a long time) of his own story.[120] By recognizing himself in Heinrich's expression of selfishness, he is not only reminded of his own ethically questionable behaviour and his feelings of annoyance towards her family ('Nur irgendetwas störte ihn, ohne daß er gleich wußte, was es wäre. Ach ja, … der Besuch in der Paulanergasse, die trübseligen Räume, der kranke Vater, die verletzte Mutter' (WiF927) (Only something troubled him without his immediately knowing what it was … Oh yes, the visit in the Paulanergasse, the depressing rooms, the ailing father, the aggrieved mother),[121] but also of the stereotypical quality of his actions, which are mirrored in Heinrich's story and in various others.[122]

If we go back to the mirror image of Nürnberger and Heinrich, another reading of the passage seems possible: the two mirrors that keep throwing back and forth the images of both writers in an endless line of *mise en abyme* could be understood as reference to Georg himself, and in fact to his specifically aesthetic function as literary character and protagonist. The passage is striking in its poetic language and emblematic quality: it is one of several moments in the novel where the

---

118 Schnitzler, *Road into the Open*, 393.
119 Schnitzler, *Road into the Open*, 394.
120 I will return to this aspect, and particularly its decisive Romantic colouring later on in this study.
121 Schnitzler, *Road into the Open*, 373.
122 Another young man in the novel, Oskar Ehrenberg, enjoys the company of a working-class girl whom he has no intention of marrying even though he has taken her out of the secure situation of a previous engagement. His statement reads like a premonition of the further development of the novel that shows the analogy between his and Georg's love affair: 'Solche Sachen dürfen nicht länger dauern als höchstens ein Jahr' (WiF676) (Things like this oughtn't to last longer than a year at the outside). See Schnitzler, *Road into the Open*, 1913b: 52. As a matter of fact, the action of the novel and with that the relationship between Georg and Anna lasts exactly one year.

'projection' of an image interrupts the flow of narrative and plot in a way that is reminiscent of Romantic writers.[123] Particularly, the way in which it just appears in front of his eyes seems to be taken straight out of one of the narratives by E. T. A. Hoffmann, in which the motif of the suddenly appearing image occurs repeatedly.[124] Moreover, the endless series of mirror images brings to mind Friedrich Schlegel's definition of the function of Romantic poetry:

> Nur sie [Romantic poetry] kann gleich dem Epos ein Spiegel der ganzen umgebenden Welt, ein Bild des Zeitalters werden. Und doch kann auch sie am meisten zwischen dem Dargestellten und dem Darstellenden […] auf den Flügeln der poetischen Reflexion in der Mitte schweben, diese Reflexion immer wieder potenzieren und wie in einer endlosen Reihe von Spiegeln vervielfachen.[125]
> Only Romantic poetry can, like the epos, become a mirror of the entire world by which it is surrounded, an image of the age. And yet it can, more than any other form of writing, float on the wings of poetic reflexion in the middle between the object represented and he who represents; it can potentiate this reflexion time and again and multiply it like an endless series of mirrors.

The fact that both men in Georg's dream image are literary writers, and that Georg has just witnessed a discussion between them regarding the functions of literature when the image occurs to him, makes it plausible to read it as a metafictional reflexion. Schlegel's remark on the self-reflective function of literature would thus indeed fit here: while literature should aim at representing the world, it is first and foremost able to mirror itself, which is nevertheless more than just a poetological reflection but a reflection on what it means to know oneself.[126] This, however, can never be fully achieved: 'Schlegels Vergleich dieser Selbstreflexion mit einem sich spiegelnden Spiegel weist zugleich darauf hin, dass die Suche der Literatur nach sich selbst nie zu Ende kommen kann. Der Versuch, über sich selbst zu wissen, bleibt notwendig eine Aufgabe, ein Projekt' (Schlegel's comparison between this self-reflection and a mirror that mirrors itself shows that literature's search for

---

123 See Webber, Andrew J. (1996), *The Doppelgänger: Double Visions in German Literature*, Oxford: Oxford University Press, 115.
124 On the image in Hoffmann, see Kohns, *Die Verrücktheit des Sinns*, 194.
125 Schlegel, Friedrich (1967), 'Athenäum: Fragmente,' *Kritische Friedrich-Schlegel-Ausgabe: Zweiter Band*, ed. by Ernst Behler, Munich [et al.]: Verlag Ferdinand Schöningh, 182–183.
126 See Kohns, Oliver (2007), *Die Verrücktheit des Sinns: Wahnsinn und Zeichen bei Kant, E.T.A. Hoffmann und Thomas Carlyle*, Bielefeld: transcript, 152.

itself can never come to an end. The attempt to know about oneself necessarily has to remain a project).[127]

It is this impossibility of completion that is expressed in Georg's oneiric image and in his resulting feeling of dizziness: 'Kannte da einer noch den anderen, kannte da einer noch sich selbst?' (WiF934) (but did either of them really know the other, did either of them really know himself?)[128] This reflection of (self-)recognition is again linked to the discussion between Heinrich and Nürnberger on the possibility of an objective stance in literature, in which the latter complains about Heinrich's attempt at being 'fair' when writing his play:

> In solch einem Stück, das eine Zeitfrage behandelt, oder gar mehrere, wie es Ihre Absicht war, werden Sie mit Objektivität nie etwas erreichen. Das Publikum im Theater verlangt, daß die Themen, die der Dichter anschlägt, auch erledigt werden, oder daß wenigstens eine Täuschung dieser Art erweckt werde. Denn natürlich gibt es nie und nimmer eine wirkliche Erledigung. Und scheinbar erledigen kann eben nur einer, der den Mut oder die Einfalt oder das Temperament hat, Partei zu ergreifen. Sie werden schon drauf kommen, lieber Heinrich, daß es mit Gerechtigkeit im Drama nicht geht. (WiF929)
> In a piece like that, which deals with a question of the day, or indeed several questions, as you really intended, you'll never do any good with a purely objective treatment. The theatre public demands that the subjects tackled by the author should be definitely settled, or that at any rate some illusion of that kind should be created. For of course there never is a real solution, and an apparent solution can only be made by a man who has the courage or the simplicity or the temperament to take sides. You'll soon appreciate the fact, my dear Heinrich, that fairness is no good in the drama.[129]

To take up a position is here understood merely as a strategic, and almost aesthetic, move to cover up the impossibility of objective representation. Heinrich, in turn, rejects Nürnberger's criticism: 'Ich stehe auch nicht über den Parteien, sondern bin gewissermaßen bei allen oder gegen alle. Ich hab' nicht die göttliche Gerechtigkeit, sondern die dialektische' (WiF929) (I do not stand above parties either, but I belong to them all in a kind of way, or am against them all. I have not got the divine but

---

127 Kohns, *Die Verrücktheit des Sinns*, 152.
128 Schnitzler, *Road into the Open*, 381.
129 Schnitzler, *Road into the Open*, 375.

the dialectical fairness).[130] With this remark, Heinrich suggests that his refusal to take up a position in his play, to write in an, as it were, programmatic way, is not at all an attempt at coming to an objective mode of representation. The expression 'dialectic justice' implies precisely the never-ending chain of reflections expressed in Schlegel's fragment as well as in Georg's 'dream image', and refuses any attempt at the kind of *Erledigung* (completion) Nürnberger is requesting. Rather, it sounds like Heinrich is highlighting the inability to reach a point of completion and making of this a central aspect of his writing. This corresponds to the concept of Romantic irony as the knowledge of the impossibility of giving an adequate representation of the world and its infinite connectedness: 'So wird Ironie die latente Sprachhaltung des Endlichen, der vom Unendlichen reden will' (In this way, irony becomes the attitude for the man, who is finite, but wants to speak of infinity).[131] This relativist (or maybe resigned) position in Romantic irony is expressed through meta-poetic reflections in the text, which make the reader aware of its own constructedness and fictional quality. By letting Heinrich and Nürnberger have this conversation, Schnitzler's text does precisely that, reminding readers of the aesthetic and fictional quality of what they are reading, which produces the effect of a *mise en abyme* and thus potentially a similarly endless mirror effect to that described in Georg's 'dream image'. We are reading a literary text in which the characters are discussing a literary text which is explicitly not *erledigt* (completed), but dialectically structured, which makes it possible to assume that it might contain a similar self-referential scene, creating a virtually endless chain of 'mirror images'.

Again, very much like in the passage in which Leo and Heinrich discuss 'the Jewish question', Georg is here merely a witness, an observer and listener, and not an active participant in the discussion. He is the medium through which the reader gets access to the discussions precisely without being confronted with a predominant position, because Georg does not have one. His function is to receive passively, rather than produce, as he realizes himself towards the end of the novel with regard to his art:

[N]icht schöpferische Arbeit, – die Atmosphäre seiner Kunst allein war es, die ihm zum Dasein nötig war; kein Verdammter war er wie Heinrich, den es immer trieb, zu fassen, zu formen, zu bewahren, und dem die Welt in Stücke zerfiel, wenn sie seiner gestaltenden Hand entgleiten wollte. (WiF921)

---

130 Schnitzler, *Road into the Open*, 376.
131 Gockel, Heinz (1979), 'Friedrich Schlegels Theorie des Fragments,' *Romantik: Ein literaturwissenschaftliches Studienbuch*, Ernst Ribbat, Königstein/Ts.: Athenäum, 22–37, 28.

[I]t was not creative work – it was simply the atmosphere of his art which was necessary to his existence. He was not one of the damned, like Heinrich, who always felt driven to catch hold of things, to mould them, to preserve them, and who found his world fall to pieces whenever it tried to escape from his creative hand.[132]

In this, Georg resembles very much the artist figure in Hoffmann's writings, as he is the one who 'receives' images, as if outside of his control.[133] Indeed, Georg has a few moments when images like that of the endless mirror sequence between Heinrich and Nürnberger appear without his active volition in front of his eyes.[134] However, he is unable to conjure up any image when he explicitly tries to do so as he visits again the house in which Anna gave birth to their dead child. He almost expects to see a 'ghost' of his former self on the balcony: 'Der Georg dieses Sommers, der dort gewohnt hatte? Dumme Einfälle. Der Balkon blieb leer, das Haus war stumm, und der Garten schlummerte tief. Enttäuscht wandte Georg sich ab' (WiF954) (the George of this summer who had lived up there. Silly fancies. The balcony remained empty, the house was silent and the garden was deep asleep. George turned away disappointed).[135]

---

132 Schnitzler, *Road into the Open*, 366.
133 See Kohns, *Die Verrücktheit des Sinns*, 194.
134 Another striking passage in this respect is the moment in which Georg anticipates the trip to Italy he has planned with Anna because of her pregnancy. Significantly, he imagines himself not only alone without Anna, but also deeply immersed in his work: 'Und wie ein Bild, von einer Laterna magica an einen weißen Vorhang geworfen, erschien ihm seine eigene Gestalt: er sah sich auf einem Balkon sitzen, in beglückter Einsamkeit, vor einem mit Notenblättern überdeckten Tisch; Äste wiegten sich vor den Gitterstäben; ein heller Himmel ruhte über ihm, und tief unten zu seinen Füßen, in traumhaft übertriebenen Blau, lag das Meer' (WiF763) (His own form appeared before him like a picture thrown onto a white screen by magic lantern: he saw himself sitting on a balcony in happy solitude, in front of a table strewn with music paper. Branches rocked in front of the railings. A clear sky hung above him, while below at his feet lay the sea, with a dreamy blueness that was quite abnormal). See Schnitzler, *Road into the Open*, 162. It might be subtly ironic that this fantasy of productivity is once more an utterly passive experience in the sense that the image just appears in front of him without his active or conscious decision-making.
135 Georg's anticipation of seeing himself is highly reminiscent of Romantic *Doppelgänger* scenes, as in Adelbert Chamisso's 'Erscheinung' (Apparition, 1828) or Heinrich Heine's,'Der *Doppelgänger*' (The Double, 1828). See Schnitzler, *Road into the Open*, 406; Adelbert Chamisso (1975b), 'Erscheinung,' *Sämtliche Werke*, vol. 1, ed. by Jost Perfahl, Munich: Winkler, 383–384, Heinrich Heine (1973), 'Buch der Lieder: Die Heimkehr, 20,' *Werke*, vol. 1, ed. by Stuart Atkins, Munich: Beck, 172–173, 172f.

Georg's failed attempt at receiving an image – which in this case appears like the hope for a sign for the future or an explanation for what has happened – highlights his passivity. Georg is a medium, not a producer, nor an active analyst. Through him, the reader is indeed presented with a picture that brings together different elements, 'Zeitfragen' (questions of the day) and 'ewige Probleme [...]: Tod und Liebe' (WiF930) (eternal problems, death and love).[136] However, Georg's perspective does not offer a synthesis of these elements, except for the aesthetic one, the combination of them in a picture created by the narrative of the novel.

The text therefore defies the request for *Erledigung* (completion) and inscribes itself into a literary tradition that understands the striving for this kind of completion as inadequate. This does not mean that the novel takes on an Aestheticist position. It not only highlights its own fictional and constructed quality, but also that of the cultural narratives inherent in stereotypes that generally appear very much as *erledigt* (completed) and thus indisputable. In this way, it demonstrates how these cultural narratives, despite their constructed quality, nevertheless have a real impact on people's lives. They are exposed as ordering structures that are essentially used to define the norm, and with that a sense of self. In this way, Schnitzler's text is very much about what it means to 'know about oneself', comparable to Schlegel's definition of Romantic literature. 'Knowing about oneself' is revealed as not only a never-ending process of mirror images, but also as one that depends on drawing lines between 'self' and 'other'. *Der Weg ins Freie* (Road into the Open) displays the psychic mechanism and use of cultural narratives involved in the process of drawing these lines. This, however, remains for the most part unconscious for the protagonist.

This chapter has sketched out how Schnitzler's novel plays with the way stereotypes can take on a fate-like function for the typecast individuals. Moreover, the text shows that not even the privileged position of the norm is completely free of determining cultural narratives. In the texts discussed in the following chapters, this aspect will become even more prominent. Feeling increasingly restricted by the cultural narratives that determine their own bourgeois male identity, the protagonists are drawn to the idea of an alternative destiny that transcends the restrictive boundaries of normativity. The idea that one's identity is determined and restricted by cultural narratives is much more unsettling than the idea of a higher power of destiny, which is why Georg and his friends, but also other Schnitzler protagonists, are so eager to embrace the latter. As we have seen in Georg's case, his status of a noble

---

136 Schnitzler, *Road into the Open*, 376.

man leads to the suspicion of dilettantism, which he seeks to overcome through his connection to Jewish circles. What emerges here ever so subtly is the mystification of the social position of the stereotyped 'other' as a tempting alternative destiny to the privileged position within the norm. This romanticization of 'otherness', however, glosses over the essential difference between the conception of an individual destiny and the social position of the stereotyped 'other': the former implies the idea of 'chosenness', of being assigned an individual path, while the determining character of stereotypes function precisely in the opposite way, as it denies any form of individual development. The seductive pull of the position of the 'other' thus neglects the precarity of that position and therefore turns out to lead the protagonists to a dead end. As we will see in the next chapter, this is particularly the case in the novella *Flucht in die Finsternis* (Flight into Darkness) in which the yearning for a meaningful destiny on the one hand and a seductive play with the social position of the 'other' become ultimately overwhelming for the protagonist.

Two Madness and Investiture in *Flucht in die Finsternis* (Flight into Darkness)

Illness is the night-side of life, a more onerous citizenship. Everyone who is born holds dual citizenship, in the kingdom of the well and in the kingdom of the sick.[1]

Schnitzler's *Wahnsinnsnovelle* (novella of madness) as he called it in his journal,[2] describes a transition from relative mental health into illness. In a process of an increasing loss of a sense of reality, the *Sektionsrat* (head of section in a ministry) Robert becomes more and more overpowered by his own delusional ideas which lead him to the murder of his brother and finally also to his own death. The narrator sums up the events of the novella: 'Die Aufzeichnungen, die man in seiner Reisetasche fand, wurden dem Gericht übergeben und auszugsweise veröffentlicht. Der Fall in all seiner Düsterkeit lag so klar wie möglich: Verfolgungswahn, wer konnte daran zweifeln?' (FiF114) (The memoirs which were discovered in his traveling-bag were handed over to the legal authorities, and extracts were published. The case, sinister as it was, was clear as could be. Persecution mania. Who could doubt it?)[3]

---

1 Sontag, Susan (1991), *Illness as Metaphor & AIDS and Its Metaphors*, London: Penguin, 3.

2 Schnitzler, Arthur (1983), *Tagebuch 1913–1916*, ed. by Kommission für Literarische Gebrauchsformen der Österreichischen Akademie der Wissenschaften and Werner Welzig, Wien: Verlag der Österreichischen Akademie der Wissenschaften, 88.

3 Schnitzler, Arthur (1931), *Flight into Darkness*, trans. by William A. Drake, New York: Simon & Schuster, 152. All translations for *Flight into Darkness* are taken from the translation by William A. Drake (1931), sometimes with added explanations, where I find it necessary. All other translations from the German are my own.

The key word *Fall* (case) seems to promise a representative character to what has been told, in the sense of a case study or case history.[4] As we would probably always expect from a literary text that it somehow goes beyond an individual pathological report, but should tell about something of a more general interest, this might at first not be particularly remarkable. The question is then: 'Unser Text muss also mehr erzählen als eine bloße Krankengeschichte: aber was?' (Our text has to tell more than just a pathological case history: but what?)[5]

I will show in this chapter that *Flucht in die Finsternis* (Flight into Darkness) displays a close connection between the psychical crisis and a threatening loss of secured and legitimate social status. The fact that the protagonist seems to be in a transitional state for the larger part of the narrative makes it possible to analyze this connection.[6] It will become clear that the protagonist no longer feels that he fits into his social role, particularly his symbolic function as *Sektionsrat* (head

---

4   In Schnitzler's manuscripts (CUL A199,3) one can find a newspaper clipping from the *Neue Freie Presse* (03.05.1913) which reports on a fratricide in an asylum. The fictional 'case' thus had a factual equivalent. A later draft is furnished with the generic subtitle *Eine novelistische Studie* (A novelistic study), which could suggest a literary case study.

5   Wünsch, Marianne (2004), 'Logische Argumentation und erkenntnistheoretische Probleme am Beispiel von Arthur Schnitzlers *Flucht in die Finsternis*,' *Littérature et théorie de la connaissance 1890–1935*, ed. by Christine Maillard, Strasbourg: Presses universitaires de Strasbourg, 302–317, 302.

6   Hannelore Schlaffer writes that medical case histories provide rich material for the literary genre of the novella, particularly when they are situated on the threshold of the norm: 'Gerade solche Fälle aber, die die Grenze des Gesetzes und der Normalität tangieren, sind die bevorzugten Stoffe der Novelle' (Precisely such cases, which touch on the borderline of the law or that of normalcy, are the most typical subjects of the novella. See Schlaffer, Hannelore (1993), *Poetik der Novelle*, Stuttgart: Metzler, 227. For the function of the transition period in *Flucht in die Finsternis* (Flight into Darkness), see above all Horst Thomé's extensive examination of the psychiatric knowledge that informs the representation of this case of mental illness in the novella. Thomé argues that the transitional state allows the novella to evaluate ethical implications of Robert's case which would be impossible if it displayed an advanced state of mental illness. He demonstrates that the clinical picture of the protagonist does not correspond to the contemporary medical knowledge of mental illness, but is based on Richard von Krafft-Ebing's model of Paranoia Persecutoria, which was already regarded as obsolete when Schnitzler wrote the novella. The aetiology described by Krafft-Ebing assumes a small window in which the patient can actively work against the illness and avoid succumbing to it, as opposed to theories that stated a clear biological predisposition which made the outbreak of the illness inevitable. According to Thomé, this allows Schnitzler to explore an ethical perspective of the case: the fact that the protagonist is ultimately overpowered by his delusions is partly due to his own individual failure to confront himself with the threat of illness and take over responsibility. See Thomé, Horst (1993), *Autonomes*

of section in a ministry), but also more generally as representative of the bourgeois order. We will see that he is threatened with losing his secured position within the norm. In this context, the possible diagnosis of mental illness takes on a fate-like quality: not only a neutral description of symptoms and assumed aetiology, it also marks the diagnosed subject as 'other' and in this way 'seals' their destiny as excluded from the norm. While this is of course frightening to the protagonist, the stereotypes attached to mental illness are not exclusively threatening and punitive but also yield a certain kind of promise: madness appears as a way to escape the bourgeois order, which is no longer capable of providing him with a secured position.[7] The 'role of the madman' is associated with a certain form of creativity outside of the prescriptive patterns of bourgeois existence. Correspondingly, the protagonist shows an affinity with performance arts, in that he repeatedly plays with stereotypes of madness by half-consciously re-enacting them. At the same time, he clings to the bourgeois order and its representations of the norm. The more advanced his delusions become, the more he tries to reassure himself of his legitimate position within the norm. Significantly, he turns increasingly to the belief in the higher power

---

Ich und 'Inneres Ausland'. Studien über Realismus, Tiefenpsychologie und Psychiatrie in deutschen Erzähltexten (1848–1914), Tübingen: Niemeyer, 694–722. While my reading is compatible with Thomé's argument, I would suggest that the question of guilt and individual responsibility is less central to the novella than the influential power of cultural narratives that prevent the individual from taking over responsibility. See also the articles by Segar, Kenneth (1988), 'The Death of Reason: Narrative Strategy and Resonance in Schnitzler's *Flucht in die Finsternis*,' *Oxford German Studies* 17: 97–117, 101; Schmidt, Harald (2000), 'Grenzfall und Grenzverlust: Die poetische Konstruktion des Wahns in Arthur Schnitzlers *Flucht in die Finsternis*,' *Literatur als Geschichte des Ich*, ed. by Eduard Beutner and Ulrike Tanzer, Würzburg: Königshausen & Neumann, 185–204, 189, 199: for Segar, the transitional state makes possible an empathetic reaction in the reader. Schmidt interprets the poetical description of a transitional state as rejection of the *Grenzverwischungsfahren* (method of blurring boundaries) of psychoanalysis, which according to him illegitimately integrates the highly pathological within the boundaries of normalcy. He nevertheless concedes that Schnitzler's psychologically motivated narrative technique itself comes quite close to the method of blurring. As Schmidt seems to draw the inherent critique of psychoanalysis mainly from remarks Schnitzler made elsewhere and since there do not seem to be any clear references *in* the text itself that suggest such a reading, I find this interpretation doubtful. However, I too will argue in this chapter that the blurring of boundaries between norm and 'other' is indeed a central concern of the text.

7   That Robert's crisis is tightly linked to his post-enlightened bourgeois identity, which is based on the exclusion of the 'other,' is also seen by Meyer, Imke (2010), *Männlichkeit und Melodram: Arthur Schnitzlers erzählende Schriften*, Würzburg: Königshausen & Neumann, 175.

of destiny, which provides him with a sense of legitimacy and individuality. This turning to metaphysical determinism demonstrates
how much the protagonist depends on some sort of ordering frame,
which the social order seems to fail to provide. However, I do not want
to suggest that the causality of the psychical conflict displayed in the
novella can be reduced to the external influence of a pathogenic and
pathologizing social environment.[8] Rather, I am interested in the interplay between psychical symptoms, legitimate and secured statuses
within the social order, stereotypical cultural narratives of madness,
and internalized expectations of social roles. In order to parse these
interactions in their finer detail, I will take into account the specific
literary quality of the representation of mental illness in the novella. In
the second half of this chapter, I will show that the protagonist's symptoms are those of Romantic madness and that the protagonist himself
can be seen to some extent as a Hoffmannesque protagonist, as has
already been indicated at the end of the last chapter. One of the central Romantic elements in the novella is the repeated occurrence of the
sensation of *Grauen*. It will become clear that in *Flucht in die Finsternis*
(Flight into Darkness) this *Grauen* is a reaction to a crisis of investiture,
which I will now set out in the first section.

A Crisis of Investiture

For my analysis of the novella I draw on Eric L. Santner's study *My
Own Private Germany*, where he examines Daniel Paul Schreber's
prominent case of mental illness.[9] The similarities between the Schreber case (at least as approached by Freud) and *Flucht in die Finsternis*
(Flight into Darkness) have been noted in the scholarship, but never
fully explored.[10] I argue that the so-called 'crisis of investiture', which
Santner detects as lying at the root of Schreber's delusional system

---

8   In the context of the anti-psychiatry discourse of the 1970s, Heide Tarnowski-Seidel
    suggests such a clear causal connection between environment and illness in
    Schnitzler's text. Using an approach based on communication theory, she ana-
    lyzes Robert's symptoms as a result of a pathological family constellation, particu-
    larly his neurotic relationship to his brother. Tarnowski-Seidel also draws from
    biographical information about Schnitzler's own family history, which has been
    convincingly deemed too speculative by other scholars. See Tarnowski-Seidel,
    Heide (1983), *Arthur Schnitzler, 'Flucht in die Finsternis': Eine produktionsästhe-
    tische Untersuchung*, Munich: Fink, 97–110.
9   Santner, Eric L. (1996), *My Own Private Germany*, Princeton: Princeton University
    Press.
10 See Perlmann, Michaela L. (1987a), *Der Traum in der literarischen Moderne: Unter-
    suchungen zum Werk Arthur Schnitzlers*, Munich: Fink, 169; Thomé, *Autonomes Ich
    und 'Inneres Ausland,'* 721; Schmidt, 'Grenzfall und Grenzverlust,' 185–204, 189.

of ideas, also plays a role in Schnitzler's literary case study of mental illness.[11] Highlighting the fact that the main outbreak of Schreber's delusions appeared when he was appointed *Senatspräsident* (president of the senate) of the Supreme Court of Saxony, Santner argues that Schreber's crisis had strong 'resonances with the larger social and cultural crises of his era'.[12] Schreber's psychotic system thus gains an exemplary status beyond the representational function of the pathological case study as undertaken by Freud: Santner's study aims at bringing to the surface the 'connections between the "private" domain of psycho-pathological disturbances and the "public" domain of ideological and political forces and realities'.[13]

In a circular fashion, the social rites and procedures that endow individuals with a legitimate status ensure the functioning of the social and political system which engendered them in the first place. This is paradigmatically the case when an individual is appointed a function and a corresponding title by virtue of a performative speech act. These performances are acts of symbolic investiture and confirm the individual's position within the norm of the dominant order, his or her symbolic function. The symbolic function thus primarily means those aspects of one's social role with which one is officially endowed by social and institutional authority through acts of investiture, e.g. appointments, degrees, and marriages. When, however, this symbolic function is disavowed, for example through a pathologizing diagnosis, this loss of the symbolic function threatens the legitimate status within the norm and, by extension, the social order in general.

In *Flucht in die Finsternis* (Flight into Darkness), this aspect of symbolic investiture takes up a prominent – even though at first not conspicuous – position in relation to the pathological symptoms of the protagonist. In fact, this connection already becomes clear in the first two sentences of the novella:

Es klopfte; der *Sektionsrat* erwachte, und auf sein unwillkürliches 'Herein' erschien ohne weiteres der Kellner mit dem regelmäßig für acht Uhr bestellten Frühstück in der Tür. *Roberts* erster Gedanke war, daß er gestern abend nun doch wieder vergessen hätte, die Tür zu versperren [...]. (FiF5 [emphasis added])
[The head of section] was awakened by a knock on the door. 'Come in', he said involuntarily, and the waiter appeared with his breakfast, ordered, as usual, for eight o'clock. Robert's first thought was: 'So I did forget, last night again, to lock the door!'[14]

11 See Santner, *My Own Private Germany*, 16.
12 Santner, *My Own Private Germany*, xiv.
13 Santner, *My Own Private Germany*, xiv.
14 Schnitzler, *Flight into Darkness*, 3.

The novella begins without the classic frame narration: the beginning *in medias res*, akin to Kafka's *Der Process* (The Trial) and *Die Verwandlung* (The Metamorphosis), projects the reader directly into the scene of waking in disorientation. The protagonist is initially introduced as *Sektionsrat* (head of section), thus through his symbolic function.[15] In the second sentence the narrator switches without transition to his proper name, his first name even, which not only points to the individual behind the official social role but also evokes a certain form of privacy and intimacy. The abrupt change of appellation, however, causes a moment of perplexity where the reader is uncertain about whether title and name refer to the same person. Thus, in the very beginning of the narrative, the identity of symbolic function and individual, and with that the question of legitimacy, is revealed as being at stake.

Robert is depicted as caught in a rather private moment – that of just waking up. In this slightly embarrassing situation – which is also Robert's own fault, as he forgot to lock the door – he is actually presented much less in his professional role as *Sektionsrat* (head of section) than as what one could call his private self. As we learn later, he is also currently on sick leave, thus indeed officially suspended from his symbolic function. The immediate switch from the official term of the professional occupation to the first name can be understood as a corrective through which the misnomer of the first sentence becomes apparent. The text performs the process of suspension by taking away the official title and replacing it with the first name, Robert. In this way, the beginning of the novella already introduces one of its key questions: what happens when one is deprived of one's symbolic status? Or, in other words, how does the deprivation of the symbolic function affect one's position within the norm of the bourgeois order?

The protagonist's first name then prefigures the critical psychic state that will become the main topic of the novella. Robert's first thought ('erster Gedanke') is addressed to the absent-mindedness of forgetting to lock the door, which, as we will come to know later, is a symptom of his mental instability. In this way, deprivation of symbolic status and symptom are presented as interrelated, which might be understood as a hint to look more closely at the apparently simple causal connection between illness and leave from duty. Indeed, it appears later in the novella as if Robert's symbolic function had been weakened to the point of dispensability even before his nervous breakdown made it impossible for him to keep up his work in the ministry. His friend and physician, Leinbach, repeatedly and pointedly refers to Robert's privileged

---

15 Interestingly, the translator William A. Drake chose to correct this irritation, by translating *Sektionsrat* (head of section) simply with 'Robert'.

position which allows him to take time off, while 'Andererseits gibt es viele Leute, denen einfach nur die Zeit mangelt, verrückt zu werden' (FiF20) (On the other hand, there are plenty of people who simply haven't the time to go crazy).[16] This not only suggests that Robert's illness is not to be taken seriously, but also that his position in the ministry is uncalled-for, in the sense that his absence does not make a difference, that no one is really calling him on duty.[17] And even Robert himself seems to think similarly of his own occupation. In an attempt to resist the compulsion of paranoid ideas, he forces himself to think of something irrelevant: 'Er setzte seinen Weg fort und zwang sich an etwas Gleichgültiges zu denken. Er versuchte, sich den Inhalt seiner letzten Arbeit – zur Statistik des niederösterreichischen Volksschulwesens – ins Gedächtnis zu rufen' (FiF31) (Robert continued on his way, forcing himself to think of unemotional matters [matters he was indifferent about, M.K.]. He tried to recall the contents of his last report, statistical data on the public schools of Lower Austria).[18] On the other hand, the inactivity of his sick leave makes him miss the routine of his work life:

Robert verspürte Heimweh nach seinem Kanzleiraum, nach dem großen Schreibtisch, dem bequemen, schwarzledernen Lehnsessel, den hohen Regalen mit den Aktenfaszikeln, den gelblichen Wänden mit den Landkarten und Tabellen, er sehnte sich nach einem Wirkungskreis, wo es ihm beschieden wäre wahrhaft Nützliches zu leisten und die Anerkennung eines Vorgesetzten, vielleicht gar ein Lob aus des Ministers eignem Munde zu erringen, was ihm nicht nur zur Befriedigung seines Ehrgeizes, sondern auch aus einem anderen, ihm nicht gleich deutlich werdenden Anlaß von Wichtigkeit zu sein dünkte. (FiF32)
Robert felt homesick for his office, for the big desk, the comfortable black leather armchair, the tall cabinets with the files of documents, the yellow-white binders of maps and charts. He

---

16   Schnitzler, *Flight into Darkness*, 24. See also: '"Ja", seufzte Leinbach, "wer auch sechs Monate Urlaub nehmen könnte! Wenn unsereiner solange seine Freiheit haben wollte, müsste er geradezu durchbrennen"' (FiF53) ('Yes,' Leinbach sighed. 'Anybody who could take six months' leave! If one of us wanted his freedom so long he would just have to run off). See Schnitzler, *Flight into Darkness*, 68.

17   The title 'Sektionsrat' (head of section) in the first sentence of the novella might refer to the perspective of the waiter, who would still be addressing him as such. However, this only reproduces the sensation of the emptiness of the title that in the context of being 'off-duty' is a mere mode of address and does not refer to Robert's actual function.

18   Schnitzler, *Flight into Darkness*, 39.

longed for a sphere of activity where it would be possible for him to accomplish something really useful and win the recognition of his superiors, perhaps even the praise from the Minister's own mouth.[19]

Without the task of doing something useful, the subject does not have a legitimate position in the world and is in that sense homeless. Robert's *Heimweh* (home sickness) demonstrates that the deprivation of his symbolic status makes him feel out of joint, useless, even unreal.[20] The recognition by a superior that he so desperately craves is linked to what Santner describes as 'symbolic resources that human societies depend upon to assure their members that they are "legitimate"'.[21] Even in the later stages of his illness, Robert hangs on to this promise of investiture to convince himself and others that he is still needed, and thus a legitimate member of society. When his brother mocks him about his travel plans with his fiancée ('Du heiratest wohl nur, um wieder dafür einen Vorwand zu haben?' (FiF88) ('Are you marrying only to have an excuse to get away again?)),[22] he defends himself: 'Keine sehr lange [Reise] diesmal [...]. Ich kann nicht wieder für ein paar Monate Urlaub nehmen' (FiF88) (Not a long trip this time. I can't get two months' leave right away).[23] Whether this is true – the willingness with which Robert's superior grants him the freedom to take days off may suggest the opposite – remains unclear, but the statement underlines how important it is to Robert to at least keep up the appearance of having a secured position and a task. That this is precisely not the case becomes clear when he does return to work after his long period of leave: he finds out that he has been replaced and will from now on assist another magistrate who is preparing to retire (see FiF55). These examples give the impression that Robert's work is somewhat superfluous to needs, which makes his position as *Sektionsrat* (head of section) a shallow nomination.

That this sensation of not being needed intensifies Robert's crisis is not surprising, as it not only calls into question the legitimacy of his own symbolic status, but also that of the entire order of which he is a representative. The connection between one's own legitimate status

---

19 Schnitzler, *Flight into Darkness*, 39.
20 See also the passage in which a conversation with his soon-to-be-fiancée Paula makes him realize his 'Sehnsucht nach Arbeit und Betätigung' (FiF46) (longing for work and activity). See Schnitzler, *Flight into Darkness*, 59 and his hope to be 'endlich wahr werden' (FiF47) ([to be] finally restored to reality). See Schnitzler, *Flight into Darkness*, 59.
21 Santner, *My Own Private Germany*, 144.
22 Schnitzler, *Flight into Darkness*, 116.
23 Schnitzler, *Flight into Darkness*, 116.

and the legitimacy of the system of social reality one is surrounded by particularly applies to Robert, as his workspace is a place where this social reality is administered. Its unembellished functionality demonstrates its occupation with the 'factual': official documents, maps, and charts are all supposed to refer to objective facts of reality. However, the administrative work in the ministry not only organizes given social facts in a certain way, it also *creates* or *engenders* these facts by the very act of performing the rules of the society's legal system.

Referring to Benjamin's essay 'Zur Kritik der Gewalt' (Critique of Violence), Santner points to a lack of justification at the origin of legal systems, which is covered up by a self-referentiality expressed in the tautological enunciation 'The law is the law'.[24] Bureaucratic administration is the performative realization of that tautology because by acting out the rules and prescriptions it establishes them as facts. Performative speech acts take up an important position in this system of self-realization as they constitute social reality by transferring symbolic power by virtue of investiture. However, at the origin of this chain of performances and investitures, there is a gap, which – at least in secular societies – cannot be closed and makes necessary the tautology, 'The law is

---

24 See Santner, *My Own Private Germany*, 10. There is no explicit reference to this tautology in Benjamin's essay, but he describes how the law manifests itself through performance, particularly in the case of the death penalty: 'For in the exercise of violence over life and death more than in any other legal act, law reaffirms itself. But in this very violence something rotten in law is revealed, above all to a finer sensibility, because the latter knows itself to be infinitely remote from conditions in which fate might imperiously have shown itself in such a sentence'. See Benjamin, Walter (1986), 'Critique of Violence,' *Reflections: Essays, Aphorisms, Autobiographical Writings*, ed. by Peter Demetz, New York: Schocken Books. According to Santner this refers to the lack of a legitimate origin of the law:

> What manifests itself as the law's inner decay is, […], that the very space of juridical reason within which the rule of law obtains is established and sustained by a dimension of force and violence that, as it were, holds the place of those missing foundations. At its foundation, the rule of law is sustained not by reason alone but also by the force/violence of a tautologous enunciation – "The law is the law!" – which is for Benjamin the source of a chronic institutional disequilibrium and degeneration. See Santner, *My Own Private Germany*, 10.

> Judith Butler offers a similar argument: '"It is the law!" becomes the utterance that performatively attributes the very force to the law that the law itself is said to exercise.' See Butler, Judith (2000), *Kinship between Life & Death*, New York, Chichester: Columbia University Press, 21.

the law'. Santner's claim is that this knowledge of the missing link, this void at the root of every legal system, is normally repressed into the (collective) unconscious but threatens to emerge, especially in times of heightened social antagonism or crisis.[25] The action of *Flucht in die Finsternis* (Flight into Darkness) is set in precisely such a time of crisis: the late era of the Habsburg Monarchy. By dint of his position in the ministry, Robert is particularly exposed to the crumbling structures of the system. The end of the passage in which Robert imagines himself as being convicted for murder seems to refer to the aspect of performativity in the legal system and the danger for authority when this aspect becomes palpable: 'Ein dröhnendes Lachen geht durch das ganze Auditorium, daß alle Fenster klirren. Ich bitte um Ruhe, schreit der Richter, hier ist kein Theater. Ich werde den Saal räumen lassen' (FiF49) (Thunderous laughter went through the courtroom, rattling the windows. 'Order!' shouted the judge 'This is no theatre! I shall have the room cleared!').[26]

To be clear, I do not want to suggest that the case of mental illness described in *Flucht in die Finsternis* (Flight into Darkness) is a pure crisis of investiture, unequivocally caused by the external factors of a rotten society that, as a result, produces deranged individuals. However, the text gives enough clues to enable us to assume a link between the symbolic function and Robert's symptoms, also in the ambiguous relationship to his brother, Otto, which is central to the development of his delusional ideas and has probably received the most attention in the scholarship.[27] Robert's feelings of ambivalence, oscillating between competition and admiration are closely linked to Otto's superior capability to conform to his social role and symbolic function:

Denn von Jugend auf hatte er sich dem älteren Bruder gegenüber bei äußerlich glänzenden Eigenschaften als einen Menschen von geringerem Wert erkannt, und er verhehlte sich nicht, daß sein eigener bürgerlicher Wandel von Otto zwar mit Nachsicht, oft aber mit Ungeduld und Unmut betrachtet wurde. Und Robert begriff das sehr gut. Ottos pflichtenschweres Dasein, der Ernst seines Berufes, bei dessen Übung es um so wesentliche Dinge wie um Leben und Gesundheit ging, sein sicheres und zugleich opfervolles Ruhen in der Familie, all das stellte sich für Robert in so hehrem Lichte dar, daß ihm dagegen seine eigene Existenz,

25 Santner, *My Own Private Germany*, 16.
26 Schnitzler, *Flight into Darkness*, 62.
27 See Thomé, *Autonomes Ich und 'Inneres Ausland,'* 714; Tarnowski-Seidel, Arthur Schnitzler, 'Flucht in die Finsternis,' 97–110; Allerdissen, Rolf (1985), *Arthur Schnitzler: Impressionistisches Rollenspiel und skeptischer Moralismus in seinen Erzählungen*, Bonn: Bouvier, 128–152, particularly 132.

wenn sie auch in den Rahmen eines Amts gespannt war, oft genug wie ohne rechte Würde und ohne tieferen Sinn erschien. (FiF10f.) From childhood he had regarded himself, in spite of superficially more brilliant qualities, as of less worth than his brother, and he did not conceal from himself the fact that his social life was viewed by Otto seldom with indulgence, more often with impatience and anger. And Robert understood that very well. Otto's heavy responsibilities, the seriousness of his profession, in which such matters as life and well-being were at hazard, and his steady and self-denying domesticity, exalted him in the eyes of Robert, whose own existence, though not free from cramping obligations of an official, often enough seemed to him without true worth or deeper meaning.[28]

While Robert's *Amt* (office) does not provide him with enough security about the legitimacy of his existence, Otto's symbolic function appears secured in multiple ways – not only through the indisputable necessity of the medical profession, but also through the dutiful manner in which he seems to carry out his tasks as doctor, husband, and father. His 'sicheres und zugleich opfervolles Ruhen in der Familie' (steady and self-denying domesticity) might extend to the social community in which he dutifully reiterates the performances of his symbolic mandate ('opfervoll' – self-denying) and in return gains reassurance ('sicheres Ruhen' – steady domesticity) about his legitimate status. Correspondingly, Otto is introduced in the beginning through a letter to Robert in which he mentions his recent investiture as extraordinary professor (FiF5). His name remains unknown until the second chapter, which might underline his strong symbolic function. This subtle counter-position of the two brothers on the very first page – one being deprived of symbolic status, the other being invested with an additional symbolic mandate – creates a tension that is going to be played out further in the novella until it reaches its culmination in the final fratricide.

Central to this dynamic between the two brothers is obviously also the asymmetrical distribution of power between them. As his doctor, Otto is in a position to diagnose his brother, which – similar to an act of investiture – is also a certain form of performative speech act. In this way, the act of diagnosis can take on the quality of a prophecy: not only in the sense of a medical estimation of the course of the disease, but also in the sense of a prognostic social destiny, comparable to (but also in opposition to) those social destinies assigned by virtue of symbolic investiture.

---

28 Schnitzler, *Flight into Darkness*, 10–11.

Diagnosis as Destiny

A diagnosis can only be uttered by a person who is invested with the power to do so – by virtue of an official doctor's degree. In this context it might not be surprising that Robert uses the word 'Urteil' as a synonym for diagnosis when he wonders whether he might have played down his symptoms in front of Otto, 'in der unbewußten Hoffnung, auf diese Art ein gelinderes Urteil zu erfahren' (FiF10) (in the unconscious hope of thus securing a milder sentence).[29] This aspect of diagnosis as judgement also becomes clear through Robert's reaction to Otto's diagnosis of their mutual friend Höhnburg. The speech act of diagnosis appears here like a prophecy of destiny:

Auf dem Heimweg aber hatte Otto den Bruder beiseitegenommen und ihm anvertraut, daß ihr gemeinsamer Freund Höhnburg – was die andern noch nicht ahnten, er selbst als Arzt aber seit etlichen Tagen mit Bestimmtheit wußte – unheilbaren Wahnsinns verfallen sei und in spätestens drei Jahren unter der Erde liegen werde. Robert lehnte sich zunächst gegen die Zumutung auf, in dem jungen Kavallerieoffizzier, der ein solches Bild ungetrübter, ja gesteigerter Gesundheit bot und der zudem ein Freund war, einen *Gezeichneten*, einen *Verurteilten* zu erblicken. (FiF14 [emphasis added])

But on the way home, Otto had taken his brother aside and told him confidentially what no one else suspected as yet, but what Otto, as a physician, had known with absolute certainty for many days – that his friend Höhnburg was uncurably insane and would be dead in three years at the longest. Robert at first refused to believe that the young cavalry officer, who was the picture of robust health and his friend besides, was a marked, a condemned man.[30]

The comparison of the diagnosis with a juridical judgement points up the structural similarity between both performative speech acts. Moreover, the word *Gezeichneter* (marked) underlines the stigmatic, but also fate-like quality of those speech acts. At another point in the narrative, Robert makes his understanding of madness as destiny explicit by referring to the word *Wahnsinn* (madness) as 'schicksalsvolle Wort' (fateful word) (FiF16). This, in turn, brings to mind Bourdieu's[31] description of institutional investitures and acts of naming as proclamations of social destinies:

---

29 Schnitzler, *Flight into Darkness*, 10.
30 Schnitzler, *Flight into Darkness*, 17.
31 Bourdieu, Pierre (1992), *Language and Symbolic Power: The Economy of Linguistic Exchanges*, ed. by John B. Thompson, Cambridge: Polity Press, 122.

'Become what you are': that is the principle behind the performative magic of all acts of institution. The essence assigned through naming and investiture is, literally, a fatum. [...] All social destinies, positive or negative, by consecration or stigma, are equally fatal – by which I mean mortal – because they enclose those whom they characterize within the limits that are assigned to them and that they are made to recognize.

Social stigmatizations as well as social appreciations or appointments can thus be understood as a kind of prescription of habitus. Both are accompanied by a definition of a certain social role with given codes of conduct and a determined social position.

While an official appointment is obviously an act of consecration, a medical diagnosis can become a stigma. As Susan Sontag has analyzed in her essay *Illness as Metaphor*, some diseases are associated with specific character traits, which in turn give the diagnosis a moralizing effect. She also highlights the punitive impact of this assumed connection between illness and character on those diagnosed with these diseases.[32] This moralizing interpretation of illness therefore stereotypes the people suffering from these illnesses. These stereotypes carry cultural narratives within them that go beyond a neutral scientific description of symptoms. A medical diagnosis can thus function like a judgement or investiture, not only in the sense that it implies assumptions about the course of the illness, which can have a prophetic, fate-like quality, but also in the sense that the culturally engendered ideas and fantasies inherent to the stereotype of the illness prescribe a certain social role to the diagnosed individual. Moreover, the diagnosis of mental illness is tightly linked to the individual's position in relation to the social norm: it assigns to the diagnosed individual a negative social status, which denies a legitimate position within the realm of the norm: the diagnosis of mental illness relegates the individual to the periphery of the 'other'. This is why this social destiny is fundamentally different from other institutional performative acts, which ascribe a social destiny: it is this 'non-place' of the 'other' which negates the membership of the social order. This is particularly important in cases when juridical and medical knowledge systems meet, i.e. when the question of guilt and accountability is at stake.

We can understand Robert's ambivalent fantasy that he might have murdered his former lover Alberta and could be convicted for this

---

32 See Sontag, *Illness as Metaphor & AIDS and its Metaphors*, 47.

crime in this context.[33] As long as a subject can be punished and held responsible for his or her actions, he or she is still considered as part of the norm, still as a legitimate subject. While being punished is obviously a frightening idea to Robert, a certain longing and an aspect of self-fashioning lies in the way his fantasies are played out as a medial projection:

> Plötzlich sah er sein eigenes Porträt vor sich, mit Überzieher, Zylinder und Stock, so wie er sich in Wirklichkeit nie hatte photographieren lassen; ganz in der Art eines nachlässig vervielfältigten Bildes in einer Tageszeitung, und darunter las er mit großen Lettern die Worte: Ein neuer Blaubart. Er roch das Papier und die Druckerschwärze. Gleich darauf sah er sich vor Gericht stehen als Angeklagten. Er leugnete. Er schwor zu Gott, daß er niemals einen Menschen umgebracht habe. Es ist nur ein Wahn von mir, meine Herren Geschworenen. Wie darf man mich denn wegen eines Wahns vor Gericht stellen? Ich bin krank, meine Herren Geschworenen, aber ich bin kein Verbrecher. Die Umstände sprechen gegen mich. (FiF48)
>
> Suddenly he saw a portrait of himself, in a guise in which he would never have let his picture be taken, with overcoat, top-hat and stick; a typical badly reproduced newspaper photograph, and underneath, in great letters, he read the caption: 'A New Bluebeard'. He could smell the paper and the ink. Immediately afterward he saw himself standing before the judge as an accused criminal. He denied the charge. He swore to God that he had never killed any one. 'It is only a delusion of mine, gentlemen of the jury. How can a man be brought to trial for the events of a delusion? I am ill, gentlemen of the jury, but I am not a criminal. Circumstances are against me'.[34]

The contradictory quality of these sentences underlines not only Robert's ambivalent feelings about this compulsive idea, but also the complexity of the different aspects it contains. When he insists on his

---

33 The women in Robert's life play a decisive role for the development of his psychical symptoms: he also fears that he might be responsible for the death of his wife, who died many years before the narrated time of the novella. During the course of action he meets and gets engaged to the rational and deliberate Paula, whom he imagines as his saviour. He repeatedly uses her as confirmation of his own sanity. Before getting engaged to Paula, he has a sexual encounter with a piano teacher, who becomes a central part of his later delusions. In the last section of this chapter, I will analyze the passage with the piano teacher in more detail.

34 Schnitzler, *Flight into Darkness*, 61.

innocence, he significantly does not only refer to the murderous deed, but also to the extenuating illness itself. This can be understood as an attempted defence against the collapsing of diagnosis and judgement analyzed above.[35] However, both the fact that he mentions that the circumstances speak against him and the way in which he imagines his portrait in the newspaper suggest that the passage can also be read as a kind of wishful thinking. In the context of Robert's unsatisfactory position in the ministry and his desire to be 'wanted', the idea of being persecuted by the law can be seen as displaced wish fulfillment: as long as he can be considered guilty, he can feel secured of his place within the norm, even though this might result in his conviction.[36]

This also addresses the topic of individual responsibility, which stands in opposition to the state of mental illness.[37] It is Robert's most pressing concern that 'eine Geistesstörung den Menschen zum willenlosen Sklaven des Schicksals erniedere'(FiF15) (insanity, robbing him of his will, reduced him to a helpless dependence on fate).[38] Destiny seems to mark the non-place that the diagnosis of mental illness entails. Although used in a negative way here, it is already clear that the idea of a metaphysical destiny begins where the social order ends. The loss of accountability means the loss of one's secured position within the norm. In order to avoid this loss of accountability at all costs, he asks Otto to promise him to commit an act of euthanasia should he ever notice the first signs of mental illness in his, Robert's, behaviour. In this way, he transfers all responsibility about his life to Otto. Interestingly, this is done in the manner of investiture:

---

35   The manner in which Robert imagines his own image, as a typical badly reproduced newspaper photograph, might hint at the influence of stereotypes on his perception: not only does the newspaper print evoke the literal meaning of the stereotype – a letter mould that made the reproduction of text possible – the formulation 'nachlässig vervielfältigt' (badly reproduced) also points up the serial quality of stereotypes, which deny an individual development. Moreover, the multiplication/reproduction of self-images may also already pre-figure the ego-dissociation and encounter with mirror images, which is yet to come and which I will analyze later on.

36   The fantasy of being convicted can be understood as a compulsive return of the ideological interpellation which, according to Althusser, engenders the subject. See Althusser, Louis (1971), 'Ideology and Ideological State Apparatuses,' Lenin and Philosophy and Other Essays, London: New Left Books, 127–188, 174. As Butler has noted with regard to the Althusserian concept, the process of becoming a subject is always linked to a certain kind of guilt. See Butler, Judith (1997b), The Psychic Life of Power: Theories in Subjection, Stanford, CA: Stanford University Press, 107. This may underline once more Robert's desire for a secured symbolic status.

37   Thomé's reading focuses on the question of accountability and mental illness and their poetic function in the novella. See Thomé, Autonomes Ich und 'Inneres Ausland'.

38   Schnitzler, Flight into Darkness, 17.

Robert sets up 'trocken, geradezu geschäftsmäßig, den Empfang jenes Versprechens bestätigte' (FiF16) (a cold and business-like document, recording promise).[39] The reassurance that Robert feels immediately after that is, however, only a transient one. Doubts about Otto's faultlessness begin to form in his mind, which eventually build up to an essential calling into question of Otto's own mental health and so of his accountability. All this leads Robert deeper and deeper into a paranoid state, which finally has him become his brother's murderer. It becomes clear that Robert tries to compensate for his insecurity about his symbolic function through the 'investiture' of his brother: he transfers the power to decide about the legitimacy of his position within the norm to Otto. However, since Otto, as we have seen, is for Robert a representative of the social order that has become unable to provide him with a feeling of security about his legitimate status, he cannot provide Robert with the right assurance either. On the contrary, it becomes clear how much this elevation of Otto's power, which puts him in an almost God-like position, increases the pressure Robert finds himself under. Robert experiences here the missing link of legitimization: he cannot be sure whether Otto is really capable of diagnosing his symptoms correctly, which leads to his increasing doubt. His question as to whether Otto is sure that he can 'die Grenze immer bestimmen zu können' (FiF60) (always draw the line [between health and insanity]?)[40] demonstrates his anxiety about the power he has given to his brother. This anxiety becomes so determined that he develops the paranoid idea that Otto in turn might have become insane and could be planning to kill him. At the same time, Otto takes on the function of Robert's super-ego, which leads to advanced feelings of anxiety, for example when Robert catches himself wanting to test Otto's medical competence: 'Zugleich aber fühlte er diesen Vorsatz wie von einer unbestimmten Angst durchzittert, ungefähr so, als wenn er etwas Unrechtes begangen hätte und zumindest eines Verweises, wenn nicht gar einer Strafe gewärtig sein müßte' (FiF13) (But at once he felt this resolution shaken by an indefinable fear, somewhat as if he had committed a misdeed and must expect reprimand, if not punishment).[41] That Robert once more anticipates punishment from Otto underlines the fact that Otto not only functions as some sort of father figure for Robert, but also as a representative of the social law and order in its entirety.

---

39 Schnitzler, *Flight into Darkness*, 18.
40 Schnitzler, *Flight into Darkness*, 78.
41 Schnitzler, *Flight into Darkness*.

To a substantial extent, Robert has internalized this law, which is for example demonstrated in the way he thinks about Otto's superiority in the passage quoted above, and also by his immediate censorship of the idea of testing Otto's competence. On the other hand, Robert seems dissatisfied by the interpretative patterns of the dominant order and the explanations offered by Otto as a representative of the latter. In this context, one could read the 'hehres Licht', in which Otto's devotion to his professional duties appears to Robert, as an allusion to the Enlightenment.[42] Correspondingly, he turns out to share the Enlightenment understanding of madness as absence of rationality: 'Du bist nun hoffentlich endgültig vernünftig geworden' (FiF94) (I hope you have finally become sensible).[43] This notion of *Vernunft* (reason) marks the crucial conflict in the narrative because it is closely linked to the claim of free volition, upon which post-Enlightenment societies are based. There is something paradoxical about this claim to autonomy and the way subject constitution works through appellation and the iteration of performative investitures.[44] If we take Bourdieu's description of social roles as destiny seriously, the subject's capacity for autonomy appears highly restricted.[45] This hidden contradiction has an uncanny effect, which plays a significant role in *Flucht in die Finsternis* (Flight into Darkness).

The production of symbolic identities depends on the performance of institutional rites and speech acts. All these investitures and pronunciations of social status are calls to order, which inform the individual's identity and in turn require a 'regulated series of social performances, rituals, behaviours, that corresponds to that symbolic position in the community'.[46] The knowledge of this dependency on the performative reiteration of social identity is usually repressed, but when it emerges in times of instability, the performances are experienced as an uncanny repetition compulsion 'when one's actions appear to be controlled by a demonic force, lending those actions a mechanical, automatic quality'.[47] This feeling of being driven to an endless chain of repetition, recalling the endless chain of mirror images in *Der Weg ins Freie*, is expressed in an idea uttered by Robert's friend and doctor Leinbach, which becomes crucial to Robert's delusions:

---

42 It also reproduces the metaphorical light–dark dichotomy for mental health and illness, which is already implied in the novella's title. I will return to the function of this imagery later in this chapter.

43 Schnitzler, *Flight into Darkness*, 123.

44 See Santner, *My Own Private Germany*, 145.

45 See also Foucault's elaborations on the mechanisms of the disciplines as 'systems of micro-power,' which are the complementary side to liberties established by the Enlightenment. See Foucault, Michel (1991), *Discipline and Punish: The Birth of the Prison*, London: Penguin, 222.

46 Santner, *My Own Private Germany*, 11.

47 Santner, *My Own Private Germany*, 126.

Er [Leinbach] hatte damals einen Beweis gefunden, daß es eigentlich keinen Tod auf der Welt gebe. Es sei ja zweifellos, erklärte er, daß nicht nur für Ertrinkende, sondern daß für alle Sterbenden im letzten Augenblick das ganze Leben mit einer ungeheuren, für uns andere gar nicht zu erfassenden Geschwindigkeit noch einmal sich abrolle. Da nun dieses erinnerte Leben natürlich auch wieder einen letzten Augenblick habe und dieser letzte Augenblick wieder einen letzten, und so weiter: so bedeute das Sterben im Grunde nichts anderes als die Ewigkeit – unter der mathematischen Formel einer unendlichen Reihe. Robert erinnerte sich noch, wie erbittert Otto dieses Gefasel zurückgewiesen hatte; Robert aber, ohne sich für Leinbachs Auffassung geradezu einzusetzen, hatte keineswegs vermocht, sie völlig unsinnig zu finden. (FiF24f.)

Leinbach had discovered proof that there really is no death. It is beyond question, he had declared, that not only the drowning, but all the dying, live over again their whole past lives in the last moment, with a rapidity inconceivable to us others. This remembered life must also have a last moment, and this last moment its own last moment, and so on; hence, dying was itself Eternity: in accordance with the theory of limits one approached death, but never got there. Robert still remembered with what acerbity Otto had rejected this as twaddle. Robert, however, though he did not accept Leinbach's proposition, had not been able to pronounce it entirely nonsensical.[48]

This can be understood as the radicalized version of the repetition compulsion of the symbolic function, which becomes important for Robert when he finds himself tormented by delusional thoughts: 'Zum wievielten Male schritt er jetzt wohl diese Treppe hinauf? Wie oft war sie der arme Höhnburg hinaufgegangen [...]? Und ging sie immer noch, und mußte sie ewig gehen –?!' (FiF25) (How many times had he gone up these steps? Hundreds, thousands? How often had poor Höhnburg gone up them [...]? And would he go again and eternally?)[49] The idea of an eternal reiteration of life is obviously an attack upon the concept of free will, which is why it is not surprising that it is vehemently rejected by Otto. For Robert, however, it to some extent seems to resonate with his experiences, referring to the empty completion of the performances his social destiny forces him to repeat. It becomes clear that Robert has already felt dissatisfied with the compulsive repetition of the symbolic

48   Schnitzler, *Flight into Darkness*, 30.
49   Schnitzler, *Flight into Darkness*, 30–31.

function of his bourgeois identity for a long time. During the years of his marriage with his deceased wife Brigitte, it was not only the precept of monogamy that made him feel trapped and on edge:

> Doch das Schlimmste für ihn war ihr Klavierspiel gewesen. Ohne zureichende Begabung, aber mit der ihr eigenen Beharrlichkeit hatte sie die Gewohnheit ihrer Mädchenjahre beibehalten, täglich eine Stunde lang zu üben; und ihre Art, Mozartsche und Beethovensche Sonaten mit kindischen, dicken Fingern herunterzuspielen, hatte den Gatten, während er nach dem Abendessen rauchend und lesend im Nebenzimmer saß, manchmal in den Zustand wahrer Verzweiflung versetzt. (FiF39) But worst of all, for him, had been her piano-playing. With very little talent, but with the persistence characteristic of her, she had retained her girlhood habit of practising an hour every day. Her way of thumping off Mozart and Beethoven sonatas with childishly clumsy fingers had often reduced her husband, as he sat in the next room after dinner, smoking and reading, to a state of actual despair.[50]

What annoys Robert here is the repetitive structure of Brigitte's piano practice that does not have any other goal than to re-constitute her bourgeois identity which demands that every young daughter learn the basics of piano playing. In this way, Robert's fear of being turned into a 'slave of destiny' suddenly seems to be not just a symptom of mental illness any more, but an essential part of his bourgeois identity. This is made unequivocally clear when Robert thinks back to his married life as 'unentrinnbare Sklaverei' (FiF39) (unescapable slavery).[51] From this perspective, the 'otherness' of insanity suddenly appears a form of escape, as will be shown in the next section.

Seductive Stereotypes of Madness

In his own piano playing, as opposed to Brigitte's mechanical exercises, Robert indulges in 'musikalischen Kaffee- und Havannaphantasien' (FiF27) (coffee and Havana improvisations),[52] thus in a free and not too ambitious form of improvisation. This coincides with Otto's slightly reproachful understanding of Robert's mental instability, which he describes as a 'Neigung zur Verspieltheit, zur Unwahrheit, zur Komödianterei, kurz, ein unanständiges Bestreben, vom wirklichen Ernst des

---

50 Schnitzler, *Flight into Darkness*, 49.
51 Schnitzler, *Flight into Darkness*, 49.
52 Schnitzler, *Flight into Darkness*, 34.

Lebens abzurücken, und unbequeme Verantwortlichkeiten abzuleh-
nen' (FiF60) (a desire to play, to mystify, to make-believe – in short, as an
improper effort to escape from the real seriousness of life and to shirk
disagreeable responsibilities').[53] The moral judgement in this statement,
which highlights the debasing aspects of the stereotype of insanity, is
clearly discernible and refers to the rejection of responsibility. Besides
these punitive aspects of the stereotype of insanity that make the diagnosis appear like a moral conviction, it also contains an idealizing
mystification. Sontag describes how tuberculosis and its visible symptoms were perceived in a glamorized way that 'spiritually refined' the
person suffering from it: the idea that people became more 'conscious'
when confronted with the possibility of near death made tuberculosis
patients more 'interesting', making the healthy appear banal or vulgar.
After tuberculosis was de-mystified through the improvement of heal-
ing methods, a new 'fashionable' disease had to be found: 'In the twentieth century, the repellent, harrowing disease that is made the index of
superior sensitivity, the vehicle of "spiritual" feelings and "critical" dis-
content, is insanity'.[54] Influenced also by these idealizing stereotypes,
'madness' appears to Robert as a way to escape the bourgeois order and
to question the post-Enlightenment primacy of rationality: 'Und ist es
denn gar so wünschenswert, vernünftig zu sein. [...] Vielleicht bin ich
sogar verrückt. [...] Aber wenn ich es bin, so fühle ich mich sehr wohl
dabei' (FiF94) (And is it so desirable to be sensible? [...] Perhaps I really
am crazy. [...] But if I am, I like it very well).[55]
      The close connection between diagnosis and destiny that has been
analyzed above is permeated by the ambivalence of fear and fascination
linked to the punitive *and* idealizing stereotypes of 'madness'. While
Robert fears the outbreak of a mental illness, it also has a kind of 'elevating' quality. By compulsively seeking signs of destiny, he constructs an
individual narrative for himself that seems to compensate for his lack of
identification with his symbolic function and bourgeois existence in general. When Robert thinks back to the evening when Otto had diagnosed
his friend Höhnburg, it becomes clear that he identifies strongly with his
friend: 'Denn mit grausamer Deutlichkeit stieg vor Roberts Sinnen der
längst vergangene Frühlingsabend auf, an dem nicht nur des Freundes,
sondern – wie er tief erschauernd fühlte – vielleicht auch sein eigenes
Schicksal geheimnisvoll sich angekündigt hatte' (FiF14) (With cruel
clarity arose the memory of that spring evening of long ago, when his
friend's fate, and possibly his own also [he felt, and shuddered deeply,

53 Schnitzler, *Flight into Darkness*, 78.
54 Sontag, *Illness as Metaphor & AIDS and its Metaphors*, 36.
55 Schnitzler, *Flight into Darkness*, 123–124.

M.K.], had announced itself in such dread fashion).[56] While Robert's emotions are dominated by fear, the sensation of *Schauer* (shudder), particularly in combination with the adjective *geheimnisvoll* (mysterious), does not seem to be exclusively negative, but may also have an awestruck connotation.[57] In his precarious situation, in which the coercive quality of his social role emerges, the state of mental illness suddenly appears not exclusively as a threat, but also as a certain kind of promise.

The playful tendency not only suggests a relation between a certain lack of maturity or childishness and mental instability, but also – especially in conjunction with *Komödianterei* (playing comedy) – hints at a performative aspect of Robert's illness, thus linking it also to artistic and aesthetic practices such as acting, creative writing, and music. This gives way to the sentimentalizing or idealizing image of mental illness, which also plays a role in Robert's perception of his symptoms and which turns out to be no less problematic than the moralizing and pejorative verdicts. It lends the diagnosis not only the connotation of (moral) doom but also of seduction. This positive interpretation of mental illness is rooted in its cultural stereotypes. With the rather glamorous connotations of madness, the mentally unstable personality becomes a somewhat appealing role. The ambivalent stereotype of the madman may thus entail the seductive promise of a way to act out, a certain form of creativity and thus agency outside of the lacklustre repetitive patterns of the bourgeois symbolic function. This mystification of the position of the 'other', which we have already encountered in *Der Weg ins Freie* (Road into the Open), where Georg feels tempted to emulate his Jewish friends, is a recurring motif in Schnitzler's writings and will continue to play a central role for the argument of this study.

Robert's identification with Höhnburg and the idea that his friend's symptoms had already prefigured his own destiny become something close to a self-fulfilling prophecy.[58] It becomes clear relatively early in the novella that he repeatedly plays with stereotypes of madness by half-consciously re-enacting them, for example when he emulates Höhnburg's symptoms.[59] In this context, his affinity with performance arts

---

56 Schnitzler, *Flight into Darkness*, 16.
57 I will return to this sensation of *Schauer* (shudder) as a reference to German Romanticism in the next section.
58 See Lukas, Wolfgang (1996), *Das Selbst und das Fremde: Epochale Lebenskrisen und ihre Lösung im Werk Arthur Schnitzlers*, Munich: Fink, 234f. and 274.
59 The theatrical aspect of Robert's illness has been pointed out by Thomé, *Autonomes Ich und 'Inneres Ausland,'* 710. On the comedic quality of Robert's symptoms, see also Allerdissen, *Arthur Schnitzler: Impressionistisches Rollenspiel und skeptischer Moralismus in seinen Erzählungen*, 131. Both authors also note that the 'enactment' of the role of the madman brings some relief for Robert, but they do not refer to the impact of the stereotypical cultural narratives of madness that are at work here.

becomes interesting. During a theatre performance Robert finds himself 'kindlich erfreut, als ihm der erste Komiker mitten im Couplet von
der Bühne herab vertraulich zunickte' (FiF19) (He felt a boyish delight
when the principal comedian bowed confidentially to him in the middle of a stanza).[60] The fact that he feels a kind of complicity with the
comedian suggests that the idea of a non-bourgeois existence appeals
to Robert. Since a higher creativity and artistic affinity are aspects of the
positive stereotype of mental illness, the seductive quality of the role of
the 'madman' is underlined here. The gesture of nodding is repeated in
a further moment of apparent connection between Robert and another
performance artist – a piano player in a night bar,[61] to whom Robert gives
a very generous tip: 'Der Pianist nickte zum Dank' (FiF24) (The pianist
nodded his thanks).[62] The large-handed tip turns out to be an act of identification with the manic Höhnburg, who, on the day of Otto's fatal diagnosis, had appeared in particularly high spirits, while giving the waiter
an unusually big tip (FiF14). At the same time, the tip is also a parapraxis:
after Robert has drawn unwanted attention to himself by laughing too
loudly, he quickly decides to leave the bar, calls for the waiter and thinks:
'Ich werde nicht so dumm sein und ihm zehn Gulden Trinkgeld geben'
(FiF23) (I shall not be such an idiot as to tip him ten gulden).[63] In this
way, he negates his connection to Höhnburg and his symptoms. However, when he finds out that the bill has already been paid by a friend, he
displaces the act of tipping from the waiter to the pianist: 'In den Teller
auf dem Deckel des Pianos legte er zu den dort schon gesammelten kleineren Münzen ein goldenes Zehnkronenstück, ärgerte sich zugleich,
wagte aber nicht, es zurückzunehmen' (FiF24) (In the plate on the piano
top, which was filled with much smaller coins, he placed a gold ten kro-
nen piece. At once he was vexed with himself, but he dared not take the
coin back).[64] Thus, the performative play with the role of the madman
seems to have got out of control and to run the risk of becoming a repetition compulsion. In this way, the escape into illness as alternative to his
bourgeois existence is already here announced as a dead end.

This corresponds to Robert's experience in the further course of the
novella's action, when compulsive thoughts and actions begin to overpower him. In an, albeit transient, moment of clarity, Robert reflects on
this at one point:

---

60 Schnitzler, Flight into Darkness, 22.
61 The piano player in a night bar as 'door man' to a realm that appears like an
    alternative to the bourgeois order returns in Traumnovelle, as we will see in the
    fifth chapter of this study.
62 Schnitzler, Flight into Darkness, 29.
63 Schnitzler, Flight into Darkness, 28.
64 Schnitzler, Flight into Darkness, 29.

Von seinem eigenem Leben gleichsam im Stich gelassen, im Innersten leer geworden, hatte er allzu willig, ja, mit einer gewissen Selbstgefälligkeit, eine Art Rolle für sich zu spielen begonnen, die wachsende Gewalt über ihn erlangt und allmählich angedroht hatte, sein innerstes Wesen zu zerstören. (FiF46f.)
Left in the lurch, as it were, by his own life, become empty in his innermost being, he had all too willingly, even with a certain complacency, begun to play for himself a rôle which had exerted control over him and threatened gradually to crowd out his true nature.[65]

In this passage, the connection between Robert's empty symbolic function and his mental illness is made explicit. When Robert compares himself with Otto and contrasts Otto's significant position as doctor with his own, he misses a 'tieferen Sinn' in his existence. We can recognize here a curious hint at the gain he derives from his pathological constitution, as it is one of his striking symptoms to look for and construct deeper meaning behind everything he experiences. This quest for a deeper meaning is significantly linked to the idea of a metaphysical destiny: everything Robert experiences becomes potentially meaningful, becomes a possible sign linked to the plan of a higher power. This gives his clinical picture a decisive aesthetic and literary quality, which is underlined by elements in the text that allude to literary genres other than that of the psychological novella, particularly German *Schauerromantik* (Dark Romanticism). In the next section, I will explore this aesthetic functionalization of madness and show how Robert's tendency to over-interpret events is both undermined and mirrored by the text.

Signs of Destiny

Robert tends to interpret random events as meaningful signs of destiny, as either warnings or positive anticipations of the future. 'So entschloß er sich, den beabsichtigten Besuch vorläufig zu verschieben, um Otto [...] erfrischt, in gehobener Stimmung und womöglich – denn auch dies erschien ihm nicht ohne Bedeutung – bei gänzlich aufgehelltem Wetter zum erstenmal wieder gegenüberzutreten' (FiF17) (So he decided to wait and call on Otto after a good night's rest, refreshed, in better spirits, and if possible – for this seemed to him not without importance – in pleasant, sunny weather).[66] The idea that the weather could have any impact on either Otto's judgement of Robert's condition of health or even of his future life in general could maybe be taken as a curious effect of spleen rather than a serious symptom of mental instability.

---

65 Schnitzler, *Flight into Darkness*, 59.
66 Schnitzler, *Flight into Darkness*, 20.

However, this tendency to the pathetic fallacy becomes more salient the more he becomes overpowered by delusional ideas.[67] We have already seen that Robert constructs for himself a narrative of destiny by linking his life to that of Höhnburg, which develops into a kind of self-fulfilling prophecy over which Robert increasingly loses control. In this way, the text undermines Robert's interpretations of the world in terms of signs of destiny. At the same time, the text itself is obviously aesthetically constructed and thus invites the *reader* to look for hidden meanings. Robert's way of looking at the world is, in fact, reminiscent of the perspective of the literary critic who tries to decipher symbolic meanings in poetic texts. Ironically then, we have to adopt a similar perspective to that of Robert in order to understand how the text undermines this very same perspective. Throughout the novella there seems to be a double structure of Robert's practice of composition and interpretation and the narrative itself which provides its own mesh of references. At times, both structures seem to be absolutely congruent, when the narrative perspective comes to be identical with that of Robert.[68] Only at rare points is there a clearly distinguishable distance between the two perspectives, when the narrator points out the falsity of Robert's perceptions;[69] but most of the time, the narrative structure is a potentially uncanny *Doppelgänger* of Robert's thinking patterns, ironically undermining the latter by using the same strategies of referencing.

Nevertheless, the practice of overcharging everything with an additional 'meaning' is clearly a coping strategy for Robert. He tries quite literally to come to 'terms' with what is happening to him by finding

---

67 The tendency to suspect a hidden meaning in both positive or negative ways is recurrent throughout the novella, e.g.: 'Mit den Knaben trieb er allerhand Kurzweil, nahm den kleineren auf den Schoß und hatte dabei das Gefühl einer Vorbedeutung, ja eines heiter-trostreichen Zukunftsbildes' (FiF56) (He romped with the little boys, took the younger one on his knee, and thought fondly of the time when he should have children of his own [literally: and had the feeling of a premonition, even of a happy-comforting vision of the future, M.K.]). See Schnitzler, *Flight into Darkness*, 73.
68 See Thomé, *Autonomes Ich und 'Inneres Ausland,'* 717.
69 The two most unequivocal examples are when Robert tells his fiancée Paula about his escape plan ('Sie stand vor ihm, totenblaß und mit einem verzerrten Lächeln. Aber er merkte nicht, daß ihre Züge sich so seltsam verändert hatten' (FiF100f.) (She stood before him, deathly pale, and with a tortured smile. But he did not notice that her features had altered so strangely). See Schnitzler, *Flight into Darkness*, 134) and when Otto tries to take him into his arms right before being shot ('In seinen Augen war Angst, Mitleid und Liebe ohne Maß. Aber dem Bruder bedeutete der feuchte Glanz dieses Blickes Tücke, Drohung und Tod' (FiF113) (In his eyes were anxiety, sympathy, and love unbounded. But the twinkling moisture in those eyes meant to his brother fraud, menace and death). See Schnitzler, *Flight into Darkness*, 150).

new formulations, signifiers, for his mental behaviour: 'Und doch laufen meine Gedanken immer aufs neue nach dieser Richtung hin, ohne Sinn und Zweck, wie auf ein totes Geleise. Auf ein totes Geleise, wiederholte er. Ja, das ist es. Und das Vergleichswort, das er gefunden hatte, beruhigte ihn beinahe' (FiF66) (And yet my thoughts always, always run in this direction, without sense and purpose, along this single track. Single track!' he repeated. 'Yes, that is it!' And the expressiveness of the phrase almost reassured him).[70] The fact that Robert chooses a metaphorical term, which reassures him, fits in well with his habit of interpreting random experiences and events metaphorically. With the attempt to find a metaphor for what he experiences, he seems to become more active as he not only deciphers the hidden meaning of the world around him, but also *creates* meaning and signification, behaving perhaps not only like a literary critic but also like a writer.

Freud's essay on creative writing and daydreaming, *Der Dichter und das Phantasieren* (Creative Writers and Day-Dreaming, 1908), comes to mind here. Freud points out the parallels between childhood play, the daydreaming of adults and the process of creative writing. Freud considers daydreaming and unsatisfied wishes which drive the resulting fantasies as a source for the ideas of the creative writer. However,

If phantasies become overluxuriant and over-powerful, the conditions are laid for an onset of neurosis or psychosis. Phantasies, moreover, are the immediate mental precursors of the distressing symptoms complained of by our patients. Here a broad by-path branches off into pathology.[71]

This metaphorical byway is rendered literal in *Flucht in die Finsternis* (Flight into Darkness), when Robert becomes completely lost in the elaborate system of his delusional ideas: 'Morgen mit dem ersten Zug fahre ich weiter, gehe dann an einer Zweigstation auf eine andere Strecke über, irgendwohin, wo mich niemand vermutet, und dort setze ich meine Anklage- oder Verteidigungsschrift sorgfältig auf' (FiF110) (Tomorrow I'll take the first train out of here, to some way-station on another branch of the road – and any place where no one would expect to find me. There I will write, very carefully, my defense – or accusation).[72] While Robert is consciously thinking in clearly juristic terms, his plan to change trains at a *Zweigstation* (way-station with branching tracks) not

70   Schnitzler, *Flight into Darkness*, 86.
71   Freud, Sigmund (2001), 'Creative Writers and Daydreaming,' *Standard Edition*, vol. IX, ed. by James Strachey, Alan Tyson, Alix Strachey, Anna Freud, and Angela Richards, London: Vintage, 147.
72   Schnitzler, *Flight into Darkness*, 146.

only recalls Freud's pathological bypath, but also Robert's own metaphor of *totes Geleise* (dead-end track). Moreover, the train motif holds a specific connotation related to mental instability in the contemporary discourse: Sander Gilman describes how the train, or more specifically the trauma of train accidents, 'became a means of understanding the traumatic nature of hysteria at the turn of the century'.[73] The idea that hysteria was caused by a trauma similar to that caused by train accidents was quite predominant in the medical discourse of the late nineteenth century. This connection between train, trauma, and hysteria also had a symbolic quality, as 'in the 1890s, the railroad became the sign of the overloading of the nervous system through the pressures of modern life'.[74] Robert's perspective is thus undermined by the narrative structure. Last but not least, the train and rail track imagery also connotes a predetermined, unchangeable destiny.[75] Thus, while the text exposes

---

73   Gilman, Sander L. (1995), *Freud, Race, and Gender*, Princeton, NJ: Princeton University Press, 123.
74   Gilman, *Freud, Race, and Gender*, 124.
75   See also the earlier passage in the novella, in which Robert, while on a train journey, tries to keep his fear of the diagnosis of mental illness at bay by repeating the word *Wahnsinn* (madness) until it loses its meaning – a strategy interestingly also adopted by Daniel Paul Schreber as we will see in the next chapter. See Schreber, Daniel Paul (1995), *Denkwürdigkeiten eines Nervenkranken nebst Nachträgen*, Berlin: Kadmos, 163–164. The rhythmic sound of the train wheels assists Robert here: 'Und wirklich begann es [the word] allmählich leerer und nichtiger zu werden, war am Ende nichts als ein zufälliges Nacheinander von Buchstaben, willkürlich aneinandergereiht, nicht sinnvoller als unter dem heimrasenden Zug das Singen der Räder, mit dem es sich vermischte und in dem es sich endlich für den mählich Entschlummernden völlig verlor' (FiF11) (And presently indeed it began to lose its substance, its import; finally it was nothing but an insignificant succession of letters, arbitrarily strung together, meaning no more than the rumble of the wheels under the homeward-rushing train. String of letter and rumble of wheels blended together and at last were lost completely as the man sank gradually into sleep. See Schnitzler, *Flight into Darkness*, 12. While Robert is thus able to repress the threat of mental illness at this point, the text suggests that this strategy of avoiding responsibility by regressing into a childhood-like state (the singing of the wheels being reminiscent of a lullaby) cannot be successful. If the train is the symbol for everything that threatens mental wellbeing, it appears that in the moment that Robert refuses to confront the seriousness of his condition and surrenders to the soothing sounds of the train, he already gives himself over to the powers that lead him inevitably in the direction of madness. The 'singing' of the train wheels could also allude to the fatal temptation of sirens. Although the word 'madness' itself is in general regarded as threatening in this passage, it rings out earlier in the passage ('klingen' (FiF11) (sound)), which also suggests a musical sound. Both formulations seem to point to the dangerously tempting possibility of giving himself over to the 'runaway train' of madness. For a comment on this avoidance of responsibility and its ethical implications in the novella, see Thomé, *Autonomes Ich und 'Inneres Ausland,'* 716.

Robert's compulsive search for signs of destiny as pathological, it never-theless suggests through the rail track metaphors that Robert is indeed 'doomed', in the sense that he will not reach a state of lucidity again. A similar effect is yielded through the light–dark dichotomy that illustrates metaphorically Robert's transition into a delusional state. Already at the beginning of the novella, the imagery of darkness is connected to the threatening doom of mental illness: 'Als er auf den Stufen der Arena stand, vom entweichenden Tagesschein umflossen, stieg, gleich einer dunklen Mahnung, aus der Tiefe des ungeheuren Kreises der Abend zu ihm empor' (FiF9) (As he stood on the top circle of the ruined arena, in the fading light of the sunset, out of the depth of the immense bowl night seemed to rise up to him, like a dark admoni-tion).[76] Robert's perspective and that of the narrator are not distinguish-able here. Thus, while Robert's ongoing compulsive search for signs is clearly part of his pathology, the reader is nevertheless invited to follow the model: Robert's psychical constitution is indeed metaphorically expressed through the imagery of light and dark, and the presentation of nightfall as admonition of the looming illness – or *Dämmerzustand* (FiF30) (somnambulistic state) as Robert himself has it – prefigures the *Grauenhafte* (the horrific) (FiF113) that is yet to come.

With this imagery of light and dark that illustrates Robert's psychical condition, as already emphasized in its title, the text also evokes the atmosphere of Romanticism, particularly the German *Schauerromantik* (Dark Romanticism): the greyness of shadows and half-shadows, break-ing dusks and dawns, the doubling of faces, uncanny forms of *mise en scène* where inner psychic processes are merged with land- and city-scapes feature prominently in the novella.[77] The greyness (*Grau-en* as it were) of *mise en scène* is linked to the feeling of the motif of *Grauen* which at once refers to a psycho-physical sensation of shuddering (*Schauder/ Schauer*) and also to the half-light of breaking dawn (*Morgengrauen*).[78]

---

76 Schnitzler, *Flight into Darkness*, 8.
77 Artis Fioretos remarks, '[d]er romantische Dichter wandte sich [...] vorzugs-weise jenem als Mittelalter bezeichneten Halbschatten zu' (Romantic poets pre-ferred that half-shadow, which is generally referred to as the middle ages). See Fioretos, Artis (2004), 'Eine Studie in Blau (Novalis),' *Bilder-Denken. Bildlichkeit und Argumentation*, ed. by Barbara Naumann and Edgar Pankow, Munich: Fink, 139–152, 140. On the shadow and the double as generic markers of the Gothic 'physiognomy,' see also Webber, Andrew J. (2012), 'About Face: E. T. A. Hoff-mann, Weimar Film, and the Technological Afterlife of Gothic Physiognomy,' *Popular Revenants: The German Gothic and Its International Reception, 1800–2000*, ed. by Andrew Cusack and Barry Murnane, Rochester, New York: Camden House, 161–180, 163.
78 On the affective colouring of *Grauen* (horror) as contraction of *Schauer* (shudder) and 'greyness' with regard to Hoffmann and the Romantic influences on Wei-mar film, see Webber, 'About Face,' 162–163.

The function of *Grauen* as a recurring motif in Schnitzler will be an ongoing concern in this study, particularly when discussing the novellas compiled in the volume *Dämmerseelen* (Dozing Souls, 1907) in the third and fourth chapters. Recall that the Romantic motif of *Grauen* occurs when a subject is confronted with a fading of difference, which had been taken as given and secure before: 'Die Romantik erfand die Ästhetik des Grauens als beobachtetes Fading von Differenzen'[79] (Romanticism invented the aesthetics of *Grauen* as an observation of fading differences). This applies precisely to Robert whose symptoms make it increasingly hard for him to differentiate between reality and his delusional ideas. Moreover, the threshold state between mental health and illness, in which he is caught for the large part of the novella, negates Otto's confirmation that the lines of demarcation between health and illness are always clearly distinguishable.

As discussed previously, when Robert feels, 'tief erschauernd' (deeply shivering/shuddering deeply) (FiF14), the signs of his destiny, this sensation has an ambivalent quality. *Grauen* (horror) seems to be tightly related to this feeling of *Schauer* (shudder) and indeed appears to have a 'prophetic' quality – but this time for the reader. It seems to prefigure a state of real anxiety or terror – an announcement of a terrifying presence that has not yet fully materialized or become conscious to the protagonist. The following passage anticipates Robert's irreversible succumbing to his mental illness and features a feeling of *Grauen* as a transient moment between the playful toying with the role of the madman, which is experienced as exciting, and the real fear of losing control over this game:

In dieser Wirtsstube, wo ihn zu dieser Stunde niemand vermuten konnte, im Dämmer eines frühen Dezembernachmittags, erschien er sich wundersam losgelöst von allen, mit denen er diesen Morgen noch sich nach Menschenart verbunden gewähnt hatte; alle, Braut, Bruder und Freunde, waren wie Schatten der Vergangenheit; und zugleich war ihm, als müßte auch er jenen allen in dieser Stunde nur als blasses Bild durch die Erinnerung schweben. Dies war ihm zuerst nur wie ein seltsamer, fast süßer Schauer, der sich aber allmählich in ein leises Grauen verwandelte; endlich stieg in ihm eine Angst an, die ihn aufjagte und durch die dämmernde, menschenleere, feuchte Allee gegen die Stadt zurücktrieb, als hätte jeder Schritt, der ihn dem Lebensgetriebe näher brachte, zugleich die Kraft, sein blasses Erinnerungsbild in den Herzen der Menschen, die ihn liebten, in ein schärferes und lebendigeres zu wandeln. (FiF84)

79 Schneider, Manfred (1999), 'Das Grauen der Beobachter: Schriften und Bilder des Wahnsinns,' *Bild und Schrift in der Romantik*, ed. by Gerhard Neumann and Günter Oesterle, Würzburg: Königshausen und Neumann, 237–253,248.

In this tap-room, where no one could expect to find him at this hour, in the dusk of an early December afternoon, he felt himself wonderfully delivered from all the human ties by which this morning he had still felt himself bound. All, fiancée, brother, and friends, were like shadows of the past. At the same time he felt that he too must float through the memories of all these only as an indistinct image. At first the idea gave him a strange, almost delicious sensation. Then he shuddered. Finally a fear rose up in him which drove him forth and through the fog, along deserted promenades, back toward the city. It seemed that every step which brought him nearer the hustle and bustle of life could make his image more clear and living in other people's minds.[80]

Striking in this passage is the reference to shadows and images of people, which appear almost like ghostlike projections. The detachment from social bonds is then ultimately linked to a fading of vision, thus, a fading mutuality of recognition. The removal of the self from social structures is at first experienced as liberating – expressed in the sensation of an almost sweet shiver[81] – but then accompanied by the notorious *Grauen* that quickly manifests itself as fear. We can understand this transition from pleasant shudder to quiet horror as a realization of the elements of 'otherness' in the self: while at first, this playful removal of the self from social settings appears like a newfound freedom, supported by the positive stereotypes linked to madness, the crossing into the realm of the 'other' is, of course, above all terrifying.

The entire setting in this passage is reminiscent of the gloomy atmospheres of Romantic *Schauerliteratur*: the dusk (*Dämmern*) of an early winter afternoon. We see here how the text uses the same technique as Robert does, in the sense that the external conditions of the weather become meaningfully linked to his internal psychic processes. This direct connection between internal processes and external settings is even made figuratively explicit in Robert's musings, when suddenly the image of the piano teacher, with whom he spent a single night earlier in the narrative, appears in front of his eyes: 'Daß die Erscheinung irgend etwas zu bedeuten hatte, wenn sie auch nur aus seiner eigenen Seele in den Nebel dieses Tages emporgestiegen war, daran konnte er nicht zweifeln' (FiF84) (That the apparition had some meaning, even if his own imagination had only created it from the murky uncertain light

---

80 Schnitzler, *Flight into Darkness*, 111.
81 The expression of 'süße[r] Schauer' (sweet shivers) underlines my interpretation that it is an ambivalent feeling when Robert thinks he recognizes in Höhnburg's symptoms, 'tief erschauernd' (deeply shivering), the signs of his own destiny.

of this murky day, he could not doubt).[82] The image of the piano teacher is thus a projection from his soul into the fog of the day, which is in itself an interesting formulation that leaves open whether the fog is in fact the real fog of December or rather, like the image, a creation of Robert's mind, and one that provides a Gothic *mise en scène*.[83]

As argued in the last chapter on *Der Weg ins Freie* (Road into the Open), this kind of apparition corresponds to the way in which Hoffmannesque artist figures 'receive' images without their intention or control. That Robert is particularly prone to understanding these images as 'signs of destiny' corresponds in fact to a Romantic theory of aesthetic production. As the figure of the stranger in Hoffmann's *Doge und Dogaresse* (Doge and Dogaressa) describes:

Es ist ein eignes Geheimnis, daß in dem Gemüt des Künstlers oft ein Bild aufgeht, dessen Gestalten, zuvor unkennbare körperlose im leeren Luftraum treibende Nebel, eben in dem Gemüte des Künstlers erst sich zum Leben zu formen und ihre Heimat zu finden scheinen. Und plötzlich verknüpft sich das Bild mit der Vergangenheit oder auch wohl mit der Zukunft, und stellt nur dar, was wirklich geschah oder geschehen wird.[84]

It is a secret in itself that the artist's mind often receives an image whose figures – initially nothing but illegible, disembodied fogs floating in the empty space of air – seem to come to life and find their home only in the artist's mind. And suddenly, this image is linked to the past or possibly even to the future and represents what was or what will be.

The correspondence to the passage in which Robert sees the images of the piano teacher in the fog, and the fact that he understands it as a prophetic sign, is striking. The artwork represents here human destinies either mimetically or providentially.[85] Significantly, there is no necessity of an authorial intention or even knowledge of the historic or futural

---

82 Schnitzler, *Flight into Darkness*, 110.
83 In my reading of *Andreas Thameyers letzter Brief* (Andreas Thameyer's Last Letter) in Chapter Three, I return to the motif of the grey fog as Gothic element by comparing the text to passages of Bram Stoker's *Dracula*.
84 Hoffmann, E. T. A. (2001), *Doge und Dogaresse, Sämmtliche Werke*, vol. 4: *Die Serapionsbrüder*, ed. by Hartmut Steinecke and Wulf Segebrecht, Frankfurt a. M.: Deutscher Klassiker Verlag, 429–483, 430–431.
85 Neumann, Gerhard (1999), 'Narration und Bildlichkeit. Zur Inszenierung eines romantischen Schicksalsmusters in E.T.A. Hoffmanns " Doge und Dogaresse",' *Bild und Schrift in der Romantik*, ed. by Gerhard Neumann and Günter Oesterle, Würzburg: Könighausen und Neumann, 107–142, 112.

quality of these imaginations. It is this idea that seems to be dominant in Robert's attempts at making sense of his symptoms.[86] This seems also to be underpinned by the adjective *geheimnisvoll* (mysterious), which sounds like an invitation to solve the riddle, to reveal this secret inherent to the sign. In this way, Robert can be understood as akin to Hoffmann's protagonists, who also often set out to solve a riddle, to form, like the artist in *Doge and Dogaresse* (Doge and Dogaressa), a synthesis out of the myriad of signs they receive.[87] However, Schnitzler's post-Romantic protagonists prove to be unable to form such a synthesis through conscious and active reflection, as I have already demonstrated in the last chapter on *Der Weg ins Freie* (Road into the Open). Rather they become overpowered by signs and meaning that they are unable to control or construct themselves.[88] This is precisely what is happening to Robert: while he is indeed confronted with a series of images (and self-images), he struggles to bring them together to form a 'bigger picture' that actually makes 'sense'. His final interpretation, the metaphysically charged tale of two brothers, one of whom had to go 'ins Dunkel' (into darkness) certainly cannot be called a successful synthesis. Here, like Georg, he corresponds to Hoffmann's protagonists, who are unable to synthesize what they receive in a meaningful way. In this way, the representation of mental illness in *Flucht in die Finsternis* (Flight into Darkness) has a decisively aesthetic quality. It seems to inscribe itself into the literary tradition of Romanticism, which, in a way, can be linked to the practice of stereotyping in the sense that character formations seem to be reproduced by the aesthetic convention of a literary style.

Romantic Madness

The topic of madness is of course itself a central theme in the fiction of the *Schauerromantik*. Moreover, Robert's negation of contingency corresponds to the symptoms of Romantic madness: 'Zu den Symptomen des romantischen Wahnsinns zählen: Auslöschung von Kontingenz, Mißbrauch von Wörtern (und Zeichen), Fading der Grenzen zwischen innerer und äußerer Realität, automatisches Handeln' (The symptoms of Romantic madness include: elimination of contingency, abuse of words (and signs), fading of the demarcating lines between internal

---

86 Recall the stereotype of the mentally ill as 'spiritually more refined': the cultural narrative that links insanity to mantic qualities is at work here and seems also to influence Robert's perception of his symptoms. See Sontag, *Illness as Metaphor & AIDS and its Metaphors*, 32.

87 See Kohns, Oliver (2007), *Die Verrücktheit des Sinns: Wahnsinn und Zeichen bei Kant, E.T.A. Hoffmann und Thomas Carlyle*, Bielefeld: transcript, 195.

88 See also my elaborations in Chapter One.

and external reality, automated conduct).[89] All these symptoms are part of Robert's clinical picture, which underlines the aesthetic quality of the case of mental illness represented in *Flucht in die Finsternis* (Flight into Darkness). The aesthetic functionalization of mental illness is stressed further by the repeated occurrence of *Grauen*, which is connected to the symptoms of Romantic madness: the abolition of contingency has to be understood as escapism, and as an attempt at avoiding the *Grauen* in everyday life: 'Der Wundersinn ersetzt den Kontingenzsinn, um den Verstand vor dem Grauen zu bewahren' (The sense of magic replaces the sense of contingency, in order to protect reason from the sensation of horror/*Grauen*).[90] This sensation of *Grauen* in turn is triggered, as argued in the last section, by the experience of a fading of differences, in *Flucht in die Finsternis* (Flight into Darkness), particularly between norm and 'other' (or self and 'other'). This is also connected to the last symptom of Romantic madness, i.e. automated conduct. If automated conduct (which could be also called a form of stereotypy) is on the one hand a symptom of madness, but on the other an essential part of identity construction in the form of repeated performances, then the difference between the healthy norm and the mad 'other' are indeed fading. *Grauen* thus marks a moment in which categories, norms, and interpretative patterns of the dominant order seem to fail.

This is also the case when Robert 'recognizes' his own mirror image in Otto's features and the sensation of *Grauen* returns:

Und plötzlich, mit Grauen, erblickte er ein Antlitz, das er kannte. Es war das gleiche, das ihm neulich nachts aus dem Spiegel entgegengestarrt hatte, sein eigenes, blaß, mit weitaufgerissenen Augen und um die Lippen einen schmerzlich entsetzten Zug. Diese Ähnlichkeit war so außerordentlich, so zwingend, daß ihn der Gedanke durchzuckte, ob es nicht wirklich das Bild seines Bruders und nicht sein eigenes gewesen war, das ihm damals warnend oder drohend aus dem Spiegel entgegengeblickt hatte. War es vielleicht die ewige Macht der Blutsverwandtschaft gewesen, die in einem bedeutungsvollen Augenblick durch ein solches geheimnisvolles Zeichen sich ankündigte? (FiF89)
Suddenly, with horror, he beheld the countenance which had stared out at him, at night, from the mirror – his own, pale, with

---

89   Schneider, 'Das Grauen der Beobachter,' 239.
90   Interestingly, Schneider finds this concept of Romantic madness also expressed in the memoirs of Daniel Paul Schreber, who abolishes the sense of contingency as well. See Schneider, 'Das Grauen der Beobachter,' 249.

widely distended eyes, and around the lips a line of pain. The resemblance was so extraordinary, so compelling, that the thought shuddered through him: was it really the image of his brother, and not his own, which had glared its threat or warning from the mirror? Was that mysterious sign an all-important moment of proof of the eternal power of blood-relationship?[91]

This passage undergoes a rapid transition from canniness to uncanniness in Robert's perspective: immediately before this moment of *Grauen*, Robert had felt 'ein wundersames, lange nicht genossenes Gefühl von Geborgenheit durch die Seele fließen' (FiF89) (Robert had the delightful feeling, not unknown to him, of being taken care of, coddled),[92] as Otto reminisced about their shared childhood and parental home. The motif of the uncanny 'other' breaking into the canniness of the bourgeois home is obviously a highly prominent feature of German *Schauerromantik*, particularly of Hoffmann's writings.[93] The face that Robert recognizes in Otto's features had appeared earlier in the novella in Robert's own mirror image. Significantly, he had identified this face as his 'true face' 'hinter den gepflegten Masken des Alltags' (FiF76) (under the mask assumed for every day),[94] thus hinting at an identity separate from the symbolic function. This 'true face', however, is also the face of the 'other', 'in das alle Ängste eingegraben waren, die ihn sein Leben lang verfolgt [...] hatten' (FiF76) (the face deeply engraved with the marks of all the anxieties which had persecuted him half his life).[95] When Robert recognizes this physiognomy in Otto's features, Otto, the representative of the bourgeois order who seems to be so securely anchored by this symbolic function, suddenly also appears 'infected' with 'otherness'. It is after this moment in which Otto irreversibly loses the authority as his bourgeois role model that Robert irrevocably succumbs to his delusional ideas.

The entire passage creates the impression of a *Doppelgänger* (double) relationship between the two brothers. Andrew J. Webber has analyzed such *Doppelgänger* (double) moments in Hoffmann's writings and claims that 'the principal threat is that the double will *see* the self as other than itself, diagnosing its pathological estrangement both from the world and from its own identity'.[96] Otto is then particularly

---

91 Schnitzler, *Flight into Darkness*, 117.
92 Schnitzler, *Flight into Darkness*, 117.
93 *Der Sandmann* is here obviously the paradigmatic example.
94 Schnitzler, *Flight into Darkness*, 100.
95 Schnitzler, *Flight into Darkness*, 100.
96 Webber, Andrew J. (1996), *The Doppelgänger: Double Visions in German Literature*, Oxford: Oxford University Press, 119.

'predestined' for this role because of the close family bond between them: it is indeed Robert's fear that Otto might diagnose him as 'other' – from himself and from the bourgeois order he represents. That Otto is cast into the role of the double is underpinned by the symbiotically close relationship between the brothers: 'es kam doch immer wieder ein Ereignis, das [...] sie beide ihre Zusammengehörigkeit als unzweif-elhaft und unauflöslich empfinden ließ' (FiF5) (something was always coming up which [...] made these two feel the force and constancy of their attachment).[97] In this way, while Robert himself has also stated the difference between them particularly with regard to their bourgeois lifestyle, the diagnosis by Otto would betray this inner bond between them that makes them fundamentally equal to each other. At first, Otto's position as Robert's double is reassuring – as long as Otto sees in him a representative of the norm, the danger seems to be contained. However, as Otto is closely identified with the bourgeois order that has lost credibility for Robert, his authority seems to become questionable as well.

The possibility of being banished into the realm of the 'other' by Otto becomes an increasingly disconcerting necessity: what is revealed here is that the *Doppelgänger* (double)-relationship is never an equal one, but inherently structured by a master–slave dynamic.[98] This is also reflected in Robert's metaphysically charged musings about his and Otto's destiny toward the end of the novella: 'Wir beide vielleicht Erscheinungsformen ein und derselben göttlichen Idee? Einer von uns beiden mußte ins Dunkel. Es ward über ihn verhängt, obwohl früher meine Schale herüberneigte' (FiF106) (The two of us perhaps a split manifestation of one and the same divine idea? One of us must be destroyed [had to go into darkness, M.K.]. He was chosen, though formerly it seemed to be my side of the balance that tipped).[99] That one of the two parts has to become the 'other' is the fundamental ele-ment of Hegel's master and slave topos, following directly after the movement of mutual recognition.[100] This assumption of what is a (in Robert's perspective metaphysical) necessity allows him to displace his inner conflict onto the mystified relationship to his brother, which also becomes clear when he speaks of the 'ewige Macht der Blutsver-wandschaft [...], die in einem bedeutungsvollen Augenblick durch ein

---

97 Schnitzler, *Flight into Darkness*, 4.
98 Webber, *The Doppelgänger*, 119. For the Hegelian passage on the master slave dia-lectic, see Hegel, G. F. W. (1988), *Phänomenologie des Geistes*, ed. by H.-F. Wessels and H. Clairmont, Hamburg: Meiner, 128–136.
99 Schnitzler, *Flight into Darkness*, 141.
100 The master–slave dialectic seems to be also expressed at another point: 'Und er [Otto] wäre der Sieger. Der Sieger? Ist es denn ein Kampf?' (FiF102) (And he [Otto] would be the victor. The victor? Is it a duel?). See Schnitzler, *Flight into Darkness*, 135.

solches geheimnisvolles Zeichen sich ankündigte'.[101] Robert thus turns most emphatically to the higher power of destiny after the *Grauen* has become ultimately unbearable. It turns out to be a coping strategy that covers up the fact that he is in the process of crossing the boundary between norm and 'other'.[102]

The passage in which the image of the piano teacher appears before Robert's eyes describes the onset of this process. The 'vision' of her image initiates the sensation of *Grauen* as alienation from his social bonds in the passage in which all other people appear only as shadows of the past. As a widowed, childless, middle-aged woman without any substantial funds to rely on, the piano teacher's status in society appears precarious. Also her profession as teacher of performance skills, which, at least to Robert, makes her a member of the non-bourgeois night-side of life, marks her as a representative of the 'other'. While the other people in his life appear only as pale images, the apparition of the piano teacher is so clear that she seems almost real to Robert. He hence feels particularly connected to her:

> Und er empfand, daß von allen Menschen, die lebten, sie vielleicht das Wesen war, das am allerstärksten zu ihm gehörte und dessen Schicksal mit dem seinigen geheimnisvoll zusammenstimmte; und daß ihre beiden Daseinslinien sich einmal hatten kreuzen müssen, um dann sofort wieder für alle Zeiten auseinanderzustreben, das schien ihm einen verborgenen Sinn, eine in die Zukunft weisende Bedeutung in sich zu bergen. (FiF83)
> He felt that of all living persons, she perhaps was the one who truly belonged to him, whose fate truly coincided with his own. There seemed to be a hidden meaning, a prophecy, in the fact that lines of their lives had had to cross, only to proceed further and further apart.[103]

The connection between their destinies could be explained by her 'otherness', from the bourgeois perspective. As Robert feels unable to identify with his 'social destiny' as representative of the bourgeois

---

101 Schnitzler, *Flight into Darkness*, 117. Fred Lönker seems to take over Robert's perspective, assuming that the fratricide is already pre-destined ('schicksalhaft angelegt') in the relationship of the brothers. See Lönker, Fred (2006), '"Flucht in die Finsternis": Wahnsinn – psychologisches Fatum oder metaphysische Logik?' *Interpretationen: Arthur Schnitzler: Dramen und Erzählungen*, ed. by Hee-Ju Kim and Günter Saße, Stuttgart: Reclam, 240–251, 251.

102 That Robert increasingly becomes the 'other' of the male bourgeois has also been mentioned by Meyer, *Männlichkeit und Melodram*, 174.

103 Schnitzler, *Flight into Darkness*, 110.

order, she seems to stand for the realm of the 'other'. Robert wonders later whether the encounter with the piano teacher could have been a decisive turning point for the worse in the development of his illness (see FiF110). Robert thinks of his lack of sympathy with the woman, and he seems to understand his unethical behaviour as furthering his psychical symptoms. He reproduces here the moralizing, punitive aspect of the stereotype of 'madness' by stating his own ethical failure and marking it as a possible point of no return to the realm of the norm.

The ethical failure seems then linked to the crisis of investiture analyzed in the first section of this chapter: as has already been said, the dependency of social identities on repeated performative rites of institution poses a paradox, as it contradicts the Kantian claim of autonomy upon which the post-Enlightenment bourgeois order relies. Once this dependency emerges, it is experienced as usurpation of one's own authority and autonomy. It makes it impossible to fulfil the demand of practical reason, which implies a full identification with the moral law: 'heteronomy signifies a merely mimetic relation to morality resulting from a failure to be oneself the legislator of the moral law. [...] Heteronomy results, in other words, from the subject's failure to identify fully with the transcendental locus of the moral law'.[104]

The capability of self-legislation is expected from anyone within the norm, but it is completely denied to those classified as 'other'. In Schnitzler's times, women and Jews were said by some to be incapable of moral autonomy and were at best able to imitate moral behaviour, but never occupy that transcendental locus that would inform their ethical choices and actions.[105] The transcendental locus, however, is, as we have seen in the first section, that which Benjamin calls the 'Morsches im Recht' (something rotten in the law) covered up only by the tautology 'The law is the law!' This 'rottenness' at the root of the law is fantasized as infectious, Santner argues: the experience of one's own heteronomy propels the self into the vicinity of 'otherness', particularly that of Jewishness and femininity. That Robert thinks of the sexual encounter with the piano teacher as a turning point may then be understood also on another level, as it entails the potential danger of infection – literally with syphilis and metaphorically with 'otherness'. Through this rather random act of extra-marital intercourse, Robert at least temporarily crosses the line of the bourgeois norm.

---

104 Santner, *My Own Private Germany*, 139–140.
105 This is for example expressed in Otto Weininger's elaborations on Jewishness and femininity in his notoriously misogynistic and anti-Semitic work *Geschlecht und Character* (Sex and Character). See Weininger, Otto (1903), *Geschlecht und Charakter: Eine prinzipielle Untersuchung*, Vienna and Leibzig: Wilhelm Braunmüller, 257.

Through his feeling of connection with the woman combined with the implicit threat of syphilis and the overall theme of madness in the novella, the aspect of Jewishness as otherness may be very subtly introduced here as well. Gilman writes, '[t]he linked dangers of sexuality, syphilis, and madness were constantly associated with the figure of the male Jew'.[106] In this context, the way he imagines himself in the memory of the parting with the piano teacher, and the fact that even he himself realizes that this does not correspond to reality, seems particularly interesting: 'Doch sah er sich völlig anders als er in diesem Augenblick oder überhaupt jemals ausgesehen haben konnte. Übergroß und hager stand er da in einem fliegenden dunklen Mantel und warf einen schwarzen Schatten weit vor sich hin' (FiF110) (Very, very tall and lean, he stood there in a flying black cloak and threw a dark shadow which stretched out long and thin before him).[107] This description is certainly recognizable as the cliché of the general villain in different literary genres, but the selection of attributes, especially the dark coat, might also evoke the stereotypical image of the Jew or even hint more specifically at depictions of the 'Wandering Jew'.[108] This admittedly rather speculative interpretation is supported by other passages in which the text seems to link Robert's symptoms to an imagery that is reminiscent of representations of the 'Wandering Jew', who 'is not so much a man in search of fortune as one driven to wander in search of a cure for the compulsion to wander'.[109] Robert's restlessness is repeatedly pointed out and is as much understood as therapeutic function (in the form of his travels) as a symptom ('"Unruhiger Geist", rief Marianne [Otto's wife] ihm zum Abschied nach' (FiF30) ('Uneasy spirits!' Marianne called after him in parting)).[110] Robert's symptoms of mental illness seem to project him into the realm of the 'other' and in this way may bring him closer to other forms of 'otherness', such as Jewishness and femininity, as well.[111] In a way, 'madness' appears as a marker and also a form of legitimization of 'otherness', rather than as an individual category of otherness itself: in Schnitzler's times, social groups already labelled as belonging to the realm of the other, particularly women and Jews, were said to

---

106 Gilman, *Freud, Race, and Gender*, 61–62.
107 Schnitzler, *Flight into Darkness*, 146–147.
108 The Wandering Jew was usually depicted as wearing a long coat. See Anderson, George K. (1965), *The Legend of the Wandering Jew*, Providence: Brown University Press, 42.
109 Santner, *My Own Private Germany*, 112.
110 Schnitzler, *Flight into Darkness*, 38.
111 See also Imke Meyer's reading of the novella, which focuses on the aspect of 'otherness' in Robert's personality, particularly his stereotypically rather feminine features. See Meyer, *Männlichkeit und Melodram*, 172–174.

have a higher risk of becoming mentally ill than the male gentile representatives of the norm.[112]

Bourdieu argues that the 'performative magic' of acts of institutions works to keep the subjects from crossing the border into the realm of the 'other' and to make them stay within the realm of the norm. When the dominant order fails to address its subjects properly, and when they then 'cease to believe in themselves', they 'begin to cross the line into the wrong direction'.[113] Robert's identification with the piano teacher, but also the subtle allusion to the 'Wandering Jew' in the text, and not least his early identification with his friend Höhnburg, all suggest that this process is in motion in *Flucht in die Finsternis* (Flight into Darkness). The experience of this process is of course unsettling and triggers the by now familiar *Grauen*. Through the use of such uncanny Romantic elements, Schnitzler's text then highlights the fluidity of demarcation lines: the boundaries around the norm suddenly appear to have become permeable, which unsettles the sense of security not only of the protagonist's own status but also of the post-Enlightenment bourgeois order he represents. In order to contain this increasing sense of insecurity, which is expressed through the Romantic effect of *Grauen*, Robert turns to a search for meaning and signs of the higher power of destiny. However, Schnitzler's text is far from an endorsement of irrational or mysticist tendencies. Rather it exposes them as a form of Romantic madness, thus as a symptom rather than a cure.

With what I have called the narrative double structure in the text that undermines and mirrors Robert's constant search for signs and meaning, *Flucht in die Finsternis* (Flight into Darkness) brings to attention its own constructed quality, which, again, can be seen as a Romantic, or more particularly Hoffmannesque element.[114] Moreover, the text not only emphasizes its own constructed quality, but also that of the cultural narratives that in turn construct social reality: the claim of the autonomous subject as well as stereotypical narratives of madness, be they punitive or idealizing. As argued in the previous chapter, these stereotypical cultural narratives make 'fast, firm and separate what is in reality fluid and much closer to the norm than the dominant value system cares to admit'.[115]

As Foucault argues in *Madness and Civilization*, the concept of madness as 'otherness' is essential for the maintenance of that of reason and

---

112 See Gilman, *Freud, Race, and Gender*, 93; Santner, *My Own Private Germany*, 140.
113 Bourdieu, *Language and Symbolic Power*, 112.
114 See Matt, Peter von (1989), *... fertig ist das Angesicht: Zur Literaturgeschichte des menschlichen Gesichts*, Frankfurt a. M.: Suhrkamp, 236–237.
115 Dyer, Richard (2002), *The Matter of Images: Essays on Representation*, London: Routledge, 16.

in this way necessary for the functioning of post-Enlightenment culture.[116] Thus, the lines of demarcation between the rational norm and the mad 'other' must be clearly drawn. In the preface of the 1969 German edition,[117] Foucault points to a static figure which appears in the definitions of 'madness' as benightedness: 'die einfache Trennung zwischen Tag und Dunkelheit, zwischen Schatten und Licht, zwischen Traum und Wachsein, zwischen Wahrheit der Sonne und den mitternächtlichen Kräften. Dies ist eine elementare Figur, die die Zeit nur als unbegrenzte Wiederkehr der Grenze wahrnimmt' (The simple distinction between day and darkness, between shadow and light, between dreaming and waking, between the sun's truth and the midnight powers. This is an elemental figure, which perceives time exclusively as an infinite return of the demarcation line).[118] However, the introduction of psychology as a scientific discipline in the nineteenth century resulted in an integration of the so-called 'dark side' into the human psyche, thus made it into something interior to every human being rather than exterior. At the beginning of the twentieth century, psychoanalysis, with its conceptualization of the unconscious, obviously took this development even further. With Robert's state of transition he is a paradigmatic case for the general unsettledness of the post-Enlightenment bourgeois identity. Schneider's definition of *Grauen* as a fading of differences is applicable here: the boundaries between self and 'other', between the enlightened bourgeois rational subject and the mad 'other' have become blurred.[119]

This is what seems to be pointed at in the ending of the novella, with the often-cited quotation from Leinbach's journal. 'Wir aber reden von Zwangsvorstellungen! Ob wir dazu berechtigt sind, dieses Wort – wie so manche andere – nicht eigentlich eine Ausflucht bedeutet –

---

116 Foucault, Michel (1989), *Madness and Civilization: A History of Insanity in the Age of Reason*, London, New York: Routledge, xii.

117 The preface has been substantially shortened in the English translation and lacks the equivalent passage. In the recent French edition, the preface has been replaced altogether. The German translation I am quoting from is based on the French original edition from 1961.

118 Foucault, Michel (1969), *Wahnsinn und Gesellschaft: Eine Geschichte des Wahns im Zeitalter der Vernunft*, Frankfurt a. M.: Suhrkamp, 14.

119 '"Und bist du auch sicher, die Grenze [between health and insanity] immer bestimmen zu können?" "Gewiß bin ich das, sonst hätte ich meinen Beruf längst aufgegeben"' (FiF60) ('Are you sure you can always draw the line?' 'Of course I am. Otherwise I should have given up medical practice a long time ago'). See Schnitzler, *Flight into Darkness*, 78. Otto's emphasis on the possibility of drawing a clear line of demarcation between mental health and illness underlines once more his position as representative of a bourgeois order threatened by decay. That he is in fact not able to draw the line of demarcation between mental health and illness is demonstrated by the course of events in the novella, when he recognizes much too late the severe stage of his brother's symptoms.

eine Flucht ins System aus der friedlosen Vielfältigkeit der Einzelfälle –, das ist eine andere Frage' (FiF115) (But we speak of obsessive ideas. Whether we have any right to do so – whether this term, like so many others, is not really an evasion, a flight into system out of complexity of individual cases, is another question).[120] The practice of labelling – in this case by virtue of diagnosis – is described as an escape from a chaotic and not fully commensurable reality. This corresponds to the way stereotypes function as perceptual ordering tools.[121] It is important to note that a diagnosis is not of itself a stereotype, of course, but it can function in the same way when punitive or sentimental cultural narratives are linked to and legitimized by it. A medical diagnosis is also the primary way of labelling something or someone as abnormal. This practice can be ideologically exploited in order to pathologize certain groups and in this way exclude them from the norm – which is the case in the stereotype of a Jewish predisposition to mental illness. Gilman's definition of stereotyping as a form of cultural practice was quoted before:[122] much as we have to indulge in it in order to preserve a clear and secure concept of the self, this practice runs the risk of becoming – and the choice of word is particularly interesting in our context here – 'pathological', when the ability to differentiate between stereotype and individual becomes lost. That the line between these two forms of stereotyping is as constructed (and therefore also subject to blurring) as that between the concept of self and 'other', which stereotypes seek to secure, has already been argued in the reading of *Der Weg ins Freie*. The difficulty in distinguishing clearly between the so-called pathological and normal form of stereotyping is rooted in the problem of drawing a clear line between the pathological and the normal, as discussed above.

It is, however, this pragmatic acceptance that we can also find in Schnitzler's text. While Leinbach is given the last word in the novella, his character is presented as rather unreliable throughout the text.[123] It might also be important to note that his remarks are broken off mid-sentence ('Und ein Fall, wie der meines armen Freundes –' (FiF115) (And a case like that of my poor friend ...)),[124] as if the narrator had

---

120 Schnitzler, *Flight into Darkness*, 152.
121 See Gilman, Sander L. (1985), *Difference and Pathology: Stereotypes of Sexuality, Race, and Madness*, Ithaca, London: Cornell University Press, 18.
122 See Gilman, *Difference and Pathology*, 3.
123 See Thomé, *Autonomes Ich und 'Inneres Ausland,'* 713; Allerdissen, *Arthur Schnitzler: Impressionistisches Rollenspiel und skeptischer Moralismus in seinen Erzählungen*, 136. Only Tarnowski-Seidel proposes that Leinbach becomes Schnitzler's mouthpiece and should thus be understood as authority in the text. This, however, does not seem to be supported by the text. See Tarnowski-Seidel, *Arthur Schnitzler, 'Flucht in die Finsternis,'* 119–121.
124 Schnitzler, *Flight into Darkness*, 152.

decided to terminate his testimony. The text thus does not condemn the practice of ordering systems as such, but underlines their construct-edness and the dangerous effects when they become 'naturalized' and 'cemented' as evident truths. In this way, one could read Schnitzler's last published novella as a plea for a new kind of rationalism, but with a grain of salt: an acceptance of the 'otherness' within the norm, an acceptance of the necessity of certain demarcation lines, but with an awareness of their constructedness.

This acceptance seems to be crucial in order to avoid either becoming overwhelmed by an uncontrollable *Grauen* or lost in succumbing to an alleged higher power of 'destiny'. In all five novellas of the *Dämmer-seelen* (Dozing Souls) collection, which will be the focus of the next two chapters, the protagonists experience a moment of *Grauen* at at least one point. All these moments seem to be deeply connected to encounters with an unfathomable, inaccessible 'other' and the feeling of losing control over one's own life – or rather of the narrative the protagonists have consciously or unconsciously constructed for themselves. As we will see, all these narratives are linked to the belief in a higher power of destiny and to the ambivalent function of stereotypes of 'otherness'.

Three Race and Destiny in *Die Weissagung* (The Prophecy) and *Andreas Thameyers letzter Brief* (Andreas Thameyer's Last Letter)

Apparently some of Schnitzler's contemporary reviewers already observed that his volume *Dämmerseelen* (Dozing Souls, 1907) features allusions to German Romanticism, particularly to E. T. A. Hoffmann. Josef Körner, however, vehemently opposed this interpretation:

> Schnitzlers 'Dämmerseelen' sind, [...] wiederholt mit den Gespenstergeschichten der deutschen Romantiker, insbesondere mit denen E.T.A. Hoffmanns verglichen worden; ein sehr unglücklicher und völlig unzutreffender Vergleich. Der Romantiker sieht Wunder, von denen Schulweisheit sich nichts träumen läßt, mit gläubigem Gemüt, hofft gerade von der Nachtseite der Seele her in ihr Geheimnis eindringen zu können, er schaut in den grauesten Alltag die goldensten Phantasien hinein, weil sich in jedem Endlichen ihm das Unendliche spiegelt. Von all dem ist beim Verfasser der 'Dämmerseelen' im geringsten nicht die Rede. Der unheimliche Zweifel, ob ein nüchtern-natürlicher Zusammenhang zwischen den Dingen besteht, dieser Zweifel, der den Leser Hoffmannscher Spukgeschichten hin und her schaukelt, bis ihm schwindelig wird, kommt bei Schnitzler kaum auf. Oder doch nur ein einzigmal: in der technisch meisterhaften Schicksalsnovelle 'Die Weissagung'.[1]

---

1 Josef Körner (1921) and Michael Imboden (1971) both point out that *Die Weissagung* is comparable to Hoffmann's *Nachtstücke*. See Körner (1921), *Arthur Schnitzlers Gestalten und Probleme*, Zurich, Leipzig, Vienna: Amalthea, 176; Imboden (1971), *Die surreale Komponente im erzählenden Werk Arthur Schnitzlers*, Bern: H. Lang, 95. See Imboden, Michael (1971), *Die surreale Komponente im erzählenden Werk Arthur Schnitzlers*, Bern: H. Lang, 95.

Schnitzler's 'Dozing Souls' has been repeatedly compared to the ghost stories of German Romanticism, particularly those of E. T. A. Hoffmann; an extremely infelicitous and completely unjustified comparison. The Romanticist's faithful mind accepts miracles, which rational, conventionally educated people cannot even imagine. He hopes to be able to access the secrets of the soul precisely from its dark side, he projects the most golden fantasies into the greyest of all quotidian lives, because for him, the eternal is mirrored in each and every finite being. The uncanny doubt, whether there is a sober-natural causal connection between the things – this doubt, which rocks the reader of Hoffmann's phantom narratives back and forth until he feels rather dizzy, this doubt never emerges in Schnitzler's stories. Or, at least, only one single time: in the expertly crafted novella of destiny, 'The Prophecy'.

While Körner's assessment that Schnizler's texts do not endorse an affirmative fascination with mysticism is certainly correct, he over-looked the fact that the Romanticist's faithful mind is nevertheless to be found in the texts – not on the authorial level, but on that of the characters. Schnitzler's texts display a tendency to mystical beliefs, par-ticularly the emphatic evocation of destiny, through the perspective of their protagonists. And because the narratives are very often rendered entirely in this perspective of the unreliable protagonists, readers can indeed at times find it hard to decide whether the text confronts them with a realistic setting or not, particularly in the novellas compiled in *Dämmerseelen* (Dozing Souls).[2] Körner was, however, right to stress a fundamental difference between Schnitzler and the Romantics. Schnit-zler's texts do not promote any kind of 'new mythology' as a reaction to the Enlightenment and its degradation of the mythos as pre-rational form, as was the case in the theoretical and meta-poetic works of the Romantics.[3] However, like many other scholars, Detlef Kremer stresses that Romanticism is not only to be understood in contrast to the Enlightenment, but rather as a form of self-reflection of Enlightenment itself ('Selbstreflexion der Aufklärung'). This aspect of self-reflection can certainly be found in Schnitzler's texts as well. They introduce and expose the irrational tendencies of the rationalist, post-Enlightenment bourgeois ideology. In fact, Schnitzler's texts critically address the 'myths of today', following Roland Barthes,[4] particularly those hidden in the form of stereotypes of 'otherness'. The narratives in the volume

---

2   Another paradigmatic example here would be *Das Tagebuch der Redegonda* (Redegonda's Diary, 1911), which is not part of the volume.

3   See Kremer, Detlef (2007), *Romantik: Lehrbuch der Germanistik*, Stuttgart: Metzler, 108.

4   Barthes, Roland (1972), *Mythologies*, London: Vintage, 109.

Dämmerseelen are concerned with the influence of these stereotypical 'myths' in connection with the fate-like function of 'social destiny' in the Bourdieusian sense on the one hand and the belief in a metaphysical destiny on the other.

This chapter is concerned with stereotypes of race addressed in the narratives *Die Weissagung* (The Prophecy) and *Andreas Thameyers letzter Brief* (Andreas Thameyer's Last Letter).[5] In *Die Weissagung* (Die Prophecy), which will be the main focus of the chapter, anti-Semitic stereotypes are incorporated in an ostensibly fantastic tale about the higher power of destiny. *Andreas Thameyers letzter Brief* brings to the fore the influence of stereotypes of Blackness in connection with the 'fatal' force of 'social destiny': being confronted with the impossibility of bringing his own individual situation into congruence with the requirements of the bourgeois male norm, the protagonist experiences the fate-like necessity of his suicide as a last performance of masculinity. Both texts avail themselves of elements alluding to *Schauerromantik*, which underlines their own fictional quality and brings to the fore the constructedness of the stereotypical cultural narratives they address. That this kind of self-referentiality is in itself an essential element of Romantic irony has already been argued in the first chapter on *Der Weg ins Freie* (Road into the Open). The first narrative I will analyze, *Die Weissagung* (The Prophecy), for which even Joseph Körner concedes a Hoffmannesque character, is in turn probably one of the most paradigmatic examples of irony in Schnitzler's texts.

Destiny and Stereotypes of Jewishness in *Die Weissagung* (The Prophecy)

The short narrative *Die Weissagung* (The Prophecy) was first published under the simple title *Erzählung* (Narrative) in the Christmas issue of the journal *Neue Freie Presse* in 1905, before it was included in the 1907 collection of narratives, *Dämmerseelen* (Dozing Souls). The text contains three narrative perspectives: first, the first-person narrator, second, the protagonist Umprecht in the story-within-a-story, and third, the fictional editor, who provides an after-word claiming that everything told in the story is true. In the beginning, the narrator tells the reader that he has written a play for the art lover and *Freiherr* (baron) von Schottenegg. On the day of the performance, Schottenegg's nephew Franz von Umprecht, who also is the lead actor in the play, tells the narrator the following story: ten years before, to the day, he was confronted by the

---

5   All translations of *Die Weissagung* (Prophecy) are my own. All translations of *Andreas Thameyer* are taken from the translation by Frederick Eisemann. See Schnitzler, Arthur (1913a), 'Andreas Thameyer's Last Letter,' *Viennese Idylls*, translated by Frederick Eisenmann, Boston, MA: John W. Luce & Co., 107–120.

Jewish magician Marco Polo with an allegedly prophetic image, which showed him on his deathbed, surrounded by a mourning woman and two children, exactly ten years from the premonition. The so-called prophecy took place in a rather isolated Polish village, where Umprecht was based as a lieutenant of the Austrian army. From then on, Umprecht lived his life in fear and tried at all costs to prevent this destiny from coming true. However, only when he learned about the narrator's play did he feel that there was hope: the last scene appears to be identical with the prophetic image. He then hopes that by playing the lead role, thus enacting the prophecy in a fictional setting, he will prevent the realization of his destiny. Although doubtful at first, the narrator is finally convinced of the truthfulness of Umprecht's story. For him, one curiosity seems to suffice as evidence: Umprecht even knows of a character who had appeared in the last scene of a draft version of the play, but had been erased in the final version. Later, when this character nevertheless actually appears on stage at the appointed moment (in the person of a flautist from the orchestra), the narrator accepts this as the realization of Umprecht's destiny. And indeed, despite all his attempts at avoiding the prophecy, Umprecht dies on stage.[6]

The novella has been extensively discussed with regard to the opposition of determinism and free will, which is raised by implication of this narrative elaboration on the topic of destiny. In Schnitzler's papers on *Die Weissagung* (The Prophecy), one note reads: 'Prophezeiungen, [sic] die, wenn sie sich erfüllen, eine andere Bedeutung annehmen, als man anfangs geglaubt' (CUL A255,2) (Prophecies, which, when they come true, adopt a meaning different to what one had initially assumed). This effect is indeed yielded by the narrative in terms of the reading expectations it evokes. Almost no critic fails to quote Freud's judgement of the narrative, in which he claims it left the reader dissatisfied and with a feeling of having been betrayed, because it initially pretended to stay in the realistic realm only to then include fantastic elements, which 'flirt' ('liebäugeln') with the supernatural.[7]

Earlier critics seem to follow Freud, when they lament Schnitzler's 'Unentschiedenheit'[8] (indecisiveness) or speak of an 'Unklarheit'[9] (lack

---

6   Even more clearly than in *Flucht in die Finsternis* (Flight into Darkness), we find here the model of a self-fulfiling prophecy. See Lukas, Wolfgang (1996), *Das Selbst und das Fremde: Epochale Lebenskrisen und ihre Lösung im Werk Arthur Schnitzlers*, Munich: Fink, 232.

7   Freud, Sigmund (1947b), 'Das Unheimliche,' *Gesammelte Werke*, vol. 12: *Werke aus den Jahren 1917–1920*, ed. by Anna Freud, Edward Bibring, Willi Hoffer, Ernst Kris, and Otto Isakower, London: Imago, 227–268, 266.

8   Just, Gottfried (1968), *Ironie und Sentimentalität in den erzählenden Dichtungen Arthur Schnitzlers*, Berlin: E. Schmidt, 126.

9   Imboden, *Die surreale Komponente im erzählenden Werk Arthur Schnitzlers*, 96.

of clarity) which derived from the usage of occult elements. Most of the later critics, however, seem to agree that the play with the occult in the novella has to be read ironically.[10] Several critics interpret this irony as a satirical criticism of mysticism and occult tendencies. Many scholars also share the assumption that Umprecht's own acceptance of the prophecy has to be understood as the driving force of the apparently fateful events and their deadly outcome.[11] This (unconscious) participation of Umprecht leads some critics to find a relativist position between

---

10 See Allerdissen, Rolf (1985), *Arthur Schnitzler: Impressionistisches Rollenspiel und skeptischer Moralismus in seinen Erzählungen*, Bonn: Bouvier, 156; Perlmann, Michaela L. (1987a), *Der Traum in der literarischen Moderne: Untersuchungen zum Werk Arthur Schnitzlers*, Munich: Fink, 90; Weigel, Robert (1996), 'Schnitzlers Schicksalserzählungen *Die Weissagung* und *Die dreifache Warnung*,' *Die Seele ... ist ein weites Land: Kritische Beiträge zum Werk Arthur Schnitzlers*, ed. by Joseph P. Strelka, Bern, Berlin, Frankfurt a. M., New York, Paris, Vienna: Peter Lang, 149–162, 150; Rohrwasser, Michael (1999), 'Arthur Schnitzlers Erzählung "Die Weissagung": Ästhetizismus, Antisemitismus und Psychoanalyse,' *Zeitschrift für deutsche Philologie* 118: 60–79, 63 (Sonderheft: *Zur deutschen Literatur im ersten Drittel des 20. Jahrhunderts*, ed. by Norbert Oelers and Hartmut Steinecke); Gerrekens, Louis (2011), *'Die Weissagung oder wie aus schlecht erzähltem Theater eine spannende Novelle wird,'* *Theatralisches Erzählen um 1900: Narrative Inszenierungsweisen der Jahrhundertwende*, ed. by Achim Küpper, Heidelberg: Universitätsverlag Winter, 89–102, 106. Only Martin Brucke rejects an ironic reading, highlighting the 'ernste Kontext des Hypnotismus' (serious context of hypnotism) and the tragic ending of the text. See Brucke, Martin (2002), *Magnetiseure: Die windige Karriere einer literarischen Figur*, Freiburg im Breisgau: Rombach, 123. See also Gert K. Schneider's more recent monograph. Schneider, Gert K. (2014), *Grenzüberschreitungen: Energie, Wunder und Gesetze: Das Okkulte als Weltanschauung und seine Manifestationen im Werk Arthur Schnitzlers*, Vienna: Praesens. While Schneider explores Schnitzler's personal position with regard to occultism in the first part of his study, the second, more extensive part provides a detailed collection of occult elements in Schnizler's literary works. Although Schneider does not overlook the often ironic representation of these elements, he nevertheless detects the presence of a 'kosmische Urkraft' (cosmic primal force) in Schnitzler's texts.

11 Critics differ here as to the degree of psychologization and pathologization of Umprecht: Lawson detects an unconscious death wish linked to latent homoerotic tendencies. See Lawson, Richard H. (1963), 'An Interpretation of "Die Weissagung", *Studies in Arthur Schnitzler*, ed. by Herbert Reichert and Herman Salinger, Chapel Hill: The University of North Carolina Press, 71–78, 74. Allerdissen speaks of a compulsive idea, which is condensed into reality. See Allerdissen, *Arthur Schnitzler: Impressionistisches Rollenspiel und skeptischer Moralismus in seinen Erählungen*, 154. Perlmann agrees that it is possible to detect in Umprecht's behaviour first signs ('Ansätze') of a mental illness even before his encounter with Marco Polo. See Perlmann, *Der Traum in der literarischen Moderne*, 92. Brucke does not necessarily assume an initial pathological condition, but stresses the possibility of post-hypnotic suggestion. See Brucke, *Magnetiseure: Die windige Karriere einer literarischen Figur*, 123.

human autonomy and determination of fate in the novella.[12] Others even claim that a completely rational explanation of the events is possible. According to Louis Gerrekens, even the entire debate about free will and determinism in the novella does not make any sense: in fact, there is no prophecy in *Die Weissagung* (The Prophecy), because all three narrative perspectives deconstruct themselves in the end by virtue of various inconsistencies and signals of irony.[13] It is certainly true that the narrative displays a large set of paralogisms and inconsistencies that should alert the reader to question the credibility of the three narrators and their insistence on the presence of a 'higher power' being involved in the course of events. An affirmative reading of the superstitious narrative perspectives is therefore indeed misplaced. However, it is nevertheless important to interrogate the *function* of the play with fantastic or occult elements and the topic of destiny in the text, which – as it seems to me – addresses more than a rejection of mysticism and a defence of rationality. Also in this text, the protagonist's fascination with destiny is linked to a weakened identification with his own position in the social order. Anti-Semitic stereotypes serve again as compensation for this insecurity. And just like in the previous chapters, the position of the stereotyped 'other' has nevertheless also a certain seductive effect, which informs the idea of a higher power of destiny.

Destiny as Revenge of the 'Other'

Umprecht, who does not hide his anti-Semitic attitude, and the narrator, who sympathizes with Umprecht, both accept the presence of a higher power as an explanation of the events. Michael Rohrwasser has pointed out that this links anti-Semitism to irrationality and superstition, which highlights its anti-modern tendencies.[14] This link between the representation of anti-Semitism and the question of destiny in the text can be carried further. It has been convincingly argued

---

12 See Allerdissen, *Arthur Schnitzler: Impressionistisches Rollenspiel und skeptischer Moralismus in seinen Erzählungen*, 157; Weigel, Robert (1997): 'Schnitzlers Schicksalserzählungen "Die Weissagung" und "Die dreifache Warnung",' *Die Seele ... ist ein weites Land. Kritische Beiträge zum Werk Arthur Schnitzlers*, ed. by Joseph P. Strelka, Bern [et al.] Peter Lang, 149–162; Brucke, *Magnetiseure: Die windige Karriere einer literarischen Figur*, 124.

13 Gerrekens provides an extensive analysis of the logical inconsistencies and ironical contradictions of the three narrative perspectives in the text. Perlmann also mentions the unreliability of all three narrators. See Gerrekens, '*Die Weissagung* oder wie aus schlecht erzähltem Theater eine spannende Novelle wird,' 104ff.; Perlmann, *Der Traum in der literarischen Moderne*, 92ff.

14 See Rohrwasser, 'Arthur Schnitzlers Erzählung "Die Weissagung",' 71.

that Marco Polo's premonitions serve as a form of revenge against the anti-Semitic slurs of the military officers.[15] However, the aspect of revenge in the narrative goes beyond the simple immediate payback: I see here the link between this revenge for anti-Semitism and the topic of destiny.

After having been threatened by the colonel of the regiment and called pejoratively 'Jud' (W605) (Jew) by another lieutenant, Marco Polo foretells the colonel's lethal destiny. The reaction of the bystanders is significant: 'ich versichere Sie, uns allen war, als ob der Oberst in diesem Moment gezeichnet worden wäre' (W606) (I assure you, we all felt as if the colonel had been marked in this very moment). The idea of being marked and thus being assigned an unchangeable destiny recalls the way Jewishness had become a marker of difference that is comparable to an unchangeable destiny.[16] Marco Polo's prophecy therefore mirrors the effects that anti-Semitic discourse has on the Jews. This is underlined by the fact that the first prophecy of the Oberleutnant's death follows directly on an act of insulting mimicry on his part: challenging Marco Polo to read his hand, the colonel imitates Marco Polo's Yiddish accent when he says: 'Nu, lesen Sie' (W605) (Go ahead, read).

Shulamit Volkov has suggested that we should understand anti-Semitism at the beginning of the twentieth century as a cultural code well accepted in Austria and Germany rather than an extremist political movement.[17] Marco Polo's prophecies are also mimicries of this cultural code, particularly with its implications of biological difference: central for the development of anti-Semitism at the beginning of the twentieth century was the debate about the 'biology of the Jews', and thus genetic predispositions associated with Jewishness as a 'race'.[18] A biological predisposition is inescapable, and cannot be shed like a religious confession or lost like the citizenship of a nation state. Thus, no matter what a Jewish person does, no matter how they may strive for 'assimilation' or 'acculturation', if the racial difference is established as biological fact, they will remain excluded from the non-Jewish norm. This established difference can then be ideologically used to legitimate the marginalization and denial of recognition of Jews in an anti-Semitic

---

15   See Brucke, *Magnetiseure: Die windige Karriere einer literarischen Figur*, 126.
16   See also my analysis of physiognomy in *Der Weg ins Freie* (Road into the Open) in Chapter One, as well as my reading of *Flucht in die Finsternis* in Chapter Two, in which the diagnosis of mental illness appears like a stigmatic mark.
17   See Volkov, Shulamit (2006), *Germans, Jews, and Antisemited Trials in Emancipation*, New York: Cambridge University Press, 115; Lipphardt, Veronika (2008), *Biologie der Juden: Jüdische Wissenschaftler über 'Rasse' und Vererbung 1900–1935*, Göttingen: Vandenhoeck & Ruprecht, 21.
18   See Lipphardt, *Biologie der Juden*, 74.

society. This is precisely played out in Umprecht's description of Marco Polo. Although Umprecht clearly perceives his appearance as utterly strange, it nevertheless bears unequivocal signs of the assimilated Jew: he has shaved his beard and wears elegant western clothes, a top hat and waistcoat under a dark coat.[19] Umprecht indicates that 'seine Erscheinung augenblicklich auffiel' (W604) (his appearance was immediately noteworthy) due to the 'lächerlichen Eleganz' (W604) (ridiculous elegance) of his apparel. In the perspective of the anti-Semite Umprecht, the assimilation fails completely. Marco Polo's apparent striving to get rid of the typical Jewish attributes not only makes him ridiculous in Umprecht's eyes but also seems to aggravate other traits associated with the stereotype of 'the' Jew, above all that of weakened masculinity: as 'ein kleiner, magerer, bartloser Mensch' (W604) (a short, skinny, beardless person), Marco Polo hardly fulfils the ideal of the masculine norm. The appellation 'Jud' is thus not only pejorative, it also produces a reduction of every aspect of the individual to Jewishness. Even though Marco Polo demonstrates with his appearance that he is not religious, his identity is perceived by the colonel and the others as dominated by his Jewishness. When Marco Polo refuses to accept the injurious appellation by insisting on the name he has given himself ('Mein Künstlername ist Marco Polo' (W605) (My stage name is Marco Polo)), he is not only defending himself against the anti-Semitic insult, but also insisting upon his right to an individual and freely chosen identity. The appellation 'Jud' was an attempt to put Marco Polo in his place, to remind him of the social status he has as a Jew and of the limited potential of individual development, and 'marking' the colonel with the prophecy is thus a direct payback.[20]

---

19 See for example Joseph Roth's (1976) description of the assimilated Jews in *Juden auf Wanderschaft*: 'guterzogene, glattrasierte Herren in Gehröcken und Zylindern, die das Gebetbuch in den Leitartikel des jüdischen Leibblattes packen, weil sie glauben, man erkenne sie an diesem Leitartikel weniger als an dem Gebetbuch' (well-mannered, clean-shaven gentlemen in coats and top hats, who wrap their prayer books in the front page of the favourite Jewish newspaper, because they think that this paper is less recognizable than the prayer book). See 'Juden auf Wanderschaft,' *Werke*, vol. 3, ed. by Hermann Kesten, Cologne: Kiepenheuer & Witsch, 305). See also the following passage: 'Die meisten frommen Juden verurteilen einen Mann aufs schärfste, der sich den Bart rasieren läßt – wie überhaupt das rasierte Gesicht das deutliche Merkmal für den Abfall vom Glauben darstellt' (Most religious Jews utterly judge a man, who has his beard shaved – as the clean shaven face is generally the clearest indication for apostasy). See Roth, 'Juden auf Wanderschaft,' 308.

20 Recall the way Bertolt Stauber in *Der Weg ins Freie* (Road into the Open) was silenced by the anti-Semitic insult 'Jud, halt's Maul' (WiF657) (Hold your jaw, Jew). See Schnitzler, *Road into the Open*, 28. Calling Marco Polo 'Jud' can be seen as an attempt to exclude him as a subject of discourse. By marking the colonel, Marco Polo seems to (re-)assert himself as subject.

Anti-Semitic Stereotypes as Coping Mechanism

Marco Polo is not presented as a real character – we only get to know him through Umprecht's perspective. This narrative effect exposes the Jew's function as complementary 'other' that is used to define the norm and endow its representatives with a clear sense of self. However, this mechanism is disrupted from the beginning. The situation in which Umprecht receives the prophetic image is significantly one in which representatives of the 'norm' – non-Jewish Austrian males – find themselves isolated and in the minority.

> Unsere Kaserne lag außerhalb des Dorfes, das aus höchstens dreißig verstreuten Häusern bestand; die nächste Stadt, eine Reitstunde entfernt, war schmierig, widerwärtig, stinkend und voll von Juden. Notgedrungen hatten wir manchmal mit ihnen zu tun – der Hotelier war ein Jude, der Cafetier, der Schuster desgleichen. Daß wir uns möglichst beleidigend gegen sie benahmen, das können Sie sich denken. Wir waren besonders gereizt gegen dieses Volk, weil ein Prinz, der unserem Regiment als Major zugeteilt war, den Gruß der Juden – ob nun als Scherz oder aus Vorliebe, weiß ich nicht – mit ausgesuchter Höflichkeit erwiderte und überdies mit auffallender Absichtlichkeit unseren Regimentsarzt protegierte, der von Juden abstammte. (W603f)[21]

> Our barrack was located outside a village, which consisted of at most thirty scattered houses; the next town, an hour on horseback away, was sleazy, disgusting, smelling and full of Jews. Out of necessity we sometimes had to engage with them – the hotelier was a Jew, the owner of the coffee house, the shoemaker and so on. You can imagine that we treated them as insultingly as possible. We were particularly irritated by this people, because the prince, who had been allocated to us as our major, always responded to the Jews' greetings with a special politeness. Moreover, he was particularly protective of the regiment's physician, who was Jewish.

What is striking in the first instance is the casual way in which the narrative introduces anti-Semitism: when Umprecht tells the narrator the background story of the prophecy, not only Umprecht's own anti-Semitic sentiments but those of the entire regiment are exposed. The description of the Polish village evokes the stereotypical picture of the Eastern-Jewish way of life.[22] The Eastern-European Jew as the

---

21   The Jewish physician, who has intimate insight into the soldiers as patients and has a diagnostic power over them, may be seen as a counterpart to Marco Polo.

22   See Brucke, *Magnetiseure: Die windige Karriere einer literarischen Figur*, 124.

ultimate target of anti-Semitism was a commonplace in Schnitzler's time,[23] so that Umprecht's description of the offensive behaviour towards them might have indeed not be surprising for contemporary readers. Umprecht's anti-Semitism is not problematized by the narrator, who later speaks of the 'günstigen Eindruck, den ich von der Person des Herrn von Umprecht gewonnen hatte' (the positive impression which Umprecht had made on me, W615). Schnitzler's novella thus imitates the cultural code of anti-Semitism by using the voices of the narrator and Umprecht. However, by 'quoting' this code, the text also displays its inherent paralogisms or logical shortcuts: anti-Semitism does not have to explain itself any more because it is handled as a given ('daß wir uns möglichst beleidigend gegen sie benahmen, können Sie sich denken' – you can certainly assume that we treated the Jews as offensively as possible). Readers of 1905 might have recognized the anti-Semitic discourse as something so familiar that it could even pass unnoticed, so that 'können Sie sich denken' (you can certainly assume) would implicitly also address them. Used to trusting the authority of the narrator, the readers might follow the initial invitation of the text and identify with Umprecht. Only when it could already be too late, at the end of the novella, might they realize their mistake – that they are like Umprecht himself deeply 'im Unrecht' (in the wrong).[24] As the ending of the novella suggests, Umprecht's mistake lies in the assumption that by performatively re-enacting what he saw in the image, he can avoid any real consequences. Playing a role may be understood metaphorically in the context of Umprecht's social status which turns out to be less secure than his privileged position as representative of the norm (as opposed to Marco Polo's position as 'other') might initially suggest.

In this context, it seems significant that Umprecht mentions the emptiness of the military service, 'der nicht immer anstrengend genug war' (which was not always exhausting enough, W603). This state of boredom does not sufficiently distract from the restrictions of individual choices. It is crucial to notice Umprecht's somewhat hopeless situation when he meets Marco Polo: he and the other soldiers in the regiment are confronted with their lack of autonomy, as they are 'kept' in the village by the anonymous authority of the military. This seems to produce an uncanny, almost Kafkaesque sensation of being held in place by an obscure bureaucratic power – 'Überdies hatte man die Möglichkeit vor Augen, jahrelang hier festsitzen zu müssen' (W604) (Moreover, one was faced with the possibility of being stuck here for years). The exercises of the military service start

---

23 See Gilman, Sander L. (1985) *Difference and Pathology: Stereotypes of Sexuality, Race, and Madness*, Ithaca, London: Cornell University Press, 178.
24 The connotation of the name has been pointed out by Perlmann, *Der Traum in der literarischen Moderne*, 91.

to appear like empty performances which have no other purpose than keeping the military system alive. While the military structures are obviously based on a certain amount of open coercion, their functioning nevertheless depends on a general acceptance of the necessity of this coercion. If this is no longer fully the case, as in the situation described by Umprecht, the very legitimacy of one's own function and of the system in its entirety becomes questionable, which is bound to produce feelings of anxiety.

This is also how we have to understand the irritation Umprecht and his comrades feel against the Jews precisely when their superior proves to be strikingly respectful towards the Jews. To witness this form of mutual recognition (in the Hegelian sense) between the prince and the Jews seems to upset the members of the military company. The prince's respectful treatment of the Jews is perceived as an attack on the stability of their own social status. When Marco Polo enters the officers' mess, they are surprised not only by his appearance but also by his non-submissive attitude. The fact that the prince not only invited the Jew but greets him by a handshake (an act of mutual recognition) is interpreted by Umprecht as provocation: 'Er [Marco Polo] wandte sich dabei an den Prinzen, der auf ihn zutrat und ihm – natürlich ausschließlich, um uns zu ärgern – die Hand schüttelte' (W604) (With this, he addressed the prince, who came up to him and shook his hand – of course only to irritate us). Umprecht and his comrades seem to be irritated by the shift of what they perceive as the normal world order: the Jews, by whom they find themselves surrounded, get the protection and recognition of the authority, instead of being subject to discrimination. In this way, the order imposed by the self–other recognition is here challenged. The recognition between the prince and Marco Polo points to the arbitrariness of the positions within the social order and reveals its instability. Umprecht and his comrades, then, feel surrounded by Jews whom they habitually think of as inferior, and are irritated by their major's respectful attitude towards the Jews. The dismissive typecasting of the Jews can thus be understood as a poor attempt at regaining security concerning their own status.

Transgressions of the Norm

This general insecurity explains the range of incidents in the village, in which several members of the regiment transgress the normative boundaries of their social roles in the form of alcoholism, uncontrolled violence, insanity, and even suicide:

> Mein Regiment lag damals in einem öden polnischen Nest. An Zerstreuungen gab es außer dem Dienst, der nicht immer anstrengend genug war, nur Trunk und Spiel. Überdies hatte man die Möglichkeit vor Augen, jahrelang hier festsitzen zu müssen, und nicht alle von uns verstanden es, ein Leben in dieser

Trostlosigkeit mit Fassung zu tragen. Einer meiner besten Freunde
hat sich im dritten Monat des dortigen Aufenthalts erschossen.
Ein anderer Kamerad, früher der liebenswürdigste Offizier, fing
plötzlich an, ein arger Trinker zu werden, wurde unmanierlich,
aufbrausend, nahezu unzurechnungsfähig und hatte jenen
Auftritt mit einem Advokaten, der ihm die Charge kostete. Der
Hauptmann meiner Kompanie war verheiratet und, ich weiß
nicht, ob mit oder ohne Grund, so eifersüchtig, daß er seine Frau
eines Tages zum Fenster hinunterwarf. Sie blieb rätselhafterweise
heil und gesund; der Mann starb im Irrenhause. Einer unserer
Kadetten, bis dahin ein sehr lieber, aber ausnehmend dummer
Junge, bildete sich plötzlich ein, Philosophie zu verstehen,
studierte Kant und Hegel und lernte ganze Partien aus deren
Werken auswendig, wie Kinder die Fiebel. (W603)
My regiment was stationed then in a boring Polish one-house
town. We had nothing to distract us except for the service which
was not always exhausting enough. Moreover, one had to face
the possibility of being stuck here for years. Not everyone knew
how to maintain their composure living in such desolation. One
of my best friends shot himself at the end of his third month there.
Another comrade, previously the nicest officer, suddenly began
to drink heavily, he lost his manners, became choleric, almost
unaccountable and finally had this encounter with an advocate,
which cost him his charge. The captain of my company was married
and – whether he had reason for it I don't know – he was so jealous
that one day he threw his wife out of the window. Magically, she
wasn't injured in the process, but her husband died in an asylum.
One of the cadets, up until then a very nice, but exceptionally
stupid boy, suddenly thought himself capable of understanding
philosophy – he studied Kant and Hegel and learnt entire passages
from their works by heart, like children do with their textbooks.

These cases of 'acting out' demonstrate the threat of a general state
of crisis, which becomes urgent when members of the norm begin to
cross the boundaries into the realm of the 'other'.[25] While philosophical

---

25 Bourdieu writes that it is 'the function of all magical boundaries [...] to stop
those who are inside, on the right side of the line, from leaving, demeaning
or down-grading themselves'. See Bourdieu, Pierre (1992), *Language and Symbolic Power: The Economy of Linguistic Exchanges*, ed. by John B. Thompson,
Cambridge: Polity Press, 122. See also Santner, Eric L. (1996), *My Own Private
Germany*, Princeton, NJ: Princeton University Press, 12. Moreover, see my analysis of Robert's identification with the piano teacher in *Flucht in die Finsternis* in
the previous chapter.

reading does not necessarily strike one as 'deviant behaviour', the way the cadet seems to engage with the texts, by learning whole passages by heart, appears more like lacklustre repetition compulsions than the active understanding process of the autonomous enlightened subject. In fact, the practice of the cadet is strikingly reminiscent of a strategy adopted by Daniel Paul Schreber, whose psychical symptoms can be interpreted as a reaction to his crisis of investiture, as we know from the last chapter:

Ich habe eine größere Anzahl von Gedichten, namentlich Schiller'sche Balladen, größere Abschnitte aus Schiller'schen und Göthe'schen [sic] Dramen, aber auch Opern-Arien und Scherzgedichte [...] auswendig gelernt, die ich dann im Stillen *verbotenus* [sic] aufsage. Auf den poetischen Werth der Gedichte kommt es dabei natürlich an und für sich nicht an; jede noch so unbedeutende Reimerei [...] ist als geistige Nahrung immer noch Goldes werth gegenüber dem entsetzlichen Blödsinne, der sonst meinen Nerven anzuhören zugemuthet wird.[26]

I have learned by heart a large number of poems, particularly Schiller's ballads, longer passages from Schiller's and Goethe's plays, but also opera arias and joke rhymes. The aesthetic value of these poems is rather insignificant; every meaningless rhyme [...] as food for my mind is worth a ton of gold as compared to the terrible nonsense which my nerves have to listen to otherwise.

Schreber thus counters the feeling of heteronomy engendered through his compulsive repetitive thoughts by the active and self-inflicted repetition of poetic language.[27] Similarly the cadet might counter the automated repetition compulsion of the military service with the mindless repetition of the works of Kant and Hegel. That he chooses these two out of all philosophers might be understood as a hint that the crisis present among the regiment has to be regarded in a broader context: I have already mentioned in the last chapter that the dependency of social identities on repeated performative rites of institution poses a paradox, as it contradicts the Kantian claim of autonomy upon which the post-Enlightenment bourgeois order relies. The Kantian subject does not just carry out a mimetic repetition of the moral law, but has to

---

26 Schreber, Daniel Paul (1995), *Denkwürdigkeiten eines Nervenkranken nebst Nachträgen*, Berlin: Kadmos, 163–164.

27 See Santner, *My Own Private Germany*, 12; Schneider, Manfred (1999), 'Das Grauen der Beobachter: Schriften und Bilder des Wahnsinns,' *Bild und Schrift in der Romantik*, ed. by Gerhard Neumann and Günter Oesterle, Würzburg: Könighausen und Neumann, 237–253, 244.

become the law himself. The mimetic repetition of the law as an externally imposed system is in turn a marker of 'otherness' – the practice of
women and Jews who were denied the capability of active self-legislation and accordingly had to 'act as if'.[28] Thus, the cadet's philosophical
reading habit fits cleanly into the list of transgression into the realm of
the 'other' committed by the others in the regiment.

In contrast to these rather remarkable 'exits', Umprecht's behaviour
seems to follow quite the opposite 'strategy'. He does not 'act out',
even though he describes his own reaction idiomatically as boredom
close to madness: 'Was mich anbelangt, so tat ich nichts als mich lang-
weilen, und zwar in einer so ungeheuerlichen Weise, daß ich an manchen Nachmittagen [...] fürchtete, verrückt zu werden' (W603) (As
where I was concerned, I did nothing but feel bored, and I was bored
in such a terrible way that I feared on some days that I would lose my
mind). This might still hint at unstable mental health, as various critics have pointed out,[29] but with regard to the numerous other cases of
mental health problems around him, it is important not to reduce the
plot of the novella to the description of an individual pathology, but
rather to stress that this instability appears to be a symptom of that
of the dominant order and its interpretative patterns. If the performative demands of one's social role begin to feel like a heteronomous
force, its fate-like quality becomes palpable, which seems to produce
the desire to 'act out' in one way or the other. We have already seen in
the last chapter that this desire, which results from a weakened identification with one's own social position, may lead to an idealizing mystification of the place of the 'other'. This explains the rather uncanny
and ambivalent role of Marco Polo: he appears as both challenger and
seducer by unsettling the (power) structures of the dominant order
and by promising insight into a realm inaccessible to those aligned
with the norm.[30]

---

28   Santner, *My Own Private Germany*, 140. That this differentiation is not as clear-
cut as the post-Enlightenment social orders want to admit is already implied by
Kant when he writes: 'Der Mensch handelt nach der Idee von Freiheit, als ob er
frei wäre, und eo ipso ist er frei' (Man acts according to the idea of freedom, as if
he were free, and eo ipso he is free). See Kant, Immanuel (1972), 'Philosophische
Religionslehre nach Pölitz,' *Kants gesammelte Schriften*, vol. 5, ed. by Akademie
der Wissenschaften zu Göttingen, Berlin: de Gruyter, 1068.

29   See Lawson, 'An Interpretation of "Die Weissagung",' 74; Allerdissen, *Arthur
Schnitzler: Impressionistisches Rollenspiel und skeptischer Moralismus in seinen
Erzählungen*, 154; Perlmann, *Der Traum in der literarischen Moderne*, 92.

30   The character of the Eastern-Jewish 'gate keeper' who promises access to a
realm lying beyond normative boundaries returns also in Schnitzler's *Traumnovelle* (Dream Story), which I will analyse in the fifth chapter of this book.

The Seductive Horror of 'Otherness'

Marco Polo's performance is accompanied by the obligatory moment of *Grauen* (horror): 'Nicht ohne Grauen sahen wir alle zu, wie der philosophische Kadett, in Schlaf versetzt, den Befehlen des Zauberers gehorchend, zuerst durchs offene Fenster sprang' (W605) (We observed, not without a feeling of horror, how the philosophical cadet was put into a somnambulist state and, following the magician's orders, jumped out of the window). The uncanny moment is thus engendered by a demonstration of one of them succumbing to a heteronomous force: without even knowing, the cadet obeys Marco Polo's orders and displays a completely automated conduct under the suspension of his autonomy. This is, then, a classical uncanny moment that brings to the surface what is familiar and known but has been repressed, particularly in evidence in the compulsion to repeat.[31] The confrontation with this performance of heteronomy touches on the repressed repetition compulsion connected to the symbolic function of the members of the military and their social destinies in the broader sense. Thus, the *Grauen* (horror) sets in because the automated conduct displayed by the cadet is a symptom of (Romantic) madness, as we have seen in the last chapter, but is at the same time also uncannily familiar to their own life in the barracks. The prince's question, with which he comments on the events during Marco Polo's performance, is crucial in our context: 'Wo fängt das Wunder an?' (W606) (Where does the miracle begin?). According to Manfred Schneider, the 'Wundersinn ersetzt den Kontingenzsinn, um den Verstand vor dem Grauen zu bewahren' (the sense for miracles replaces the sense for contingency, in order to protect reason from horror).[32] In this narrative too, then, the complete abolition of any sense of contingency follows an experience of *Grauen* (horror), when Umprecht from this moment on experiences everything in relation to his 'destiny'.

The fact that Marco Polo presents himself as puppet master is a further threat to the superior position of the gentiles. This is stressed even more when Marco Polo goes on to assume the role of Umprecht's challenger by implicitly calling him a coward: 'Der Herr Leutnant haben Angst' (W606) (You are afraid, Lieutenant). For Umprecht, this challenging statement may release a repressed fear of the revenge of the suppressed 'other', in line with the Hegelian master–slave dialectic. By performing a speech act that he (as both a civilian and a Jew) officially has no legitimate right to perform, Marco Polo also undermines the

---

31 See Freud, 'Das Unheimliche,' 251.
32 Interestingly, Schneider finds this concept of Romantic madness also expressed in the memoirs of Daniel Paul Schreber, who abolishes the sense of contingency as well. See Schneider, 'Das Grauen der Beobachter,' 249.

power of investiture. While the right to perform certain acts – like a challenge for a duel – depends on the symbolic function of the individual, performing an act one is not legitimately allowed to not only functions as a form of appropriation of that right but also points to the 'missing link' at the origin of the chain of performances in every legal system.[33] Umprecht's reaction is conditioned by the military code of honour: to feel fear might be understood as cowardice, which is not acceptable for a lieutenant. Thus he turns around quickly, to see whether anyone could have heard the magician's verdict – 'aber wir waren schon durch das Kasernentor geschritten und befanden uns auf der Landstraße' (W606) (but we had already gone through the gate of the barack and were standing on a country road). Marco Polo has led him out of the realm of military structures and it seems as if the codes and rules have momentarily lost their power. In this way, Marco Polo threatens not only Umprecht individually but also the entire system, in which the latter is a representative of the norm while Marco Polo is restricted to the place of the 'other'.

While this place of the 'other' is represented in Schnitzler's narratives generally as precarious, a certain element of freedom also appears to be suggested in this novella. Umprecht and his comrades are entrenched in the village, while Marco Polo travels, returning to the village only during the summer. This might explain why, while on the surface of it Marco Polo seems to repulse Umprecht and the other members of the regiment, they also seem to be fascinated by the magician. Especially when Umprecht asks him secretively to foretell his future, the encounter between the two men seems almost of an erotic intimacy.[34] Before presenting Umprecht the prophetic image, he tells him: 'Kommen Sie hinaus, [...] in den Hof. Mir is lieber bei Mondschein' (W606) (Come outside, Lieutenant, into the courtyard. I prefer the moonlight). And von Umrecht remembers: 'Er hielt mich an der Hand, und ich folgte ihm durch die offene Tür ins Freie' (W606) (He was holding my hand, and I followed him through the open door outside). Marco Polo leads Umprecht outside of the determining military structures into the court, scene for a certain kind of 'courtship'. The seductive element of this moonlight encounter lies in the possible mystification of the outsider position of the 'other', which seems to hold a space for freedom and emancipation independent from the restrictions of social norms, but is also linked to knowledge. Marco Polo seems to have access to an understanding of something that lies outside the social order, because

---

33 See Chapter Two.
34 For a reading focused on the homoerotic subtext of the novella see Lawson's psychoanalytically informed interpretation. See Lawson, 'An Interpretation of "Die Weissagung"'.

he himself is not securely located within it. His knowledge (or alleged knowledge) is seductive, because he promises to make sense of a chaotic and incommensurable reality: by foretelling Umprecht's destiny, he would assure him of a life individually mapped out for him, of a secured position in the world, which seems to be no longer provided by his status in the military.

We see here once more how the stereotype of the 'other' is ambivalently charged and also contains elements of idealizing mystification. The position of the 'other' stands outside of the norm and is thus obviously precarious. However, as seen in the previous two chapters, for Schnitzler's protagonists, there seems to be a potential freedom of transgression associated with this position, which gives 'otherness' an additional positive connotation. For Umprecht, Marco Polo seems to have the 'privilege' of not being determined by a symbolic function within the norm due to his position of alterity. It thus appears once more that the actual higher power that determines the behaviour of people like Umprecht is attributable to the performative restrictions and instructions of their social role. This would also explain why – despite his initial aversion – Umprecht actively seeks out Marco Polo and asks him to tell him his future.

The Higher Power of Destiny and the Enlightened Subject

I suggest that we should understand Umprecht's acceptance of Marco Polo's image as his destiny in this way: the assumption of a metaphysical higher power gives an explanation for the feeling of restraint and brings relief from the claim of autonomy the post-Enlightenment order relies on. When Umprecht claims, 'Und mir war es immer klarer, daß ich mit irgend einer unbekannten höhnischen Macht in einem ungleichen Kampf begriffen war' (W612) (and it became clearer and clearer to me that I was fighting an uneven battle with an unknown taunting power),[35] this is strikingly reminiscent of the 'obscene and malevolent presence that appears to have a direct hold on one's inner parts' of which Santner speaks with regard to the repetition compulsion of social destinies.[36] Umprecht's belief in destiny is thus presented in the novella as a form of escapist coping strategy: while others around him escape into alcoholism, madness, and death, Umprecht becomes obsessed with the idea of the power of destiny. Even though seeing himself on his deathbed is obviously uncomfortable on a conscious level, the fact that Umprecht accepts the image as prophecy so willingly, and that he from then on arranges his life accordingly, hints at the possibility that he also

---

35 The 'unbekannte, höhnische Macht' (unknown, taunting power) can be seen as a distinctly Hoffmannesque formulation.
36 See Santner, *My Own Private Germany*, xii.

gains something from this terrifying idea: not only does the assumption of destiny give an explanation for the feeling of heteronomous coercion without calling the dominant order into question, it also provides Umprecht with the sensation of being somewhat 'special' or 'chosen'. In this way, it reassures him of his individuality as opposed to the uncanny feeling of being reduced to performing a social role, while being denied any individual agency.

Moreover, unlike the other forms of escapism, the belief in destiny does not require any form of 'acting out' or transgression: it becomes clear in the text that Umprecht is most concerned with hierarchical structures and the code of honour. There is a range of passages in which he is afraid that his behaviour might be seen as deviating from the requirements of the norm. Thus, while others around him escape from the uncomfortable situation via transgression, Umprecht clings to the social structures. In this way, Marco Polo's allegedly prophetic image turns out to be the perfect replacement for the weakened function of his social destiny. In the end, it literally provides him with a new role, including stage directions and the requirement of repetitive performances: 'Wir probieren seit einigen Wochen Tag für Tag, ich habe die Situation, die mir heute bevorsteht, schon fünfzehn- oder zwanzigmal durchgemacht' (W613) (We have been practising every day for a few weeks, I have gone through the situation, which is lying ahead of me today, already fifteen to twenty times). This is, ironically, highly reminiscent of the repetitive exercises of the military service that Umprecht dreaded so much at the time.

Umprecht's life is highly influenced by maintaining appearances, giving performances, in order to play the part of the independent self-determined male subject that the norm requires him to be. It has to be ascribed to this role when he desperately stresses his autonomy, claiming: 'Vor allem war es mir klar, daß ich mein Schicksal vollkommen in der Hand hatte' (W609) (above all, it was clear to me that I was in full control of my destiny). It is striking that this statement, which is the direct reaction to Marco Polo's image (read from his hand), mirrors and contradicts his other, later utterance quoted above: 'Und mir war es immer klarer, daß ich mit irgend einer unbekannten höhnischen Macht in einem ungleichen Kampf begriffen war' (W612) (and it became clearer and clearer to me that I was fighting an uneven battle with an unknown taunting power). Significantly, both utterances seem to describe what Umprecht perceives as reality: 'it was clear to me' can be used as a synonym for 'I knew', which generally implies that what the subject thinks to be true actually *is* true. Thus, Umprecht as narrator does not maintain any authorial distance to what he is recounting retrospectively: in both cases he presents what he thought to be true as knowledge so that it sounds as if he still believes it to be true.

It is the tension between these two contradictory sentences that marks Umprecht's conflict. He is supposed to represent the rational and enlightened subject, thus expected to be responsible for his own actions, to be autonomous in his decisions. The first of the sentences can thus be seen as a kind of knee-jerk reaction in which Umprecht reminds himself of his social role: he claims his rationality and autonomy as an enlightened male subject. The second sentence demonstrates that this feeling of autonomy has become unstable. This is why we could read Umprecht's conflict as the looming sensation of his incapability to fulfil the demands of the role of the Kantian subject, which I have already mentioned earlier and which Santner has proposed to be 'the central paradox of modernity: that the subject is solicited by a will to autonomy in the name of the very community that is thereby undermined, whose very substance thereby passes over into the subject'.[37] While the secular societies of the post-Enlightenment eras are based on the idea of the autonomous subject, the functioning of the same societies depends on the submission of individuals to norms and regulated performances. This is why too radical an understanding of autonomy threatens the social order. In order to maintain the idea of the enlightened and autonomous subject, the community, i.e. the social order, has to 'pass over into the subject',[38] thus be fully internalized and incorporated as 'natural essence' on the one hand, or freely chosen on the other. The process of internalization is obviously not only the case in modern and post-modern societies, but rather seems to be the foundation of any social order. However, the claim of autonomy requires a much higher level of identification with the given structures and one's own position within them. When those structures cease to be able to address the subjects sufficiently, this identification is weakened.

In Umprecht's case, it becomes clear that despite his strong conscious identification with the social norms, he nevertheless also feels the urge to overcome the role of the enlightened male subject and that the insecurity concerning his social status is not only tied to the specific situation in the Polish village. Even years after the frustrating military service, when he is married and can call himself a proud land owner, he seems to feel the longing to escape this bourgeois existence. Significantly, the looming fulfilment of the prophecy gives him the licence to have thoughts of transgression. Since the prophetic image showed him on his deathbed surrounded by mourning wife and children, he imagines: 'wenn ich mich von meiner Frau und den Kindern trennte, so müßte ja all die Gefahr schwinden und ich hätte das Schicksal zum

---

37   Santner, *My Own Private Germany*, 145.
38   Santner, *My Own Private Germany*, 145.

Narren gehalten' (W610) (if I left my wife and children, all the danger would have to vanish, and I would have fooled destiny). The use of the word 'destiny' may have a double meaning here. It obviously refers to the higher power Umprecht assumes to be behind Marco Polo's proph-ecy. However, what this fantasy entails is in fact the avoidance not only of what he assumes to be his metaphysical destiny but also of his *social* destiny in the Bourdieusian sense. While he does not give in to the temptation and tries to rationalize his superstitious fears, and so, at this point, remains within the boundaries of the norm, such a transgressive act is precisely the scenario he re-enacts in the play written by the nar-rator: here, a man finds himself suddenly longing for adventures and leaves his family behind. However, alone on the first day of his escape he experiences so many atrocities that he decides to return home only to fall victim to a murder.

Thus, the moral of the play seems to be: if you fail to perform the duties of your social role (in this case, head of the family, husband, father), you will be punished. However, this is not congruent with Schnitzler's narrative itself, even though it does conclude with Umpre-cht's real death. Taking into account the conventional narrative style of *Die Weissagung* (The Prophecy), we might suspect another, rather ironic narrative voice behind the apparent one of the narrator, which exposes the narrator and his perspective as conservative and narrow-minded.[39] Thus, while the play within the novella condemns the urge to trans-gress the boundaries of the norm, the novella itself does not give an equally clear-cut moralistic answer. Umprecht's eagerness to play the role can be explained by the fact that the play allows him to transgress the boundaries of the norm in a fictional frame – thus to make believe. At the same time, he has a role to play, to follow the script and stage directions – to do what he has been assigned to do. Nevertheless, his participation in the play makes it possible for him to keep up the illu-sion of his own autonomy: after all, playing the part is understood as a strategy to beat his destiny at its own game. In this way, he presents himself as an active subject who takes his destiny into his own hands. However, all of Umprecht's strategies to regain a secured sense of his own position within the norm as autonomous subject turn out to be a dead end. Schnitzler's protagonist never reaches a critical position towards the normative restrictions of his social role, which is why he proves to be indeed unable to escape his destiny. That this failure has much to do with the power of cultural narratives will become clear in the next section.

---

39 See Rohrwasser, 'Arthur Schnitzlers Erzählung "Die Weissagung",' 63.

Recognition Scenes

The definite turning point, sealing Umprecht's inferior position in view of the power of destiny, is the moment when Umprecht receives his scar: in his premonition he sees himself on his presumed deathbed, bearing a scar on the forehead. In the years following the premonition he tries to avoid situations in which he is more likely to be injured in the face. However, perhaps significantly on a train journey,[40] Umprecht becomes the victim of an apparently arbitrary attempted act of assassination. A sharp stone thrown through the window of the speeding train injures him on the forehead, which results in the dreaded scar. For Umprecht, this signifies the definite turning point, which seems to seal his defeat against the malicious power of destiny. The scar belongs to the classic properties of a recognition scene, and we might understand this passage as such: Umprecht recognizes the scar as a further completion of what he assumes to be a prophecy. When he looks into a mirror, he recognizes his own face as the one he saw in the image induced by Marco Polo. Terence Cave describes recognition scenes as a shift from ignorance to knowledge,[41] and Umprecht seems indeed to experience precisely such a shift:

> Nach ein paar Wochen leuchtete sie [the scar] auf meiner Stirn an derselben Stelle, wo ich sie in jenem Traume gesehen hatte. Und mir war es immer klarer, daß ich mit irgend einer unbekannten höhnischen Macht in einem ungleichen Kampf begriffen war, und ich sah dem Tag, wo das letzte in Erfüllung treten sollte, mit wachsender Unruhe entgegen. (W612)
>
> After a few weeks the scar was shining on my forehead precisely on the spot which I had seen in my dream. And it became clearer and clearer to me that I was fighting an uneven battle with an unknown taunting power, and so I anticipated the day when the last part should become true with increasing dread.

We have already seen that this statement is paired with an earlier one, directly after he is confronted with Marco Polo's prophetic image: 'Vor allem war es mir klar, daß ich mein Schicksal vollkommen in der Hand hatte' (W609) (above all, it was clear to me that I was in full control of my destiny). This indeed seems to mark, then, a shift from ignorance to knowledge ('klar' – 'klarer', 'clear' – 'clearer'), but we have also seen that the second sentence does not fully erase the truth-value of the first

---

40 See the implications of the train motif in Chapter Two.
41 See Cave, Terence (1988), *Recognitions: A Study in Poetics*, Oxford: Oxford University Press, 27.

one, as Umprecht also does not distance himself from it. This, however, seems to be in line with Cave's description of recognition scenes, as the knowledge provided through them is always a shifting one:

> [...] recognition scenes in literary works are by their nature 'problem' moments rather than moments of satisfaction and completion. Anagnorisis seems at first sight to be a paradigm of narrative satisfaction: it answers questions, restores identity and symmetry, and makes a whole hidden structure of relations intelligible. Yet the satisfaction is somehow excessive, the reassurance too easy; the structure is visibly prone to collapse. An ignorance which was never wholly innocent turns for the moment into an implausible and precarious knowledge; the apparently opposite poles of knowledge and ignorance meet in surreptitious complicity [...].[42]

Umprecht's quick jump to the conclusion that the scar proves that there is a higher power at work can be understood as such an 'excessive' recognition scene. It provides Umprecht with an ordering frame and a prompt explanation for his feeling of lack of autonomy. If we bear in mind that this negation of contingency can be considered a symptom of Romantic madness that is supposed to keep the sensation of *Grauen* (horror) at bay, it is safe to assume that the causal structure Umprecht constructs here is indeed 'prone to collapse'.

Umprecht's death, finally, is the result of a very similar excessive recognition scene: in his prophetic image, he sees a bald man with a green shawl and glasses running towards the death scene. However, while this is not part of the narrator's script, it turns out that he had planned initially that 'der wahnsinnige Vater der Frau, von dem im ersten Akt die Rede ist, [...] zum Schluß auf die Szene stürzen sollte' (W614) (the woman's insane father, who is mentioned in the first act, was supposed to run on stage at the end of the play). When Umprecht performs the last scene of the play, a man who perfectly fits the description actually appears on stage. He turns out to be the flautist in the orchestra. The wind has blown away his wig, and, as he runs after it, he involuntarily and unknowingly takes on the role of the 'insane father'. This seems to seal Umprecht's fate: 'seine Blicke sind starr, wie verzückt auf den Mann gerichtet; er will etwas reden – er vermag es offenbar nicht – er sinkt zurück' (W617) (his gaze is transfixed on the man, almost rapt; he tries to speak – is apparently unable to do so – he is sinking back).[43]

---

42 Cave, *Recognitions: A Study in Poetics*, 489.
43 The motif of the fixed gaze can also be seen as a Hoffmannesque 'stock image'.

Umprecht recognizes the man as the last detail of his vision. The bald man is thus the figure that explains Umprecht's death in both readings: for Umprecht himself, and as the narrator suggests, he is proof that a force outside the grasp of rationality must have been at work in the line of events that necessarily leads to his death. Critics have argued convincingly that this must be the moment where Umprecht completely surrenders, accepts his 'fate', and accordingly he dies, as Robert Weigel puts it, 'medizinisch gesprochen durch Herzversagen' (from the medical perspective, because of heart failure).[44] This statement implies that we have to assume that the novella's course of events can be attributed to the phenomenon of autosuggestion. Seen in this way, we can find a rational explanation of Umprecht's death: he *believes* that his fate has been sealed, when he sees the bald man, and this is why he dies, not because there is actually a higher power at work. However, it seems to me that such a rationalist approach would be more appropriate if we were confronted with a newspaper report that turned out to be a hoax ('this is not what actually happened, what actually happened is this ...'). As Schnitzler's text is a work of fiction, we should perhaps be less concerned with finding a way to explain what 'actually' happened, but rather with the way the text itself highlights its own fictional quality: the scenes of recognition that only seemingly motivate the plot as well as the three narrators, precisely by claiming plausibility and authenticity, draw the reader's attention on the paralogical structure of the narrative.

The novella as a whole fits Cave's description of recognition very nicely: in various moments the three narrators seem to provide evidence for the inevitability and truthfulness of the events, which do not hold out against a closer scrutiny.[45] Moreover, the text provides multiple recognition scenes for the *reader*, especially on the level of genre and the association thereof with certain reading expectations. Freud's comment on the text implies that it initially had him expect a realistic setting, which made him wait for the rational explanation in the end. Stylistic elements, like the conventional narration or the description of social milieus and issues (military hierarchy, anti-Semitism), must have raised that expectation – they were recognized as markers of a certain narrative genre. At the same time, the text introduces more and more

---

44 Weigel, 'Schnitzlers Schicksalserzählungen *Die Weissagung* und *Die dreifache Warnung*,' 160. A similar approach can be detected in Perlmann's interpretation, which is otherwise convincing. See Perlmann, *Der Traum in der literarischen Moderne*, 91.

45 See Gerrekens, '*Die Weissagung* oder wie aus schlecht erzähltem Theater eine spannende Novelle wird,' 104ff.

elements generally attributed to fantastic fiction and that of *Schauerro-mantik*, which invites a completely different reading. Thus, the reader, like Umprecht, is confronted with moments of apparent recognition ('first I thought this was a realistic narrative, but now I recognize that it must be a case of fantastic literature'), which, however, do not provide complete satisfaction. This is why neither an affirmative reading of the text as fantastic novella, nor the completely rational denouement of the events,[46] seems absolutely convincing.

For Cave, the motif of recognition can be seen as synechdoche for literature as a whole, in the sense that it 'represents the most quintes-sentially fictional type of plot: it is the signature of a fiction, the local detail that stands for the whole'.[47] This means that recognition scenes *within the plot* are also recognition scenes on the level of narrative struc-ture – narrative turns that we recognize for what they are and that we are ready to accept in and as fiction. This yet again engenders an effect of Romantic irony, in the sense that the literary text itself refers to its own constructedness. And indeed, besides the moment of *Grauen* (hor-ror) already mentioned, we recognize in the text a range of Romantic and Hoffmannesque elements: through the play-within-a-story as well as the story-within-a-story-within-a-story (evoked by the three narra-tive perspectives of the editor, the narrator, and Umprecht himself), the aesthetic and fictional quality of the narration is emphasized.[48] And of course, Umprecht's strategy to transform the prophetic image into an aesthetic one by re-enacting it on stage takes up Hoffmann's fasci-nation with the scenic and spectacle.[49] Moreover, this transformation from a prophetic image into an aesthetic one is precisely the process described by the stranger in Hoffmann's *Doge und Dogaresse* (Doge and

---

46 Perlmann claims that this is possible. See Perlmann, *Der Traum in der literarischen Moderne*, 92.

47 Cave, *Recognitions: A Study in Poetics*, 492.

48 Schnitzler toys with the element of the fictional editor in several prose texts, e.g. also in his novella *Der letzte Brief des Literaten* (The Writer's Last Letter, 1917). In his interpretation of the intertextual references in this text, Achim Aurnhammer argues convincingly that in contrast to Goethe's (1787), the play with different narrative levels is used to highlight the unreliability of the narrator's voice. This calls into question the possibility of finding one unequivocal truth: 'Der Leser gerät damit in die Rolle eines Analytikers, der aufgrund des projektiv und inter-textuell überformten Materials die Wahrheit zu ermitteln sucht oder erkennen muss, dass es mehrere Wahrheiten gibt' (Therefore, the reader is put into the position of the analyst, who, confronted with the projectively and intertextually overdetermined material, tries to find the truth – or who has to accept that there is more than one truth). See Aurnhammer, Achim (2013), *Arthur Schnitzlers inter-textuelles Erzählen*, Berlin; Boston, MA: De Gruyter, 157.

49 Webber writes that Hoffmann's writings are often 'interrupted by the figurative terms of theatrical production, drama, opera, puppet play, and *tableau vivant*'. See Webber, *The Doppelgänger: Double Visions in German Literature*, 115.

Dogaressa) already mentioned in the last chapter: the artist 'receives' an image ('daß in dem Gemüt des Künstlers ein Bild aufgeht')[50] and thus inspired creates the artwork. The artist and his artwork, then, become a sort of medium through which reality becomes perceivable: according to this kind of Romantic theory, art is understood as 'wahrne-hmungsermöglichendes und wahrnehmungserweiterndes Organ' (an institution/organ, which enables and amplifies cognition).[51] The artist thus functions as medium of a higher power, while art is a mimetic or providential representation of human destinies.

This understanding of art became popular again in Schnitzler's time.[52] Also the narrator in *Die Weissagung* (The Prophecy) is clearly influenced by it. He admits that he is partly glad to accept Umprecht's account of a higher power, as it allows him to see himself as an instrument 'eines über uns waltenden Willens' (W615) (a will ruling over us). However, through the multiple inconsistencies in the novella that seem to undermine both the narrator's and Umprecht's perspective, Schnitzler's text mocks the tendentious mystification easily deduced from this kind of reflection on art. Thus, besides the boundary between norm and 'other', *Die Weissagung* (The Prophecy) also addresses another kind – that between life and art or between reality and fiction. The theme of bringing images to life and capturing life in aesthetic images is prefigured in the performances at the estate of Freiherr von Schottenegg: the narrator remembers Umprecht from his participation in 'lebenden Bildern' (W601) (living images). Also, Umprecht's attempt at avoiding his real death by enacting it on stage, and the failure of this attempt, bring to the fore the blurred demarcation lines between reality and fiction.[53]

As in *Flucht in die Finsternis*, we are confronted here with an uncanny fading of differences. As this merging of play and reality reaches its climax when Umprecht really dies just moments after performing his death on stage, it might not be surprising that the sensation the narrator feels as a witness is the by now notorious *Grauen* (horror): 'Ich selbst bin am selben Abend noch ins Tal hinuntergeeilt, von Ent-setzen geschüttelt. In einem sonderbaren Grauen habe ich mich nicht

---

50 Hoffmann, E. T. A. (2001), *Doge und Dogaresse, Sämmtliche Werke*, vol. 4: *Die Serapionsbrüder*, ed. by Hartmut Steinecke and Wulf Segebrecht, Frankfurt a. M.: Deutscher Klassiker Verlag, 429–483, 430.
51 Neumann, Gerhard (1999), 'Narration und Bildlichkeit. Zur Inszenierung eines romantischen Schicksalsmusters in E. T. A. Hoffmanns " Doge und Dogaresse",' *Bild und Schrift in der Romantik*, ed. by Gerhard Neumann and Günter Oesterle, Würzburg: Königshausen und Neumann, 107–142, 138.
52 The most famous representatives of this idea are Rainer Maria Rilke and the George circle.
53 See Rohrwasser, 'Arthur Schnitzlers Erzählung "Die Weissagung",' 63.

entschließen können, das Schloß wieder zu betreten' (W618) (I myself hurried down to the valley on the same night, shivering with terror. Feeling a strange horror, I have not been able to make myself set foot in the castle again). It has become clear by now that the *Grauen* (horror) is a recurring Romantic element in Schnitzler's texts. It thus engenders a moment of recognition for the reader, referring both to the Romantic fiction it seems to be 'borrowed' from and also to other Schnitzler texts that feature similar scenarios of Romantic affect. It therefore takes on the function of the scar motif in classical recognition plots: 'The scar is a mark of treacherously concealed narrative waiting to break the surface and create a scandal, it is a sign that the story, like the wound, may always be reopened'.[54]

I would like to suggest that *Grauen* (horror), like the scar, also refers to the 'scandal' that disturbed Freud and other critics. The fading of differences between reality and fiction (or between a realistic and a fantastic plot on the level of the reader), which occurs in *Die Weissagung* (The Prophecy), is a necessary part of our perception of reality. 'We all create images of things we fear and glorify', Gilman writes about the production of stereotypes, '[t]hese images never remain abstractions: we understand them as real-world entities'.[55] The merging of constructed images and our experience of reality is thus a process that is happening all the time. However, when this process becomes conscious it can obviously have an unsettling effect on our perception of the social reality around us and of our position within it. The way *Die Weissagung* (The Prophecy) plays with the blurring of generic boundaries may remind us of the presence of this process in our own perceptions of reality.

As we will see in what follows, the short narrative *Andreas Thameyers letzter Brief* is also concerned with the blurring of boundaries and the fading of differences on several levels, resulting in the familiar sensation of *Grauen* (horror). While this text does not explicitly play with the fantastic, it nevertheless uses Gothic elements precisely when the protagonist is confronted with the shattering of the boundaries that secure the 'self' as distinct from the 'other'.

Male Suicide as Destiny and Stereotypes of Blackness in *Andreas Thameyers letzter Brief* (Andreas Thameyer's Last Letter)

The short narrative *Andreas Thameyers letzter Brief* (Andreas Thameyer's Last Letter) was first published in 1902 in *Die Zeit*. In contrast to *Die Weissagung* (The Prophecy) with its three narrative levels, this text

---

54 Cave, *Recognitions: A Study in Poetics*, 24.
55 Gilman, *Difference and Pathology*, 15.

is not framed by any authorial narrative voice and consists only of the suicide note of the lower-middle-class bank accountant Andreas Thameyer. He claims that he has to commit suicide in order to re-establish his honour and that of his wife, who has given birth to a Black child.[56] Despite the fact that he and his wife are both white, Thameyer dismisses any rumours of her infidelity. Referring to the allegedly scientifically confirmed phenomenon of maternal impression ('Versehen der Frauen' – literally: female 'mis-seeing'), he argues that the reason for the child's skin colour is the shock his wife experienced when looking at a group of Black men who were camping in the Viennese Prater. This is certainly a reference to the so-called 'Völkerschauen' (Peoples Shows) between 1896 and 1901, where members of the Ashanti people were literally exhibited and allegedly 'authentically' staged on open display for the Austrian onlookers.[57] To support his point, Thameyer mentions so-called scientific sources and other writings, which all promote the theory of maternal impression: the possibility of an unborn child taking on the looks of someone or something who or which had left a deep impression on the pregnant woman. Thameyer's theoretical sources range from anecdotes by Martin Luther and the French philosopher Nicolas Malebranche (1638–1715) to writings by the contemporary scientists Julius Preuss and Gerhard von Welsenburg, who indeed published studies on the hypothesis of maternal impression in

---

56 I capitalize 'Black' in order to express that it is not understood 'as merely a color of skin pigmentation, but as a heritage, an experience, a cultural and personal identity, the meaning of which becomes specifically stigmatic and/or glorious and/or ordinary under specific social conditions'. See MacKinnon, Catharine A. (1982), 'Feminism, Marxism, Method, and the State: An Agenda for Theory,' *Signs* 7 (3): *Feminist Theory*, 515–544, 516. Conversely, I chose not to capitalize 'white,' following Kimberlé Williams Crenshaw, who argues that capitalizing both 'seems to presume a greater parallelism between these racial designations than their histories suggest. Of the myriad differences is the fact that while white can be further divided into a variety of ethnic and national identities, Black represents an effort to claim a cultural identity that has historically been denied.' See Kimberlé, Williams Crenshaw (2011), 'Twenty Years of Critical Race Theory: Looking Back To Move Forward,' *Connecticut Law Review* 43 (5): 1253–1352, 1255.

57 Several scholars have pointed out the intertextual reference in Schnitzler's novella to Peter Altenberg's *Ashantee* (1897). See Meyer, Imke (2010), *Männlichkeit und Melodram: Arthur Schnitzlers erzählende Schriften*, Würzburg: Königshausen & Neumann, 76–84, 85; Boehringer, Michael (2011), 'Fantasies of *White Masculinity* in Arthur Schnitzler's *Andreas Thameyers letzter Brief* (1900),' *The German Quarterly* 84 (1): 80–96, 83, 90–91; Aurnhammer, *Arthur Schnitzlers intertextuelles Erzählen*, 103, 119.

the 1890s.[58] Despite his own proclaimed conviction of his wife's fidelity and the theoretical backup for this conviction, however, Thameyer insists on the necessity of his suicide. Only his death, it seems, can seal the re-establishment of his family's reputation and honour.

My reading of this short text will be tripartite. First, I will focus on the power of social destiny that is expressed in the text through Thameyer's insistence on the absolute necessity of his suicide. Compared with the other Schnitzlerian protagonists analyzed in this study, Thameyer represents an interesting exception: he does not explicitly turn to his metaphysical destiny in order to escape the normative pressure of his social destiny. Rather, he embraces his social destiny with such devotion that he decides to sacrifice himself when he is no longer able to fulfil it. Thameyer's letter demonstrates that social destinies are indeed *'fatal* – by which I mean mortal', as Bourdieu would have it.[59] The second part of my reading is thus concerned with how the text addresses the way these knowledge systems inform the cementation of stereotypes. The ironical use of the theory of maternal impression points up the way stereotypes are reinforced through concepts of biological difference, but are challenged when biological sameness between self and 'other' becomes evident. The third section of my analysis will then turn to the way the text blends not only literary and non-literary discourses, but also blurs generic boundaries. I will show that the text uses elements of the Gothic to negotiate Thameyer's unsettling experience with 'otherness'.

Necessity and the Compulsive Performance of Social Destiny

Similar to Marco Polo's challenging of the military officers in *Die Weissagung* (The Prophecy), the unknown father of the child has performed a right he does not have in *fin de siècle* Viennese society. By doing so, he has challenged boundaries that forbid such a transgression in the first place. The individual transgression makes visible the possibility of transgression of social boundaries in general and exposes the

---

58 Preuss's study *Vom Versehen der Schwangeren: Eine historisch-kritische Studie* was published in 1892 and Welsenburg's book from 1899 had the title *Das Versehen der Frauen in Vergangenheit und Gegenwart und die Anschauungen der Ärzte, Naturforscher und Philosophen darüber.* (See Schnyder, Peter (2002), 'Im Netz der Behausung: Arthur Schnitzlers Erzählung *Andreas Thameyers letzter Brief* in kulturwissenschaftlicher Perspektive,' *Akten des X. Internationalen Germanistenkongresses Wien 2000: 'Zeitenwende: Die Germanistik auf dem Weg vom 20. ins 21. Jahrhundert,'* vol. 6: *Epochenbegriffe: Grenzen und Möglichkeiten; Aufklärung – Klassik – Romantik; Die Wiener Moderne,* ed. by Peter Wiesinger, Bern: Peter Lang, 419–425, 425. Aurnhammer reveals that Georg von Welsenburg was a pseudonym of the German sexologist Iwan Bloch. See Aurnhammer, *Arthur Schnitzlers intertextuelles Erzählen,* 123.
59 Bourdieu, *Language and Symbolic Power,* 122.

boundaries around the privileged norm as constructed. Accordingly, the legitimacy of Thameyer's position within the norm has become questionable. The birth of the child clearly has confronted Thameyer with an experience in which the boundaries between self and 'other' become blurred. As Michael Boehringer puts it: 'Via a progeny that signifies the "other", [...], the protagonist's masculinity can no longer pass by without notice; rather, his gendered self, his experience of being a man, becomes marked and open to interrogation'.[60] Thameyer's letter may therefore be understood as an arguably failed performance of masculinity, which seeks to rehabilitate this status. Similarly to Schnitzler's famous *Leutnant Gustl* (Lieutenant Gustl, 1900), we encounter here a male subject whose legitimate status (as a military officer in Gustl's case, as a bourgeois patriarch in Thameyer's) has been challenged in such a disruptive manner that self-annihilation seems the only possible solution to protect that status. Thus, the text demonstrates how social destinies can in fact be 'fatal'.[61] While Thameyer does not refer to his metaphysical destiny, he presents his situation as one that does not leave him any choice:

Die Menschen sind dumm und armselig, sie können, wie ich mich ausdrücken möchte, in unser Inneres nicht hineinblicken, sie sind schadenfroh und höchst gemein! Aber nun werden sie alle verstummen ... ja nun werden sie alle sagen: wir haben unrecht [sic] getan, wir sehen es ein, deine Frau ist dir treu gewesen, und es war gar nicht notwendig, daß du dich umbringst ... Aber ich sage euch: es ist notwendig! (AT516)

But people are stupid, and they cannot, as I should like to say, peer into our inner selves. They are malignant and mean. But now they will all be quiet.... Yes, now they will all say: 'We have done wrong, we see now that his wife was faithful and it was not necessary for him to do away with himself.'... But I tell you it is necessary![62]

The emphasis on necessity, with which Thameyer repeatedly explains his suicide, implies that there is a higher power at work, which leaves him no alternative. Thameyer presents his suicide as the only possible defence of his wife's honour. However, Thameyer concedes that the suicide cannot speak for itself either: 'Aber ich habe das alles aufgeschrieben, denn ich finde es notwendig, daß diese Sache völlig klargestellt

60 Boehringer, Michael (2011), 'Fantasies of *White Masculinity* in Arthur Schnitzler's *Andreas Thameyers letzter Brief* (1900),' *The German Quarterly* 84 (1): 80–96, 81.
61 Bourdieu, *Language and Symbolic Power*, 122.
62 Schnitzler, 'Andreas Thameyer's Last Letter,' 122.

were. Würde ich das nicht tun, wer weiß, ob die Leute nicht in ihrer Erbärmlichkeit nicht endlich noch sagten: er hat sich umgebracht, weil seine Frau ihn betrogen hat' (AT519) (But I have written this all down, for I want it to be perfectly clear to the world. If I did not do it, who knows but that people in their wickedness would say: 'He killed himself because his wife deceived him').[63] In this way, the suicide becomes a performative act which is supposed to constitute a reality, while the letter is an attempt at regulating the most obvious interpretation of the suicidal act. Of course, the mere existence of the letter is evidence of the failure of this performance: if a performative act needs further explaining it has missed its goal. Interestingly, the same can be said about art. If an artist needs to provide a manual on how the artwork has to be read, one would probably assume that the latter has failed, at least in the sense of bringing across the authorial intention. The fact that *Andreas Thameyers letzter Brief* is told without any narrative frame can therefore be understood as implicit aesthetic comment that the letter – in the form of a literary text – does indeed speak for itself.[64] Thameyer's complaint that people are too stupid to understand his inner motives becomes confuted in the way that the text practically deconstructs itself before the reader's eyes, laying open Thameyer's real fears behind the official reasons for his suicide. As readers of the novella we are able to interpret Thameyer's motivations and thus can at least try to look into his 'inner self'.

Thameyer's letter displays his struggle for agency and against the experience of loss of control. It is striking that his attempts at re-establishing his wife's, and so his own, honour have a pointedly performative and theatrical character: 'Daher frage ich laut: (ich gebrauche diesen Ausdruck absichtlich, obwohl dies schriftliche Aufzeichnungen sind) – ich frage mit vernehmlicher Stimme: Was soll ich tun? Was bleibt mir übrig?' (AT517) (Therefore, I asked [sic, present tense in the original German] out loud (I use this expression on purpose) – I asked

---

63   Schnitzler, 'Andreas Thameyer's Last Letter,' 199.
64   As one can see in the unpuplished drafts, Schnitzler had at first added, similar to the ending of *Die Weissagung*, the note of a fictional editor, which explains that the letter was found in the pocket of a young man, who had hung himself in the Wienerwald (CUL A 153, 3, pp. 42 and 43). See also Aurnhammer, *Arthur Schnitzlers intertextuelles Erzählen*, 109. The fact that this topical generic marker of the literary letter has been left out in the final published version may support my interpretation that the letter is indeed supposed to speak for itself. Moreover, as I have argued elsewhere, it is significant that Thameyer's suicide itself is not confirmed for the reader, as it gives the narrator an un-dead – and therefore hauntingly ghostlike – quality. See Kolkenbrock, Marie (2018), 'Gothic Infections: Arthur Schnitzler and the Haunted Culture of Modernism,' *MLR* 113 (1): 150–170, 162.

in an audible voice: 'What shall I do? What is there left for me?').[65] With this emphasis on vocal articulation, Thameyer seems to adopt the position of the righteous Christian man who will not give up his stance even at the cost of his own life. It is certainly not coincidental that he mentions Martin Luther as one of his warrantors: the stylistic phrasing of his pseudo-rhetorical questions is reminiscent of proverbial utterance attributed to the latter: 'Hier stehe ich und kann nicht anders, Gott helfe mir, Amen' (Here I stand. I cannot do otherwise. Amen). In this way, Thameyer invokes a higher power by creating, as it were, a *mise en scène* of destiny. He inscribes himself into the tradition of white Christian masculinity, culminating in an act of self-sacrifice, which evokes, of course, the passion of Christ. Boehringer also claims that 'Thameyer performs a final act of masculinity: he utilizes self-sacrifice, the ultimate discursive formulation of maleness, to prove his own manhood'.[66]

While this is certainly a convincing interpretation of Thameyer's intention, I would suggest that the gendering of the sacrificial suicide is already less unequivocal than it might seem. As Elisabeth Bronfen demonstrates, there is a long tradition in cultural representations of female (self-)sacrifice for the sake of the re-establishment of the patriarchal order.[67] In this way, we could say that even the suicidal act as alleged 'seal' for Thameyer's assertions of masculinity is ambivalent in its gendered coding. If Thameyer's suicide can function as a reaffirmation of masculinity, it is as a general concept, but not for this male subject himself: the child is not only proof of his wife's transgression, but also a sign of his emasculation. His position as representative of the bourgeois male norm is not compatible with a Black child. Since he is no longer able to fulfil the requirements of an ostensibly superior white bourgeois masculinity, his annihilation protects the norm, but evidently not his own status within it.

For Thameyer himself, it appears that the theatrical performance of bourgeois masculinity suffices – barely – to secure his escape from the no longer bearable confrontation with the requirements of the bourgeois norm and his own insufficiency. While the transgression of the

---

65 Schnitzler, 'Andreas Thameyer's Last Letter,' 115.
66 Boehringer, 'Fantasies of *White Masculinity* in Arthur Schnitzler's *Andreas Thameyers letzter Brief* (1900),' 82.
67 See also my reading of *Traumnovelle* in Chapter Five, where Bronfen's argument will become interesting for the interpretation of the function of the dead female body in the text. Bronfen, Elisabeth (1992), *Over Her Dead Body: Death, Femininity and the Aesthetic*, Manchester: Manchester University Press, 181–204.

norm in his own family is the reason for the social shame he has to face, he then uses the same social structures to get the threat to his family's reputation back under control. Although his suicide does not prove any of his unconvincing arguments for his wife's faithfulness, he might be right in one point, at least to some extent: 'denn wenn ich tot bin, werdet ihr meine Frau nicht mehr verhöhnen und werdet über mich nicht lachen' (AT519) (for when I am dead you will not scoff at my wife, and you will not laugh about me).[68] The social code which forbids speaking ill of the dead might indeed rein in the worst of the gossip. It will, of course, not change what people think about Thameyer's fatherhood, but this seems to matter less, as long as the public shaming comes to an end. In this way, the text demonstrates how the social conventions, which are (no longer) apt to provide stability or reassure the individual of their secured status, nevertheless reproduce themselves through the subject.[69] Therefore, his social destiny becomes a compulsive performance that is supposed to culminate in his own annihilation.[70]

The fact that Thameyer's coping with the threatening de-legitimization of his social status does not explicitly involve the invocation of his individual metaphysical destiny may be linked to his slightly less privileged position. As a bank accountant, his social status may be described as slightly lower than the noblemen and upper-middle-class bureaucrats, doctors, and businessmen in the other prose texts. The idea of being destined for something special is a feeling of entitlement that the other characters easily accept and pursue, but it does not even occur to the less privileged Thameyer. His need to be normal is clearly much stronger than his need to be 'special'. In want of a metaphysical higher power, he has to cling to his social destiny and to the knowledge systems that defend his legitimacy in the realm of the norm by reinforcing stereotypical ideas of racial and sexual difference.

---

68 Schnitzler, 'Andreas Thameyer's Last Letter,' 120.
69 Although Meyer is obviously right when she mentions that the body of the child remains a visible disruption of the semiotic system of white bourgeois constructions of identity and enforces a continuing reflection on the foundation of bourgeois life which has been previously considered as unquestionable. See Meyer, *Männlichkeit und Melodram*, 102.
70 Schnitzler describes a similar process in his novella *Spiel im Morgengrauen* (Game at Dawn, 1927). See also Thomé, Horst (1984), 'Kernlosigkeit und Pose: Zur Rekonstruktion von Schnitzlers Psychologie,' *Fin de Siècle: Zur Naturwissenschaft und Literatur der Jahrhundertwende im deutsch-skandinavischen Kontext*, ed. by Klaus Bohnen, Uffe Hansen, and Friedrich Schmöe, Kopenhagen and Munich: Fink, 62–87, 75–76.

Biological Difference and the Stereotypes of 'Otherness'

Instead of seeking solace from a priest, Thameyer turns to his family doctor, who indeed provides a form of superficial comfort through the studies of Welsenburg and Preuss and the theory of maternal impression. Thameyer tries to negate the possibility of an active female eroticism, which would accord his wife a sexual desire independent of him, through this theory of maternal impression. This, however, must fail, as the theory implies that the woman's gaze becomes an active force, which seems to overpower the male role in the process of reproduction.[71] Moreover, in Thameyer's case, the theory does only negate the actual intercourse between his wife and another man, but not the overpowering effect of the mere presence of the Black men. Thameyer's description of the 'Riesenmenschen mit den glühenden Augen und den großen schwarzen Bärten' (AT519) (giants with glowing eyes and long black beards)[72] barely hides the fear of a superior Black potency, which corresponds to the stereotype of 'the black as the icon of sexuality' in Schnitzler's time.[73] In fact, this stereotype can also be found as early as in Lavater's physiognomic fragments which I have discussed in the first chapter of this book. In Lavater's study, the Black man is attributed 'einem sonderbaren Gemische stumpfer Tierheit im intellektuellen, und Stärke der Leidenschaften im physischen Sinn' ('a curious mix of animality in the intellectual and powerful passions in the physical sphere').[74] This racist narrative clearly influences Thameyer's ideas of Blackness.

Thameyer's own deficient masculinity is thus contrasted with, and further threatened by, the stereotype of Black vitalistic sexuality.[75] Disguised as a less fatal representation in contrast to purely pejorative depictions of Blackness, this stereotype is nevertheless based on the assumption of a fundamental biological difference and banishes the Black, by virtue of mystification, from the realm of the norm into that of the 'other'. Gilman writes: 'Fin-de-siècle Austrian liberalism trained

---

71 See Meyer, *Männlichkeit und Melodram*, 91; Aurnhammer shows in some detail that Thameyer's account ignores the aspect of active female sexuality raised in the very sources (e.g. in Malebranche) he uses to construct his argument, which indicates Thameyer's repression of female eroticism. See *Aurnhammer, Arthur Schnitzlers intertextuelles Erzählen*, 123.

72 Schnitzler, 'Andreas Thameyer's Last Letter,' 118.

73 Gilman, *Difference and Pathology*, 120; Boehringer, 'Fantasies of White Masculinity in Arthur Schnitzler's *Andreas Thameyers letzter Brief* (1900),' 92.

74 Lavater, Caspar David (1968–1969), *Physiognomische Fragmente zur Beförderung der Menschnekenntnis und Menschenliebe: Eine Auswahl mit 101 Abbildungen IV*, Zurich: Orell Fussli, 320.

75 Since his marriage has remained childless for four years, the possibility of Thameyer's impotence can be considered. See Meyer, *Männlichkeit und Melodram*, 98.

its attention on the black as possessing an alternative, perhaps even utopian, human sexuality. The sense of difference dominates this discourse, as it does the discourse of other writers, writers whose view of human nature stresses biology and downplays culture'.[76]

We encounter here once again the ambivalent function of the 'other': the threat as well as the lure of difference. The liberal idealization of Black sexuality also relies on the assumption of a fundamental – and, in fact, biological – difference, just as much as the conservative more openly pejorative stereotypes of Blackness. Like the interplay of anti-Semitic stereotypes and scientific explorations of the so-called 'biology of the Jew' (discussed in the previous section of this chapter), this cementation of biological racial difference in the stereotype of Blackness provides another example of the functionalization – or, following Louis Althusser, 'exploitation' – of science for the manifestation of power structures.[77] Moreover, besides the assumption of a heightened and more potent sexuality, the stereotype of Blackness also contained, like that of the Jew, the higher risk of mental illness, which, in contrast to the idea of the more alive, more natural Black, enforced the ambivalent notion of the seductive and at the same time dangerous 'other'.

This is brought into sharper relief when one considers that in Weininger's notoriously racist and sexist work *Geschlecht und Charakter* (Sex and Character), maternal impression is paralleled with a related phenomenon, which he calls 'Infektion' (infection).[78] According to him, women who in the past had had intercourse with a Black man could

---

76 Gilman, *Difference and Pathology*, 120.
77 Althusser claims that ideology has the tendency to exploit science for the cementation of given power relations. See Althusser, Louis (1990b), *Philosophy and the Spontaneous Philosophy of the Scientists & Other Essays*, London, New York: Verso, 120.
78 Weininger, Otto (1903), Geschlecht und Charakter: Eine prinzipielle Untersuchung, Vienna and Leipzig: Wilhelm Braunmüller, 308. This connection to Weininger has also been made by Meyer and Aurnhammer. See Meyer, *Männlichkeit und Melodram*, 101; Aurhhammer, *Arthur Schnitzlers intertextuelles Erzählen*, 130. Aurnhammer provides a stimulating reading of the novella's genealogy and literary and cultural-historical intertexts: by comparing Thameyer's sources and the way he uses them to construct the argument of his wife's fidelity, Aurnhammer shows how much Thameyer struggles to even convince himself of his own narrative. Although Aurnhammer's own analysis critically reveals Thameyer's racist perspective, I find it problematic that he reproduces this perspective without necessity, by using its terminology outside of direct quotations. See Aurnhammer *Arthur Schnitzlers intertextuelles Erzählen*, 118, 119, 125, 129.

become permanently infected and would from then on give birth to Black children, even if the actual father was white.[79] In their introduction to the anthology *Bakteriologie und Moderne* (Bacteriology and Modernism), the editors Philipp Sarasin, Silvia Berger, Marianne Hänseler, and Myriam Spörri stress the central role of bacteriology for the rhetoric of discourses concerned with setting boundaries between self and 'other', such as colonialist and anti-Semitic discourses, but also discourses on class and gender.[80] The idea of a healthy body of the norm (e.g. 'Volkskörper', i.e. the 'body' of the nation) that had to be protected from the 'invasion' of germs and parasites was a very common image here. The idea of an infectious Blackness in particular corresponds on the one hand to the paranoia of colonialist Europeans. Ironically, the 'colonized was perceived as invader', as Donna Haraway has pointed out: 'the "coloured" body of the colonized was constructed as the dark source of infection, pollution, disorder, and so on, that threatened to overwhelm white manhood (cities, civilization, the family, the white personal body)'.[81] On the other hand, the fear of becoming infected with 'otherness' also resonates with the unsettling effects of the new scientific discoveries in the field of germ theory at the time. In her study *Membranes: Metaphors of Invasion in Nineteenth Century Literature, Science, and Politics*, Laura Otis shows how the discovery of infectious microbes as cause for illness in the late nineteenth century revealed 'the arbitrariness of social boundaries and the meaninglessness of social differences in the light of biological sameness', as the pathogens could cross all socially constructed borders and infect individuals from all social classes and ethnic backgrounds.[82] At the same time, Otis reveals how much the concept of identity around 1900 relies precisely on the ability to draw boundaries, which, as we have seen, is further supported by the scientific discourses of the time.[83] The transgressive quality and the invisibility of germs are linked to an imagination of boundaries, of their potential permeability, and of the need to defend them. The transgression of Thameyer's wife and the unknown father of the child have a similar effect with regard to social boundaries: it highlights biological sameness rather than difference and therefore constitutes the permeability of these boundaries.

---

79 See Weininger, *Geschlecht und Charakter*, 307–308.
80 See Sarasin, Philipp, Silvia Berger, Marianne Hänseler, and Myriam Spörri (eds) (2007), *Bakteriologie und Moderne: Studien zur Biopolitik des Unsichtbaren 1870-1920*, Frankfurt a. M.: Suhrkamp, 38–39.
81 Haraway, Donna (1991), *Simions, Cyborgs, and Women: The Reinvention of Nature*, New York: Routledge, 223.
82 Otis, Laura (1999), *Membranes: Metaphors of Invasion in Nineteenth Century Literature, Science, and Politics*, Baltimore and London: The Johns Hopkins University Press, 119.
83 See Otis, *Membranes*, 4–5.

Blurred Boundaries and the Horror of 'Otherness'

This potential alliance between two forms of 'otherness', Black masculinity and white femininity, is threatening for Thameyer, as it makes
his own status as representative of the white masculine norm precari-
ously expendable. The text illustrates Thameyer's overwhelming fear
of the Black men with aesthetic devices, which are once more borrowed
from the *Schauerromantik* (Dark Romanticism). Thameyer's terror
becomes fully apparent in his description of his wife's allegedly traumatic encounter with the Black men. No fewer than three times on the
same page he mentions the 'Grauen' (horror, AT518) which she must
have felt, 'als sie im August mit ihrer Schwester im Tiergarten war, wo
diese fremden Leute ihr Lager hatten, diese unheimlichen Schwarzen'
(AT517) (when she was with her sister in the Tiergarten last August
where those miserable [rather: uncanny, M.K.] blacks had their encamp-
ment).[84] However, it is clearly Thameyer's own fear that becomes evident in his account of the events:

> Hier füge ich bei, daß ich selbst diese Leute später gesehen habe
> [...] im September [...]. Anna wollte durchaus nicht mit, ein
> solches Grauen war ihr zuückgeblieben seit jenem Mittwoch. Sie
> sagte mir, niemals in ihrem Leben habe sie ein solches Grauen
> empfunden als an dem Abend, da sie allein bei den Negern war
> ... (AT518)
> And here let me add that I myself saw these people later [...]
> in September [...]. Anna absolutely refused to go, as she still
> shuddered [Grauen, M.K.] whenever she thought of that
> Wednesday. She told me that never in her life had she felt such
> a fear [Grauen, M.K.] as when she found herself on that evening
> alone with the blacks ...[85]

Here again the sensation of *Grauen* (horror) marks a feeling in which
the boundaries that secure the perception of social reality, of norm
and 'other', appear to dissolve. Thameyer feels *Grauen* (horror) at his
lack of words, at something that cannot be expressed except for the
repeated label of *Grauen* (horror). Again, the *Grauen* (horror) marks
a moment of *Entsetzen* (horror), which may also here subtly refer to
the experience of being deposed or deposited, thrown from one's
position.[86]

---

84 Schnitzler, 'Andreas Thameyer's Last Letter,' 115.
85 Schnitzler, 'Andreas Thameyer's Last Letter,' 117.
86 See Santner, Eric L. (2011), *The Royal Remains: The People's Two Bodies and the End-
    games of Sovereignty*, Chicago: University of Chicago Press, 49.

Thameyer's description of the setting in which his wife's encounter took place is surprisingly detailed, considering the fact that he was
not there himself. Moreover, the language becomes suddenly almost
poetic:

> Es war ein nebliger Abend, wie sie im Spätsommer zuweilen
> vorkommen; ich für meinen Teil gehe abends nie ohne Überrock
> in den Prater … ich erinnere mich, daß da auf den Wiesen oft
> graue Dämpfe liegen, in denen sich die Lichter spiegeln … Nun,
> solch ein Abend war es an jenem Mittwoch, und Fritzi [the sister]
> war plötzlich fort, und meine Anna war allein – mit einem Male
> allein … wer begreift nicht, daß sie unter diesen Umständen
> ein ungeheures Grauen vor diesen Riesenmenschen mit den
> glühenden Augen und großen schwarzen Bärten empfinden
> mußte? (AT519)
> It was a foggy evening, as one often finds in the late summer;
> I for my part never go to the Prater in the evening without an
> overcoat … for I remember that there are often gray mists rolling
> over the fields … Well, Wednesday was that sort of an evening,
> and Fritzi was suddenly gone, and my Anna was alone – all at
> once alone … Who cannot conceive what a terrible fear [Grauen,
> M.K.] she must have had to find herself among these giants with
> their glowing eyes and long black beards![87]

No longer just a subjective sensation of Thameyer's wife, the *Grauen*
(horror) seems already inherent in the grey mists ('*graue* Dämpfe') lying
on the lawn.[88] In this way it becomes uncontrollably transgressive: in
its non-corporeal quality it cannot be banished or fought, but can cross
any boundary, even enter the body by way of mouth and lungs. This
seems to evoke the idea of a miasmatic infection, which was part of the
bacteriological discourse and thought to bring diseases such as typhus,
diphtheria, cholera, or tuberculosis.[89] The grey steam takes on a ghost-
like quality, which gives the scene, complete with will-o'-wisps, the
atmosphere of a Romantic *Schauernovelle* (shudder novella) or, indeed,
a Gothic novel.

---

87 Schnitzler, 'Andreas Thameyer's Last Letter,' 118.
88 See also Freud's wordplay with *Grauen* (horror) in *Die Traumdeutung*. Freud,
    Sigmund (1942), 'Die Traumdeutung,' in *Gesammelte Werke*, vols 2 and 3: *Die
    Traumdeutung/Über den Traum*, ed. by Anna Freud, Edward Bibring, Willi Hoffer,
    Ernst Kris, and Otto Isakower, London: Imago, 1–642, 481.
89 See Sarasin, Phillip (2007), 'Die Visualisierung des Feindes: Über metaphorische
    Technologien der frühen Bakteriologie,' *Bakteriologie und Moderne: Studien zur
    Biopolitik des Unsichtbaren 1870–1920*, ed. by Philipp Sarasin, Silvia Berger, Mari-
    anne Hänseler, and Myriam Spörri, Frankfurt a. M.: Suhrkamp, 427–461, 28.

In their respective introductory essays to the volume *Popular Reve-nants* (2012), Andrew Cusack (1–9) and Barry Murnane (10–43) describe the Gothic as a mode of literary writing, rather than as a distinct genre of a certain time period. This allows the authors to define the genres of the *Schauerroman* (shudder novel) and the literature of the *Schauerro-mantik* (Dark Romanticism), but also certain texts of the Realist period as forms of the German Gothic. As the Gothic imaginary experiences a sort of revival in many literary works around 1900,[90] *Thameyers let-zer Brief* seems to respond ironically to these modern forms of Gothic fiction. Not only can the colour grey be counted as a typical element of *Schauerromantik*, but the motif of steam, fog, or smoke as an uncanny medium of transgression of the evil 'other' is also a recurring motif of Gothic fiction.[91]

Particularly Bram Stoker's *Dracula* may function as a source of inspira-tion in Thameyer's imagination of Blackness. We might compare, for exam-ple, the passage in which Thameyer imagines his wife's encounter with the Black men in the park with that in *Dracula* when the vampire gains access to Mina's bedroom in the form of a foggy steam-like substance:

> The gaslight which I had left lit for Jonathan, but turned down, came only like a tiny red spark through the fog, which had evidently grown thicker and poured into the room. Then it occurred to me that I had shut the window before I had come to bed. I would have got out to make certain on the point, but some leaden lethargy seemed to chain my limbs and even my will. I lay still and endured, that was all. I closed my eyes, but could still see through my eyelids. [...] The mist grew thicker and thicker and I could see now how it came in, for I could see it like smoke, or with the white energy of boiling water, pouring in, not through the window, but through the joinings of the door. It got thicker and thicker, till it seemed as if it became concentrated into a sort of pillar of cloud in the room, through the top of which I could see the light of the gas shining like a red eye.[92]

---

90   See Murnane, Barry (2012), 'Haunting (Literary) History: An Introduction to German Gothic,' *Popular Revenants: The German Gothic and Its International Recep-tion, 1800–2000*, ed. by Andrew Cusack and Barry Murnane, Rochester, NY: Camden House, 10–43, 23.

91   See for example E. T. A. Hoffmann's *Der Sandmann* (1816), in which the colour grey is evidently linked to the uncanny figure of Coppelius or the grey man in Adelbert von Chamisso's *Peter Schlemihl* (1813). The fog as a marker of danger and horror also appears in Edgar Allen Poe's *The Narrative of Arthur Gordon Pym of Nantucket* (1838).

92   Stoker, Bram (2011), *Dracula*, ed. by Roger Luckhurst, Oxford: Oxford University Press, 241–242.

We find all the properties from the *Dracula* passage – fog, dim lights and even the uncanny glowing eye – in Thameyer's imagination of the scene in the park.[93] While it may go too far to suggest Stoker's novel as an unequivocal intertext here, the parallels nevertheless reveal the stereotypical cultural sources that inform Thameyer's perception of 'otherness'. In this way, the text demonstrates the fictional quality and the narrative character of the stereotypes that function as cognitive ordering tools in Thameyer's perception.

Thameyer's account of the events thus Gothicizes the Black men and makes them appear as vampire-like creatures. Moreover, the big black beards that Thameyer observes on the men in the park seem more likely to be attributes of Eastern-European Jews. The possibility that Thameyer may here be conflating the two types of 'otherness', Blackness and Jewishness, supports the co-reading with *Dracula*: as several scholars have pointed out, the figure of Dracula bears many characteristics of the stereotype of Eastern-European Jewry.[94] Moreover, the correlation of infectious diseases with migration movements from the East (caused, for example, by the expansion of trade or anti-Semitic pogroms) was one of the most common theories at the time.[95] This fear of infection with 'otherness' is also taken up in *Dracula*, when van Helsing tells Mina: 'He have [sic] infect you oh, forgive me, my dear'.[96] And in *Nosferatu: Eine Symphonie des Grauens* (1922), F. W. Murnau's film adaptation of Stoker's novel, the vampire is even explicitly a carrier of the plague. RecallingWeininger's contextualization of the phenomenon of maternal impression with that of 'Infektion' (infection), the interpretation that Schnitzler's text plays with similar elements of the cultural imaginary as Stoker's novel becomes plausible.

---

93 See also the passage in which Mina surprises Dracula as he feeds on Lucy, which, in addition to the gleaming eyes also seems to give a connotation to the 'long black beards' of the Ashanti: '[t]here was undoubtedly something, long and black, bending over the half-reclining white figure. I called in fright, "Lucy! Lucy!" and something raised a head, and from where I was I could see a white face and red, gleaming eyes'. See Stoker, *Dracula*, 241–242.

94 See the overview on 'Vampires and Anti-Semitism' in Gelder, Ken (1994), *Reading the Vampire*, London & New York: Routledge, 13–17.

95 Through Arthur Schnitzler's own medical practice, he was of course aware of these discourses. Schnitzler, Arthur (1988), *Medizinische Schriften*, ed. by Horst Thomé, Vienna: Zsolnay, 282. Particularly his survey of medical daily news and notes ('Tagesnachrichten und Notizen'), which includes two entries concerned with the cholera epidemic, is particularly interesting. Schnitzler cites here from a decree by the Austrian Prime Minister addressed to the Galician governor. Galicia is asked to act as a 'Schutzwall' (protective barrier) against the threat coming from the North-East in order to prevent the 'Eindringen' (invasion) of the illness into Austria. On this kind of militarist metaphor in the language of bacteriology, see Sarasin, 'Die Visualisierung des Feindes,' 459.

96 Stoker, *Dracula*, 299.

The mystification of the Black man as vampire allows Thameyer to see his wife in the same innocent light as the virtuous Mina in Stoker's novel. However, in light of the highly sexual connotations in the *Dracula* passage, Mina's character is much more ambivalent than it first might seem: she is certainly unconsciously corrupted by the virile force of Dracula, while her fiancé Jonathan is left significantly emasculated by his encounter with the vampire.[97] Thus, the threat of the infectious evil other is not fully contained and persists even after the assumed victory of day over night at the end of the novel. Therefore, not even this utter demonization of the Black men is able to provide Thameyer with the complete reassurance of his wife's faithfulness.

The function of the play with Gothic elements in Schnitzler's text corresponds to Eve Kosovsky Sedgwick's suggestion that 'articulations of male paranoia' are typical properties in Gothic fiction.[98] While Kosofsky Sedgwick refers here in particular to the heterosexual male's homophobic fear of detecting homosexual desires within himself, one may extend this observation: as any norm is defined by its excluded 'other', the norm's integrity depends on clearly drawn demarcating lines that divide self from other. Reinforced by the idea of a sexual and racial biological difference, Thameyer's cognitive ordering tools, stereotypes of Blackness and femininity, promise such a clear line of demarcation. However, by dint of the skin colour of his child, Thameyer is confronted with the transgressability of these boundaries. Thameyer's attempts at finding clarity in so-called scientific works give way to the overwhelming sensation of an unspecified horror (*Grauen*) of a strikingly literary quality. Moreover, the Gothic elements in the novella also have a meta-fictional function: they interrupt the realist narrative flow of the text and in this way could be called a form of generic infection. As Halberstam has argued, 'Gothic is the disruption of realism and of all generic purity'.[99] Thameyer's attempt to draw clear lines of demarcation between self and 'other' is thus also undermined on the generic level of the text.

For Thameyer, this permeation – or 'infection' – with 'otherness' is tantamount to 'social death'. Thameyer's proclamation of the 'necessity' of his suicide does after all reflect a reality: after the persistently visible transgression of his wife, it is impossible for him to continue existing within the limits assigned to him by his 'social destiny' as

---

97   See Kittler, Friedrich A. (1993), *Draculas Vermächtnis: Technische Schriften*, Leipzig: Reclam, 27.
98   Sedgwick, Eve Kosofsky (1985), *Between Men: English Literature and Male Homosocial Desire*, New York: Columbia University Press, 97.
99   Halberstam, Judith (1995), *Skin Shows: Gothic Horrors and the Technology of Monsters*, Durham and London: Duke UP, 11.

representative of the bourgeois male and white norm. As the analysis in this chapter has shown, his suicide can be seen as a realization of the 'fatal' force of 'social destinies' described by Bourdieu.[100]

Peter Schnyder concludes in his reading of Schnitzler's text that as well as arguably ridiculing the theory of maternal impression, the text could also be read by supporters of the hypothesis as a criticism of the petty bourgeois gossip from which Thameyer suffers. He writes, 'Schnitzler selbst hat nicht zuletzt durch den Verzicht auf jeden auk-torialen Kommentar offen gelassen, welche Lesart er selbst favorisiert hätte' (Not least by omitting any form of authorial commentary, Schnit-zler himself has left it open, which of the two readings he himself would have preferred).[101] However, since the theory had already been scien-tifically falsified around 1900, Aurnhammer's interpretation is more convincing that the text has to be understood as a parodic criticism of attempts to re-establish it – like those of Preuss and Welsenburg's.[102] Moreover, I find it difficult to detect any signals in the text that would allow an interpretation in favour of the theory of maternal impression. Rather, as I hope to have shown in my reading, Thameyer's case demon-strates that both the theory *and* the gossip stem from the same source: a rigid concept of the bourgeois norm of white masculinity, which the narrative calls into question. The theory of maternal impression is pre-sented in the text as part of a larger cultural knowledge system of pseu-do-scientific and socio-scientific theories which inform the stereotypical perception of biological difference. They therefore serve the idea of a clearly delineated norm that is, as it were, 'immune' against the infiltra-tion of 'otherness'. Schnitzler's text undermines this idea, not only on the level of content, but also on a stylistic level through the play with Gothic elements that usurp the realist narrative form of the text.

We have encountered this generic 'impurity' also in the text dis-cussed in the previous section of this chapter, *Die Weissagung* (The Prophecy). We have seen in both sections of this chapter that the pro-tagonists apply stereotypes of racial difference, in order to defend their legitimate position within the norm. However, both texts unsettle these stereotypes of 'otherness' by pointing up their constructed qual-ity. Both texts present the inescapability of social destinies and their mortal quality. While Umprecht's death appears like the result of the escapist invocation of his metaphysical destiny, Thameyer's emphasis on necessity, with which he repeatedly explains his suicide, invokes the higher power of social destiny. We will see in the next chapter how

---

100 Bourdieu, *Language and Symbolic Power*, 122.
101 Schnyder, 'Im Netz der Behausung,' 424.
102 See Aurnhammer, *Arthur Schnitzlers intertextuelles Erzählen*, 113.

the protagonist in *Die Fremde* constructs the necessity of his suicide as destiny in order to conceal the fact that it is actually rather an escapist decision.

Stereotypes are always clichés, but not all clichés are stereotypes.[103] Clichés are, by the same token, cognitive simplifications in the form of transfixed images of social reality that avoid reflection. While clichés, as a form of 'human expression (in words, emotions, gestures, acts)',[104] can have a reassuring effect of recognition, and understanding that *goes without saying*, they may also produce a sense of dissatisfaction. A phrase or image becomes a cliché because of its repetitive quality that empties out the original meaning. This sense of cliché may be linked to what has been said above about the feelings of repetition compulsion when the identification with one's social 'destiny' is weakened. The performances carried out to uphold one's social identity may then be experienced as a sort of cliché. Cave writes, '[t]he sense of cliché is the sense of being cheated, of being brought to a moment of fullness only to find that it is empty. It is also the sense of repetition, a compulsive returning to the "same" place, a place already known, as if one were discovering it for the first time'.[105] This sense of being 'cheated' evokes Freud's comment on *Die Weissagung* (The Prophecy) and his feeling of betrayal. Indeed, Freud seems to accuse Schnitzler of a sort of cheap narrative trick here: as a creative writer, he can always use the supernatural as a – one could say literal – *deus ex machina* in order to resolve the plot. It is thus seen as a disappointing reading experience in which the constructedness of literature emerges and the reader's absorption in the plot becomes disturbed. The same sense of cliché can be experienced when one becomes aware of narrative constructions that influence and engender social reality. This raises the desire for more 'original' and individualized experiences.

So far, the discussion here has mainly concerned repetitive performances required by the symbolic function, thus related to the 'professional' and more openly institutionalized aspects of social roles. If this symbolic function fails to address the subject, the desire for originality and individuality may be sought in social interactions outside the institutionalized realm of the social order. However, the emphatic evocation of one's destiny, which is supposed to bring reassurance about one's individuality, is no less pervaded by the repetition compulsion of stereotypical cultural narratives – clichés. Particularly, when individual

---

103 See Zijderveld, Anton C. (1987), 'On the Nature and Function of Clichés,' *Erstarrtes Denken: Studien zu Klischee, Stereotyp und Vorurteil in englischsprachiger Literatur*, ed. by Günther Blaicher, Tübingen: G. Narr, 26–40, 28.
104 Zijderveld, 'On the Nature and Function of Clichés,' 28.
105 Cave, *Recognitions: A Study in Poetics*, 459–460.

destiny is equated with the ultimate 'cosmic fate' of romantic love, the emphatic claims of originality may be undermined by their own serial quality. In the next chapter I will explore this tension between originality and seriality in the narratives *Die Fremde, Das Schicksal des Freiherrn von Leisenbohg,* and *Das neue Lied,* which complete the compilation *Dämmerseelen.*

Four Love as Destiny and Cliché in *Die Fremde* (The Stranger), *Das Schicksal des Freiherrn von Leisenbohg* (Baron Leisenbohg's Destiny) and *Das neue Lied* (The New Song)

Es ist immer wieder beschämend, in einem eigenen Erlebnis, dessen Einzigartigkeit man eben zu empfinden glaubte, das hundertmal Dagewesene, den typischen Kern zu erkennen.[1]

It is always embarrassing to recognize in your own experience a typical core, to recognize it as something that has happened a hundred times before, even though it felt unique and original just a moment ago.

Arthur Schnitzler

The idea of love as cosmic destiny predates modern concepts. As a passionate force sent from a cosmic power, it was thought to be disruptive in pre-modern societies: 'it uproots the individual from the mundane', writes Anthony Giddens, 'seen from the point of view of social order and duty it is dangerous'.[2] In the modern concept (since the late eighteenth century) of romantic love, this cosmic force of destiny does not stand in opposition to the force of social destinies and the order they

---

1 Schnitzler, Arthur (1985), *Aphorismen und Notate: Gedanken über Leben und Kunst*, Leipzig and Weimar: Gustav Kiepenheuer, 33f.
2 Giddens, Anthony (1992), *The Transformation of Intimacy: Sexuality, Love, and Eroticism in Modern Societies*, Oxford: Polity Press, 38. See also Luhmann, Niklas (1995), *Liebe als Passion*, Frankfurt a. M.: Suhrkamp, 96.

constitute. Romantic love is based on the idea that it has a complementing function through which 'the flawed individual is made whole'.[3] In this way, it has a stabilizing effect, which provides orientation and the sensation of an individually laid out path of life.[4] Romantic love can thus compensate for insecurities occurring in the social order and in this way it stabilizes not only the individual subjects, but also the dominant order in its entirety: when one feels less addressed by one's symbolic function for example, the individualizing reassurance of a romantic relationship may keep one in one's 'place', so to speak.[5] When love is institutionalized in the form of marriage, it itself becomes a symbolic function (one is 'pronounced' husband or wife by an institutional authority) and thus also takes on the form of a social destiny which is fully integrated into the bourgeois order. However, since the concept of romantic love incorporated elements of the *amour passion* (as opposed to the pre-modern concept of marriage not being based on love at all due to its disruptive qualities), there seems to remain the risk of 'deregulation', of love unfolding its dangerous, uprooting potential.[6] The construct of *amour fou* implies the possibility that love can become a road to 'otherness', bearing the same ambivalence of seduction and danger we have already encountered in the previous chapters.

The main focus of the chapter will lie on the narrative *Die Fremde* (The Stranger), which will be supplemented by readings of the shorter texts *Das Schicksal des Freiherrn von Leisenbohg* (Baron Leisenbohg's Destiny) and *Das neue Lied* (The New Song). All three narratives are concerned with the individualizing quality of love. In the first two narratives, love appears indeed as a deregulated force close to madness that is no longer containable within the boundaries of the norm. Through stereotypes of enigmatic femininity and the clichéd promise of love as an original experience, the protagonists seem to try to find an alternative to their social destiny in the Bourdieusian sense. As already shown in the previous chapters, particularly in *Flucht in die Finsternis* (Flight into Darkness), this mystification of 'otherness' as an alternative, more original way of existence is a dead end, however. Accordingly, both narratives end with the protagonist's demise, mediated by the mystifying work of stereotypes. In the third narrative, the protagonist is able to remain within the realm of the norm, although he too indulges in mystified stereotypes of 'otherness', but only at the expense of a socially inferior woman.

---

3   Giddens, *The Transformation of Intimacy*, 45.
4   On socio-structural conditions that determine the need for individualization through relationships, see Luhmann, *Liebe als Passion*, 15–17.
5   This is also hinted at in *Flucht in die Finsternis* (Flight into Darkness), when Robert gets engaged to Paula with the hope she might 'save' him.
6   See Giddens, *The Transformation of Intimacy*, 38.

Destiny and Stereotypes of Enigmatic Femininity in *Die Fremde* (The Stranger)

Originally published under the title *Dämmerseele* (Dozing Soul) in 1902 in the *Neue Freie Presse*, *Die Fremde* (The Stranger) seems to have inspired the title of the entire compilation volume. The new title under which it was integrated into the volume already introduces the topic of 'otherness' per se. On the face of it, it is a tale of enigmatic and dangerous femininity of which the male protagonist becomes the victim: Albert, a 'Vize-Sekretär' (vice-secretary) in a ministry, falls in love with Katharina, whom he perceives as an enigmatic, almost otherworldly creature. This, however, seems to rather increase his fascination with her and when the opportunity appears, he proposes to her. She agrees and they get married, but on the fourteenth day of their honeymoon, Katharina disappears, leaving behind only an ambiguous note in their hotel room in Innsbruck. This is the actual beginning of the novella, while everything that has happened before is told from Albert's perspective as he reminisces about his relationship with Katharina. It turns out that he had anticipated this moment and already decided to commit suicide when it arrived.

Before Albert meets Katharina in person, he hears rumours that attribute to her both mantic qualities and symptoms of insanity. We encounter here again the stereotype of the mentally ill as 'spiritually more refined'.[7] This gives way to the mystification of insanity as 'otherness', which is always ambivalent: Katharina seems at once fascinating and highly uncanny. It is a decisive property of stereotypes that they say more about the one who entertains them than those they speak about.[8] It is thus safe to assume that the narrative, which is told entirely from Albert's perspective (apart from very few comments from the authorial narrator), does not provide us with any reliable information about Katharina as an individual character, but is more telling about Albert whose perception of her is highly influenced by stereotypes.

Earlier critics have at least partly accepted Albert's perspective, by either emphasizing Katharina's mysteriousness,[9] which is not explained through an authorial narrator,[10] or even by blaming her for Albert's death because of her alleged 'schuldhaftes Versagen im

7 Sontag, Susan (1991), *Illness as Metaphor & AIDS and its Metaphors*, London: Penguin, 32.
8 See Zijderveld, Anton C. (1987), 'On the Nature and Function of Clichés,' *Erstarrtes Denken: Studien zu Klischee, Stereotyp und Vorurteil in englischsprachiger Literatur*, ed. by Günther Blaicher, Tübingen: G. Narr, 26–40, 27.
9 See Fliedl, Konstanze (2005), *Arthur Schnitzler*, Stuttgart: Reclam, 160.
10 See Just, Gottfried (1968), *Ironie und Sentimentalität in den erzählenden Dichtungen Arthur Schnitzlers*, Berlin: E. Schmidt, 116.

Sozialen' (culpable failure in inter-personal relationships).[11] Imke Meyer
is the first to point out that, by mainly adopting Albert's perspective,
the text is not concerned with rendering a clear picture of Katharina.
Instead, the main topic is how Albert constructs a patriarchal image
of femininity as an attempt to contain his own crisis of masculinity.[12]
Meyer emphasizes that Albert uses his object of desire, Katharina, both
to secure his self-image of masculinity and to escape his own mediocre
bourgeois identity. He is thus, like so many of Schnitzler's characters,
caught in the paradoxical situation of feeling the desire to transgress
the boundaries of the norm and yet to secure his position within them.
These attempts at self-reassurance, however, have to fail due to another
paradox that constitutes the entire endeavour: woman has to be the
'other' to man in order to mark a clear line of distinction that defines
man as self. However, this 'other' has to be domesticated in order to
contain the threat that absolute 'otherness' imposes on the norm. Yet
this domestication can never be complete, so that the 'other' retains
its liminal status in the bourgeois order.[13] The somewhat contradictory
urge to both transgress and secure the boundaries around the conception of 'self' within the norm is linked to a simultaneous demonization
and idealization of the 'other'. On the one hand, Albert perceives Katharina as the source of his downfall; on the other, he has to elevate her
in order to confirm the insurmountable gap between them, so that she
stays the inaccessible stranger he needs her to be.

The focus of my reading of *Die Fremde* (The Stranger) will fall on
how Albert uses the emphatic evocation of love as destiny to regain
a sense of individuality. Moreover, I will analyze how this very sense
of individuality is in turn undermined by a looming realization of the
seriality of experience, which is induced by the emergence of the cultural narratives that are at work in Albert's perceptions. These cultural
narratives draw upon literary material, particularly Romantic conceptions of femininity, love, and sexuality. I will only briefly sketch out
how Albert constructs Katharina as 'other' and uses this construction
of her to overcome his own bourgeois existence, in view of Meyer's
convincing discussion of these matters.

Social Destiny and Love as Cosmic Fate

Very early in the novella, it becomes clear that Albert feels restrained
by his social destiny in the Bourdieusian sense. Compared with *Flucht
in die Finsternis* (Flight into Darkness), there is less evidence about the

---

11   Gutt, Barbara (1978), *Emanzipation bei Arthur Schnitzler*, Berlin: Spiess, 70.
12   See Meyer, Imke (2010), *Männlichkeit und Melodram: Arthur Schnitzlers erzählende
      Schriften*, Würzburg: Königshausen & Neumann, 53.
13   See Meyer, *Männlichkeit und Melodram*, 47.

failure of the symbolic function to properly address the subject, which
would provide him with a secured and meaningful position within society. However, it is telling that once again, the protagonist, like Robert,
works in a ministry. His mediocrity is pointedly stressed in the description of his character, but also his paradoxical position that seems to be
at once secured but also devoid of meaning:

> Er hatte sein anständiges Auskommen und konnte als
> Junggeselle ein recht behagliches Leben führen, aber Reichtum
> hatte er von keiner Seite zu erwarten. Eine sichere, aber gewiß
> nicht bedeutende Laufbahn stand ihm bevor. Er kleidete sich
> mit großer Sorgfalt, ohne jemals wirklich elegant auszusehen, er
> redete nicht ohne Gewandtheit, hatte aber niemals irgend etwas
> Besonderes zu sagen, und er war stets gerne gesehen, ohne jemals
> aufzufallen. (F553)
> He had a decent salary and, as a bachelor, he could lead a rather
> comfortable life, but not in any way could he expect to become
> wealthy. A secured, but certainly not significant path was lying
> ahead of him. He dressed with great care, but without ever
> looking really elegant, he was articulate, but never had anything
> special to say, he was always well received by everyone, without
> really being noticed.

Albert's life seems to be laid out in front of him, without any possibility of individual self-realization. The security of his bourgeois existence
appears to be intertwined with a distinct feeling of constraint. At the
same time, Albert's position might be less secured than it initially seems.
The word 'Laufbahn' (path/track) evokes the topographical quality of
destiny, a journey with a 'destination', a train running on pre-determined tracks.[14] In this way, the text indicates that Albert is unable to
identify with his social role and as a consequence feels restricted by it.
The protagonist thus becomes aware of his heteronomy, which, as we
have seen in the last chapters, is already a sign of crisis. In contrast to
that, Katharina seems to be completely free of determination:

> Denn wenn sie über die Zukunft redete, so tat sie das nicht
> wie jemand, dem ein vorgezeichneter Weg ins Weite weist;
> vielmehr schien ihr alle Möglichkeiten nach wie vor offen zu
> stehen, und nichts in ihrem Verhalten deutete auf innere oder
> äußere Gebundenheit. So wußte Albert eines Tages, daß ihm ein

---

14 See also the traintrack scenes in *Flucht in die Finsternis* (Flight into Darkness)
    and *Die Weissagung* (The Prophecy) discussed in Chapters Two and Three in this
    book.

unsicheres und kurzes Glück bevorstand, daß aber auch alles, was folgen könnte, wenn Katharina ihm einmal entschwunden war, jeglicher Bedeutung für ihn entbehrte. Denn sein Dasein ohne sie war vollkommen undenkbar geworden, und es war sein fester Entschluß, einfach die Welt zu verlassen, sobald ihm Katharina verloren war. In dieser Sicherheit fand er den einzigen, aber würdigen Halt während dieser wirren und sehnsuchtsvollen Zeit. (F556)

When she talked about the future, she did not talk like someone who has a predetermined path ahead of them; rather, all the possibilities seemed to be still open for her, and nothing in her behaviour gave him the impression that she felt any form of commitment. Thus, Albert realized one day that he had an insecure and brief moment of happiness in front of him, but that everything which would come after the moment when he would have lost Katharina was completely irrelevant to him. Because his existence without her had become entirely inconceivable, and therefore it was his unwavering decision to just leave the world as soon as Katharina was lost to him. This security provided him with the only form of stability in this time full of confusion and longing.

In the same way as Marco Polo appeared to be less restricted than von Umprecht and the other members of his regiment, Albert imagines Katharina as enjoying a freedom that is denied to him. While Katharina's future appears to Albert to be free of restrictive determinations, it is precisely this indefiniteness of hers that gives Albert a fixed framework and a clear path of life. In this way, he uses her 'otherness' to make sense of his own 'destiny'. Without her, his path lies predictable in front of him, but does not give him a secured sense of legitimacy and individual identity. Katharina's freedom, attributed by Albert to her enigmatic personality, in fact seems to be linked to her lack of a symbolic function: as a fatherless, unmarried young woman known for problems with mental health, her position is precisely the opposite of the 'sichere Laufbahn' that Albert has to face. That her situation is a rather precarious one is ignored by Albert's perception of her as a creature as if from 'einer anderen Welt' (F553) (a different world).[15] Katharina seems to promise not only escape from the rigid structures of his social reality, but also access to something lying beyond these structures: 'Sie sprach nicht viel, und ihre Augen pflegten oft, wenn sie in Gesellschaft war, wie in eine für die anderen unzugängliche Ferne zu blicken' (F553) (She did not talk much, and when she was around other people, her eyes seemed to

---

15 See Meyer, *Männlichkeit und Melodram*, 62.

gaze into a distance which was inaccessible to the others). Albert's fascination for Katharina is closely linked to the idea of freedom and knowledge which he attributes to her 'otherness'. As we have already seen in
the last chapter, the idealized freedom of the 'other' is a result of being
excluded from the norm: Like Marco Polo, Katharina does not seem to
be obliged to follow any rules or conventions – social or logical – nor to
be confined to any predetermined destiny. The freedom of the 'other'
is thus exposed and contrasted to Albert's feeling of being completely
subjected to an unchangeable destiny. This in turn mirrors Umprecht's
feeling of being stuck in a military service without purpose.

Albert thus feels restricted by his social destiny, which is completely
independent of his relationship to Katharina. However, the emphatic
way in which he invokes his individual metaphysical destiny as insep-
arably linked to Katharina reveals its function as a coping mechanism.
We have already seen in the last chapters that the conventionalized
modes of conduct that the social destinies require can be seen as a threat
to the possibility of original experience and one's sense of individuality: if one's actions and patterns of behaviour and perception begin
to appear imposed by pre-formed, external structures, the longing for
alternative, individualized ways of existence becomes stronger. It is
one of the main properties of the concept of love that it provides such
an alternative: it can be seen as the individualizing currency par excellence.[16] Based on the idea of exclusivity and the uniqueness of each of
the two partners, it promises a realization of one's individual destiny
and an ongoing recognition of one's individual status and value. Moreover, it is conventionally seen as following a logic independent from
and thus alternative to that of reason, which seems to make it an ideal
escape from the demands of the post-enlightened order to prove oneself as an autonomous subject of reason – demands which, as we have
seen, appear increasingly impossible to fulfil. While – at least on the
conscious level – Robert in *Flucht in die Finsternis* (Flight into Darkness)
still fears becoming a 'slave of destiny', Albert practically embraces this
kind of slavery from the beginning: a 'slave of love' is equally a 'slave
of destiny', because love appears as 'cosmic fate'.

While, on the face of it, Albert proceeds with the performances
required by his bourgeois role – proposal, marriage, honeymoon – it
nevertheless becomes clear that his understanding of love is of a rather
pre-modern quality: instead of romance, the emphasis lies on passion,
which was said to pose a threat to the stability of the dominant order
by uprooting 'the individual from the mundane',[17] 'generating a break

---

16   See Luhmann, *Liebe als Passion*, 123–61, 222.
17   Giddens, *The Transformation of Intimacy*, 38.

with routine and duty'.[18] In this view, love is perceived as disruptive for the social order, as is expressed in Albert's musings: 'Er [...] begriff mit einem Male alle Gefahren und allen Wahnsinn, in die heftige Leidenschaft den besonnensten Mann zu stürzen vermag' (F553) (He suddenly understood that even the most level-headed man could be thrown into danger and insanity by deep passion.

Albert's identification with the bourgeois order is so weakened that the institutionalized form of individualization through love is not enough for him. He yearns for an experience that cannot be provided by a domesticated 'otherness' of sexual difference, but only by an encounter with a more radical form of 'otherness'. The love incorporated into the bourgeois order is no longer able to provide a satisfactory sense of individuality and originality of experience.[19] However, while he seeks this individuation in the relationship with Katharina, it turns out that he is highly dependent on cultural narratives of 'otherness' that are always products of the dominant order they define by virtue of their exclusion. The 'other' cannot be thought of without its relation to the norm. In this way, the text undermines Albert's 'narrative' of his individual 'destiny' as a product of pre-formed cultural fantasies. The text, as I will show in the next section, reveals Albert's construction of Katharina as the enigmatic 'other': a stereotype of femininity that seems to have a decisively literary and aesthetic quality. Albert thus seems to 'fictionalize' – and thus aestheticize – his own life in order to suspend the social reality around him. That this strikingly corresponds to the 'symptoms' of one of the most dominant literary movements of the Viennese *fin de siècle* should alert the reader: *Die Fremde* (The Stranger) can be read as an implicit critique of the Aestheticism of Viennese *décadence*.

Masochistic Courtly Love and the Suspense of Reality

Albert's infatuation with Katharina is highly literary in character. In the way that it depends on her constant inaccessibility, it takes on the form of courtly love: the insistence on Katharina's freedom, with the corresponding emphasis on his dependence on her, follows the logic of the servile knight's love for his lady. Correspondingly, Katharina appears in Albert's perspective as a higher being: 'Katharina trug sich immer einfach, aber ihre hohe Gestalt und ganz besonders ihre einzige, ja königliche Weise, das Haupt zu neigen, wenn sie jemandem

---

18   Giddens, *The Transformation of Intimacy*, 40.
19   This corresponds to Robert's memories of his married life in *Flucht in die Finsternis* (Flight into Darkness), but is also hinted at in von Umprecht's fantasy of leaving his wife and children, as we have seen in the last chapter. It may also be one explanation for Georg's inability to commit to Anna in *Der Weg ins Freie* (Road into the Open).

zuhörte, verlieh ihr eine Vornehmheit von ganz eigener Art' (F553) (Katharina's demeanour was always simple, but her tall figure and particularly the unique, even regal manner, in which she used to bow her head when listening to someone, gave her a completely unique elegance). Even after their wedding, Katharina has to stay out of reach for Albert to maintain this impossibility of their relationship, the quintessence of the knight's relationship to the lady. In his study *The Metastases of Enjoyment: On Women and Causality*, Slavoj Žižek points out that the Lady has to be someone 'with whom no relationship of empathy is possible'.[20] Katharina's apparent lack of empathy ('Vielleicht lag es daran, das Katharina diesen Dingen [his past and family history] nicht das geringste Interesse entgegen brachte' (F554–55) Maybe it was because Katharina showed not the slightest interest in these matters) and her behaviour that does not seem to follow any conventional or logical rules offer enough material for Albert to construct his image of her as such an incommensurable, sovereign being for whom he is 'zu jedem Opfer bereit' (F553) (ready to make any possible sacrifice).

Meyer also describes how Albert elevates Katharina, but without reference to the conventions of courtly love. Interestingly, however, she situates *Die Fremde* (The Stranger) within the discourse of femininity in the tradition of Sacher-Masoch's *Venus im Pelz*.[21] Žižek, in turn, points out how courtly love is rooted in masochism, 'a specific form of perversion articulated for the first time in the middle of the last century in the literary works and life-practice of Sacher-Masoch'.[22] The transformation of romantic love into 'perverted', often sado-masochistic forms, is typical for the literature of *décadence* around 1900, which is accompanied by an increasing demonization of femininity.[23] In her 1986 study, *Marmorbilder: Weiblichkeit und Tod bei Clemens Brentano und Hugo von Hofmannsthal*, Marlies Janz has analyzed the connection between the literature of German Romanticism and the *décadence* of 1900 with regard to imaginations of femininity.[24] In *Die Fremde* (The Stranger) this

---

20 Žižek, Slavoj (1994), *The Metastases of Enjoyment: On Women and Causality*, London, New York: Verso, 90.
21 See Meyer, *Männlichkeit und Melodram*, 60.
22 Žižek, *The Metastases of Enjoyment*, 91.
23 See Hilmes, Carola (1990), *Die Femme Fatale: ein Weiblichkeitstypus in der nachromantischen Literatur*, Stuttgart: Metzler, 15.
24 Marlies Janz shows for the examples of Brentano and Hofmannsthal that 'Erfahrung des Ich-Zerfalls und der Identitätsauflösung bei beiden Autoren aufs engste verknüpft ist mit Bildern einer mortifizierten Weiblichkeit' (for both writers, the experiences of ego dissociation and disintegration of identity are tightly linked to images that associate femininity and death). See Janz, Marlies (1986), *Marmorbilder: Weiblichkeit und Tod bei Clemens Brentano und Hugo von Hofmannsthal*, Königstein/Ts.: Athenaeum, 9.

connection is played out in Albert's attempt to suspend social reality through his relationship with Katharina.

Žižek stresses the theatrical aspect of masochism and the importance of the masochist's agency: 'It is the servant, therefore, who writes the screenplay [...]: he stages his own servitude'.[25] This seems to be what Albert does, when he inverts the relation of power and dependence between Katharina and himself: he ignores the fact that Katharina is in quite a precarious situation – a woman of poor means and without the protection of a male relative – and is thus actually dependent on a man like Albert to secure her social status through marriage. In other words, by staging Katharina's unavailability as well as his own dependence on her ('Aber je unfaßlicher ihm ihr Wesen zu entgleiten schien, umso hoffnungslos dringender rief seine Sehnsucht nach ihr' (F555) - However, the more her essence seemed to slip away from him, the more hopelessly urgent became his longing for her), Albert stages a theatrical, masochistic game that suspends the reality of the bourgeois order and its inherent power structures, in which Katharina does not come close to the privileged position he attributes to her.

What distinguishes Albert from the average masochist described by Žižek is his inability to keep this suspension of reality within the boundaries of a setting based on a contract or any other clear-cut frame which would mark the game as fictional. Normally, 'the surrealistic passionate masochistic game, which suspends social reality, none the less fits easily into that everyday social reality'.[26] It is thus not per se subversive but rather an institutionalized outlet that, by deflecting disruption into that contained space, in the end actually protects and thus confirms the social order. In Albert's case, the game soon begins to permeate every part of his life and leads to a permanent suspension of reality. However, since the game is rooted in the values of the same order it tries to suspend, it can also only lead to the annihilation of the subject. We thus encounter here the familiar fading of differences between reality and fiction, as well as between norm and 'other', with the attendant sensation of *Grauen* (horror).

At one point, Albert realizes that Katharina does not differentiate between life and art. When she sees the painting of a landscape in a gallery, she incorporates it into her memory:

Einmal besuchte sie mit Albert das Künstlerhaus und stand lang mit ihm vor einem Bild, das eine einsame grüne Höhenlandschaft mit weißen Wolken darüber vorstellte. Ein paar Tage darauf

---

25   Žižek, *The Metastases of Enjoyment*, 92.
26   Žižek, *The Metastases of Enjoyment*, 92.

sprach sie von dieser Gegend, als sei sie in Wirklichkeit über
die Höhen gewandelt, und zwar als Kind in Gesellschaft ihres
verstorbenen Bruders. (F555)
One time, she and Albert went to the art gallery, and she spent a
long time looking at a painting which depicted a mountainous
landscape with white clouds in the sky above. A few days later,
she talked about this landscape, as if she really had strolled
over these heights, when she was still a child together with her
deceased brother.

Significantly, Katharina's apparent access to the realm unreachable
for normal people seems to go hand in hand with the blurring of the
boundary between fact and fiction, or more precisely between social
and aesthetic space. Katharina constructs her childhood memory with
the help of the aesthetic image. In the same way as she incorporates the
painted landscape into her memory, she does not seem to distinguish
between real, imagined, or aesthetic experiences:

Doch alles, was sie berichtete, Erzählungen wirklicher
Geschehnisse und Geständnisse ferner Träumereien, schwebte
wie im gleichen matten Schimmer vorüber, so daß Albert nicht
wußte, was sich in ihrem Gedächtnis lebendiger eingeprägt:
jener Orgelspieler, der sich vom Kirchturm herabgestürzt hatte,
der junge Herzog von Modena, der einmal im Prater an ihr
vorübergeritten war, oder ein Van Dyckscher Jüngling, dessen
Bildnis sie als junges Mädchen in der Liechtenstein-Galerie
gesehen hatte. (F555)
But everything she talked about, stories about actual events or
confessions about distant daydreams, everything floated past
in the same soft shimmer, so that Albert could not know what
appeared more realistic in her memory: the organ player, who
had ended his life by jumping from a church tower, the young
count of Modena, who in the Prater had once ridden past her on
his horse, or the young man painted by Van Dyck, whose portrait
she had seen in the Lichtenstein Gallery when she had been a
young girl.

It is then that Albert realizes 'wie sich sein Staunen in ein schmerzliches
Grauen zu verwandeln begann' (F555) (how his wonder began to turn
into painful horror). This *Grauen* (horror) derives from the uncanny
dissolving of the boundaries that secure the social reality: the differences between inner and outer worlds, between aesthetics and reality,
are beginning to fade. Moreover, the sensation also refers uncannily,
in the Freudian sense, to something well known that should have

remained hidden. Katharina's practice of incorporating aesthetic experiences into her life can be seen as a perfect mirroring of Albert's own 'strategy': his construction of his dependent relationship with Katharina and her inaccessible 'otherness' is, after all, precisely that. The narrative he constructs, drawn from pre-existing cultural fictions, as will become clearer in the next section, starts to take over his existence, and his loss of control over it can only be glossed over by the final action that leads to his own death.

Romantic Imagery of Femininity and the State of Transition

In order to uphold his self-image as enlightened bourgeois subject, Albert attributes this fading of differences solely to Katharina, as if she had infected him with her 'otherness'. In fact, she appears to have an almost drug-like, sedating effect on him: 'Und da ihm jede Kraft gebrach, sie aus ihrer verschwommenen Art des Daseins emporzuziehen, fühlte er endlich, wie ihn der verwirrende Hauch ihres Wesens zu betäuben und wie sich allmählich seine Weise zu denken, ja selbst zu handeln, aller durch das tägliche Leben gegebenen Notwendigkeit zu entäußern begann' (F556) (And since he did not have the strength to pull her out of her fog-like existence, he finally felt how the confusing breath of her being began to sedate him and how his thinking and even his actions began to dispose of all quotidian responsibilities).

The use of terms associated with opiates and sedatives is striking, as well as Katharina's 'fog-like existence' as opposition to the necessities of everyday life, thus the bourgeois order. The pointedly poetic language in this passage highlights the fact that Albert's perception of Katharina and his imagination of her as his destiny is influenced by literary clichés of love and stereotypes of femininity.[27] As in *Die Weissagung* (The Prophecy), the narrative stages here several 'recognition scenes' for the reader through the use of motifs and imagery familiar from Romantic literature, but also from the contemporary literature of Aestheticism influenced by it.

The word 'emporziehen' (pull up) evokes the myth of the water spirit Undine, who, in the eponymous fairy-tale novella by the Romantic author Friedrich de la Motte Fouqué, causes the demise of her

---

27 A similar effect can also be observed in Schnitzler's *Das Tagebuch der Redegonda* (Redegonda's Diary) and, as we will see in the next section, *Das Schicksal des Freiherrn von Leisenbohg* (Baron Leisenbohg's Destiny). Both novellas also feature variations of courtly love, in terms of the man's undying admiration for an inaccessible woman, and in both cases the texts refer not only to their own fictionality, but also introduce characters who are so influenced by literary clichés and stereotypes that they are unable to emancipate themselves from them and finally fall victim to their own constructed narratives.

human husband. The association of femininity with narcotic effects is in turn highly reminiscent of Brentano's fusion of beauty and inebriation as a compensation for the dissociated self who rejects the bourgeois order. The dissolving boundaries of art and life also are a typical feature of Brentano's writings, or more precisely, the dissolution of the self in aesthetic experience.[28] This, in turn, is also one of the main features of Viennese Aestheticism at the fin de siècle. Schnitzler's text not only seems to bring out the Romantic inheritance of the writing practices of contemporary literary tendencies, but also to distance itself ironically from them. By revealing Albert's image of Katharina as a constructed one that not only fully depends on Albert's own perspective, but also on the influence of literary concepts of love and femininity, the text undermines Albert's claim that his individual metaphysical destiny is 'responsible' for the events.

Albert's aestheticization of his own life through Katharina and its deconstruction are pointedly revealed in the passage regarding their honeymoon:

Sie reisten miteinander ins Gebirge. Durch sommerliche Täler fuhren sie, die sich weiteten und engten; ergingen sich an den milden Ufern heiter bewegter Seen und wandelten auf verlorenen Wegen durch den raunenden Wald. An manchen Fenstern standen sie, schauten hinab zu den stillen Straßen verzauberter Städte, sandten die Blicke weiter den Lauf geheimnisvoller Flüsse entlang, zu stummen Bergen hin, über die blasse Wolken in Dunst zerflossen. (F556)

They went on a holiday in the mountains. They drove through summery valleys, which widened and narrowed; they walked by the soft shores of cheerful choppy lakes and strolled on lost paths through the murmuring woods. They would stand by different windows, looking down onto the quiet streets of enchanted towns, sent their gazes further along the course of mysterious rivers, over the silent mountains, where the pale clouds dissolved into mist.

In Katharina's presence, the obviously pleasant but not necessarily arcane experience of travelling through beautiful landscapes becomes overloaded with fairytale-like and mystic signifiers: lost paths, murmuring woods, enchanted towns, and enigmatic rivers. This other-worldly setting, however, is undermined by the following sentences, which bring the whole passage down to the rounded figure

---

28 See Janz, *Marmorbilder*, 72.

of a tourist brochure: 'Und sie redeten über die täglichen Dinge des Daseins wie andere junge Paare, spazierten Arm in Arm, verweilten vor Gebäuden und Schaufenstern, berieten sich, lächelten, stießen mit weingefüllten Gläsern an, sanken Wange an Wange in den Schlaf der Glücklichen' (F556–7) (And they talked about the everyday matters of life like other young couples, wandered around arm in arm, lingered by buildings and shop windows, had discussion, smiled, cheered with wine-filled glasses, happily fell asleep cheek to cheek).

The emphasis on their comparability to others ('wie andere junge Paare', like other young couples) and the descriptions of quite a mundane tourist trip seem at first to be continuous with the travels through an apparently magical landscape. Together they appear to draw the picture of a perfect honeymoon that is only overshadowed by Katharina's occasional outbursts of strangeness:

> Manchmal aber ließ sie ihn allein, in einem matthellen Gasthofzimmer, darin alle Trauer der Fremde dämmerte, auf einer steinernen Gartenbank unter Menschen, die sich des duftenden Blütentags freuten, in einem hohen Saal vor dem gedunkelten Bild eines Landsknechts oder einer Madonna, und niemals wußte er in solcher Stunde, ob Katharina wiederkehren würde oder nicht. (F557)
>
> But sometimes she left him alone, in a half-lit hotel room, in which the melancholy of foreignness began to dawn/doze, on a stony garden bench among people who enjoyed the fragrant blossoming day, in a hall with high ceilings in front of a darkened painting of a farm hand or a Madonna, and he never knew in these hours, whether Katharina would return to him or not.

While Katharina's behaviour seems to interrupt the unlimited happiness of their vacation, a closer look shows that the real interruption is in fact this short episode of normalcy, which threatens to destroy Albert's construction of a destiny meant to be fully determined by Katharina's otherness. That they indeed talk about the 'täglichen Dinge des Daseins' (everyday matters of life) stands in contrast to Albert's decision not to discuss his financial situation with Katharina, because 'er jede Aussprache über dergleichen Dinge für überflüssig hielt' (F556) (he thought any discussion about things like that unnecessary). Albert's claim is that 'der verwirrende Hauch ihres Wesens' (confusing breath of her being) is to blame, when he feels that 'sich allmählich seine Weise zu denken, ja selbst zu handeln, aller durch das tägliche Leben gegebenen Notwendigkeiten zu entäußern begann' (F556) (his thinking and even his actions began to dispose of all quotidian responsibilities). Should it turn out that Katharina is actually capable of normality, this construction of a higher necessity would crumble. Those cherished moments, in which he and Katharina cannot be distinguished from any other young couple, are only enjoyable to Albert as long as they are embedded in the mysterious framework of her underlying strangeness.

Moreover, the formulation that describes his loneliness when Katharina leaves him temporarily on their trip is only on the face of it purely negative: the hotel room, 'darin alle Trauer der Fremde dämmerte' (in which the sadness of foreignness began to dawn), evokes the properties attributed to Katharina. The 'Fremde' (foreignness), here indicating the foreign land, nevertheless connotes the title and thus Katharina herself. With 'dämmern' (dozing/dawning), Albert also describes Katharina's state of being ('Und so dämmerte auch jetzt ihr Wesen hin' (F555) - And thus also dozed her entire being), which obviously also alludes to the novella's original title and that of the volume *Dämmerseelen* (Dozing Souls). In this way, being left alone in the hotel room allows Albert to enter into his imagination of Katharina. However, grammatically he still projects the 'Dämmerzustand' (state of dozing) onto an incorporeal 'Trauer der Fremde' (melancholy of foreigness). In this way, Albert, like Robert in *Flucht in die Finsternis* (Flight into the Darkness), seems to enjoy a sort of transition state, which allows him an existence at once inside and outside of the bourgeois order. This, however, is only 'enjoyable', as long as the narrative of his fatal destiny is still perceived as an inevitable truth. Should it turn out that it was possible to lead a bourgeois marriage with Katharina, 'wie andere junge Paare' (like other young couples), then the idea of his individually laid out metaphysical destiny, as opposed to his social destiny, would be in danger. This is why Katharina abandoning him without further notice is actually a reassuring proof of his own construction of destiny: 'Denn unablässig und untrüglich in ihm wie der Schlag seines Herzens war das Gefühl, daß nichts sich geändert hatte seit dem ersten Tag, daß sie frei war wie je und er ihr völlig verfallen' (F557) (He had the persistent feeling, unerring like his own heartbeat, that nothing had changed since the first day, that she was free, while he had completely and irreversibly fallen for her).

Seriality, Replication, and Originality of Experience

What has emerged from the analysis so far can be summarized as a tension between seriality and originality of experience. Albert's fascination with Katharina's strangeness is above all an attempt to elevate his own existence, to free it from mediocrity and transform it into something 'special'. In the description of their honeymoon the 'threat' of seriality is already present – the formulation 'wie andere junge Paare' (like other young couples) as well as the use of plural forms without determining articles ('verweilten vor Gebäuden und Schaufenstern [...], stießen mit weingefüllten Gläsern an' lingered in front of buildings and shop windows, cheered with wine-filled glasses) not only evoke the stereotypical quality of their experiences in the sense that many others have done and will do the same, but also the fact that, during the short journey, they themselves already fall into a seriality of repetitive actions which form their experience together and mark it as 'happy' ('Schlaf der Glücklichen' – 'sleep of the happy'). Happiness seems already to be typecast, something that it is only possible to have by virtue of recognition – and therefore cannot be an original or unique experience.[29] The possibility of original experience thus seems to be drawn into question by the novella. At the same time, the text exposes Albert's intense longing for precisely that. The use of Romantic topoi seems to underline the aspect of seriality and the inability to avoid repetition, quotation, and reference. More poignantly still, the text not only plays with Romantic topoi, but rather seems to take on a stance of second-order repetition – the quotations are not direct quotations of Romantic texts, but rather of the neo-Romantic discourse of Aestheticism: not homage as such, but a parody of homage.

This effect of repetition and mirroring is subject to further complication: the construction of Albert's apparently so unique fate is also undermined by two other cases of male suicide mentioned in the novella. The first is Katharina's brother, who squandered his father's entire estate in addition to his mother's allowances and left his mother and sister stranded after his death. The second is mentioned in connection with the rumour of Katharina's mystical abilities: one night she dreamed of the death of the famous organ player Banetti, whom she had allegedly admired, and on the same day it turned out that Banetti had thrown himself off a church tower. The information about these two suicides, more or less connected to Katharina, is given to Albert, before he starts courting her. In this way, she seems fit to become constructed as femme fatale in the literal sense of the word – a woman that seals a fatal destiny for the men around her.

Moreover, Banetti's death may also refer to another literary 'case' of male suicide: Nathanael's lethal jump from the 'Ratsturm' (tower of the city hall) in Hoffmann's *Der Sandmann*. In this way, the seriality would occur not only within the text, but point to a – literary – tradition of male suicide connected to a suspension of reality, to a fading of differences, and particularly to a form of constructed femininity. Besides the allusions to the Romantic texts already mentioned, Albert can be seen as a sort of latter-day Nathanael whose love for the

---

29   This question of originality of experience is most famously addressed, of course, in Schnitzler's *Reigen* (La Ronde, 1900).

automaton Olimpia turns out to be merely projections of his own self. I have said that the compulsory inaccessibility of Katharina creates the impression of courtly love, and Žižek stresses that the incommensurable Lady functions as 'a kind of automaton'.[30] While Nathanael ironically feels understood by the actual automaton Olimpia, Albert stresses at any opportunity Katharina's lack of interest in him as a person and her general incommensurability. In this way, she appears somehow 'soulless', in a similar way to the automaton Olimpia. This radical 'otherness' is strikingly expressed in both cases through the motif of voice, as in the description of Katharina's beautiful but expressionless singing, with echoes of Olimpia: 'Zuweilen sang Katharina mit einer angenehmen Stimme, aber beinahe völlig ausdruckslos, einfache, meist italienische Volkslieder, zu denen er sie auf dem Klavier begleitete' (F554) (Sometimes Katharina sang simple, mostly Italian folk songs, with an agreeable voice, almost completely devoid of expression).

While both strike the right note, there seems to be something missing: the expression of feeling or inwardness, in short, subjectivity. As Mladen Dolar writes, referring to Kempelin's 'Sprech-Maschine' (speech machine), a voice is 'the most human of effects, an effect of "interiority"',[31] which makes a machine that is able to imitate a human voice in a believable way highly uncanny. When a person, who is supposed to be human, lacks this distinctly human effect of the voice, they in turn become uncanny. Katharina's mechanical soullessness seems once more rather an effect of Albert's projections. In *Die Fremde* (The Stranger) it is not the automaton that functions as woman, but the woman as automaton – or artwork. Through this parallel to Hoffmann's text with regard to the male construction of femininity, *Die Fremde* (The Stranger) seems to relay a Romantic position that undermines the male gaze. Hoffmann's texts already developed a critical and ironic distance to the Romantic constructions of femininity and exposed them as projections of the unsettled male self.[32] In this way, the second-order repetition in Schnitzler's text becomes two-fold: on the one hand, it takes up an opposition to the literary discourse of Aestheticism and *décadence* by mocking the Romantic influences on these texts. On the other hand, *Die Fremde* (The Stranger), like other Schnitzler texts we have seen, features touches of the 'Hoffmannesque', which seem to underline the text's ironic distance. These meta-textual references to the repetitive structure of the text not only count once more as a sign of Romantic irony in

---

30 Žižek, *The Metastases of Enjoyment*, 90.
31 Dolar, Mladen (2006), *A Voice and Nothing More*, Cambridge, MA: MIT Press, 10.
32 See Hilmes, *Die Femme Fatale*, 16 and 37.

Schnitzler's texts, they also further undermine Albert's attempts at proclaiming his uniquely individual destiny. Achim Aurnhammer finds similar parallels between Schnitzler's novella *Der letzte Brief des Literaten* (The Writer's Last Letter, 1917) and Hoffmann's *Rat Krespel* (Councillor Krespel, 1818) and *Der Sandmann* (The Sandman, 1917).[33] Aurnhammer shows that the intertextual reference to Hoffmann's texts reveals how Schnitzler's protagonist longs to achieve a sense of authenticity 'im inszenierten Nachgefühl' (by engendering real emotions through the theatrical staging of experience).[34] This can also be said about Albert in *Die Fremde* (The Stranger).

Katharina's preference for Italian folk songs seems to be another reference to German Romanticism: particularly in early Romantic literature, Italy appeared as a cipher for the idealized home of art and art lovers.[35] Katharina demonstrates a general affinity for Italy: the organ player Banetti, whom Katharina is said to have adored for a while, not only has an Italian-sounding name, but also committed suicide 'in einem kleinen lombardischen Dorf' (F552) (in a small Lombardian village). Moreover, the man from whom Katharina will be expecting a child at the end of the novella is also Italian, Andrea Geraldini from Verona. And last but not least, Theoderic, whose statue seems to induce a trance-like fascination in her, was not only king of the Ostrogoths but also became the ruler of Italy in AD 493.[36] This fascination for Italy seems to express a certain sentimental longing for the ideal of romantic love that Albert only knows in its 'perverted' form of distanced, courtly love. In the sense that Italy was perceived in Romanticism as idealized *locus amoenus*, Katharina's affinity for it could be understood as a mirroring of Albert's yearning for an exotic 'otherness': she in turn might be longing for a place of security and wholeness that she is only able to find in art (paintings and music), as expressed in her incorporation of the painted landscape mentioned earlier. In this context, Albert's feelings of inadequacy with regard to the ideal of masculinity seem to be confirmed through Katharina. Her fascination with the statue of Theoderic the Great can be understood as a longing for a type of

---

33 See Aurnhammer, Achim (2013), *Arthur Schnitzlers intertextuelles Erzählen*, Berlin, Boston, CA: De Gruyter, 150–153.

34 Aurnhammer, *Arthur Schnitzlers intertextuelles Erzählen*, 153.

35 See Battafarano, Italo Michele (1996), *Deutsche Romantik-Sehnsucht nach Italien: Wackenroders Auffassung der Kunst der italienischen Renaissance in den 'Herzensergießungen eines kunstliebenden Klosterbruders,' 'Italien in Germanien': Deutsche Italienrezeption 1750–1850*, ed. by Frank-Rutger Hausmann, Tübingen: Narr, 351–371, 357.

36 See Lafferty, Sean D. W. (2013), *Law and Society in the Age of Theoderic the Great: A Study of the Edictum Theoderici*, Cambridge: Cambridge University Press, 5.

masculinity belonging to the era of the *ancien régime*, which has become unreachable for the bourgeois man.[37]

The passage with the statue is told strictly from Albert's perspective. The narrator renders Albert's account of the scene in the internally focalized narrative mode. It is certainly convincing that Albert identifies with Theodoric (or rather, with his own interpretation of the statue), whose 'Haltung war von erhabener Müdigkeit, als sei er sich der Größe und Zwecklosigkeit seiner Taten bewußt, und als ging sein ganzer Stolz im Schwermut unter' (F558) (posture was of a sublime tiredness, as if he were aware of the greatness and purposelessness of his deeds, and as if his entire pride were drowning in his melancholia).[38] Theodoric stands for an ideal of patriarchal masculinity that seems to belong to a time long gone and is no longer able to give orientation but only represent tired resignation for the modern man. At this point, the novella addresses most explicitly the contemporary father–son conflict so overtly present in other writing of the time.[39] Theodoric the Great in this text seems to fulfil the same function as Alexander the Great in Hofmannsthal's *Märchen der 672. Nacht* (Fairytale of the 672. Nights):[40] the ideal of the great father that cannot be reached, except that here the

---

37   In his essay on Schnitzler's *Traumnovelle* (Dream Story), which I will turn to in Chapter Five, W. G. Sebald remarks that the ideal of masculinity that influenced the wishes and expectations of the bourgeois woman at the beginning of the twentieth century was already threatened by extinction: 'Bemerkenswert ist zunächst die Tatsache, daß das erotische Leitbild des Kavaliers, auf das die bürgerliche Frau ihre Wunschvorstellungen projiziert, für sie in der Regel gar nicht mehr erreichbar war, weil das ersehnte Wesen selber einer im Aussterben befriffenen Spezies angehörte beziehungsweise, wie der Fall Leutnant Gustl zeigt, bloß als seine eigene leere Hülle herumparodierte' (Of course it is noteworthy that the erotic ideal of the cavalier, which functions as projection screen for the sexual wishes of the bourgeois woman, was normally unachievable, because the desired creature belonged to a species that was either about to be extinct or, as the case of Lieutenant Gustl shows, he represented nothing more than a parody in his own empty shell). See Sebald, W. G. (1985), *Die Beschreibung des Unglücks. Zur Österreichischen Literatur von Stifter bis Handke*, Salzburg: Residenz, 48.
38   See Meyer, *Männlichkeit und Melodram*, 67.
39   See Brittnacher, Richard (2000), 'Welt ohne Väter: Söhne um 1900. Von der Revolte zum Opfer,' *Kursbuch* 140: 19–31.
40   The 'Kaufmannssohn' (son of a sales man) in Hugo von Hofmannsthal's *Das Märchen der 672. Nacht* keeps reading and fantasizing about the 'große König der Vergangenheit' (great king of the past). The narrative, however, brings out the failure of the protagonist to reach the requirements of this ideal of masculinity. See Hugo von Hofmannsthal (1975), 'Das Märchen der 672. Nacht,' *Sämtliche Werke*, vol. XXVIII: *Erzählungen 1*, ed. by Ellen Ritter (Frankfurt a. M.: Fischer), 13–30, 18.

resignation that Albert feels is already projected onto the figure of the king. In ordering a copy of the statue as a last present to Katharina, he seems to erect a monument for himself – or rather for the idea of masculinity he wished but failed to represent. This failure is – by virtue of the statue – directly linked to imitation: he obviously cannot buy the original but has to order a copy. The fact that he is not even the original ordering customer, but only takes over the statue somewhat like a 'hand-me-down' from a deceased lord whose heirs refused to pay for the order, intensifies the seriality and lack of originality of the courtly gesture. It also introduces the aspect of class differences, signifying that in his striving to overcome his bourgeois identity, Albert reaches for the crumbs left behind by the nobleman. Moreover, we can understand this refusal of the lord's heirs to take over the statue as a hint that the concept of masculinity – that Albert struggles to fulfil, tries to overcome, and still cannot let go of – is outdated.

However, we must not overlook Katharina's fascination with the statue. If we accept that Theodorich stands for the old ideal of masculinity, it follows that Katharina is as much determined by the traditional gender order as Albert. This fits in well with her preference for older men, which Albert observes before their marriage: 'Die jüngeren Herren behandelte sie mit einiger Unachtsamkeit, lieber unterhielt sie sich mit reiferen Männern von Rang oder Ruf' (F553) (She treated the younger gentlemen with disregard, she preferred to talk to more mature men with a respectable status and reputation). This preference might well have a lot to do with Katharina's precarious social and financial situation, but that does not exclude the interpretation that here the failing of the 'Sohnesgeneration' (generation of sons) to reach the standards set by the fathers also plays a role. Particularly the attribute 'von Rang und Ruf' (with a respectable status and reputation) puts the emphasis on symbolic rather than economic capital.

The ending of the narrative provides a moment of deconstruction of both Albert's and Katharina's idealized, mystified, and stereotypical conceptions of 'otherness': the now strictly authorial voice of the narrator tells the reader that Katharina, after briefly looking at Albert's copy of the Theoderic statue, sits down to write a letter to the father of her unborn child, Andrea Geraldini, but, as the narrator knows, will never receive a reply. The ideals of romantic love and masculinity could thus not be found in the man with the promising Italian-sounding name either. Moreover, for this stranger, Katharina seems not to have had a comparable effect of mystery, which ultimately confirms her function as Albert's projection screen. In these last sentences, the precarity of her situation, which Albert had ignored in his perception of her, because it would not have fitted into his narrative of courtly love, is made plainly visible.

Albert in turn has already been buried for weeks. With his suicide, he has indeed fulfilled his 'destiny': as an act of honour according to the moral code of the dominant order, aping that of the courtly regime, it confirms his place within the norm, which he would not have been able to keep had he stayed alive. In this way, here too, social destinies are indeed 'mortal'. As we shall now see, in *Das Schicksal des Freiherrn von Leisenbohg* (Baron Leisenbohg's Destiny), the ironic play with the concept of courtly love encountered in *Die Fremde* (The Stranger) is taken to a further extreme. Similarly to *Die Weissagung* (The Prophecy), this text toys with fantastic elements, allowing it to challenge the cliché of love as destiny in a more radical, parodic way.

Courtly Love and Seriality in *Das Schicksal des Freiherrn von Leisenbohg* (Baron Leisenbohg's Destiny)

Das Schicksal des Freiherrn von Leisenbohg (Baron Leisenbohg's Destiny) was first published in 1903 under the title *Novelette* in the *Neue Freie Presse*. The novella tells of the unrequited love of the Freiherr von Leisenbohg for the opera singer Kläre Hell. Leisenbohg has to witness how Kläre engages in various love affairs without ever considering him as a potential lover. After the death of her greatest love, the Fürst von Bedenbruck, Kläre seems to have lost all interest in romance. However, when the Norwegian singer Sigurd Ölse arrives in town for an engagement at the Vienna Opera, Leisenbohg fears Kläre might turn to him, and is even more joyfully surprised when she finally responds to his own ten years of courtship and spends the night with him. However, his moment of bliss is cut short the next morning when he learns that Kläre has left the city without leaving so much as a note. Heartbroken and confused, Leisenbohg starts travelling around aimlessly until he is reached by an urgent telegram from Ölse, containing the plea to come see him in Norway immediately. Upon arrival he learns that Ölse had met Kläre on the train and had become her lover. Yet now Ölse fears that he is doomed: the Fürst Bedenbruck had uttered a curse on his death bed, condemning the first man Kläre should ever take as her lover to 'Wahnsinn, Elend und Tod' (SL596) (madness, calamity, and death). Leisenbohg drops dead on the spot.

Love as Individualizing Destiny

Leisenbohg's love for Kläre takes on the form of courtly love in a similar way to Albert's infatuation with Katharina in the sense that it is based on her unattainability. While Kläre indeed rejects Leisenbohg and is thus inaccessible to him in a much more literal sense than Katharina is to Albert, the masochistic game of courtly love is here again constructed by the 'servant' himself. Leisenbohg aligns himself and his life completely with Kläre: he gives up his career in order to be near her, ends relationships with women as soon as she seems to become available (only to be disappointed again) and uses his contacts to arrange her engagement at the Vienna Opera. In short, he constructs his life as a tale in which the sacrificial behaviour will have to be rewarded in the end.

However, his unrequited love for Kläre has a latent, secondary gain of 'illness': it allows him to live a life on the margins of bourgeois existence: during his ten year long courtship of Kläre, she enjoys several love affairs. Leisenbohg also allows himself relationships with other women, but deliberately keeps them uncommitted in order to be free and ready as soon as Kläre might finally turn her love to him: 'Immer, wenn er einen in ihrer Gunst wanken sah, hatte er seiner Liebsten den Abschied gegeben, um für alle Fälle und in jedem Augenblick bereit zu sein' (SL584) (Whenever he saw that her current lover was losing grace, he had ended his current love affair, in order to be ready just in case). Moreover, it turns out that the career he sacrificed in order to be close to Kläre was 'eine vielversprechende Staatskarriere' (SL582) (a very promising career in the civil service). Reading the narrative on its own, this might not appear like significant information, but since Leisenbohg is now, after Robert and Albert, the third 'Ministerialbeamter' (SL581) (civil servant in a ministry) who seems to feel not fully identified with his symbolic function, it is possible to recognize a pattern here.[41] It is thus safe to assume that Leisenbohg, too, constructs this narrative of love as destiny here as an attempt at overcoming his social destiny. His love allows him to construct the narrative of an individualized destiny for himself. The late success with Kläre and her numerous erotic encounters before him are turned around and embraced as proof that it is the destiny of both of them to be with each other: the delayed fulfilment becomes the 'notwendige Abschluß seiner bisherigen Beziehungen zu Kläre' (the necessary conclusion of his relationship to Kläre) and he has

---

41 One can find another similar case in *Die Weissagung* (The Prophecy), where von Umprecht's uncle, the art lover Freiherr von Schottenegg, who provides the setting for the narrator's fatal drama, has led a sort of 'double existence'. When very young he had attempted an acting career, but then had given it up,

> um noch ohne erhebliche Verspätung in den Staatsdienst treten zu können und damit dem Beruf seiner Vorfahren zu folgen, den er dann auch zwei Jahrzehnte hindurch treu, wenn auch ohne Begeisterung erfüllte. Aber als er, kaum vierzig Jahre alt, gleich nach dem Tode seines Vaters das Amt verließ, sollte sich erst zeigen, mit welcher Liebe er an dem Gegenstand seiner jugendlichen Träume noch immer hing. (W598)

in order to become a civil servant and in this way follow his ancestors' footsteps. He fulfilled his official duties diligently, but without passion for two decades. However, when he left his office at just about forty, right after his father's passing, it became clear how much he was still attached to the matters of his youthful dreams.

the impression that 'es gar nicht anders hätte kommen können' (SL588) (another outcome would not have been possible). Moreover, the belief in the higher power of destiny is then explicitly linked with the claim of exclusivity and originality: 'Und er ahnte den Tag voraus, da Kläre ihm sagen würde: Was waren mir alle anderen? – Du bist der einzige und erste, den ich je geliebt habe [...]. Gewiß; sie hatte keinen geliebt vor ihm, und ihn vielleicht immer und in jedem!' (SL588) (And he anticipated the day when Kläre would tell him: What did the others even mean to me? – You are the first and only one whom I have loved. Certainly, she had not loved anyone before him, and maybe she had always loved him in each of her previous lovers).[42]

The idea of true love as exclusive, individualizing experience can be seen as the key theme of the narrative. All characters seem to be in one way or the other 'infected' by this idea: Kläre assigns unique status to her love for Prince Bedenbruck as the one true love, as expressed by 'jene seltsame Handbewegung [...], mit der sie seit dem Tod des Fürsten alle Andeutungen von der weiteren Existenz leidenschaftlicher oder zärtlicher Beziehungen auf Erden abgewehrt hatte' (SL586) (that strange hand gesture, with which, since the prince's death, she had dismissed all further existence of passionate and affectionate relationships,). Of course, Bedenbruck's curse, identified by Freud as an expression of the taboo of virginity, is also rooted in the idea of the exclusivity of love.[43] The serial repetition of this claim to the originality and exclusivity of love obviously undermines that very claim in each case. Of course, the fact that Kläre in the end 'uses' the prince's curse on Leisenbohg in order to be with Sigurd has the parodic effect of a *reductio ad absurdum* that contradicts the claims of exclusivity and uniqueness made in the text.

The novella in this way exposes the impact of the cultural narratives of clichés on the experience of reality. While Leisenbohg, very much like Albert in *Die Fremde* (The Stranger), strives for an original and individual experience of love, he is confronted with its serial quality that seems to turn his feelings and gestures of affection into a cliché. While he apparently sought to escape the repetitive performances and conventional forms of conduct of his social destiny, it turns out that even the 'cosmic fate' of love is structured by pre-formed narratives, conventionalized modes of conduct, and the repetition compulsions of cliché. When Leisenbohg finds out about Kläre's betrayal, this is the moment

---

42 This cliché of looking for the one true love in other love affairs returns in *Traumnovelle* (Dream Story), as we will see in the next chapter.

43 See Freud, Sigmund (1947a), 'Das Tabu der Virginität,' *Gesammelte Werke*, vol. 12: *Werke aus den Jahren 1917–1920*, ed. by Anna Freud, Edward Bibring, Willi Hoffer, Ernst Kris, and Otto Isakower, London: Imago, 161–180, 178.

of feeling 'cheated' by cliché, as described by Cave, 'being brought to a moment of fullness only to find that it is empty'.[44]

Horror as Experience of Seriality

Of course, this is also the point when the reader is made aware of the sensation of *Grauen* (horror). It appears when Ölse informs Leisenbohg of the curse uttered by Prince Bedenbruck on his deathbed:

> 'Erinnerst du dich des Abends', fragte Sigurd, 'an dem wir alle in Klärens Haus zu Gaste waren? Am Morgen dieses Tages war Kläre mit Fanny auf den Friedhof hinausgefahren, und auf dem Grabe des Fürsten hatte sie ihrer Freundin das Grauenhafte anvertraut.' – 'Das Grauenhafte –?' Der Freiherr erbebte. (SL595)
> 'Do you remember that night', Sigurd asked, 'when we all were at Kläre's house? On the morning of that day, Kläre had gone to the cemetery with Fanny, and by the prince's grave she told her friend about the horror.' – 'About the horror –?' The baron shuddered.

As in the case of Thameyer, *Grauen* (horror) is here related to the fear of emasculation: the curse of the Prince Bedenbruck repeats the paternal threat of castration and makes Kläre into the forbidden maternal object of desire.[45] At the same time, Kläre becomes the enigmatic and inaccessible femme fatale, whose seductive power is poisonous to her male victim. The Grauenhafte here is thus tightly linked to the deconstruction of Leisenbohg's tale of love according to which he and Kläre were 'destined' for each other. The fact that it is Ölse who brings up the *Grauen* (horror) is not contradictory to this interpretation: after all, he had the same experience when Kläre's friend Fanny told him about the curse.

Even before Leisenbohg learns about the curse, but is already stricken by Kläre's unexplained disappearance, the *Grauen* (horror) is prefigured in the way that he externalizes his depressed and, at the same time, increasingly hysterical mood: 'Über der Stadt lag es wie ein ewiger grauer Dunst; die Leute, mit denen er sprach, hatten verschleierte Stimmen und starrten ihn merkwürdig, ja verräterisch an' (SL592) (There was something like a grey mist hanging over the city; the people, whom he talked to, had veiled voices and stared at him strangely, yes, even

---

44   Cave, Terence (1988), *Recognitions: A Study in Poetics*, Oxford: Oxford University Press, 459–460.
45   Katan claims that Kläre is a mother figure for Leisenbohg. See Katan, M. (1969), 'Schnitzlers *Das Schicksal des Freiherrn von Leisenbohg*,' *Journal of the American Psychoanalytic Association* 17 (3): 904–926.

treacherously). Strikingly, the grey fog thus reappears here in a very similar way to Thameyer's description of the scene where his wife's 'Versehen' (miss-seeing, maternal impression) allegedly took place. Leisenbohg's paranoid impression of the people around him, their 'veiled voices' and 'treacherous gazes', is also reminiscent of Thameyer's paranoid ideas of hearing people talking about him and his 'case' (See AT517). Voice and gaze appear as markers of dishonesty: the 'veiled voices' might not disclose what their speakers are holding back, but nevertheless they display their veiled character and thus the presence of uncanny double-talk. The gazes are treacherous, which in itself seems to bear a double meaning: on the one hand, it implies that through the way the people stare at Leisenbohg they give something away – presumably that they know more than Leisenbohg does himself. On the other hand, their treacherous looks might imply the betrayal of Leisenbohg, in the sense that they do not tell him what they know.

This Gothic atmosphere is then retrospectively applied to the long-desired sexual encounter with Kläre. Leisenbohg tries to make sense of Kläre's disappearance by pathologizing her:

> Die eine Stunde der Lust, die er mit Kläre erlebt hatte, schien ihm wie von dunklen Schauern umweht. Es war ihm, als hätten ihre Augen in der gestrigen Nacht wie im Wahnsinn geglüht. Nun begriff er alles. Zu früh war er ihrem Ruf gefolgt. Noch hatte der Schatten des verstorbenen Fürsten Bedenbruck Gewalt über sie, und Leisenbohg fühlte, daß er Kläre nur besessen hatte, um sie auf immer zu verlieren. (SL591)
> The single hour of passion, which he had shared with Kläre, now appeared to him to be marred by dark showers. He seemed to remember that last night her eyes had glowed in madness. Now he understood everything. He had followed her call too soon. The shadow of the deceased Prince Bedenbruck still had power over her, and Leisenbohg knew that he had possessed Kläre only to lose her forever.

Leisenbohg's attempt at integrating Kläre's at this point still enigmatic behaviour into his usual interpretative patterns clearly fails. His claim to the contrary ('Nun begriff er alles' – Now he understood everything) is undermined by the strong irony of the following sentence: the idea that his ten years of courtship had not been long enough and that some strategic waiting on his part could have led to the fulfillment of his dreams must be doubtful to the reader. Moreover, we encounter here again the strikingly Gothic colouring of the passage: the 'dunklen Schauern' (dark showers) seem like a direct reference to the Gothic fiction the text evokes, again with the typological arsenal of grey fogs, glowing eyes, and, last but not least, the moment of *Grauen* (horror) itself. The sensation of *Grauen* (horror) in Leisenbohg is thus tightly linked to the deconstruction of love as individualizing experience.

However, in a similar way to *Die Weissagung* (The Prophecy), the *Grauen* (horror) here also marks a moment in which enacted performance and reality become indistinguishable: it is crucial that it is not the night with Kläre but only when he witnesses Ölse's 'performance' that leads to Leisenbohg's death. It thus seems as if the re-enacted performance of the curse in fact activates it, a logic which is reminiscent of the way the law of the social order is dependent on repeated performances and speech acts. By rendering Bedenbruck's curse in first-person narration, Ölse performatively adopts the position of the latter: 'Ich spreche [...] und ich lasse Fanny sprechen, und Fanny läßt Kläre sprechen, und Kläre läßt den Fürsten sprechen' (SL596) (I am speaking, and I am letting Fanny speak, and Fanny is letting Kläre speak, and Kläre is letting the Prince speak), he explains, after Leisenbohg could only exclaim in confused exasperation: 'Wer spricht?' (Who is speaking?). Introduced by the multiple voices and perspectives in Ölse's report, the dead Bedenbruck makes a ghost-like appearance: 'Es war ihm [Leisenbohg], als hörte er die Stimme des toten Fürsten aus dreifach verschlossenem Sarge in die Nacht klingen' (SL596) (He felt like he was hearing the Prince's voice sounding from his threefold locked-up coffin into the night). This play with the several narrative perspectives (metaphorically cast as locks on the coffin) not only ironically takes the effect of seriality to an extreme, it also self-referentially points up the fictional constructedness of the narrative itself. This, in turn, underlines the constructed quality of Leisenbohg's perception of reality, particularly of his tale of love and destiny. And it thus also brings to the fore the fictionalization and, with it, the aestheticization of life, which could be understood again as a subtle critique of Aestheticism in the text.

Fictionality and Performance

The interpretation of the text as critique of Aestheticism is supported by the interesting double-performance Ölse provides for Leisenbohg. Only at first does he take on the role of Bedenbruck and become his mouthpiece: 'Sigurd, aus dessen Mund die Stimme des toten Fürsten tönte, hatte sich erhoben, groß und feist stand er in seinem weißen Flanellanzug da und blickte in die helle Nacht' (SL596) (Sigurd, whose mouth was speaking in the Prince's voice, had raised from his seat, tall and big he stood in his white flannel suit and gazed into the bright night). Then, however, Ölse appears as a *Pierrot*, which has multiple connotations: with his white costume and the black accessories, the *Pierrot* in literature around 1900 symbolizes, according to Julia Bertschik, 'das weiße Blatt Papier, noch unbeschrieben, aber schon mit den ersten Spuren schwarzer Schrift versehen: aus der traditionellen Kunstfigur wird so eine Figuration der Dichtkunst' (the white sheet of paper, still blank, but with the first marks of black writing).[46] This underlines the aesthetic quality of Ölse's performance, but also the meta-fictional character of the entire passage. Moreover, Ölse, with his face, which 'entbehrte im Zustand der Ruhe wohl manchmal des besonderen Ausdrucks' (SL585) (in a state of calm his face sometimes lacked any special expression) becomes, in his function as Pierrot, a projection screen and mirror image for Leisenbohg. Thus, while Ölse represents, on the one hand, Bedenbruck, and thus Leisenbohg's challenger, he also stands in for Leisenbohg himself. The character of the Pierrot in the *Commedia del'arte*, with his submissive and relentless admiration for Columbine, is the epitome of unrequited love: 'Pierrot selbst agiert im Verhältnis zur dämonischen "femme fatale" Columbine unterwürfig-passiv, gewissermaßen als eine in unschuldiges Weiß gekleidete, männliche "femme fragile"' (In comparison to the demonic *femme fatale* Columbine, Pierrot himself behaves submissively and passively, one could say like a male *femme fragile*, dressed in innocent whites).[47] In this way, we can read the passage as a *Doppelgänger* scene: Leisenbohg dies the second that Ölse announces what he assumes to be his own destiny: 'der Elende, an dem sich der Fluch erfüllen soll, bin ich! ... ich! ...ich! ...' (SL596) (the wretched man, who is supposed to receive the curse, is I! ...I! ...I! ...).

If Ölse as a *Pierrot* both functions as mirror image for Leisenbohg and symbolizes *Dichtkunst* (the art of literature/poetry) per se, then Leisenbohg is confronted with his own aesthetically constructed self-image which is based on his tale of love as destiny. However, the *Pierrot* presents him with an alternative way of storytelling: while he himself has constructed his relentless courtship of Kläre as a sign of heroic determination and masculinity, which would end with a reward worthy of the long wait, he now sees himself, mirrored by Ölse, as the effeminate figure of the *Pierrot* who has become the powerless victim of the cruel game played by a demonic woman and (implicitly) more potent men than himself: the Prince Bedenbruck and, paradoxically, also Ölse. Leisenbohg has to realize that Ölse, his *Doppelgänger*-competitor, has won and that he himself has become the 'proxy figure' that had to be sacrificed to make way for Ölse as Kläre's new lover. Correspondingly, he drops dead 'lautlos [...] wie eine Gliederpuppe' (SL597) (silently, like a jointed doll). Apart from the obvious comparison to a puppet whose strings have been dropped as a metaphor for the lack of agency, the remark 'lautlos' (silently) may also imply that Leisenbohg has now

---

46 Bertschik, Julia (2005), *Mode und Moderne: Kleidung als Spiegel des Zeitgeistes in der deutschsprachigen Literatur (1770–1945)*, Köln: Böhlau, 158.

47 Bertschik, *Mode und Moderne*, 160.

fully become the *Pierrot* himself: one of the most remarkable traits of the *Pierrot* is that he has no voice, that he is silent. While Ölse's voice had initially been a marker of his virility (see SL585), it had become 'weniger voll' (SL593) (less sonorous) after his affair with Kläre. However, he significantly regains the full volume of his voice after Leisenbohg's death.[48]

The figure of the *Pierrot* can thus also be seen here as a death omen, as is the case in *Pierrot Hypnotiseur* (1892) by Schnitzler's contemporary Richard Beer-Hofmann.[49] Bertschik reads the *Pierrot* as a comment on the image of the decadent dandy of the turn of the century: 'Ob in seinem weißen oder schwarzen Kostüm, der Pierrot verkörpert als dandyistisches Subjekt theatraler Metamorphosen in jedem Fall das gefürchtete Nichts hinter vielfältigen Masken.[50] Er steht somit für die existentielle Gefährdung individueller Identität und persönlicher Autonomie' (Whether in his black or white costume, as the dandy-like subject of theatrical metamorphosis, the Pierrot embodies in any case the dreaded nothing behind various masks. He symbolizes therefore the existential danger of individual identity and personal autonomy).

This, in turn, brings together the key themes linked to the complex of 'stereotype and destiny' developed so far: the feeling of being coerced into empty repetition compulsions by one's social destiny produces precisely these feelings of a threat to individuality and autonomy. Bertschik elaborates further that the Pierrot can be understood as a symbolic figure for the cognitive practice of over-determination ('Bedeutungsüberlastung'), which ultimately culminates in an absolute emptiness of meaning ('Bedeutungsentleerung').[51] We have already come across the tendency of over-determination several times in previous chapters, and here too it plays a significant role. Already described in Leisenbohg's perception of his relationship to Kläre, it is ironically carried to extremes by Ölse, the *Pierrot*. Early on in the text, Ölse reveals his mysticist tendencies:

Unter anderem erzählte er, daß ihm auf der Herreise auf dem Schiff von einer an einen russischen Großfürsten verheiratete Araberin aus den Linien seiner Hand für die nächste Zeit die verhängnisvollste Epoche seines Lebens prophezeit worden war. […] Er hatte freilich allen Grund, an solche geheimnisvolle [sic] Beziehungen zwischen unbegreiflichen Zeichen und Menschenschicksalen zu glauben. (SL586)

---

48   For the interpretation of Ölse's voice as a sign of impotence/virility, see Katan, *Schnitzlers Das Schicksal des Freiherrn von Leisenbohg*.
49   Bertschik, *Mode und Moderne*, 166.
50   Bertschik, *Mode und Moderne*, 167.
51   Bertschik, *Mode und Moderne*, 167.

Among other things he told the story that, when travelling by ship on his journey to Vienna, he had had his palm read by an Arabian woman, who had been married to a Russian Prince. She had foretold him that the coming time would be the most calamitous period of his life. Of course, he had reason to believe in such mysterious relationships between unfathomable signs and human destinies.

This of course evokes the symptoms of Romantic madness: the denial of contingency corresponds to an over-determined understanding of meaning, while the experience of 'Bedeutungsentleerung' (emptiness of meaning) can be found in the sensation of cliché as a trivialization of meaning.[52] The idea of love as destiny, as a 'cosmic fate', leads to the practice of over-determination comparable to Romantic madness: contingency is abolished when destiny brings two lovers together. However, as has already been shown above, those claims of individuality and uniqueness of the experience of love are ironically undermined by the repetitive structure of the text, which brings to the fore their cliché-like quality and thus the threatening emptiness behind conventionalized gestures of love.

While for Imboden, *Das Schicksal des Freiherrn von Leisenbohg* (Baron Leisenbohg's Destiny) tells of the power of destiny, in the face of which the individual can only succumb,[53] Perlmann stresses that the text is not at all about the 'Evozierung des Unheimlichen, sondern [...] dessen ironische Entlarvung vermittels der Entlarvung seiner Anhänger bzw.[54] Opfer' (evocation of the uncanny, but about its ironical exposure through the exposure of its followers or victims). Fliedl also concludes that Leisenbohg is not a real 'Schicksalsnovelle' (novella of destiny), but rather a parody of that genre.[55] My reading of the text shows that all three positions are in a way right: it is certainly true that the narrative does not support mysticist tendencies and the belief in a higher cosmic power. The belief in destiny, particularly in love as destiny, is exposed as fallacy and indeed ridiculed through parodic and ironic elements. However, the text leaves the reader with a certain 'indigestible' remainder which purely rationalistic-realistic interpretations (Leisenbohg believes in destiny, which is why he dies when he learns about the curse due to autosuggestion) cannot fully resolve. And while the narrative certainly treats the topic of destiny in a parodic manner, it seems

---

52 Zijderveld, 'On the Nature and Function of Clichés,' 28.
53 See Imboden, Michael (1971), *Die surreale Komponente im erzählenden Werk Arthur Schnitzlers*, Bern: H. Lang, 86.
54 Perlmann, Michaela L. (1987b), *Arthur Schnitzler*, Stuttgart: Metzler, 119.
55 See Fliedl, *Arthur Schnitzler*, 169.

to go beyond a simple light-hearted trivialization of a literary genre. I would like to suggest that there is indeed an uncanny remainder in the text, which is tightly linked to the topic of destiny: destiny, however, is not to be understood as metaphysical force, but as a derivative of social conditioning. In this way, the text nevertheless raises uncomfortable questions of autonomy and individuality. It exposes the invocation of destiny, particularly love as destiny, as a coping mechanism to create a comforting feeling of individuation. That this promise inherent in the concept of romantic love is undermined by the irrepressible sensation of cliché calls into question the possibility of an original experience independent of pre-formed cultural narratives.

Seriality and Performance in *Das neue Lied* (The New Song)

In *Das neue Lied* (The New Song), first published under the title *Erzählung* in 1905 in the *Neue Freie Presse*, the tension between seriality and individuality can be understood as central theme. The reader recognizes very soon a rather typical seduction plot: a young woman from a poor but respectable family falls victim to the seduction of a socially superior man who abandons her as soon as the relationship demands more than an uncommitted self-indulgent love adventure. The classical 'case' is further complicated by a tragic element lying outside of the control of all characters: the woman, the singer Marie Ladenbauer, is struck by a severe case of meningitis which leaves her terminally blind. Her lover, Karl Breiteneder, the son of a successful owner of a turnery, leaves her without a word when he learns of her affliction. When he finds out by accident that Marie is giving her first singing performance after her illness, he spontaneously attends it, but afterwards he finds himself unable to talk to her and ignores her attempts at conversation. Marie then leaves the room in an unattended moment and commits suicide.

Idealizing Stereotypes of Poverty

Das neue Lied (The New Song) is thus not about the protagonist constructing a narrative of love as destiny for himself. Rather, he is able to remain detached and actually eager to stress the seriality, and thus arbitrariness, of his relationship to Marie. He is not willing to recognize her as an individual behind the stereotypical image. In contrast to the first two protagonists of the narratives discussed in this chapter, Karl does not construct a tale of love as destiny for himself. However, while Marie is not an enigmatic, unreachable femme fatale to Karl, it becomes clear nevertheless that he uses her as a way to temporarily suspend his social reality and that his perception of her is highly influenced by pre-formed cultural narratives. As a young woman from the Viennese periphery, who earns her money through performance art, she represents paradigmatically the more than familiar Schnitzlerian stereotype of the 'süße

Mädel' (sweet girl).[56] Marie's family are portrayed as respectable people who have to work hard to make ends meet. In Karl's perspective, they are set up to represent the positive stereotype of *einfache, aber gute Leute* (simple but good people). The way their honesty and cleanliness are described parallels the ethical impeccability of the poor with their capability of maintaining a clean home and outer appearance. Through the cliché 'poor but clean' we encounter here, in a more subtle way than in most of the other narratives discussed so far, the idealization of the 'other' that is contrasted with the feeling of inauthenticity in the bourgeois order. In this case, it is not the enigmatic femininity of an almost otherworldly creature, the insight of a Jewish magician or the potentially more creative lifestyle of insanity that seems to promise an alternative way of being or access to a less restricted existence, but the more authentic, more 'real' interactions and relationships of the less privileged milieu of performance artists. One could also argue that the way Karl's perspective depicts Marie and her family is reminiscent of the 'Viennese types' photo series discussed in the introduction to this book. They create for him the image of old-Viennese cosiness and reassure him of his own privileged position. All we learn about Karl's family and other social contacts is the hypocritical attitude of his father and that his acquaintances in the coffee house are less reliable than the Ladenbauers in terms of the payback of gambling debts. The things he notices in the Ladenbauers' house are almost all related to a certain kind of reciprocal engagement and commitment. It appears that Karl has used Marie and her family to create an escape from his everyday life, going beyond the conventional and almost institutionalized transgression of a little love adventure. When Marie falls ill, Karl realizes that it is expected of him to behave like a lover and friend – a role he formerly only 'performed' when it was convenient.

The escape and sanctuary which he thought existed separately from his normal existence thus comes to pose demands. And of course he fails to fulfil them. It therefore is important that it is strictly Karl's perspective when the narrator remarks about the memories of their love affair: 'So schöne Erinnerungen gab es manche, und die beiden lebten sehr vergnügt, ohne an die Zukunft zu denken' (NL622) (There were many of these beautiful memories, and both of them lived happily without thinking of the future). It is by no means clear that Marie had indeed never had the hope of becoming more serious with Karl – since she 'hing an ihm, ohne viel Worte zu machen' (NL621) (she was attached to him without making a great play of it), we only know that she conveniently never uttered any demands or claims. Karl used Marie and her family as

---

56 See Janz, Rolf-Peter and Klaus Laermann (1977), *Arthur Schnitzler: Zur Diagnose des Wiener Bürgertums im Fin de siècle*, Stuttgart: Metzler, 41–54.

mirror devices rather than engaging in an actual relationship with them. The bright and friendly atmosphere in the Ladenbauers' home invited him to imagine himself as a part of it. The short passage is full of little recognition scenes, from which Karl can gain reassurance about himself: the immediate payment of gambling debts is a form of acknowledgement of Karl as the winner. The exchange of cigars between him and Marie's brother can also be understood as a performance of male mutual recognition. Marie's behaviour towards him among the group of people is another form of recognition: 'Aber Marie sah zu Karl herüber, grüßte ihn scherzend mit der Hand oder setzte sich zu ihm und schaute ihm in die Karten' (NL621) (But Marie looked over to Karl, jokingly waved her hand at him or sat next to him and looked into his cards). The greeting as most basic form of recognition is here combined with a reassuring understanding of Karl as a person: the literal act of Marie looking into his cards can also be understood metaphorically in the sense that he feels like he has nothing to hide from her.

Uncanny Recognition Scenes

When Karl learns about Marie's terminal blindness, he is stricken by a sudden fear: 'Er hatte plötzlich Angst, Marie wiederzusehen. Es war ihm, als hätte er nichts an ihr so gern gehabt, als ihre Augen, die so hell gewesen waren und mit denen sie immer gelacht hatte' (NL622) (He was suddenly afraid to see Marie again. He felt as if he had loved nothing as much as her eyes, which had been so bright and with which she had always smiled). Marie's gaze had the reassuring impact of recognition without demanding his part of the mutual movement. When she loses her eyesight she seems to also have lost her complementary function for Karl. However, the mirroring effect seems to be restored in an uncanny way: 'Da war ihm, als ob sie ihre toten Augen in die seinen versenken wollte und als könnte sie tief in ihn hineinschauen' (NL631) (He felt like she wanted to let her dead eyes sink into his, as if she could look deeply inside him). This is obviously linked to a sensation of guilt, as she reminds him of his interpersonal failure, but her disability also makes impossible her function as perfect projection screen which never failed to invoke good feelings in him ('ihre Augen, […] mit denen sie immer gelacht hatte' (NL622) – her eyes, with which she had always smiled). The knowledge she appears to have of him becomes uncanny and threatening, in contrast to his former willingness to let her 'see his cards'. The uncanny effect of her 'dead' eyes can be read once more as a Hoffmannesque element, reminiscent as it is of Nathanael's revelation when he sees Olimpia's dark eye holes in her puppet face. The realization that Olimpia is not a real woman but an automaton is traumatic because it destroys Nathanael's illusion of recognition through Olimpia and in this way threatens his own sensation of integrity. Marie's blindness is a different form of 'otherness' than that which she represented to Karl before: it no longer provides him with a secured sense of self, but rather represents absolute otherness and in this way threatens rather than reinforces Karl's identity:

Und plötzlich fühlte er gar, wie sie seine Hand berührte und streichelte, ohne daß sie ein Wort dazu sprach. Nun hätte er so gern etwas zu ihr gesagt: irgendetwas Liebes, Tröstendes – aber er konnte nicht ... Er schaute sie von der Seite an, und wieder war ihm, als sähe ihn aus ihren Augen etwas an; aber nicht ein Menschenblick, sondern etwas Unheimliches, Fremdes, das er früher nicht gekannt – und es erfaßte ihn ein Grauen, als wenn ein Gespenst neben ihm säße ... Ihre Hand bebte und entfernte sich sachte von der seinen, und sie sagte leise: 'Warum hast du denn Angst? Ich bin ja dieselbe.' Er vermochte wieder nicht zu antworten und redete gleich mit den anderen. (NL632)

And suddenly he even felt that she was touching and stroking his hand, without saying a word. Now he would have liked to say something to her, something nice, comforting – but he could not ... He looked at her from the corner of his eye, and again it was as if something was looking at him from her eyes; but it was not a human gaze, but something uncanny, something foreign, which he had not known previously – and he was overwhelmed by a feeling of horror, as if a ghost were sitting next to him ... Her hand trembled and was removed from his, and she said softly: 'Why are you afraid? I'm just the same as I've always been.' He was unable to respond and immediately talked to the others.

The Gothic colouring of this passage with words such as 'Unheimliches' (uncanny), 'Grauen' (horror), and 'Gespenst' (ghost) is striking. A Freudian reading of the passage would suggest that Marie's blinded eyes stand symbolically for the traumatic moment when the little boy realizes that the woman is lacking a penis, assuming she must have been castrated and establishing the fear of castration in the boy's psyche. And to some extent, this interpretation might prove fruitful for the analysis of *Das neue Lied* (The New Song). If we accept that Marie used to function as a mirror device for Karl, the reflection she gives now is significantly lacking. It is her inability to return the gaze, which makes her, like Olimpia the automaton without any 'Sehkraft' (power of vision), 'ganz unheimlich' (completely uncanny).[57]

---

57 Webber, Andrew J. (1996), *The Doppelgänger: Double Visions in German Literature*, Oxford: Oxford University Press, 137. Webber describes here the uncanny effect of the automaton Olimpia.

With her urgent comment 'Ich bin ja dieselbe' (I'm just the same) Marie insists on her self-identity. This reveals her expectation of the individuality and originality of her relationship with Karl, based on the idea of love as the original experience and mutual recognition of each other's individuality. In contrast to that, Karl stresses repeatedly the aspect of seriality of their relationship, which seems to diminish its significance and also his own responsibility: the fact that Marie is a woman, 'die schon so manches erlebt hatte' (NL621) (who had quite some experience), in his reasoning makes his unexplained withdrawal after her illness less grave: 'Natürlich dachte er auch von Tag zu Tag weniger an sie und nahm sich vor, sie ganz zu vergessen. Er war ja nicht der erste und nicht der einzige gewesen' (NL623) (Of course, every day he was thinking less about her, and he decided to forget her completely. After all, he had not been the first or the only one). Karl's father, too, who expresses his dismay about his close relationship to Marie, refers to the seriality of this kind of relationship: 'in den Familien von meine Mädeln hab' ich doch nie verkehrt!' (NL621) (I have never associated with the families of my lovers). In this way, the seriality is thus even multiplied as a cross-generational phenomenon. When Marie tries to convince Karl that she is still the same person she used to be, she misinterprets Karl's fear: by insisting on her individual personality, she contradicts the typological character of their relationship. With her blindness, Marie takes on an individual trait that sets her apart from the type of the 'süße Mädl' (sweet girl) she used to represent for Karl. This, however, is exactly what Karl does not want, because it demands a real interpersonal relationship and requires him to step out of the pre-formed narrative in which he merely plays the role of the social type he represents.

Stereotypes and Social Destinies

Karl's moment of *Grauen* (horror), when he looks in Marie's blind eyes, appears to be linked to an almost ontological crisis. What has drawn him to the Ladenbauers' household in the past seems to be connected to an experience of reassurance about his own presence, an experience of belonging. While his privilege to go to work only when it suits him is obviously convenient on the face of it, we might here once again assume a failing of the symbolic function: 'Er war froh, daß er keine Verpflichtungen hatte, in die Stadt zu gehen, obzwar ihm ja sein Vater auch diesmal einen versäumten Wochentag nachgesehen hätte, wie er es schon oft getan' (NL621) (He was glad that he did not have any commitment to go into the city, although his father would have forgiven him another missed working day, as he had so often). Implied in this liberty to more or less come and go as he pleases is also the question of whether he is needed at all. Karl's social status, while it is certainly not precarious in the sense of the financial uncertainty that Marie's family has to face, seems nevertheless somehow suspended and undefined. This is underlined by the shifting ways in which he is addressed by Rebay and the Ladenbauers. They seem to performatively underline the class differences by calling him at times 'Herr von Breiteneder', which would imply that Karl is a nobleman. Besides the fact that this exaggerated sign of respect barely hides the aspect of mockery in it, it also underscores the fact that Karl in fact does not belong to the milieu of the performance artists. Marie's blindness seems to cut through the illusory farce of harmonious 'togetherness': in fact, it destroys the quality of 'Augenblick' (moment) of their relationship: 'und die beiden lebten sehr vergnügt, ohne an die Zukunft zu denken' (NL622) (and both of them lived happily without thinking of the future). In this way, Marie's loss of eyesight confronts Karl with his own insincerity and the simulatory character of his relationship to Marie and, with that, of his entire life situation, which leaves him to the prefigured path as heir of his father's turnery: 'der Vater wußte aus Erfahrung, daß sich die Breiteneders bisher noch immer zur rechten Zeit zu einem soliden Lebenswandel entschlossen hatten' (NL621) (The father knew from experience that the Breiteneders had always taken the respectable path of life when it was time to do so). Read like this, Karl's *Grauen* (horror) might also be directed at the bourgeois life he has to face after acknowledging that his relationship to Marie is not – at least from his side – based on any real interpersonal bond and responsibility. Jedek's comically recursive reassurance of Karl's 'Da-sein' (existence/being there) seems rather to call his identity into question: 'Weil ich g'wußt hab', Sie sein da, hab' ich ihr g'sagt, daß Sie da sein. Und weil sie so oft nach Ihnen g'fragt hat, während sie krank war, hab' ich ihr g'sagt: "Der Herr Breiteneder is da …"' (NL630) (Because I knew that you are here, I have told her that you are here. And because she asked for you when she was ill, I have told her: 'Herr von Breiteneder is here …'). It seems as if the fact that Marie is no longer able to see for herself whether Karl is *da* or not, makes his 'being there' in fact questionable for himself. This culminates in Karl's sudden inability to make himself heard: 'Er rief: "Marie! Marie!" Aber es hörte ihn niemand, und er hörte sich selber nicht' (He yelled: 'Marie! Marie!' But no one heard him, and he did not hear himself). He then seems to have become the 'Gespenst' (ghost) he mistook Marie for, when looking into her blind eyes.

It thus becomes clear that, also for Karl, the love affair with Marie has an individualizing function, which secured his place within the norm. In contrast to the other protagonists, he does not become seduced by the mystified stereotype of enigmatic 'otherness' and does not turn to the higher power of destiny. Nevertheless, he enjoys the temporary suspension of reality and – at least for him – secured transgression of the bourgeois norm by becoming attached to Marie. That he is able to uphold this safe boundary, however, is only due to the fact that he is not willing to engage with Marie individually and overcome the stereotypical image he has of her.[58] In this way, the stereotype does indeed become Marie's 'destiny'. As soon as she is no longer able to provide the de-individualized surface of the stereotype assigned to her, the only place left for her is that of the absolute 'other'. Accordingly, Karl perceives it as almost inappropriate when she sings one of her clichéd old songs, 'als wenn sie wirklich noch mit ihrem Schatz aufs Land gehen, den blauen Himmel, die grünen Wiesen sehen und im Freien tanzen könnte, wie sie's in dem Lied erzählte' (NL625) (as if she could still go to the country with her darling, as if she could still see the blue sky, the green fields, and as if she could still dance outdoors, as she said in the song). The new song, which Marie's accompanist Rebay wrote for her is in turn seen as the creation of an alternative position: 'Eine Existenz hab' ich dem Mädel gründen wollen! [...] Gerad mit dem neuen Lied!' (NL628) (I wanted to give the girl a livelihood! [...] Especially with the new song!). No longer able to perform the role of the carefree 'süßes Mädel' (sweet girl), Marie is now confined to performatively repeating her sad 'destiny' time and again: 'Ja freilich ist es ein trauriges Lied [...] – es ist ja auch ein trauriges Los, was ihr zugestoßen ist. Da kann ich ihr doch kein lustiges Lied schreiben?' (NL628-9) (Well, of course it is a sad song – after all it is a sad fate that has been bestowed on her). The sad song is thus considered appropriate with regard to Marie's actual sad 'destiny'. The performance of the song – and particularly the repeated performance – functions as a manifestation of the agony described in the lyrics, which is then confirmed by Karl's immediate rejection. Marie's suicide might, then, be understood not only as a direct reaction to Karl's behaviour itself, but also as a refusal to accept her 'trauriges Los' (sad fate) and the compulsion to confirm it through never-ending repeated performances.

The repetition of performances as a constituting element of social reality has emerged in all narratives discussed in this chapter, underscoring the tension between the typological and the individual as central conflict in Schnitzler's writings. This tension is negotiated through the complex of stereotype and destiny: while Albert's and Leisenbohg's proclamations of the originality and uniqueness of their destinies becomes undermined by the repetitive structure and stereotypical elements of the texts, it is in turn Karl's failure to acknowledge Marie as an individual beyond the stereotype that not only contributes substantially

---

58   Recall that the inability to distinguish the individual from the stereotyped class counts for Gilman as the 'pathological' form of stereotyping. See Gilman, Sander L. (1985), *Difference and Pathology: Stereotypes of Sexuality, Race, and Madness*, Ithaca, London: Cornell University Press, 18.

to Marie's 'trauriges Los' (sad fate), but also seems to lead to a certain form of self-alienation. While all three protagonists use romantic love outside marriage as an escape from their social destinies, in *Traumnovelle* (Dream Story), which I will discuss in the next chapter, love occurs in the institutionalized form of marriage and therefore, as a social destiny in itself.

Five Dream, Destiny and Infectious Alterity in *Traumnovelle* (Dream Story)

Ja, wenn die Prinzen wie im Märchen wären.[1]

Oh, suppose the princes were like in the fairy tales.

In 1931, the year of his death, Schnitzler published a volume encompassing a range of novellas that he had previously published elsewhere over the first quarter of the twentieth century. The title he chose for the book underlines the central position of two topics in his works: *Traum und Schicksal* (Dream and Destiny). The first novella of the volume is one of Schnitzler's most popular texts, *Traumnovelle* (Dream Story), which was first published as a series in the glamorous fashion magazine *Die Dame* (The Lady) in 1925/1926.[2] While the thematic centrality of dreams is already announced in the title, the novella's relation to the topic of destiny is much less self-evident. Accordingly, scholarly interest has been drawn to the relation of dreaming and waking in the novella, but the topic of destiny has received considerably less attention.[3]

---

1   From one of Schnitzler's early drafts (CUL A144,1) for *Traumnovelle* (Dream Story).

2   I have analyzed Schnitzler's authorial self-fashioning through this publication in a women's magazine elsewhere. See Kolkenbrock, Marie (2017), 'Der "graziöse" Autor und *Die Dame*: Arthur Schnitzlers implizite Autorschaft im Fortsetzungsroman *Traumnovelle*,' *Poetologien des Posturalen: Inszenierungen von Autorschaft in der Zwischenkriegszeit*, ed. by Clemens Peck and Norbert Christian Wolf, Paderborn: Fink, 49–65.

3   An exception is the article by Schrimpf already discussed in the Introduction of this book. See Schrimpf, Hans Joachim (1963), 'Arthur Schnitzlers *Traumnovelle*,' *Zeitschrift für deutsche Philologie* 82: 172–192.

I have argued so far that stereotype and destiny occur in Schnitzler's writings as a coping mechanism to regain a sense of individuality
which is threatened by an emerging coercive and de-individualizing
force on the part of one's social role. In *Traumnovelle* (Dream Story) this
is played out through the bourgeois discourse on love. It has already
been shown in the discussion of the *Dämmerseelen* (Dozing Souls) narratives in the previous chapter that destiny plays a central role in the
discourse of love, and that love, in turn, is the individualizing currency *par excellence*. The discourse on love yields, then, probably the
most powerful narrative of destiny as individuation: what could be
more reassuring of one's own individuality than to be destined to
fall in love with another person and to feel recognized by the other
as 'the one' in return?[4] This is already inherent in Hegel's figure of
mutual recognition as essential pre-requisite for the subject's development of self-consciousness. The individual has to recognize itself in
the other but still accept the independence of the latter. By the same
token, recognition by the other is required. According to Hegel, the
struggle between the two subjects is inevitable after the movement of
mutual recognition has been performed, where the winner will sub-
due the loser as slave. But the dialectic of the master is a predicament
because the movement of recognition becomes asymmetric, making
it impossible for him to recognize himself in the other and to gain
a proper assurance of himself.[5] Santner has analyzed Schnitzler's
novella through the Hegelian master and slave dialectic.[6] According
to Santner, Fridolin's conflict as that of Hegel's master has shown that
Fridolin's problem is that he cannot accept the 'otherness' of women
and that he has to possess them instead. This is why he is unable to
play the game of mutual recognition with an equal partner, which
makes it impossible for him to gain any real satisfaction. Santner's
adoption of Hegel's master and slave dialectic as a framework is
useful to bring the novella's central conflict into sharper focus, and
I would like to suggest that it can be developed further. By calling
Fridolin 'something of a neurotic', Santner seems to assume that the
conflict developed in the novella is about an individual pathological
case and that being trapped in the master and slave dialectic is a, as it

---

4   Sebald also points up the function of love as the secularized metaphysics of
     bourgeois societies. See Sebald, W. G. (1985), *Die Beschreibung des Unglücks: Zur
     Österreichischen Literatur von Stifter bis Handke*, Salzburg: Residenz, 38.
5   See Hegel, G. F. W. (1988), *Phänomenologie des Geistes*, ed. by H.-F. Wessels and H.
     Clairmont, Hamburg: Meiner, 128–136.
6   See Santner, Eric (1986), 'Of Masters, Slaves, and Other Seducers: Arthur Schnit-
     zler's "Traumnovelle",' *Modern Austrian Literature* 19 (3/4): 33–45, 39.

were, personal problem of Fridolin's.[7] If we recall Simone de Beauvoir's use of the Hegelian model to describe the positions of the patriarchal gender relationship, equating the male position with that of the master and the female position with that of the slave,[8] the conflict in *Traumnovelle* (Dream Story) seems to be more deeply rooted in the bourgeois gender order and corresponds to stereotypical images of femininity and their deconstruction.

Failing Recognitions

When Albertine reveals to Fridolin her capacity for an active eroticism, and thus presents herself not only as the object but also as the subject of desire, she steps out of the stereotypical role of the motherly 'domestic angel',[9] assigned to her by the bourgeois ideal of femininity, and by Fridolin as representative of the patriarchal gender order. The key moment of challenge to the patriarchal gender model is Albertine's comment to Fridolin, 'Ach, wenn ihr wüßtet' (T12) ('Oh, if you men knew!'),[10] which indicates that the common imago of femininity is insufficient, that the female is more complex than just the knowable complement of male wholeness. Correspondingly, Fridolin's self-perception and his feeling of security collapse when his wife reveals her capacity for activity beyond his knowledge. Even though both Fridolin and Albertine confess to each other that they felt attracted to another person at least once, Fridolin feels especially betrayed by his wife, which exposes the double standards of patriarchal gender roles.

The figure of mutual recognition in the form of the exchange of gazes is a dominant motif in the novella.[11] The first time it appears is right at the beginning, where it initially seems to signify a successful mutual recognition between the spouses: 'Und da sich nun auch Albertine zu dem Kind herabgebeugt hatte, trafen sich die Hände der Eltern auf der

7 Santner, 'Of Masters, Slaves, and Other Seducers,' 33.
8 Beauvoir, Simone de (1968/2009), *The Second Sex*, London: Jonathan Cape, 72.
9 I am borrowing the term from one of Elisabeth Bronfen's (1992) types of femininity, to which I will return later on, *Over Her Dead Body: Death, Femininity and the Aesthetic*, Manchester: Manchester University Press, 208.
10 Schnitzler, Arthur (1928), *Rhapsody: A Dream Novel*, London: Constable, 19. All translations for *Traumnovelle* (Dream Story) are taken from this English edition, which does not list the name of the translator. All other translations from the German are my own.
11 The centrality of the gaze in *Traumnovelle* (Dream Story) and Schnitzler's work in general has been pointed out by several scholars. See Freytag, Julia (2007), *Verhüllte Schaulust: Die Maske in Schnitzlers Traumnovelle und in Kubricks Eyes Wide Shut*, Bielefeld: transcript; Aspetsberger, Friedbert (1966), '"Drei Akte in einem": Zum Formtyp in Schnitzlers Drama,' *Zeitschrift für deutsche Philologie* 85: 285–308; Saxer, Sibylle (2010), *Die Sprache der Blicke verstehen: Arthur Schnitzlers Poetik des Augen-Blicks als Poetik der Scham*, Freiburg i. Br./Berlin/Vienna: Rombach.

geliebten Stirn, und mit zärtlichem Lächeln, das nun nicht mehr dem Kinde allein galt, begegneten sich ihre Blicke' (T5) (Albertina [sic] also bent over her, and as her hand met her husband's on the beloved forehead, they looked at each other with a tender smile not meant for the child).[12] Without overemphasizing the Hegelian topos, one could say that here the couple has a 'mutual other' in between – their daughter – which allows an equal recognition of each other. In their function as parents it is easy to accept the other as the matching part of oneself – different from the self but belonging to the same entity, both of them necessary. But when it comes to their function as sexual partners, the symmetry turns out to be much less stable. The objective situation of the initial conflict seems to be equal, as Fridolin and Albertine both encountered seductive strangers at the masked ball they attended the previous night and as they both confess to each other that they felt more seriously attracted to other persons before, during a holiday in Denmark. But while for Albertine the mutual confessions initially allow reconciliation, Fridolin does not seem to be able to forgive her:

> 'Wir wollen einander solche Dinge künftig immer gleich erzählen', sagte sie.
> Er nickte stumm.
> 'Versprich's mir.'
> Er zog sie an sich. 'Weißt du das nicht?' fragte er; aber seine Stimme klang immer noch hart.
> Sie nahm seine Hände, streichelte sie und sah zu ihm auf mit umflorten Augen, auf deren Grund er ihre Gedanken zu lesen vermochte. (T11)
> 'In the future let's tell each other such things at once,' she said.
> He nodded in silence.
> 'Will you promise me?'
> He took her into his arms, 'Don't you know that?' he asked. But his voice was still harsh. She took his hands and looked up at him with misty eyes, in the depth of which he could read her thoughts.[13]

The harshness in his voice signifies Fridolin's inability to accept Albertine's secret sexual desire. Yet, at this point he still feels superior to her and thinks that he is able to read her thoughts, which can be understood as mastery over her mind and indeed the denial of her independence.

---

12 Schnitzler, *Rhapsody: A Dream Novel*, 7.
13 Schnitzler, *Rhapsody: A Dream Novel*, 17–18.

This self-confidence and unforgiving attitude is of course linked to the patriarchal double standard that demands premarital virginity only for the woman. The narrator reflects here Fridolin's perspective through 'erlebte Rede' (experienced speech) stating that he *is* able to read Albertine's thoughts. However, the adjective 'umflort' may convey a contradiction of this legibility as it hints at a literal *veiling* of her gaze caused by tears. It is here that Albertine points out the asymmetry in their relationship and refuses Fridolin's patronizing attempt to comfort her:

> 'In jedem Wesen – glaub' es mir, wenn es auch wohlfeil klingen mag – in jedem Wesen, das ich zu lieben glaubte, habe ich immer nur dich gesucht. Das weiß ich besser, als du es verstehen kannst, Albertine.'
> Sie lächelte trüb. 'Und wenn es auch mir beliebt hätte, zuerst auf die Suche zu gehen?' Ihr Blick veränderte sich, wurde kühl und undurchdringlich. (T12)
> 'You may believe me, even though it sounds trite, that in every woman I thought I loved it was always you I was looking for – I know that better than you can understand it, Albertina.'
> A dispirited smile passed over her face. 'And suppose before meeting you, I, too, had gone on a search for a mate?' she asked. The look in her eyes changed, becoming cool and impenetrable.[14]

Fridolin's comment brings out the paradox inherent in the idea of love as destiny: while it seemingly stresses that Albertine is unique to Fridolin, in the sense that he was looking for his one true love and found it in Albertine, it also reveals that his idea of 'true love' was attached to the pre-conceptualized role of 'wife' and 'mother' that he had to 'cast'. It suggests that what Fridolin was looking for was rather the realization of an idealized idea of 'woman' rather than Albertine as an individual. In this way, the text demonstrates how the experience of love is also determined by performative demands of stereotypical role expectations, which undermine the sense of individuality.[15] The need for the uniqueness of one's own experience of love stands in steep contrast to the factual seriality of enunciations and verbalizations of love, as we have also already seen in the last chapter. Fridolin's remark already reflects its own clichéd character of this currency when he admits that it might sound cheap ('wohlfeil') and in this way hints at the seriality of the enunciation of love.

---

14 Schnitzler, *Rhapsody: A Dream Novel*, 19.
15 See also Sebald, who suggests that Schnitzler's works express a 'Skepsis gegenüber den habituellen Veranstaltungen der Liebe' (scepticism with regard to the habitus-related events of love). See Sebald, *Die Beschreibung des Unglücks*, 40.

It is this precise moment, as Albertine's eyes become impenetrable, that throws Fridolin off his balance. Albertine only now reveals her capability for an independent sexual desire to the full extent and breaks out of her role as Fridolin's complementary other:

> Er ließ ihre Hände aus den seinen gleiten, als hätte er sie auf einer Unwahrheit, auf einem Verrat ertappt; sie aber sagte: 'Ach, wenn ihr wüßtet', und wieder schwieg sie.
> 'Wenn wir wüßten -? Was willst du damit sagen?'
> Mit seltsamer Härte erwiderte sie: 'Ungefähr, was du dir denkst, mein Lieber.' (T12)
> [H]e allowed her hands to slip from his, as though he had caught her lying or committing a breach of faith. She, however, continued: 'Oh, if you men knew!' and again was silent.
> 'If we knew –? What do you mean by that?'
> In a strangely harsh voice she replied:
> 'About what you imagine, my dear.'[16]

The harshness which was used to describe Fridolin's irreconcilability now marks Albertine's reaction to his self-righteousness when he indulges in the resources of patriarchal discourse. This is underlined by the fact that Albertine, by using the plural form, seems to address not only Fridolin individually but men in general.[17] In this way, she also reproduces the de-individualizing effect of Fridolin's comment. Moreover, Albertine mirrors Fridolin's patronizing appeasement ('Don't you know that?') and turns the tables on him. The emphasis on knowledge – and the lack of it – refers to the underlying struggle for power in the marital conflict. While Fridolin is confident that he knows more about the functioning of gender roles than Albertine would ever be able to understand, she is eager to demonstrate to him his own ignorance. The passage thus describes a failure of mutual recognition, which is underlined when Albertine's gaze becomes 'kühl und undurchdringlich' (cool and impenetrable).

This introduces Fridolin's crisis-like experience, in which he begins to feel more and more alienated from himself and his previously familiar surroundings. That it is, in fact, this initial conflict that sets his crisis in motion and determines all the experiences and encounters during his ensuing nocturnal wanderings almost becomes clear to himself at one point: 'Wie heimatlos, wie hinausgestoßen erschien er sich [...] seit

---

16 Schnitzler, *Rhapsody: A Dream Novel*, 19.
17 See Scheible, Hartmut (1977), *Arthur Schnitzler und die Aufklärung*, Munich: W. Fink, 76.

dem Abendgespräch mit Albertine rückte er immer weiter fort aus dem gewohnten Bezirk seines Daseins in irgendeine andere, ferne, fremde Welt' (T27–28) (ever since this evening's conversation with Albertina he was moving farther and farther away from his everyday existence into some strange and distant world).[18]

Coping Mechanisms

The awareness of the failed mutual recognition with Albertine is bound to unsettle Fridolin's secured sense of self as a representative of the bourgeois masculine norm. Albertine's confession has blurred the boundaries between the active male self and the passive female other. As a result, the defining lines around his concept of self seem to have become penetrable and everything that represented the old reassuring order before begins to feel unstable. This corresponds to the many other crisis-like experiences of the protagonists discussed in the previous chapters: the protagonist is again confronted with an alienation of his social destiny in the Bourdieusian sense. In this case the arguably most 'naturalized' part of social essence comes to be drawn into question: that of gender. Moreover, if the romantic relationship is to be understood as a practice of individuation, in the sense that it provides one with a reassurance of one's own individuality, then becoming aware of the performative – and thus also serial and repetitive – quality of the experience of love, is highly disturbing for one's identity: the performative aspects of love are closely linked to those of gender. And when these become palpable, thus when what was experienced as one's inner essence begins to feel like externally imposed repetition compulsions, one's secured position within the norm becomes precarious. This is thus one of the moments 'in denen sich der Mensch selber fremd wird' (in which man becomes estranged from himself).[19] As the bourgeois order is tightly intertwined with patriarchal gender roles, the former also begins to lose its credibility through the disruption of the latter. Fridolin at first turns to the by now well-known coping mechanisms of stereotyping and the invocation of destiny.

Initially, he seeks to re-stabilize his position within the norm by typecasting the 'other', in this case Albertine and women in general: 'Eine ist wie die andere, dachte er mit Bitterkeit, und Albertine ist wie sie alle – sie ist die Schlimmste von allen' (T72) (They are all alike, he thought bitterly, and Albertina is like the rest of them – if not the worst).[20] That is, she is not only a serial figure, who can stand for all, but excessive in

---

18   Schnitzler, *Rhapsody: A Dream Novel*, 59.
19   Schrimpf, 'Arthur Schnitzlers *Traumnovelle*,' 175.
20   Schnitzler, *Rhapsody: A Dream Novel*, 145.

her exemplary badness. Elisabeth Bronfen describes three predominant types of literary representations of femininity, which will become useful for my reading of *Traumnovelle* (Dream Story): 'firstly, the diabolic outcast, the destructive fatal demon woman, secondly, the domestic "angel of the house", the saintly, self-sacrificing vessel, and thirdly a particular version of Mary Magdalene, as the penitent and redeemed sexually vain and dangerous woman, the fallen woman'.[21] Fridolin's image of Albertine is highly influenced by this stereotypical imagery of femininity: while she fulfilled the role of the 'domestic "angel of the house"' before, she now appears like the 'destructive fatal demon woman'. This becomes even more evident later in the novella when Albertine tells him about her dream. Fridolin does not distinguish here between dreamed and real experience, and judges Albertine for her oneiric actions as if she really had committed them: 'Da saß sie ihm gegenüber, die ihn heute nacht ruhig hatte ans Kreuz schlagen lassen, mit engelhaftem Blick, hausfraulich-mütterlich' (T76) (There she sat opposite him, the woman who had calmly allowed him to be crucified the preceding night. She was sitting there with an angelic look, like a good housewife and mother).[22]

As we will see, in all his encounters with the different women during this nocturnal odyssey, he seems to seek the self-assuring recognition he was used to getting from Albertine, but was suddenly deprived of through her refusal to remain within the boundaries of the complementary 'other' assigned to her by the patriarchal gender order. At the same time, the feeling of sudden alienation from his social role also sets in motion a fascination with 'otherness' and the temptation to cross the boundaries from the realm of the bourgeois norm into that of the 'other'. This is again linked with the invocation of destiny.

Fridolin decides only a few hours after his conflict with Albertine that from now on '[d]as Schicksal soll entscheiden' (T36) (Let fate decide the question)[23] and later he feels the temptation, 'sich mit dem Schicksal zu messen' (T57) (to match oneself against Fate).[24] However, 'Schicksal' connotes different things in the two passages. While at both times the invocation of destiny is linked to Fridolin's desire to transgress the normative boundaries of his social role, 'Schicksal' seems to indicate in the first case a possible loophole to escape the restrictive structures of the dominant order, thus an *alternative* to his social destiny in the Bourdieusian sense. In the second case, 'Schicksal' is less likely to refer to metaphysical destiny and thus to his individually laid-out path of

---

21   Bronfen, Elisabeth (1992), *Over Her Dead Body: Death, Femininity and the Aesthetic*, Manchester: Manchester University Press, 218.
22   Schnitzler, *Rhapsody: A Dream Novel*, 151–152.
23   Schnitzler, *Rhapsody: A Dream Novel*, 74.
24   Schnitzler, *Rhapsody: A Dream Novel*, 111.

life, but here actually means his social destiny, i.e. the rules of conduct imposed by his social role. The first quotation is taken from the conversation with his former fellow student Nachtigall, who will take him to the secret masked ball. Fridolin's invocation of destiny marks an eagerness to leave behind the restrictive structures of his bourgeois existence which have lost their reassuring effect. The moment can thus indeed count as an escape 'aus dem Alltäglich-Festgelegten' (from the pre-assigned quotidian),[25] and as the desire for an individually assigned path, set off from the pre-determined normalized tracks of his social role. While this might feel to Fridolin like an opportunity for a 'Durchbruch zum Eigenen' (breakthrough to a realm of one's own),[26] it is striking that this 'Eigene' (realm of one's own) is again linked to the idea of giving oneself over to a higher power: the rules of conduct imposed by the social destiny are replaced not by a claim of individual responsibility, but by the idea of a metaphysical determination of events. In the second example, however, 'Schicksal' (destiny) does not seem to have the same implications of individuation, but rather the opposite: it is actually his bourgeois existence that Fridolin wants to challenge here. The full sentence reads: 'Sollte man immer nur aus Pflicht, aus Opfermut aufs Spiel setzen, niemals aus Laune, aus Leidenschaft oder einfach, um sich mit dem Schicksal zu messen?!' (T57) (Is one always to stake one's life just from a sense of duty or self-sacrifice, and never just because of a whim or a passion, or simply to match oneself against Fate?).[27] What becomes clear here is the desire to transgress the normative restrictions of his bourgeois social role as physician, husband, and father. 'Schicksal' here refers, then, not to the idealized notion of an individual path of life, but to his social destiny.

The stereotype of the doctor seems to be particularly closely linked to the moral expectation that doctors have to be fully identified with their work, that it is in fact not only 'Beruf', but also 'Berufung',[28] which implies, strictly speaking, a willingness to give one's life for it. This willingness is obviously in the case of Fridolin rarely tested, but the expectation is implied in the formulation 'aus Pflichtgefühl [...] aufs Spiel setzen', taking risks out of a sense of duty, and is further underlined by the fact that immediately after this thought Fridolin remembers for the second time in the novella 'dass er möglicherweise schon den Keim einer Todeskrankheit im Leibe trug' (T57) (that even now the

---

25 Schrimpf, 'Arthur Schnitzlers *Traumnovelle*,' 175.
26 Schrimpf, 'Arthur Schnitzlers *Traumnovelle*,' 175.
27 Schnitzler, *Rhapsody: A Dream Novel*, 111.
28 See also my analysis of *Flucht in die Finsternis* (Flight into Darkness) in Chapter Two. Also Otto – at least in the perspective of his brother Robert – seems to fulfil this expectation of the stereotype.

germ of a fatal disease might be in his body),[29] which refers to his fear
that he might have got infected by the contagious cough of a child suffering from diphtheria. To take on risks not out of professional duty,
but just for the sake of passion or out of whim, can thus be understood
as an attempt at escaping the responsibilities and duties of his social
role. To challenge destiny in this context is, then, very closely linked
to the transgression of normative boundaries. At the same time, Fridolin's fear of infection is also a fear of this urge for transgression. By
wondering whether he might be delirious (see T57), Fridolin pathol-
ogizes his own desire to escape the restrictions of his social role. As a
consequence, only moments later, the very same role he just wished to
overcome seems like the return to a safe haven to him: 'Und mit einem
seltsamen Herzklopfen ward er sich freudig bewußt, daß er in weni-
gen Stunden schon im weißen Leinenkittel zwischen den Betten seiner
Kranken herumgehen würde' (T58) (And with a strange, happy beating
of his heart, he realized that in a few hours he would be walking around
between the beds of his patients in his white hospital coat).[30] This obviously indicates Fridolin's ambivalent needs for freedom *and* security,
for feeling 'special' *and* 'normal' at the same time.[31]

Infection of the Norm

Fridolin's fear of infection mentioned above, which turns out to be
a subtle but recurring theme in the novella, can be interpreted in yet
another way: infection as the 'invasion' of 'otherness' into the healthy
'body' of the norm.[32] As the conflict with Albertine has unsettled Fridolin's secured sense of his position as representative of the bourgeois
male norm, it does not only have a deeply frightening effect, but also
instills in him the desire to escape the normative boundaries he no
longer feels protected by. If crossing over the boundary from the realm
of the norm into that of the 'other' means losing one's secured and

---

29 Schnitzler, *Rhapsody: A Dream Novel*, 111.
30 Schnitzler, *Rhapsody: A Dream Novel*, 112.
31 Webber additionally underlines the ambivalence yielded by the formula-
    tion 'zwischen den Betten' (between the beds), which not only indicates his
    half-dreaming state but also the oscillating quality of his sense of adventure
    between the promises of Eros and the dangers of sickness and death. See Web-
    ber, Andrew (2011), 'Threshold Conditions: Benjamin, Schnitzler, and the Sleep-
    ing Disorders of Modernism,' *Die Halbschlafbilder in der Literatur, den Künsten und
    den Wissenschaften*, ed. by Roger Paulin and Helmut Pfotenhauer, Würzburg:
    Königshausen & Neumann, 275–290, 283.
32 See my discussion of the theme of infection in the section on *Andreas Thameyer*
    in Chapter Three. I have analyzed this aspect in both texts, *Traumnovelle* (Dream
    Story) and *Andreas Thameyers letzter Brief* (Andreas Thameyer's Last Letter) in
    more detail in my article 'Gothic Infections'.

privileged position within the social order, then infection with 'other-ness' is equal to a threat of 'social death'. Accordingly, all of Fridolin's encounters after the conflict with Albertine are marked by the ambiv-alence of Eros and Thanatos: the promise of transgression they seem to have in store is highly seductive and frightening at the same time.[33]

The returning motif of Denmark as site of the uncontrolled Eros may be seen as an initial source of infection.[34] The Shakespearean 'something is rotten in the state of Denmark' comes to mind and could refer to a smouldering wound in the patriarchal gender order, which becomes uncovered in the conflict with Albertine.[35] The sudden thawing of the snow, which introduces Fridolin's nocturnal odyssey, could also be understood as referring to the first signs of infection: a raised temper-ature. Immediately after Albertine's revelations, Fridolin is called to the deathbed of one of his patients, the 'Hofrat' (Privy Councillor). As a mag-istrate, the Hofrat is a representative of the social order. His doorbell has an 'altväterische [sic] Klingelton' (T14) (old-fashioned [literally: old-fa-therly, M.K.] bell),[36] which appears like a 'simulation' of the patriarchal. His death marks once more the disruption of the patriarchal order: the father is dead, the paternal law seems to be losing its power. However, Fridolin's sudden irrational idea that the Hofrat might only be seem-ingly dead and so able to hear the conversation between his daughter Marianne and Fridolin gives the corpse vampiric features. This also cor-responds to Marianne's appearance: years of taking care of her father have drained her and he seems to have 'sucked' all life from her. In this way, she appears like the distorted ideal of the complementary female, the 'domestic angel of the house', who fades away in order to provide a man with a sense of wholeness. The text refers repeatedly to the 'süßlich

33 See Lukas, Wolfgang (1996), *Das Selbst und das Fremde: Epochale Lebenskrisen und ihre Lösung im Werk Arthur Schnitzlers*, Munich: Fink, 108; Webber, 'Threshold Conditions,' 275–290, 283.

34 Both Albertine and Fridolin had seductive encounters during a holiday in Den-mark, which they confess to each other during their initial conflict. *Dänemark* (Denmark) then returns as password for the masked ball that Fridolin ille-gitimately attends and Albertine's Danish seductive stranger makes another appearance in her dream. In this way, Denmark is linked to a stereotypical idea of illicit desires. For an extensive reading of the orientalization of Denmark and its role as Austria's 'other' in the novella see Allen, Julie K. (2009), 'Dreaming of Denmark: Orientalism and Otherness in Schnitzler's *Traumnovelle*,' *Modern Austrian Literature* 42 (2): 41–59.

35 See Lange-Kirchheim, Astrid (2003), '*Déjà-vue* einer Jahrhunderwende. Psy-choanalyse als Traumatheorie. Zu Arthur Schnitzlers *Traumnovelle*,' *Geschlech-terforschung und Literaturwissenschaft*, ed. by P. Wiesinger, Bern [et. al.]: Lang, 269–274, 273.

36 Schnitzler, *Rhapsody: A Dream Novel*, 27.

faden Geruch' (T15) (indefinite [rather: stale, M.K.], sweetish scent)[37] of Marianne, which has highly morbid connotations. 'Death' seems to be inscribed all over her with the 'großen, aber trüben Augen' (T15) (large, but sad [rather: dull, murky, M.K.] eyes),[38] the dry hair and the wrinkled, yellowish neck. Fridolin also assumes that she is feverish and quickly diagnoses her with a 'Spitzenkatarrh' (T17) (catarrhous pulmonary infection, M.K.), which was considered as the onset of tuberculosis in Schnitzler's day.[39] This diagnosis reinforces the vampire motif, as the disease was one of the scientific explanations for vampire folklore in pre-modern times.[40] Marianne thus seems to be infected by a parasitic depletion, as if now that her father has drained all life from her, she needs a new source of life for herself. In fact, at one point Fridolin fantasizes about being that source, when he assumes: 'Marianne sähe sicher besser aus, wenn sie seine Geliebte wäre. Ihr Haar wäre weniger trocken, ihre Lippen röter und voller' (T16) (Marianne would certainly look better, he thought to himself, if she were his mistress. Her hair would be less dry, her lips would be fuller and redder).[41] However, her body as a potential dangerous source of contagions makes him feel rather repulsed than excited (see T19). When she professes her love to him he quickly distances himself from her by thinking of her as a hysteric. With this second medical diagnosis, as with the first one, Fridolin reassures himself in his position as a man of science who is immune to the infectious onslaught of vam-

---

37   Schnitzler, *Rhapsody: A Dream Novel*, 28.
38   Schnitzler, *Rhapsody: A Dream Novel*, 28.
39   The anonymous translator of the 1928 English edition pragmatically translated the term directly as 'tuberculosis'. See Schnitzler, *Rhapsody: A Dream Novel*, 32. In his 1887 book *Die diätetische Blutentmischung als Grundursache der Krankheiten* (The dietetic dysaemia as basic reason for diseases) the physician Heinrich Lahmann writes: 'Der bis dahin nur katarrhalische Lungenspitzenkatarrh geht damit in den tuberkulösen über (wobei man allerdings nicht glauben darf, dass der Übergang durch Untersuchungen genau zu bestimmen wäre, [...] was praktisch auch völlig gleichgültig ist, da ohne rationelles Eingreifen der Spitzenkatarrh zur Tuberkulose führt)' (the catarrhous pulmonary infection will eventually turn tuberculous (although one should not believe that this moment of transition could be precisely determined in the medical exam, which is completely irrelevant from a practical point of view, because without any rational intervention, the catarrhous infection will definitely lead to tuberculosis). See Lahmann, Heinrich (1987), *Die diätetische Blutentmischung (Dysämie) als Grundursache der Krankheiten: Ein Beitrag zur Lehre von der Krankheitsanlage und Krankheitsverhütung*, St. Goar: Reichl, 96.
40   See Sledzik, Paul and Nicholas Bellantoni (1994), 'Bioarcheological and Biocultural Evidence for the New England Vampire Folk Belief,' *American Journal of Physical Anthropology* 94 (2): 269–274.
41   Schnitzler, *Rhapsody: A Dream Novel*, 30.

piric 'otherness' represented by Marianne. However, this is immediately undermined by his rather unscientific and irrational, Gothic idea that the Hofrat might only be seemingly dead.[42]

Sebald's description of hysteria as 'die panische Reaktion des Mannes auf eine seinen Blick erwidernde Frau' (a man's reaction of panic, when a woman returns his gaze) points up the connection between Fridolin's reaction to Marianne and his conflict with Albertine.[43] This is underlined by Fridolin's immediate association: 'Flüchtig erinnerte er sich eines Romans, den er vor Jahren gelesen hatte und in dem es geschah, daß ein ganz junger Mensch, ein Knabe fast, am Totenbett der Mutter von ihrer Freundin verführt, eigentlich vergewaltigt wurde. Im selben Augenblick, er wußte nicht warum, mußte er seiner Gattin denken' (T19) (He had a fleeting recollection of reading a novel years ago in which a young man, still almost a boy, had been seduced, in fact, practically raped, by a friend of his mother at the latter's deathbed. At the same time he had to think of his wife, without knowing why).[44]

While Fridolin has no idea why he thinks of his wife immediately after recalling the fictional scene of the boy raped at his mother's deathbed, in the context of the conflict he had with her, it becomes understandable. The dead mother and her violent friend are both sides of Fridolin's stereotypical image of femininity, nurturing both the domestic angel and the voracious, diabolical outcast. They mirror Fridolin's disturbing experience of Albertine's revelations: the maternal woman that had provided a sense of wholeness and integrity has 'died' and the dangerous demonic woman figure has appeared instead. This corresponds again to the depiction of femininity in *Dracula* where the virtuous Lucy after her death is transformed into a lecherous vampire

---

42 See Aurnhammer, Achim (2013), *Arthur Schnitzlers intertextuelles Erzählen*, Berlin, Boston, MA: De Gruyter, 241. Aurnhammer calls the novella a 'Musterbeispiel' (paradigmatic example) for modernist fantastic fiction, because of the way it blends realistically possible and realistically impossible elements: while the beginning of the novella seems to be firmly rooted in realism, typical fantastic elements (masks, ruins, old houses, enigmatic messages etc.) enter the represented world incrementally so that the realistic setting becomes successively undermined. See Aurnhammer, *Arthur Schnitzlers intertextuelles Erzählen*, 240.

43 Sebald, *Die Beschreibung des Unglücks*, 43.

44 Schnitzler, *Rhapsody: A Dream Novel*, 36. Aurnhammer suggests that the literary text indirectly quoted in this passage refers to the fairy tale *Amgiad und Assad* (Amgiad and Assad) mentioned as the bedtime story of Fridolin's daughter at the beginning of the novella: here two mothers respectively desire the son of the other. However, Aurnhammer stresses that the actual source text is *Der 'Wilde Mann' und das 'Feuerzeug'* (The 'Wild Man' and the 'Lighter') by Otfried Mylius (pseudonym for Karl Müller). See Aurnhammer, *Arthur Schnitzlers intertextuelles Erzählen*, 248.

with an active desire.[45] With the act of violation the woman in the novel takes possession of the phallus as emblem of the paternal order. That Fridolin has to think of Albertine right after recalling this fictional scene suggests that this threat is already implicit to him when she confesses that she is capable of an active sexual desire. Fridolin's fear of infection is, then, tightly linked to a fear of the inversion or depletion of binary oppositions like male/female, dead/undead, self/'other'.[46]

On this note, it is not surprising that Fridolin feels relieved when he exits this place of decay: 'Er selbst erschien sich wie entronnen; nicht so sehr einem Erlebnis als vielmehr einem schwermütigen Zauber, der keine Macht über ihn gewinnen sollte' (T20) (He felt as if he had escaped something, not so much from an adventure, but rather from a melancholy spell the power of which he was trying to break).[47] Fridolin seems here to convince himself that he was able to avoid becoming infected at the 'contaminated' house of the Hofrat. However, ironically, the idea of fighting off the powers of a 'melancholic spell' seems to indicate the opposite: Fridolin, the doctor and man of science, has become 'infected' with irrational, mysticist thinking. The sensation of false security is also reflected directly afterwards, again with regard to the 'unnaturally' warm weather and to sexual activity, which also connotes the theme of potential infection in the guise of impregnation: 'Auf beschattenden Bänken saß da und dort ein Paar eng aneinandergeschmiegt, als wäre wirklich schon der Frühling da und die trügerisch-warme Luft nicht schwanger von Gefahren' (T21) ([H]e noticed, here and there on the benches standing in the shadow, that couples were sitting, clasped together, just as if spring had actually arrived and no danger were lurking in the deceptive, warm air [literally: as if the deceptive, warm air were not pregnant with danger, M.K.]).[48] Fridolin's

---

45 See Kittler, Friedrich A. (1993), *Draculas Vermächtnis: Technische Schriften*, Leipzig: Reclam, 38.

46 Elisabeth Strowick describes this effect of the inversion of binary oppositions through infection in Klabund's *Die Krankheit* (1915). See Strowick, Elisabeth (2009), *Sprechende Körper, Poetik der Ansteckung: Performativa in Literatur und Rhetorik*, Munich: Fink, 244.

47 Schnitzler, *Rhapsody: A Dream Novel*, 43.

48 A few lines before this sentence the text reads, 'in der Luft wehte ein Hauch des kommenden Frühlings' (T14) (there was a touch [literally: breath, M.K.] of spring in the air). See *Schnitzler, Rhapsody: A Dream Novel*, 29. Allerdissen and Imboden have pointed out that this 'Hauch' (breath) refers back to the 'Hauch von Abenteuer, Freiheit und Gefahr' (T7) (spirit [literally: breath, M.K.] of adventure, freedom and danger), which which Albertine und Fridolin felt during their seductive encounters. See Schnitzler, *Rhapsody: A Dream Novel*, 11. Allerdissen and Imboden also link this 'Hauch' (breath) to the 'unfaßbare Wind des Schicksals' (T7) (incomprehensible wind of fate) that Fridolin assumed behind his nocturnal adventures. See Schnitzler, *Rhapsody: A Dream Novel*, 11. See Aller-

feeling of having escaped is thus undermined by the narrative structure. While the text conveys Fridolin's perspective through internal focalization, the reader is presented with textual effects like the one just described that yield an additional level of meaning, exceeding Fridolin's conscious and intentional thoughts and actions. This might refer back to the 'speaking body' of the alleged hysteric Marianne, whose lips are 'wie von vielen ungesagten Worten schmal' (T15) (thin and firmly pressed together [rather: as if thinned out from too many words not said, M.K.]).[49] If hysteria can be understood as the 'genaue Äquivalent ihrer sonstigen Stimmlosigkeit' (exact equivalent of her general lack of voice),[50] then the bodily symptoms can be seen as speech acts that tell of what cannot be said: the hysterical body language can also be called 'rhetoric of the unconscious'.[51]

If the text, while on the face of it representing Fridolin's perspective, yields an additional level of meaning that undermines his intentional and conscious thoughts, it functions in a similar way to the body of a hysteric. The text offers the reader 'symptoms' that can be read and interpreted as performative effects that exceed Fridolin's perspective.[52] Moreover, while Fridolin at this point tries to reassure himself that he has escaped the 'schwermütige Zauber' (melancholy spell) in the Hofrat's house, the following passages suggest the opposite. Fridolin seems to lose more and more control over his own actions: he repeatedly does things unintentionally ('unwillkürlich') and his speech acts and 'performances' miss their goal more often than they are successful. He becomes 'self-conscious' in his own modes of conduct, so that what appeared 'natural' to him before suddenly feels theatrical. In other

dissen, Rolf (1985), *Arthur Schnitzler: Impressionistisches Rollenspiel und skeptischer Moralismus in seinen Erzählungen*, Bonn: Bouvier, 118; Imboden, Michael (1971), *Die surreale Komponente im erzählenden Werk Arthur Schnitzlers*, Bern: H. Lang, 48. This confirms my claim that destiny is used by Schnitzler's characters as coping mechanism when they feel the desire of transgression. Moreover, the emphasis on the semantic field of wind and breath could be read as referring again to infectious diseases transferred through miasmatic winds and the coughs of those already infected.

49 Schnitzler, *Rhapsody: A Dream Novel*, 29. Recall Bertolt's 'schmal gewordene[n] Lippen' (WiF657) (tightly compressed lips) in *Der Weg ins Freie* (Road into the Open). See Schnitzler, Arthur (1913b), *Road into the Open*, translated by Horace Samuel, London: Howard Latimer, 28.
50 Sebald, *Die Beschreibung des Unglücks*, 44.
51 See Strowick, *Sprechende Körper, Poetik der Ansteckung*, 85. See also Strowick's literature review about the discursive intersection of psychoanalysis and rhetoric. See Strowick, *Sprechende Körper, Poetik der Ansteckung*, 86, fn. 109.
52 See Strowick's discussion of performance/performativity of literary texts. See Strowick, *Sprechende Körper, Poetik der Ansteckung*, 145–193.

words, one could say that his habitus as bourgeois male subject begins to feel like 'role' rather than an expression of natural essence. If the habitus is produced and expressed through movements, gestures, facial expressions, manners, ways of walking, and ways of looking at the world,[53] it depends heavily on successful performances of 'social essence'. If those performances go awry, the re-production of one's habitus and thus the reconfirmation of one's position in the dominant order becomes questionable. And if the 'natural essence' of this position is in turn called into question, the performances attached to it may begin to feel theatrical. Already in the scene with Marianne Fridolin catches himself doing things involuntarily. While he thus performs things without the conscious decision to do so, the fact that he realizes that these things happen 'unwillkürlich' also indicates a form of self-consciousness. And in fact, not only does he realize that his behaviour seems to be somewhat 'automated', he almost seems to recognize them as the realization of cultural narratives: when he holds Marianne to comfort her he 'beinahe unwillkürlich' (T19) (almost against his will)[54] kisses her on the forehead, 'was ihm selbst ein wenig lächerlich vorkam' (T19) (an act that seemed somehow rather ridiculous).[55] This is only the beginning of a process in which Fridolin experiences his own actions repeatedly as ridiculous, which can be understood as an alienation from his own habitus. At the same time, his fear of infection accompanies him on this wandering where he nevertheless seems to above all seek a satisfying recognition scene, which would reassure him of his position within the norm and put an end to his feeling of increasing fragmentation.

The encounter with a group of fraternity students, in which Fridolin does not respond to the provocation of one of them and thus avoids a duel, is another failed movement of mutual recognition. While he recognizes the challenge as 'eine alberne Studentenrempelei' (T24) (silly encounter with a student)[56] he is nevertheless unable to shake off the feeling of his own inadequacy with regard to the still powerful ideal of military masculinity. Even though duels in the bourgeois milieu are marked in Schnitzler's work as 'theatralische Farce' (theatrical farce), to use Sebald's expression, the passage nevertheless displays 'die dem bürgerlichen Mann prinzipiell mangelnde Satisfaktionsfähigkeit' (the fact that the bourgeois man is not eligible to ask for satisfaction).[57] Sebald's choice of words is important in our context, as it points up the theatrical

---

53   See Moi, Toril (1991), 'Appropriating Bourdieu: Feminist Theory and Pierre Bourdieu's Sociology of Culture,' *New Literary History* 22: 1017–1049, 1031.
54   Schnitzler, *Rhapsody: A Dream Novel*, 36.
55   Schnitzler, *Rhapsody: A Dream Novel*, 36.
56   Schnitzler, *Rhapsody: A Dream Novel*, 49.
57   Sebald, *Die Beschreibung des Unglücks*, 49.

effect of when performances required by obsolete norms are still carried out without the necessary identification. However, if the old ideal has not been replaced by a new one, which is eminently the case with the ideal of bourgeois masculinity, the feeling of theatricality does not prevent feelings of inadequacy and shortcoming. Moreover, Fridolin's fear does not only refer to the threat of castration, as had been pointed out repeatedly, ('oder ein Auge heraus?' (T23) (Or lose an eye?)), but is also once more concerned with infection ('Oder gar Blutvergiftung?' (T23) (Or even blood-poisoning?).[58] The dreaded sepsis might result from a 'Hieb in den Arm' (T23) (cut in my arm),[59] thus an injury from the outer protective layer of the skin, which prevents the invasion of pathogenic germs. These fears can obviously be seen as completely rational considerations of the objective risks attached to a duel, but in the context of Fridolin's general fear of infection, they seem to be linked to his mental state of an emerging identity crisis in which he already feels that the protective boundaries around his sense of self have become permeable. As Judith Halberstam writes, 'Skin houses the body and it is figured in Gothic as the ultimate boundary, the material that divides the inside from the outside'.[60] One could say that Fridolin's skin has become permeable through a Gothic infection, or an infection with 'otherness'.

It is not surprising that at this point Fridolin is craving an encounter that could provide recognition and reassurance about his position within the norm of the bourgeois order. When he hears the interpellation 'Willst nicht mitkommen, Doktor?' (T24) (Won't you come with me, doctor?),[61] he turns around automatically (again: 'unwillkürlich' (T25) (involuntarily)).[62] Webber has pointed out that by assuming that the young sex worker must know – and thus *recognize* – him, Fridolin is 'enacting a version of Althusser's classic scene of subjectification by the calling power of ideology'.[63] Indeed, Fridolin seems to be desperate to accept this interpellation and in this way to be reassured of his position within the bourgeois order. For that, it is also important to be recognized individually, which explains his almost hopeful question: 'Woher kennst du mich?' (T25) (How do you know who I am?).[64] However, the illusion is exposed immediately afterwards: 'Ich kenn' Ihnen nicht, [...] aber in dem Bezirk sind ja alle Doktors' (T25) (Why, I don't know you [...], but here in this part of town they're all doctors, aren't

---

58   Schnitzler, *Rhapsody: A Dream Novel*, 48.
59   Schnitzler, *Rhapsody: A Dream Novel*, 48.
60   Halberstam, Judith (1995), *Skin Shows: Gothic Horrors and the Technology of Monsters*, Durham, NC and London: Duke UP, 7.
61   Schnitzler, *Rhapsody: A Dream Novel*, 50.
62   Schnitzler, *Rhapsody: A Dream Novel*, 50.
63   Webber, 'Threshold Conditions,' 285.
64   Schnitzler, *Rhapsody: A Dream Novel*, 50.

they?).[65] Fridolin's longing for self-consciousness (in the Hegelian sense of the word) is so strong that he ignores the arbitrariness of her recognition and tries to fulfil the mutual movement by asking for her name. Yet here again she does not make any attempt to conceal their stereotypical exchangeability in this encounter: 'No, wie wir i denn heißen? Mizzi natürlich' (T25) (Well, what do you think? Mizzi, of course).[66]

Despite this refusal to engage in a more personal discourse with him, Fridolin feels tempted by her, but also thinks immediately of the possibility of infection: 'Könnte gleichfalls mit dem Tod enden' (T24) (She might also lead to a fatal end).[67] According to Bronfen's typology of femininity mentioned earlier, we can recognize in Mizzi the type of the 'fallen woman', who is positioned between the two other types.[68] On the one hand, Mizzi, like Marianne, also bears the threat of infection and her appearance re-invokes the vampire theme: 'Es war ein zierliches, noch ganz junges Geschöpf, sehr blaß mit rotgeschminkten Lippen' (T25) (She was still a young and pretty little thing, very pale with red-painted lips).[69] On the other hand, her vitalistic youth stands in contrast to Marianne's lifelessness, which becomes clearer when Fridolin follows her home. Her room is 'behaglich' (pleasant) and 'nett gehalten' (neatly kept), 'und jedenfalls roch es da viel angenehmer als in Mariannens Behausung' (T25) (At any rate, it smelled fresher than Marianne's home).[70] He then realizes that her lips are naturally red and not made up with lipstick, which stands in opposition to Marianne's pale ones. The proliferation of terms that all connote the realm of the motherly 'domestic angel' is striking: he sits down and enjoys the lulling movement of a rocking chair (which Santner convincingly associates with a cradle),[71] and in her embrace he senses 'viel tröstende Zärtlichkeit' (T26) (comforting tenderness).[72] Nevertheless, the fear of contracting a contagious disease holds him back from sleeping with her. This is even stressed when Fridolin finds out the next day that Mizzi has been hospitalized and that he had thus in fact come very close to being infected.

In this way, the transgression of the bourgeois order through illicit sexual intercourse becomes linked to the objectively existing danger

---

65 Schnitzler, *Rhapsody: A Dream Novel*, 50.
66 Schnitzler, *Rhapsody: A Dream Novel*, 51.
67 Schnitzler, *Rhapsody: A Dream Novel*, 50.
68 Bronfen, *Over Her Dead Body*, 219.
69 Schnitzler, *Rhapsody: A Dream Novel*, 50.
70 Schnitzler, *Rhapsody: A Dream Novel*, 52. See also my reading of *Das neue Lied* in Chapter Four with regard to the cliché *arm, aber sauber* (poor but clean) as a sign of ethical impeccability. The Ladenbauers' flat is also 'nett gehalten' (nicely kept, NL621).
71 Santner (1986), 'Of Masters, Slaves, and Other Seducers,' 33–45.
72 Schnitzler, *Rhapsody: A Dream Novel*, 53.

of catching a sexually transmitted disease.[73] This reinforces the link between crossing the normative boundaries into the realm of the 'other' and infection. Becoming infected in this case also means a point of no return, which is why even only a single act of transgression holds the risk of losing one's position within the norm permanently. This is particularly the case with the etiopathology of syphilis, which 'aus dem eleganten Kavalier einen lallenden Paralytiker macht' (turns the elegant cavalier into a slurring paralytic):[74] the disease not only makes the transgression visible through symptoms, but threatens the loss of both physical and mental health, and with it the 'ultimate' form of 'otherness'.[75] While Fridolin does not commit an act of transgression by sleeping with Mizzi (which is ultimately not due to his prudence, but to her decision not to expose him to this risk), he nevertheless transgresses normative boundaries here by carrying out courtship rituals that are usually not part of the interaction with a sex worker: 'Er zog sie an sich, er warb um sie, wie um ein Mädchen, wie um eine geliebte Frau' (T27) (He put his arms around her and wooed her like a sweetheart, like a beloved woman).[76] And upon parting, again 'unwillkürlich' (T27) (involuntarily),[77] he kisses her hand, thus performatively assigning her a position equal to his own. This may already indicate that he has become more and more detached from his own position within the norm.

At the same time, Fridolin keeps insisting on his position as representative of the norm through acts of (gender) performance, but these acts appear to go wrong repeatedly, to produce a kind of surplus meaning, which undermines their intentional quality. He more than once also fails to persuade others (including the reader) that his 'posture' as bourgeois post-Enlightenment male subject is not in fact 'imposturous'. In a way, we could speak here of 'infected' performances, in the sense that Fridolin's habitus as enlightened bourgeois male subject appears to be more and more subject to pathological infiltration.[78] As we shall see, this process seems to begin with the encounter with Nachtigall.

---

73 For a further interpretation of the function of syphilis as Shibboleth that negotiates the moral implications of promiscuity, see Sebald, *Die Beschreibung des Unglücks*, 52–55.

74 Sebald, *Die Beschreibung des Unglücks*, 54.

75 The case of the young cavalry officer Höhnburg in *Flucht in die Finsternis* (Flight into Darkness) bears the signs of such a transgression.

76 Schnitzler, *Rhapsody: A Dream Novel*, 54.

77 Schnitzler, *Rhapsody: A Dream Novel*, 55.

78 Strowick develops the notion of the 'poetics of infection'. She argues that literature itself can be seen as infectious performative speech act and that the literary representation of infectious diseases provides a showcase for body politics and bodily performances and in this way enables an analysis of performativity as an act of the speaking body. See Strowick, *Sprechende Körper, Poetik der Ansteckung*.

Infected Performance

Up to this point, Fridolin has not completely left 'den gewohnten Bezirk seines Daseins' (T28) (his everyday existence).[79] For that it takes a
revenant of Marco Polo from *Die Weissagung* (The Prophecy): the piano
player Nachtigall, who tells him of the masked ball and finally pur-
veys him with the password (Denmark) to enter the tempting event.[80]
Both Marco Polo and Nachtigall thus lead the respective protagonist
temporarily outside of the structures of the dominant order to which
they are subjected. As performance artists, the two mediating figures
are also both representatives of a non-bourgeois 'half-world' and function as 'doormen' before the protagonist's entrance into dream-like
states of consciousness.[81] Certainly not coincidentally, they are both
Eastern-European Jews, thus culturally marked as 'other'. Marco Polo
is introduced as 'Sohn eines Branntweinjuden aus dem benachbarten
polnischen Städtchen' (W604) (son of a Jewish gin-shop owner in a Polish little town close by), which is the closest bigger town to the 'öde pol-
nische Nest' (small boring Polish town) where von Umprecht and his
regiment are based. When Marco Polo was younger he went at first to
Lemberg and then to Vienna, where he learned his skills in magnetism
before travelling around the world with his art. Nachtigall, in turn
'Sohn eines jüdischen Branntweinschenkers in einem polnischen Nest'
(T30) (son of a Jewish gin-shop owner in a small Polish town),[82] came
to Vienna in order to study medicine and piano, but lacking the ambition and discipline to finish either degree, he became a freelance piano
player and started travelling around. The similarities and cross-refer-
ences between the two figures are thus striking, considering the repetition not only of properties but also of identical formulations. Both
of them are contrasting figures to the protagonists who, as privileged
representatives of the norm, feel increasingly unfree and restricted
within the normative boundaries of their bourgeois role. Although the
protagonists feel socially superior to them, the itinerant performers
seem to promise a specific kind of insight and passage into a world
lying outside of the structures of the dominant order, which holds once
again a certain fascination and suggests a potential idealization of the

---

79 Schnitzler, *Rhapsody: A Dream Novel*, 59.
80 Without elaborating on it any further, the similarity between the two characters
    has been also pointed out by Peter Loewenberg. See Loewenberg, Peter (2006),
    'Freud, Schnitzler, and *Eyes Wide Shut*,' *Depth of Field: Stanley Kubrick, Film, and
    the Uses of History*, ed. by James Diedrick and Glenn Perusek, Madison: The Uni-
    versity of Wisconsin Press, 267.
81 For an extensive reading of the repeated negotiations of 'threshold conditions'
    in the novella, see Webber, 'Threshold Conditions'.
82 Schnitzler, *Rhapsody: A Dream Novel*, 63.

position of the 'other'. Accordingly, both protagonists demand entry to this world: von Umprecht's request 'Prophezeien Sie mir' (fore-tell me my future, W606) is mirrored in Fridolin's 'Nimm mich mit, Nachtigall' (T35) (Take me along, Nachtigall).[83]

And just as Marco Polo at one point appears as von Umprecht's challenger ('Der Herr Leutnant haben Angst' (You are afraid, Lieuten-ant, W606)), Nachtigall challenges Fridolin's courage by asking 'Hast du Courage?' (T34) (Have you got plenty of nerve?),[84] which can be understood to some extent as another form of interpellation, calling Fridolin's masculinity into question. Fridolin shows an offended knee-jerk reaction, in which he automatically performs that form of mas-culine conduct that he had dismissed as 'albern' (silly) and immature before: '"Sonderbare Frage", sagte Fridolin im Ton eines beleidigten Couleurstudenten' (T34) ('That's a strange question', said Fridolin in the tone of an offended fraternity student).[85] The reader is here obvi-ously immediately reminded of Fridolin's experience with the frater-nity students and recognizes the imposturous quality of this speech act. Bearing in mind that Nachtigall is a former fellow student of Fridolin, one could also think of this as a regression to their student days and the codes of conduct that were common then. Nachtigall's Jewishness brings back the question of 'Satisfaktionsfähigkeit', which the frater-nities in Austria denied to all Jews as early as 1896.[86] Confronted with Nachtigall's possibly challenging remark about Fridolin's courage,

---

83 Schnitzler, *Rhapsody: A Dream Novel*, 72. That the seductive 'otherness,' which appears to the protagonists as a less restricted alternative to the bourgeois exist-ence, is rooted above all in precarity, is hinted at in the case of Nachtigall: he has a wife and four children who live in Lemberg, where Marco Polo also spent some time before going to Vienna – 'und [Nachtigall] lachte hell, als wäre es ausneh-mend lustig vier Kinder zu haben, alle in Lemberg und alle von ein und derselben Frau' (T32) (He had a wife and four children living in Lemberg, and he laughed heartily, as though it were unusually jolly to have four children, and all of them living in Lemberg, and all of them by one and the same woman). See Schnitzler, *Rhapsody: A Dream Novel*, 67. Nachtigall's laughter expresses his awareness that he deviates here from the stereotype of the lightheaded non-committal artist who is not bound by any responsibilities. When he talks about his different not very prestigious sources of income, his need to make ends meet becomes clear: '"Aber wenn man für vier Kinder zu sorgen hat und eine Frau in Lemberg" – und er lachte wieder, nicht mehr ganz so lustig wie vorher' (T32–33) ('But if you have to provide for four children and a wife in Lemberg'– he laughed again, though not quite as gaily as before). See Schnitzler, *Rhapsody: A Dream Novel*, 68.
84 Schnitzler, *Rhapsody: A Dream Novel*, 70.
85 Schnitzler, *Rhapsody: A Dream Novel*, 70.
86 Pulzer, Peter (1997), 'Die Wiederkehr des alten Hasses,' *Deutsch-jüdische Geschichte der Neuzeit 1871–1918*, ed. by Michael A. Meyer, Munich: Beck, 193–248, 208.

Fridolin automatically invokes the military code of honour as an attempt to demonstrate that he is fulfilling the requirements of the masculine norm – and thus, of course, is courageous. By performing his 'Satisfaktionsfähigkeit' he seems not only to demonstrate his potency, but also to put Nachtigall, who, as a Jew, is excluded from this code, in his place. However, this might be an artificial and empty performance, and not merely because Fridolin avoided the duel with the fraternity brothers before. The aggression of the fraternity brothers towards Fridolin has also been interpreted as an attack of anti-Semitism, thus identifying Fridolin as a Jew.[87] In this way, Fridolin, as 'acculturated' Western Jew, would emphasize his belonging to the norm by stressing the 'otherness' of Nachtigall as an Eastern Jew.[88]

This may once more subtly allude to the corresponding passage in *Die Weissagung* (The Prophecy), when Marco Polo is confronted with the anti-Semitic attitude of the members of the regiment. Both von Umprecht and Fridolin seem to want to secure their position within the norm by marking their difference to the (Eastern) Jewish 'other'. However, Nachtigall immediately makes it clear that the institutionalized code of honour is not the kind of courage he was asking for anyway: 'Ich meine nicht soo [sic]' (T34) (I don't mean that).[89] Without specifying further

---

87   See Loewenberg, 'Freud, Schnitzler, and *Eyes Wide Shut*, 268.f. In her keynote talk at the Annual Conference of the Modern Austrian Literature and Culture Association 2011, which took place at Washington & Jefferson College in Washington, PA, Dagmar Lorenz also gave evidence for Fridolin's Jewish identity. This seems to be contradicted when Fridolin remembers his student days and recounts: 'Drei Säbelmensuren hatte er ausgefochten, und auch zu einem Pistolenduell war er einmal bereit gewesen, und nicht auf seine Veranlassung war die Sache damals gütlich beigelegt worden' (T23) (He had fought three sabre duels, and had even been ready to fight a duel with pistols, and it wasn't at *his* request that the matter had been called off). See Schnitzler, *Rhapsody: A Dream Novel*, 48 [emphasis in the original]. This suggests that either his student days were before Jews were excluded from the 'Satisfaktionsfähigkeit' or that he might not be Jewish after all. In a first draft of the text, Schnitzler (CUL A144,1) had Fridolin kill someone in a duel at the masked ball. In a later draft closer to the final version, however, Fridolin's doubts about his own lack of courage in the passage with the students are elaborated further, when he wonders, 'eine gewisse Anlage zur Feigheit steckte doch wohl in ihm' (CUL A144,3). This 'Anlage' suggests a biological predisposition and evokes the stereotype of the Jew's 'natural' lack of masculinity. One could read this then as a self-demeaning internalization of the stereotype. All in all, it seems important to keep open the question whether Fridolin is Jewish or not, which once more blurs the lines of demarcation between norm and 'other'.

88   It was indeed a common phenomenon among Western Jews to distance themselves from Eastern Jews. See Gilman, Sander L. (1995), *Freud, Race, and Gender*, Princeton, NJ: Princeton University Press.

89   Schnitzler, *Rhapsody: A Dream Novel*, 70.

what it is he means, he seems nevertheless to indicate that the rites and performances of masculinity Fridolin is used to are useless in the world he is about to be introduced to. This, as we will see later, is precisely the case when Fridolin tries to apply the normal rules of offence and satisfaction to the secret society at the masked ball. Thus, similar to Marco Polo, Nachtigall is a figure who leads Fridolin into a realm in which the rules and conventions of the dominant order do not apply any more. In this, he seems to be a 'doorman' of the realm of the metaphysical, individually laid out 'destiny'. When Nachtigall is reluctant to take Fridolin with him to the masked ball, Fridolin 'appoints' the power of decision to the force of 'destiny': 'Das Schicksal soll entscheiden' (T36) (Let fate decide the question).[90]

Fridolin's transition state between social and metaphysical 'destiny' (and between norm and 'other') in the passage with Nachtigall is already prefigured in a pronounced focus on voice and speech acts. The voice, as Mladen Dolar writes, 'holds bodies and language together' and seems thus particularly interesting when analyzing 'infected performances' of 'speaking bodies'.[91] The voice, as the 'instrument, the vehicle, the medium' of meaning, is nevertheless potentially excessive and disruptive: as soon as we become aware of the voice, its quality, timbre, accent etc., we are distracted from the meaning it conveys.[92] If it is true that the voice is 'the material element recalcitrant to meaning', and that the voice is precisely that part of the speech act 'which cannot be said',[93] then disruptions of meaning through the voice might be part of the 'rhetoric of the unconscious' mentioned earlier.[94] When Nachtigall tells Fridolin about the details of the secret ball, Fridolin exclaims: 'Nachtigall, Nachtigall, was singst du da für ein Lied!' (T34) (Nachtigall, what do you mean [rather: what kind of song are you singing, M.K.]?).[95] As singing is a cultural practice in which the voice tends to overpower the meaning of words, thus ceasing to be just a medium for meaning, but becoming the goal itself, Fridolin expresses here the fact that what Nachtigall tells him escapes signification and thus intelligibility. This already indicates that we are about to enter a realm outside of the structures of the dominant order. A further marker of deviance from the norm is Nachtigall's 'polnisch weicher Akzent mit mäßigem jüdischem Beiklang' (T29) (soft Polish accent and a slightly Jewish twang),[96] which is

---

90 Schnitzler, *Rhapsody: A Dream Novel*, 74.
91 Dolar, Mladen (2006) *A Voice and Nothing More*, Cambridge, MA: MIT Press, 60.
92 Dolar, *A Voice and Nothing More*, 15.
93 Dolar, *A Voice and Nothing More*, 15.
94 See Strohwick, *Sprechende Körper, Poetik der Ansteckung*, 85.
95 Schnitzler, *Rhapsody: A Dream Novel*, 71.
96 Schnitzler, *Rhapsody: A Dream Novel*, 62.

something which brings the voice into the vicinity of singing and a heavy accent suddenly makes us aware of the material support of the voice which we tend immediately to discard. [...] After all it is a norm which differs from the ruling norm – this is what makes it an accent, and this is what makes it obtrusive, what makes it sing – and it can be described in the same way as the ruling norm.[97]

Nachtigall's accent seems to indicate that he does not fully respond to the demands of the ruling norm, that he is not fully subjected to the dominant order.[98] Although Fridolin at first tries to conceal the fact that his excitement has been sparked, a disruption of his voice gives him away: after being assured by Nachtigall of the exquisite selection of women present at events of the secret society, he has to clear his voice: 'Fridolin räusperte sich leicht. "Und wie hoch ist das Entrée?", fragte er beiläufig' (T35) (Fridolin hemmed and hawed a little. 'And what's the price of admission?' he asked casually).[99] When Nachtigall turns out to be reluctant to take Fridolin with him, Fridolin tries to persuade him: 'Vor einer Minute hattest du noch die Absicht ... mir zu "vergennen". Es wird schon möglich sein' (T35) (But a minute ago you yourself spoke ... of being willing to ... I think you can manage alright).[100] This imitation of Nachtigall's accent is of an ambivalent nature. While it is reminiscent of the condescending way the colonel imitates Marco Polo in *Die Weissagung* (The Prophecy), it can also be seen as an awkward attempt at ingratiation: after all, it is a conscious deviation from the linguistic norm, which might indicate that Fridolin is willing to transgress normative boundaries. Much in the way that Robert in *Flucht in die Finsternis* (Flight into Darkness) plays with symptoms of mental illness before losing all control he might have had over it, Fridolin theatrically plays with crossing the line between norm and 'other' (which began already during the encounter with Mizzi, as we have seen), but also increasingly loses control over these performances. It seems as if Fridolin's decision 'Das Schicksal soll entscheiden' (T36) (Let fate decide the question)[101] becomes realized in this way.

---

97 Dolar, *A Voice and Nothing More*, 20.
98 The seductive element of Fridolin's encounter with Nachtigall is also underlined through the remark about his accent, which mirrors Albertine's seductive encounter with the stranger at the ball, 'dessen fremdländischer, anscheinend polnischer Akzent sie anfangs bestrickt [...] hatte' (T6) (whose blasé manner and apparently Polish accents had at first charmed her). See Schnitzler, *Rhapsody: A Dream Novel*, 9.
99 Schnitzler, *Rhapsody: A Dream Novel*, 72.
100 Schnitzler, *Rhapsody: A Dream Novel*, 72. The English translation does not convey Fridolin's imitation of Nachtigall's accent, but it is clear in the German original.
101 Schnitzler, *Rhapsody: A Dream Novel*, 74.

In order to commission appropriate clothing to enter the tempting masked ball, Fridolin goes to the costume dealer Gibiser where he also meets the daughter of the latter: dressed as a *Pierrette*, she gets caught in the middle of an erotic adventure with two men, costumed as vehmic judges. Her innocent youth is disturbed by her apparent promiscuity, as she seems to be available for erotic encounters with *any* man she meets (as Fridolin too feels immediately seduced by her).[102] With her promising costume, which represents a pantomime form of servant, the *Pierrette* offers her services to anyone who wants to be her master. Following my elaborations on the *Pierrot* figure in *Leisenbohg*, one could say that this costume refers to the ambivalence of femininity in the patriarchal order, functioning at once as a projection screen, and a death omen, but also as a kind of 'gender masquerade', bringing to attention the performativity of gender roles. Here again, the arbitrariness seems to undermine the fulfilment of Fridolin's longing for mastery and self-knowledge. Nevertheless, the idea of possession that the *Pierrette* promises appears so appealing to Fridolin that he imagines kidnapping her: 'Am liebsten wäre er dageblieben oder hätte die Kleine gleich mitgenommen, wohin immer – und was immer darauf gefolgt wäre' (T38) (He would have liked to stay, or, better still, to take the girl with him, no matter where – and whatever the consequences).[103] When Gibiser calls her 'eine Wahnsinnige' (T38) (deranged),[104] Fridolin tries to reassume his authority as a physician in order to protect the *Pierrette* from punishment. However, he fails miserably in front of Gibiser: Fridolin uses his (possibly even authentic) protective impulse to cover his own erotic interest in the girl, and the purveyor of masks Gibiser immediately sees through him.

There is an underlying and uncanny threat that determines the whole passage in Gibiser's house. The fact that Gibiser calls his daughter insane moves her into the realm of the absolute 'other'. As insanity represents

---

102 With the *Pierrette* Fridolin repeats his seductive encounter in Denmark where he felt tempted by an equally young, but apparently more innocent (i.e. probably sexually inexperienced) girl. For an extensive description of the stereotype of the seductive 'Kindfrau,' see Pohle, who writes: 'Die Furcht vor der aktiven, begehrenden Frau (der femme fatale) ist in der Begegnung mit der Kindfrau allein schon durch die Alters- und Erfahrungshierarchie abgewendet. Mythologisch in das Bild der Nymphe oder Meerjungfrau verpackt, fungiert die infantilisierte Weiblichkeit als Leinwand für Projektionen männlicher Phantasie' (The encounter with the child woman averts man's fear of the active female desire through the man's advantage in terms of age and experience. Through mythologized images of the nymph or mermaid, infantilized femininity becomes the projection screen for male fantasies). See Pohle, Bettina (1998), *Kunstwerk Frau: Inszenierungen von Weiblichkeit in der Moderne*, Frankfurt a. M.: Fischer.
103 Schnitzler, *Rhapsody: A Dream Novel*, 78.
104 Schnitzler, *Rhapsody: A Dream Novel*, 78.

the split subject *par excellence*, the *Pierrette's* promise to function as the complementary 'other' is undermined by the threat of dissociation. As a result, Fridolin seems to bear the signs of infection after he tries to find himself in the eyes of the girl: his own feeling of disintegration is exacerbated, as he becomes frightened by his own reflection in the mirror – a classic uncanny *Doppelgänger* experience. As Freud writes in *Das Unheimliche* (The Uncanny), the motif of the *Doppelgänger*, which in the phase of primary narcissism acts as a reassurance 'gegen den Untergang des Ichs' (against the decline of the ego), later develops 'zum unheimlichen Vorboten des Todes' (to the uncanny forbearer of death).[105]

Although the striking moment of *Grauen* (horror) discussed in the previous chapters does not occur explicitly in *Traumnovelle* (Dream Story), there are several passages with the same distinct Gothic colouring, as has already been pointed out with regard to the recurring vampire motif. The accumulation of Gothic elements finds its climax in the description of the secret society at the masked ball.[106] Fridolin does not feel a *Grauen* (horror), but repeatedly a similar sensation of *Schauer* (shudder, T21, 42), which could be read as an 'infection' on the level of the text, as if it were 'infected' by elements of *Schauerromantik* (Dark Romanticism) or the Gothic. This *Schauer* (shudder) accordingly accompanies an experience in which the conventional interpretative patterns of the protagonist start to crumble and the differences between real and oneiric experiences begin to fade.[107] The death symbolism is here built up to the extreme: the secret society travels in funeral coaches, complete with silent coachmen, which again strikingly allude to the coach that brings Jonathan Harker

---

105 Freud, Sigmund (1947b), 'Das Unheimliche,' in: *Gesammelte Werke*, vol. 12: *Werke aus den Jahren 1917–1920*, ed. by Anna Freud, Edward Bibrig, Willi Hoffer, Ernst Kris, and Otto Isakower, London: Imago, 227–268, 247. For a discussion of the death symbolisms in the passage, especially the dominant motif of the 'Totentanz' (dance of death), see Malsch, Katja (2007), *Literatur und Selbstopfer: Historisch-systematische Studien zu Gryphius, Lessing, Gotthelf, Storm, Kaiser und Schnitzler*, Würzburg: Königshausen und Neumann, 138, and also Scheible, *Arthur Schnitzler und die Aufklärung*, 84.

106 See also Hertha Krotkoff, who describes the novella's parodic play with elements of the *Schauerroman* (shudder novel). See Krotkoff, Helga (1973), 'Zur geheimen Gesellschaft in Arthur Schnitzlers *Traumnovelle*,' *German Quarterly* 46: 202–209, 202f.

107 Recalling in *Flucht in die Finsternis* (Flight into Darkness), Robert's 'süßer Schauer, der sich aber allmählich in ein leises Grauen verwandelte' (FiF84) (almost delicious sensation. Then he shuddered. Finally a fear [rather: slight horror, M.K.] rose up in him). See Schnitzler, Arthur (1931), *Flight into Darkness*, translated by William A. Drake, New York: Simon & Schuster, 111. This moment of slight horror makes Robert more and more removed from his social relations. One could assume that also the *Schauer* (shudder) Fridolin feels might be prefiguring the feeling of complete crisis later, but may at this point still be of an ambivalent, thus also exhilarating quality.

to Count Dracula, and finally, the hall is decorated with black silk.[108] Accordingly, Fridolin's thoughts circle around his death before he enters the event, even if he does not know the reason: 'Weiter meinen Weg, und wär's mein Tod. Er lachte selbst zu dem großen Wort, aber sehr heiter war ihm nicht zumut' (T42) (I must go through with this, even if it means death. And he laughed at himself, using such a big word but without feeling very cheerful about it).[109] As has been said in the first section, this rhetorically heightened fear of death can also be seen as fear of infection with 'otherness' in the sense of a 'social death' that would be the consequence of a permanent crossing of the normative boundaries of the bourgeois order. That he enters an alternative space to his bourgeois existence is made explicit when Fridolin puts on his costume, 'geradeso wie er jeden Morgen auf der Spitalabteilung in die Ärmel seines Leinenkittels zu schlüpfen pflegte' (T42) (just as he slipped into the sleeves of his white linen coat every morning in his ward at the hospital).[110]

At the masked ball, the woman, who will later sacrifice herself for him, at first bears all the signs of a threatening *femme fatale*, with her vampiric features ('Er sah den blutroten Bund durch die schwarzen Spitzen schimmern' (T44) (He saw the blood-red mouth glimmering through the black lace).[111] However, when she warns Fridolin about the danger he is in, the motif of the encounter of gazes appears again: 'dunkle Augen sanken in die seinen' (T44) (Dark eyes were fixed to him [literally: sunk into his own, M.K.]).[112] This formulation underlines the reassuring moment of this encounter. Her eyes 'sink into his' and thus seem to overcome the gap between them and complement Fridolin's fractured self again. In the middle of this lasciviously morbid event where the appearance of a diabolical woman seems most likely, Fridolin thus finally meets the perfect 'angel of the house' he has been looking for all night. She eminently fits Bronfen's definition of the first type – even though there might not be anything 'domestic' about her appearance, she evidently is 'a saintly, self-sacrificing [...] vessel'[113] with

---

108 Webber argues that this passage is a quotation from Friedrich Wilhelm Murnau's film adaptation of Stoker's novel, *Nosferatu: Eine Symphonie des Grauens* (Nosferatu: A Symphony of Horror, 1922), in which case the term *Grauen* (horror) is perhaps present by implication after all. See Webber, 'Threshold Conditions,' 287. Moreover, one is reminded of Thomas Mann's *Der Tod in Venedig* (1912), more precisely of Aschenbach's journey over the Grand Canal, where he feels a 'flüchtigen Schauder' (fleeting shudder) as the gondola reminds him of a coffin. Aschenbach's passage also combines fantasies of illicit sexuality and death. See Mann, Thomas (2013), *Der Tod in Venedig*, Frankfurt a. M.: Fischer, 41.
109 Schnitzler, *Rhapsody: A Dream Novel*, 86.
110 Schnitzler, *Rhapsody: A Dream Novel*, 85.
111 Schnitzler, *Rhapsody: A Dream Novel*, 89.
112 Schnitzler, *Rhapsody: A Dream Novel*, 89.
113 Bronfen, *Over Her Dead Body*, 218.

almost motherly features. The encounter immediately has a transformative effect on him: '"Ich bleibe", sagte er in einem heroischen Ton, den er nicht an sich kannte' (T44) ('I shall stay,' he said in a heroic voice which he hardly recognized as his own).[114] As long as the motherly protective woman is around him, Fridolin is able to be rid of his feelings of inadequacy: 'Er war berauscht [...] von sich selbst, von seiner Kühnheit, von der Wandlung, die er in sich spürte' (T48) (He was intoxicated with himself, with his boldness, the change he felt in himself).[115] That this change, however, is not permanent but linked to the reassuring recognition through the masked woman becomes immediately clear when she leaves him: 'Fridolin fand sich allein, und diese plötzliche Verlassenheit überfiel ihn wie Frost' (T49) (A sudden feeling of solitude made Fridolin shiver as if with cold).[116]

His inadequacy is then made explicit, when he is asked for the second password and does not know the answer. This refers back to the conflict with Albertine, in which she revealed to him that he could have seduced her even before their marriage had he said the right 'word'. In this way, the lack of the second password also refers to his inadequacy with regard to the potent codes of masculinity. That he is an impostor and indeed not accepted as an equal by the other male participants in the ball becomes clear when they demand atonement from him. Fridolin tries to establish a mutual recognition by relying on the rules of offence and satisfaction: 'Wenn einer der Herren sich durch mein Erscheinen gekränkt fühlen sollte, so erkläre ich mich bereit, ihm in üblicher Weise Genugtuung zu geben. Doch meine Maske werde ich nur in dem Fall ablegen, daß Sie alle das gleiche tun, meine Herren' (T50) (If my appearance has offended any of the gentlemen present, I am ready to give satisfaction in the usual manner, but I shall take off my mask only if all of you do the same).[117] However, the members of the secret society are not interested in the 'übliche Weise' (usual manner) of the master–slave game, as it is evident that he is not one of them. The fact that a woman is then able to replace him – 'ihn auszulösen' (T51) (to redeem him)[118] – may underline that Fridolin is already in the position of the 'other' for them. Fridolin's performance as representative of the male norm has thus failed here.[119]

---

114 Schnitzler, *Rhapsody: A Dream Novel*, 89.
115 Schnitzler, *Rhapsody: A Dream Novel*, 95.
116 Schnitzler, *Rhapsody: A Dream Novel*, 96.
117 Schnitzler, *Rhapsody: A Dream Novel*, 99.
118 Schnitzler, *Rhapsody: A Dream Novel*, 100.
119 Fridolin's assumption that the secret society may consist of noblemen supports the interpretation that the novella is concerned with a crisis of bourgeois identity that is linked to the fear of masculine inferiority. See Webber, 'Threshold Conditions,' 284, fn. 22; Sebald, *Die Beschreibung des Unglücks*, 58.

It is then that Fridolin tries to return to his bourgeois position and give assurance that he has in fact stopped playing a role. Significantly, he stresses his authenticity by invoking destiny: 'Ich spiele keinerlei Komödie, auch nicht hier, und wenn ich es bisher notgedrungen getan habe, so gebe ich es jetzt auf. Ich fühle, daß ich in ein Schicksal geraten bin, das mit dieser Mummerei nichts mehr zu tun hat, ich will Ihnen meinen Namen nennen, ich will meine Larve abnehmen und nehme alle Folgen auf mich' (T52) (I won't play a part [literally: comedy, M.K.], here or elsewhere, and if I have been forced to do so up to now, I shall give it up. I feel that a fate has overtaken me which has nothing to do with this foolery. I will tell you my name, take off my mask and be responsible for the consequences).[120]

Fridolin counter-poses the fate or destiny that has overtaken him with his social destiny, by offering to give his opponents his proper name, the signifier of his institutionalized identity and social destiny. This could be seen as a performative speech act that for the first time can count as an attempt at taking over individual responsibility. However, although Fridolin asserts that he is no longer playing a part, he cannot help but recite melodramatic lines: '"Nein", erwiderte [Fridolin] in erhöhtem Ton. "Das Leben hat keinen Wert mehr für mich, wenn ich ohne dich von hier fortgehen soll"' (T52) ('No,' replied [Fridolin], elevating his voice. 'Life means nothing to me if I must leave here without you').[121] The heightened tone of his voice underlines the theatricality of this utterance and contradicts his claim to authenticity. Fridolin seems to have no control over his performance and the invocation of his own individuality (name, face) qua destiny is not of interest for the secret society – he gets removed from the event and thrown back into the bourgeois world he came from.

However, this world is still not what it used to be: it seems to be 'infected' by an unfamiliar strangeness. When he arrives home he finds Albertine caught up in her dream as if in an uncanny masquerade, with an 'Antlitz, das Fridolin nicht kannte' (it was a face that Fridolin did not know), laughing 'in einer völlig fremden, fast unheimlichen Weise' (T58) (in a strange, almost uncanny manner).[122] The content of her dream takes her demonization to the extreme: in fact, it can be seen as a symmetrical inversion of the patriarchal gender order when she imagines Fridolin sacrificing himself for her. It is hardly surprising that the leader of her dream world is a queen. Moreover, in contrast to Fridolin's dreamlike experiences, Albertine's dream is an 'ungebrochener

120 Schnitzler, *Rhapsody: A Dream Novel*, 102.
121 Schnitzler, *Rhapsody: A Dream Novel*, 102.
122 Schnitzler, *Rhapsody: A Dream Novel*, 117–118.

Wunschtraum, der die Befreiung aus patriarchalischen Zwängen von Anfang bis Ende konsequent durchführt' (an unequivocal dream of wish fulfilment, which consequently realizes the liberation from the shackles of patriarchy).[123] Of course, this leads at first to a further intensification of Fridolin's identity crisis.[124]

During the following day, Fridolin repeatedly tries to regain control over what has happened by consciously assuming an authoritative male habitus. He returns to all the significant stations of the previous night in order to make sense of them and to re-establish the disrupted order. This may allude to the pattern of classical crime novels, in which the elements that disrupt the norms of the dominant order are step by step unravelled by an authoritative male protagonist – usually a detective of some sort. However, the course of events demonstrates that Fridolin is far from being the cool investigator of the case he aims and pretends to be. This becomes particularly evident in the way in which he compulsively strives for authoritative habitus: 'es war ihm angenehm, daß er seine Arztenstasche in der Hand trug, als er aus dem Haustor trat; so würde man ihn wohl nicht für einen Bewohner dieses Hotels halten, sondern für eine Amtsperson' (T69) (He was glad that he had his doctor's bag with him when he stepped out of the door, for anyone seeing him would not think that he was staying at the hotel, but would take him for some official person).[125] The doctor's bag is supposed to signify the status of the objective and distanced observer, and his hope that he will be perceived as an official person, thus a representative of the state, underlines the fact that Fridolin tries very hard to re-invoke the structures of the dominant order which have been drawn into question since the events of the previous night. Also when he returns to Gibiser's house to return the costume and to talk to him about the mental health of his daughter, Fridolin tries to incorporate an official habitus: '"Ich bin ferner hier", sagte Fridolin im Ton eines Untersuchungsrichters, "um ein Wort wegen Ihres Fräulein Tochters mit Ihnen zu reden."' (T69) ('I

---

123 Perlmann, Michaela L. (1987a), *Der Traum in der literarischen Moderne: Untersuchungen zum Werk Arthur Schnitzlers*, Munich: Fink, 193.

124 The way Albertine imagines Fridolin as a prince in her dream also expresses her dissatisfaction with his inability to fulfil the requirements of the ideal of masculinity, which is represented in her fascination with the Dane, who was a military officer. The bourgeois woman's erotic fantasies are thus focused on an image of masculinity stemming from ideals of the military and nobility. As already seen in Chapter Four, in the section on *Die Fremde* (The Stranger), these are ideals are of a somewhat anachronistic quality: 'Der erotische Idealtypus der bürgerlichen Frau ist ein vom Geschichtsverlauf relegiertes Wesen' (The erotic ideal of the bourgeois woman is a creature which has been relegated by the course of history). See Sebald, *Die Beschreibung des Unglücks*, 48.

125 Schnitzler, *Rhapsody: A Dream Novel*, 139.

would also like,' said Fridolin in the tone of a police magistrate, 'to have a word with you about your daughter').[126] However, with Gibiser, Fridolin remains as unsuccessful in his imposture as he was the night before. When he suggests that the girl should be examined by a doctor because of her alleged mental illness: 'Gibiser, einen unnatürlich langen Federstiel in der Hand hin und her drehend, maß Fridolin mit unverschämtem Blick. "Und Herr Doktor wären vielleicht selbst so gütig, die Behandlung zu übernehmen?" "Ich bitte mir keine Worte in den Mund zu legen", erwiderte Fridolin scharf, aber etwas heiser, "die ich nicht ausgesprochen habe"' (T70) ('And I suppose the doctor himself would like to take charge of the treatment?' 'Please don't misunderstand me,' replied Fridolin in a sharp [but slightly hoarse, M.K.] voice).[127] Again, it is Fridolin's hoarse voice that gives him away and undermines the meaning of his utterance: Gibiser, whose superiority is made obvious in this passage, has hit the mark.[128]

All of Fridolin's attempts to shed a light onto the events of the night before fail miserably and he seems unable to resume his position as representative of the bourgeois male norm. His feelings of alienation and self-loss reach a climax here: 'Er fühlte sich ungeschickt, hilflos, alles zerfloß ihm unter den Händen; alles wurde unwirklich, sogar sein Heim, seine Frau, sein Kind, sein Beruf, ja, er selbst' (T80) (He felt awkward and helpless. Everything he put his hands to turned out a failure. Everything seemed unreal: his home, his wife, his child, his profession, and even he himself).[129] Interestingly, this crisis-like state of mind briefly opens up a moment of reflection in which he questions his normal interpretative patterns and practices of stereotypical labelling: 'Wie man doch immer wieder, durch Worte verführt, Straßen, Schicksale, Menschen in träger Gewohnheit benennt und beurteilt' (T81) (Isn't it strange how we are misled by words, how we give names to streets, events and people, and form judgements about them, just because we are too lazy to change our habits?).[130] As a result he feels so alienated from his bourgeois existence that he half-heartedly considers leaving it all behind him: 'Ganz flüchtig, nicht etwas wie ein Vorsatz, kam ihm der Einfall, zu irgendeinem Bahnhof zu fahren, abzureisen, gleichgültig wohin, zu verschwinden für alle Leute, die ihn gekannt, irgendwo in der Fremde wieder aufzutauchen und ein neues Leben zu beginnen als ein anderer, neuer Mensch' (T80) (Then the idea occured to him – not

---

126 Schnitzler, *Rhapsody: A Dream Novel*, 140.
127 Schnitzler, *Rhapsody: A Dream Novel*, 141.
128 One could say that Gibiser, as a sort of puppet master and 'ventriloquist,' infects the vocal performance of his 'puppet' Fridolin.
129 Schnitzler, *Rhapsody: A Dream Novel*, 159.
130 Schnitzler, *Rhapsody: A Dream Novel*, 161.

deliberately but as a flash across his mind – to dive to some station, take a train, no matter where, and to disappear, leaving everyone behind. He could then turn up again, somewhere abroad, and start a new life, as a different personality).[131]

This passage is reminiscent of Robert in *Flucht in die Finsternis* (Flight into Darkness) who in fact follows through with this plan and as a result irreversibly crosses the boundary into the realm of the 'other'. Fridolin too displays, then, the first paranoid symptoms already familiar from Robert: 'In einer entfernten Ecke nahm ein Herr Platz; in dunklem Überzieher, auch sonst ganz unauffällig gekleidet. Fridolin erinnerte sich, die Physiognomie im Laufe des Tages schon irgendwo gesehen zu haben. Das konnte natürlich auch Zufall sein' (T84) (A man had just taken a seat in a distant corner. He wore a dark overcoat and inconspicuous clothes, and Fridolin thought he had seen his face before, during the day. It might, of course, be just a fancy).[132] The fact that Fridolin does not get overwhelmed by this 'infection of otherness' and at the end of the novella is able to return home to Albertine and his bourgeois existence, is due to the 'purifying' encounter with a dead woman.

Purification

When Fridolin finally reads a note in the paper about a beautiful Baroness D. who has been found poisoned in her hotel room, he immediately identifies her with his martyr of the previous night. In fact, the text does not give any unequivocal information as to whether the dead baroness is really the woman from the ball. Yet when Fridolin goes to see the corpse in the morgue it becomes clear that it is actually irrelevant whether or not he ascertains the dead woman's identity:

Denn ob die Frau, die nun da drin in der Totenkammer lag, dieselbe war, die er vor vierundzwanzig Stunden zu den wilden Klängen von Nachtigalls Klavierspiel nackt in den Armen gehalten, oder ob diese Frau irgendeine andere, eine Unbekannte [...] war, [...] was da hinter ihm lag in der gewölbten Halle, [...] ihm konnte es nichts anderes mehr bedeuten als, zu unwiderruflicher Verwesung bestimmt, den bleichen Leichnam der vergangenen Nacht. (T94f.)
It did not matter to him whether the woman – now lying on the hospital morgue – was the same one he had held naked

---

131 Schnitzler, *Rhapsody: A Dream Novel*, 160.
132 Schnitzler, *Rhapsody: A Dream Novel*, 165–166.

in his arms twenty-four hours before, to the wild tunes of Nachtigall's playing. It was immaterial whether this corpse was some other unknown woman, a perfect stranger he had never seen before. [...] [H]e knew that the body lying in the arched room [...] could only be to him the pale corpse of the preceding night.[133]

The dead woman, then, becomes the personification of the entirety of the previous night's temptations of transgression. Her dead body is tantamount to the dead body of the night. Thus, with her death, the danger of transgressing irreversibly into the realm of the 'other' seems to be contained. The individual person behind the mask is thus not of interest to Fridolin. He realizes instead that all the time it had been Albertine's face that he had imagined behind his saviour's mask. In this way, the woman's sacrifice takes on the quality of a displaced wish fulfilment for Fridolin: as Albertine's revelation has 'unmasked' the threatening side of femininity represented by the second type, the diabolical demon woman, Fridolin's logical reaction is to wish that this disturbing side of the feminine should be covered up again. That Fridolin has always imagined Albertine as the woman behind the mask demonstrates that he wants her to fulfil the part of the reassuring 'other' again: the woman's dramatic sacrifice appears like a radicalized version of the sacrificial role of the 'domestic angel' that is assigned to Albertine as mother and wife.[134]

In this way it is not surprising that, of all things, the sight of the woman's dead body re-establishes his security again and manages to suppress the disturbing images of the previous night. The flirtation with the corpse finally gives Fridolin the impression of a successful recognition scene:

Unwillkürlich, ja wie von einer unsichtbaren Macht gezwungen und geführt, berührte Fridolin mit beiden Händen die Stirne, die Wangen, die Schultern, die Arme der toten Frau; dann schlang er seine Finger wie zum Liebesspiel in die der Toten, und so starr sie waren, es schien ihm, als versuchten sie sich zu regen, die seinen

---

133 Schnitzler, *Rhapsody: A Dream Novel*, 183.
134 'Im weiteren Sinn geht es aber bei der geheimen Gesellschaft um die symbolische Darstellung jenes alltäglichen Masochismus, der das Verhalten von Albertine, Marianne und den anderen Frauenfiguren in der Novelle prägt' (In broader terms, the secret society symbolizes the everyday masochism that determines the behaviour of Albertine, Marianne and the other female characters in the novella). See Perlmann, Michaela L. (1987a), *Der Traum in der literarischen Moderne*, Munich: Fink, 187.

zu ergreifen; ja ihm war, als irrte unter den halbgeschlossenen Lidern ein ferner, farbloser Blick nach dem seinem; und wie magisch angezogen beugte er sich herab. (T92)

Fridolin touched the forehead, the cheeks, the shoulders of the dead woman, doing so as if compelled and directed by an invisible power. He twined his fingers about those of the corpse, and rigid as they were, they seemed to him to make an effort to move, to seize his hand. Indeed he almost felt that a vague and distant look from underneath her eyelids was searching his face. He bent over her, as if magically attracted.[135]

At first, Fridolin loses any control he might still have had over his own actions: again 'unwillkürlich', and this time even explicitly as if guided by an invisible power, which invokes both the topic of destiny and the vampire theme, he seems to lose himself in this recognition scene with the dead woman. Santner's claim that this experience has a cathartic impact on Fridolin is a convincing one.[136] But rather than freeing him from his former narcissism, the dead woman seems to 'purify' him from his 'infection of otherness'. The colourless gaze might refer to an empty canvas, which is underlined by the description of her face: 'es war ein völlig nichtiges, leeres, es war ein totes Antlitz' (T91) (It was a face without expression or character. It was dead).[137]

In his 1846 essay 'The Philosophy of Composition', Edgar Allan Poe famously claimed that 'the death [...] of a beautiful woman is, unquestionably, the most poetical topic in the world'.[138] Whether meant in a satirical way or not, Poe's comment suggests that the representation of female death yields a certain kind of aesthetic pleasure; that it resonates with audiences and readers in a specific kind of way which Poe calls 'most poetical'. Arguing that death and femininity are often conflated in cultural representations, in the sense that death is repeatedly inscribed in representations of women (for example as death-stricken *femme fragile* or as death-threatening *femme fatale*), Bronfen sees death to be culturally gendered as female and comes to the conclusion that '"dead woman" is a pleonasm used to confirm the social structure of gender and efface the reality of death'.[139] The aesthetic pleasure deriving

---

135 Schnitzler, *Rhapsody: A Dream Novel*, 180.
136 Santner, 'Of Masters, Slaves, and Other Seducers,' 45.
137 Schnitzler, *Rhapsody: A Dream Novel*, 178.
138 Poe, Edgar Allen (1965), 'The Philosophy of Composition,' *Literary Criticism of Edgar Allen Poe*, ed. by Robert L. Hough, Lincoln: University of Nebraska Press, 20–32, 26.
139 Bronfen, *Over Her Dead Body*, 208.

from female death implied by Poe is, then, for Bronfen fuelled by the 'desire for the death of the other',[140] and brings about a moment of 'satisfaction, since the survivor is not himself dead'.[141] Without claiming that Bronfen's argument can be blindly and generally applied to each aesthetic example of female death, I want to suggest that it proves helpful for the interpretation of the function of the female corpse in *Traumnovelle* (Dream Story). Fridolin's fear of infection, of irreversibly transgressing the boundary into the realm of the 'other' is tantamount, as already argued, to a fear of 'social death'. This fear is then experienced as mortal threat, which we have seen in the passages at Gibiser's house and in particular at the masked ball. Seeing the body of the woman reassures him of his own survival and gives him a chance to be, as it were, reborn.

After this mutual recognition scene with the dead woman, he receives an interpellation from the voice of his colleague, the ambitious and thorough man of science Doctor Adler, which wakes Fridolin 'jählings' (T93) (instantly) from his reverie.[142] Now Fridolin is ready to leave the events of the last two days behind him: in Doctor Adler's halls of science, he cleanses away all possibly remaining sources of infection and feeling of guilt: 'Fridolin trat ans Waschbecken. "Du erlaubst", sagte er und reinigte seine Hände sorgfältig mit Lysol und Seife' (T93) (Fridolin stepped up to the wash basin. 'With your permission', he said and carefully washed his hands with lysol and soap).[143] The thorough Doctor Adler then offers Fridolin one more option, 'zur Beruhigung deines Gewissens' (to quiet your conscience), by letting him look through his microscope: '"Findest du dich zurecht?", fragte er, während Fridolin ins Mikroskop schaute. "Es ist nämlich eine ziemlich neue Färbungsmethode."' (T93) ('Can you make it out,' he asked, as Fridolin looked into the microscope. 'It's a fairly new staining method').[144] This new method almost certainly refers to Robert Koch's colouring technique, which allowed bacteria to be made visible under the microscope.[145] The possibility to visualize pathogenic agents is obviously a promising step in order to understand and avoid infection. Adler's reassuring touch of reason ('Doktor Adler legte die Hand beruhigend auf Fridolins Arm'

140 Bronfen, *Over Her Dead Body*, 63.
141 Bronfen, *Over Her Dead Body*, 65.
142 Schnitzler, *Rhapsody: A Dream Novel*, 180.
143 Schnitzler, *Rhapsody: A Dream Novel*, 180.
144 Schnitzler, *Rhapsody: A Dream Novel*, 181.
145 See Sarasin, Phillip (2007), 'Die Visualisierung des Feindes: Über metaphorische Technologien der frühen Bakteriologie,' *Bakteriologie und Moderne: Studien zur Biopolitik des Unsichtbaren 1870–1920*, ed. by Philipp Sarasin, Silvia Berger, Marianne Hänseler and Myriam Spörri, 427–461, 430–434.

(T94) (Doctor Adler placed his hand on Fridolin's arm reassuringly)[146] seems to confirm Fridolin's purification. This gesture in fact mirrors Nachtigall's before: 'Und seine Hand auf Fridolins Arm legend' (T32) (Placing his hand on Fridolin's arm).[147] In this way, Nachtigall and Adler could be understood as the two extreme poles of 'norm' and 'other' between which Fridolin himself oscillates, with their contrasting 'bird names' also supporting this reading.[148]

After this experience, Fridolin can return home to Albertine who is magically restored as the motherly domestic 'angel of the house'. Even if a final uncanny moment is provided as Fridolin's lost mask is found by Albertine and laid on his pillow beside her, the threat nevertheless appears to be banished. Fridolin's reaction is that of the regretful child: he bursts into tears, feels comforted by her soft hand stroking his hair and confesses everything to her. Accordingly, it is Albertine who provides the final reassurance: '"Was sollen wir tun, Albertine?" Sie lächelte, und nach kurzem Zögern erwiderte sie: "Dem Schicksal dankbar sein, glaube ich, daß wir aus allen Abenteuern heil heraus gekommen sind – aus den wirklichen und aus den geträumten."' ('What shall we do now, Albertina?' She smiled, and after a minute, she replied: 'I think we ought to be grateful that we have come unharmed out of all our adventures, whether they were real or only a dream').[149] With this expression of gratitude that both their 'adventures' remained without consequences, which is, with regard to the dead woman in the morgue, at least questionable, Albertine becomes here the speaker of an order she – as a woman – used to be a victim of. 'Destiny' seems here to be congruent with their social destiny, because it has led both of them back into the realm of the bourgeois norm. By this token, the bourgeois ideal of romantic love as destiny seems to be re-enforced in the end, which underlines its 'complicity' with the bourgeois order. The cliché used by Fridolin in the beginning – that in all other women he had encountered he had been looking only for Albertine – has in some sense come true.

The death of the unknown woman is, then, a sacrifice that re-established the old order in a double sense: she has died not only for Fridolin, but also for Albertine, who was the actual object of Fridolin's fantasy of sacrifice. The resurrection of the old order seems certain as soon as the new day begins with a 'sieghaften Lichtstrahl durch den Vorhangsspalt und einem hellen Kinderlachen' (T97) (victorious ray of light through

---

146 Schnitzler, *Rhapsody: A Dream Novel*, 182.
147 Schnitzler, *Rhapsody: A Dream Novel*, 66.
148 In Schnitzler's first draft (CUL A144,1) of the text, the piano player is called 'Amsel' (blackbird). It seems that with the change to 'Nachtigall' (nightingale) the opposition between him and Adler (eagle) is emphasized.
149 Schnitzler, *Rhapsody: A Dream Novel*, 190.

the opening of the curtain, and a clear laughter of a child).[150] Whether this victory is absolutely desirable seems arguable in view of the dead woman who, in the novella's concluding pages, represents nothing but a void – no further mention of her is made. In this sense her task has been fulfilled exemplarily: she has faded completely in order to sustain the bourgeois patriarchal system. Accordingly both Albertine and Fridolin appear able to return to their mutually reassuring and individualizing roles within the norm. The mask on the pillow – as emblem of stereotype and performance – remains as the only reminder of the constructedness and potential instability of these roles. The ending seems to imply something between the possibility of the total reestablishment of the old unstable and ignorant security, and a small chance of a new, at once knowing and unknowing acceptance of 'otherness' and insecurity. This is indicated by Albertine's comment on feeling insecure about the future, which seems to suspend the model of destiny: 'Niemals in die Zukunft fragen' (T97) (Never inquire into the future).[151]

---

150 Schnitzler, *Rhapsody: A Dream Novel*, 191.
151 Schnitzler, *Rhapsody: A Dream Novel*, 190.

Conclusion

In a letter to Hugo von Hofmannsthal, dated 17 August 1895, Schnitzler confessed his 'große Sehnsucht' (great longing) to write a 'sehr einfache Geschichte, die in sich ganz fertig ist. Eine Flasche, die man ausgießt, ohne daß etwas nachtröpfeln darf und ohne daß etwas zurückbleibt' (very simple story, which is completely rounded and finished. A bottle, which one can pour out completely in one go, without any dribbles or leftovers remaining at the bottom).[1] This describes a satisfying consumption of the literary work as a unity. It also stands in opposition to the explicit lack of *Erledigung* (completion) defended as 'dialectic justice' by the fictional writer Heinrich Bermann in *Der Weg ins Freie* (Road into the Open) (see WiF929). Schnitzler's own prose texts, while they can certainly stand alone and be read individually, unfold an iterative structure of recurring themes, motifs, and character types, which seems to deny the possibility of *Erledigung* (completion). This repetitive structure has also emerged from the readings undertaken here, exemplified in particular through the recurring motif of *Grauen* (horror). This motif does not only refer each time to other Schnitzler texts, but, with its Gothic colouring, also to the Romantic tradition from which it is taken. The analysis of this recurring motif of the sensation of *Grauen* (horror) has underscored the central claim of this book that stereotype and destiny function as individual coping mechanisms and cultural defence strategies in Schnitzler's prose. I have shown in the readings of this book how the sensation of *Grauen* (horror) also underscores the connection between the individual crisis-like experiences of the protagonists, who, while on the face of it confronted with quite different problems (lack of creativity, mental illness, prophecies of death, illegitimate babies, enigmatic *femmes fatales*...), seem to be united by a fundamental conflict: the desire to be reassured of their privileged position within

---

1   Schnitzler, Arthur and Hugo von Hofmannsthal (1964), *Briefwechsel*, ed. by Therese Nickl and Heinrich Schnitzler, Frankfurt a. M.: Fischer, 59.

the norm and to transgress it at the same time. As it repeatedly occurs when the protagonists experience a fading of differences, particularly between self and 'other', stereotype and destiny work in order to protect the protagonists from this experience of horror.

The idea of destiny emerges precisely in these moments when the familiar becomes uncanny, i.e. when the social order and its power structures are being called into question. Therefore, it has become clear that in Schnitzler's prose, destiny works to reinforce the dominant order and prevent critical consciousness in relation to it. It thus *responds* to the protagonists' need for individual self-realization, but since it is based on the assumption of a higher power, it also negates individual responsibility and impedes self-realization in the sense of a process of becoming conscious of one's own position within the social order. In this way, the belief in destiny is to be understood as a marker of crisis, but nevertheless also as an effect that reinforces the power structures of the social order. The ambivalent problem of modernity, the subject's claim to autonomy in the face of the normative pressures of the social order, is played out in the way Schnitzler's characters struggle with their sense of individuality and originality of experience.

The same can be said about the stereotypes of 'otherness' that influence the protagonists' perception. Stereotypes as ordering tools stabilize the boundaries between norm and 'other' and work to keep subjects in their assigned positions of the social order. However, my readings of Schnitzler's texts have shown that the protagonists are not only prone to this kind of pejorative typecasting, but also to a certain stereotypical mystification of 'otherness'. This, like the invocation of destiny, is a marker of crisis, as it suggests that the identification with the normative pressures of social destinies is weakened. However, as these stereotypes of 'otherness', also in their idealized form, are dependent on the norm they help to define, they do not contain any positive or alternative concepts of identity construction, which is why they, too, prevent the protagonists from developing of a critical position. By examining the link between stereotype and destiny, this study has offered a new perspective on the concept of destiny in Schnitzler's prose. Moreover, it has provided an analysis of the way these texts engage with the power structures of the Viennese bourgeois order at the beginning of the twentieth century.

In Schnitzler's prose, these idealizing stereotypes of 'otherness' are often linked to the idea of being chosen for a unique destiny. We have seen these fatal effects in *Flucht in die Finsternis* (Flight into Darkness), when the play with idealized stereotypes of madness is accompanied by a belief in destiny that suspends contingency altogether, or in *Die Fremde* (The Stranger) and *Das Schicksal des Freiherrn von Leisenbohg* (Baron Leisenbohg's Destiny), when stereotypes of enigmatic femininity are aligned with the individual destiny of the protagonists. In *Die Weissagung* (The Prophecy), too, the stereotypical mystification of enigmatic Jewishness is linked with the idea of an inescapable individual destiny and covers up the feelings of restriction caused by the protagonist's social destiny. And in *Das neue Lied* (The New Song), Karl's idealizing gaze on the precarious life in the suburbs lets him appear more seriously involved with Marie than he actually is.

If the protagonists manage to remain in, or to return to, their position within the norm, it is to some extent always at the expense of a stereotyped 'other'. In *Der Weg ins* Freie (Road into the Open), Georg enjoys the opportunity to get insights into the world of his Jewish friends, but he does not develop any sense of real solidarity with them in the face of an increasingly anti-Semitic society. Moreover, while the idealized stereotype of maternal femininity becomes Anna's 'destiny', it prevents Georg from a critical evaluation of his behaviour towards her. In the end, his male and non-Jewish privilege allows him to venture along on his 'Road into the Open'. Albeit in somewhat different ways, stereotypes of femininity also help the protagonists in *Das neue Lied* (The New Song) and *Traumnovelle* (Dream Story) to return to their bourgeois existence. While Karl's typecasting of Marie becomes her 'destiny', Albertine is spared through the proxy figure of the dead woman who fulfils the stereotypical narrative of sacrificial femininity for her and in this way allows Fridolin to experience a stabilization of his position within the patriarchal bourgeois order.

What the readings in the five chapters of this study have shown is that this conflict applies to both representatives of the bourgeoisie and of the aristocracy. While for the former, the latter are often still subject to a certain mystification, as is hinted at in *Traumnovelle* (Dream Story) and *Die Fremde* (The Stranger), the protagonists who are in fact of noble descent turn out to be merely bourgeoises with a title: both von Umprecht and von Leisenbohg fail fatally and in the same way as their bourgeois counterparts Robert and Albert. All of them are tempted by stereotypical narratives of 'otherness', which seem to promise an escape from their social destinies. Georg von Wergenthin's actions towards his socially inferior lover are mirrored in those of Karl Breiteneder. The suicide of Karl's lover, the singer Marie Ladenbauer, returns as a motif in *Der Weg ins Freie* (Road into the Open) in the side-storyline of Heinrich Bermann's lover – the nameless actress. Both of them are, of course, representatives of the 'süßes Mädel' (sweet girl) – a (stereo)type of femininity coined by Schnitzler.

For the sake of consistency, this book has focused on the male perspective and therefore neglected to look at the key texts by Schnitzler which feature female protagonists like *Frau Bertha Garlan* (Ms Bertha Garlan, 1900), *Frau Beate und ihr Sohn* (Ms Beate and Her Son, 1913), *Fräulein Else* (Miss Else, 1924), and *Therese* (1928). Particularly *Fräulein*

Else, one of Schnitzler's best-researched texts, would lend itself paradigmatically to show how stereotypes as social destiny can indeed be fatal, as Bourdieu would have it. Her suicide (or at least suicide attempt, depending on which interpretation in the scholarship one supports), akin to the death of the unknown woman in *Traumnovelle* (Dream Story), can be seen as an expression of 'Weibliches Sterben an der Kultur' (female dying through culture) and therefore as a sacrifice that protects the patriarchal order.[2] Moreover, scholars have pointed out how much Else's perception is formed not so much by individual experiences, but by her literary reading.[3] Here she resembles male protagonists like Albert in *Die Fremde* (The Stranger) or Baron Leisenbohg or Wehwald in *Das Tagebuch der Redegonda* (Redegonda's Diary, not discussed in this book), whose expectations of love in particular are formed by literary clichés. For female characters, however, the incorporation of these cultural narratives is even more harmful, because they assign to them the objectified position of the 'other'. Else's internalization and anticipation of the male gaze and its stereotypical expectations of femininity has been well documented in the scholarship.[4] Schnitzler's novel *Therese* can be seen as another example, in which Schnitzler maps out the performative repetition compulsion of stereotypical social destinies. Therese's life is depicted as a succession of failures, which indeed take on the form of a social destiny. Her precarious position after her father's death mirrors that of other female characters in Schnitzler's prose: Katharina in *Die Fremde* (The Stranger), Maria in *Der letzte Brief des Literaten* (The Writer's Last Letter, not discussed in this book), or Paula in *Flucht in die Finsternis* (Flight into Darkness). All these women end up being exploited by the male protagonists for the theatrical *mise en scène* of their individual destiny.

Schnitzler's contemporary, the writer Auguste Hauschner, explained his insight into female perspective as a result of his own positionality as an Austrian Jew: both women and Jews had in common, Hauschner wrote, that they had belonged to the oppressed for thousands of years.[5]

---

2   Bronfen, Elisabeth (1993), 'Weibliches Sterben an der Kultur: Arthur Schnitzlers "Fräulein Else",' *Die Wiener Jahrhundertwende: Einflüsse, Umwelt, Wirkungen*, Vienna, Cologne, Graz: Böhlau.

3   Aurnhammer, Achim (2013), *Arthur Schnitzlers intertextuelles Erzählen*, Berlin; Boston, MA: De Gruyter, 185.

4   See Weinhold, Ulrike (1987), 'Arthur Schnitzler und der weibliche Diskurs: Zur Problematik des Frauenbildes in der Jahrhundertwende,' *Jahrbuch für Internationale Germanistik*, 19 (1): 110–145; Bronfen, 'Weibliches Sterben an der Kultur,' 466–467; Rabelhofer, Bettina (2006), *Symptom, Sexualität, Trauma: Kohärenzlinien des Ästhetischen um 1900*, Würzburg: Königshausen und Neumann, 210.

5   See Beier, Nicolaj (2008), *Vor allem bin ich ich: Judentum, Akkulturation und Antisemitismus in Arthur Schnitzlers Leben und Werk*, Göttingen: Wallstein, 162.

The last chapter has made visible the parallels between the Jewish characters Marco Polo and Nachtigall, which highlight above all their equivalent stereotypical function for the repetitive protagonists. They appear as Jewish 'stock figures', identified with a dangerous yet fascinating half-world, which promises a certain kind of freedom and insight inaccessible to the representatives of the non-Jewish (or, at least in Fridolin's case possibly acculturated) bourgeois norm. This stereotype is at once reproduced and demystified by Heinrich Berman, who explains to Georg:

> Wir verstehen euch jedenfalls viel besser, als ihr uns. Wenn Sie auch den Kopf schütteln! Es ist ja nicht unser Verdienst. Wir haben es nämlich notwendiger gehabt, euch verstehen zu lernen, als ihr uns. Diese Gabe des Verstehens hat sich ja im Lauf der Zeit bei uns entwickeln müssen ... nach den Gesetzen des Daseinskampfes, wenn Sie wollen. (WiF757)
> At any rate we understand you much better than you do us. Although you shake your head! Do we not deserve to? We have found it more necessary, you see, to learn to understand you than you did to learn to understand us. This gift of understanding was forced to develop itself in the course of time ... according to the laws of the struggle for existence if you like.[6]

In this way, the stereotype becomes linked to the precarious position of the Jews, which is also hinted at in *Die Weissagung* (The Prophecy) and *Traumnovelle* (Dream Story), although it is ignored by the protagonists. This emphasis on the special form of insight of the Jews brings out the link between the stereotyped figure of Marco Polo and other Jewish characters in Schnitzler's writings. As I have demonstrated in the first chapter, Georg too is affected by the ambivalent stereotype of the Jew, and, through contact with Heinrich, seeks insight into 'eine Welt, die ihm bisher ziemlich fremd geblieben war' (WiF708) (a world which had been more or less foreign to him).[7] This formulation returns in *Traumnovelle* (Dream Story), when Fridolin feels increasingly alienated from his bourgeois existence and moves 'aus dem gewohnten Bezirk seines Daseins in irgendeine andere, ferne, fremde Welt' (T28) (into some strange and distant world);[8] and here too it is the Jewish 'doorman' Nachtigall who grants access to this world.

---

6   Schnitzler, Arthur (1913b), *Road into the Open*, translated by Horace Samuel, London: Howard Latimer, 155.
7   Schnitzler, *Road into the Open*, 92.
8   Schnitzler, Arthur (1928), *Rhapsody: A Dream Novel*, [no translator named], London: Constable Publishers, 59.

The comparable function of stereotypes of Jewishness and femininity is then also underscored in *Die Fremde* (The Stranger) through the recurrence of the foreign world, which Albert attributes to Katharina. Karl, in *Das neue Lied*, is horrified at the 'Unheimliche, Fremde' (NL632) (uncanny, foreign element) that he thinks he discerns in Marie's blind gaze. And in the last stages of his illness, when Robert, in *Flucht in die Finsternis* (Flight into Darkness), flees to the countryside to escape Otto's alleged murderous intentions, the well-known scenery appears to him as a 'fremde, nie vorher geschaute Gegend' (FiF105) (a foreign land, which he had never seen before), which links his experience of mental illness to the encounters with 'otherness' made by the protagonists in the other texts. While stereotypes are designed to create tight categories of similarity and alterity, they recurrently serve to project Schnitzler's protagonists into more ambiguous territories.

The element of foreignness is tightly linked to the concept of destiny in Schnitzler's writings. As I hope to have shown in this study, however, these moments of alienation are not moments of individual self-realization. In my readings, destiny is not 'aus dem Alltäglich-Festgelegten ein Durchbruch zum Eigenen' (breakthrough to a realm of one's own).[9] It is also not at all irrelevant how these attempts at finding one's individual destiny turn out, contrary to what Schrimpf suggests: 'Dabei ist es von sekundärer Bedeutung, wie die Erzählfiguren aus der Erprobung hervorgehen' (It is here of secondary significance, how the characters emerge from the trials of fate).[10] In opposition to this, I have taken the recurring failures of the protagonists seriously. All protagonists share feelings of inadequacy and restriction, long for the originality and individuality of their experiences and are threatened by the 'stereotypy' of their actions, which often appear like repetition compulsions. These repetition compulsions seem to be mirrored in the iterative structure of Schnitzler's *oeuvre*, which can be read as a performative effect: while the protagonists proclaim that they are destined for an individual path of life, the effect of seriality in Schnitzler's writings precisely contradicts that.

One could then say that what may appear as a certain kind of 'stereotypy' in Schnitzler's writings has a poetological function,[11] which

---

9 Schrimpf, Hans Joachim (1963), 'Arthur Schnitzlers *Traumnovelle*,' *Zeitschrift für deutsche Philologie* 82: 172–192, 175.
10 Schrimpf, 'Arthur Schnitzlers *Traumnovelle*,' 176.
11 Katrin Schumacher offers a first sketch of Schnitzler's *Akte der Wiederholung* (acts of repetition) as his 'poetologisches Prinzip' (poetological principle). See Schumacher, Katrin (2011), 'Wieder. Einmal. Wieder: Arthur Schnitzlers Akte der Wiederholung,' *Contested Passions: Sexuality, Eroticism, and Gender in Modern Austrian Literature and Culture*, ed. by Clemens Ruthner and Ralleigh Whitinger, New York, etc.: Peter Lang, 197–208, 205.

brings to the fore the compulsive repetition inherent in the construction of identity or social essence. Through their repetitive structures, Schnitzler's texts create their own clichés, but they also play with the incorporation of cultural clichés and elements from other literary traditions, particularly that of Romanticism. By doing so, the texts stage recognition scenes for the readers and constantly give them the feeling of 'having been here before'.[12] We recall that the sense of cliché, as described by Cave, is the feeling 'of being cheated, of being brought to a moment of fullness only to find that it is empty'.[13] It is this feeling of being cheated that Schnitzler's texts can evoke, particularly if read together, which has also emerged from the readings undertaken here. However, this sense of betrayal goes beyond the simple recognition of a literary cliché: it is linked to a moment of irritation or dissatisfaction. To use Schnitzler's own metaphor, there seems to be a remainder in the bottle that we cannot swallow.

This is mirrored in many critical responses to Schnitzler's work: the discussion about coherence in *Der Weg ins Freie* (Road into the Open), the arguments for and against the element of choice and its ethical implications in *Flucht in die Finsternis* (Flight into Darkness), the attempts at rationalizing the fantastic elements in the *Dämmerseelen* (Dozing Souls) texts or at solving the question of whether Fridolin dreams about his adventures in *Traumnovelle* (Dream Story) or really experiences them. Schnitzler's texts seem to provoke a need to find unequivocal solutions or *Erledigungen* (completions/definite solutions). With regard to the set of readings undertaken here, I would like to suggest that, in contrast to Schnitzler's own idea of a successful art work, this lack of 'Erledigung' (completion) is part of what continues to make his writings interesting. By almost always offering the reader the perspective of the protagonists through internal focalization, these texts suggest that stereotype and destiny may be set up as coping mechanisms not only for the characters, but also for the readers. However, the protagonists' (existential or interpersonal) failures cast these mechanisms into question. And where some of the protagonists may get away with using the coping mechanism of stereotype and destiny, Schnitzler's texts give an account of the price that is paid by those stereotyped as 'other'.

---

12   This adds a further aspect to a claim by Konstanze Fliedl: if Schnitzler's work after 1900 is concerned with the question 'Wie kann die Kunst die Erinnerung retten?' (How can art save memory?), then the never-ending return to familiar places may be a way to seek to achieve it. See Fliedl, Konstanze (1997), *Arthur Schnitzler. Poetik der Erinnerung*, Vienna, Cologne, Weimar: Böhlau, 25.

13   Cave, Terence (1988), *Recognitions: A Study in Poetics*, Oxford: Oxford University Press, 458.

That stereotypes of 'otherness' continue to help define normative concepts qua exclusion seems almost too trivial a fact to be pointed out. The stereotype of magical or supernatural 'otherness', which we have encountered in *Die Fremde* (The Stranger), *Die Weissagung* (The Prophecy) and *Traumnovelle* (Dream Story), is still used in cultural productions today. In fact, the representation of the 'other' as someone who has access to the supernatural world or who provides some other form of intuitive wisdom to the protagonist is so common that cultural critics and scholars have found new names to describe these stereotypes: in mainstream Hollywood films, for instance, the frequent occurrence of the so-called 'magical Negro', a Black side-character, whose magical powers and/or spiritual insight help the white protagonist through a crisis, has been critically analyzed. Albeit ostensibly represented in a positive light, this character is nevertheless denied any individual development but seems to exist exclusively to help the white lead in his or her journey of self-realization. Therefore, this cinematic trope continues to reproduce marginalizing stereotypes of Blackness and suppress Black agency.[14] The way many films still represent female characters as complementary 'others' for the male protagonists has led to the controversial term 'Manic Pixie Dream Girl', coined by the film critic Nathan Rabin in 2007.[15] The term describes a female character who exists exclusively to help the male protagonist find their way (or 'destiny') again after an experience of crisis. Her complete availability, desirability, and lack of ambitions and desires of her own highlight the stereotypical function of this character, which is contrasted with the more individualized narrative of the male protagonist. Schnitzler's characters thus find their latter-day equivalents in contemporary culture, and what has emerged from the five readings of Schnitzler's prose in this book is a psycho-social structure that is still at work today. As Schnitzler's texts make us aware of the stereotypical cultural narratives that influence the protagonists' perceptions, they also can function as an incentive to reflect on the narratives that prevail in our own culture: we may ask whom of us these contemporary narratives exclude and stereotype in order to grant some of us the privilege of feeling normal and special at the same time.

---

14   See Glenn, Cerise L. and Landra J. Cunningham (2009), 'The Magical Negro and White Salvation in Film,' *Journal of Black Studies* 40 (2): 132–152; Hughey, Matthew (2009), 'Cinethetic Racism: White Redemption and Black Stereotypes in "Magical Negro" Films,' *Social Problems*, 56 (3): 543–577.

15   See Rabin, Nathan (2007), 'The Bataan Death March of Whimsy Case File #1: Elizabethtown,' http://www.avclub.com/article/the-bataan-death-march-of-whimsy-case-file-1-emeli-15577 (accessed on 1 June 2017).

Bibliography

Works of Schnitzler

Schnitzler, Arthur (1913a), 'Andreas Thameyer's Last Letter', *Viennese Idylls*, trans. by Frederick Eisenmann, Boston, MA: John W. Luce & Co., 107–120.

Schnitzler, Arthur (1913b), *Road into the Open*, trans. by Horace Samuel, London: Howard Latimer.

Schnitzler, Arthur (1928), *Rhapsody: A Dream Novel*, [no translator named], London: Constable Publishers.

Schnitzler, Arthur (1931), *Flight into Darkness*, trans. by William A. Drake, New York: Simon & Schuster.

Schnitzler, Arthur (1961a), *Andreas Thameyers letzter Brief, Gesammelte Werke: Die Erzählenden Schriften*, vol. 1, Frankfurt a. M.: Fischer, 514–520 (cited as AT).

Schnitzler, Arthur (1961b), *Die Fremde, Gesammelte Werke: Die Erzählenden Schriften*, vol. 1, Frankfurt a. M.: Fischer, 551–559 (cited as F).

Schnitzler, Arthur (1961c), *Das Schicksal des Freiherrn von Leisenbohg, Gesammelte Werke: Die Erzählenden Schriften*, vol. 1, Frankfurt a. M.: Fischer, 580–598 (cited as SL).

Schnitzler, Arthur (1961d), *Die Weissagung, Gesammelte Werke: Die Erzählenden Schriften*, vol. 1, Frankfurt a. M.: Fischer, 598–619 (cited as W).

Schnitzler, Arthur (1961e), *Der Weg ins Freie, Gesammelte Werke: Die Erzählenden Schriften*, vol. 1, Frankfurt a. M.: Fischer, 635–961 (cited as WiF).

Schnitzler, Arthur (1983), *Tagebuch 1913–1916*, ed. by Kommission für Literarische Gebrauchsformen der Österreichischen Akademie der Wissenschaften and Werner Welzig, Wien: Verlag der Österreichischen Akademie der Wissenschaften.

Schnitzler, Arthur (1985), *Aphorismen und Notate: Gedanken über Leben und Kunst*, Leipzig and Weimar: Gustav Kiepenheuer.

Schnitzler, Arthur (1988), *Medizinische Schriften*, ed. by Horst Thomé, Vienna: Zsolnay.

Schnitzler, Arthur (2002), *Fräulein Else*, ed. by Johannes Pankau, Stuttgart: Reclam (cited as E).

Schnitzler, Arthur (2006), *Flucht in die Finsternis*, ed. by Barbara Neymeyr, Stuttgart: Reclam (cited as FiF).

Schnitzler, Arthur (2006), *Traumnovelle*, ed. by Michael Scheffel, Stuttgart: Reclam (cited as T).

Schnitzler, Arthur and Georg Brandes (1956), *Ein Briefwechsel*, ed. by Kurt Bergel, Bern: Francke.

Schnitzler, Arthur and Hugo von Hofmannsthal (1964), *Briefwechsel*, ed. by Therese Nickl and Heinrich Schnitzler, Frankfurt a. M.: Fischer.

248   Bibliography

Other Primary Works Cited

Chamisso, Adelbert (1975a), *Peter Schlemihls wundersame Geschichte, Sämmtliche Werke*, vol. 1, ed. by Jost Perfahl, Munich: Winkler, 13–67.

Chamisso, Adelbert (1975b), 'Erscheinung', *Sämmtliche Werke*, vol. 1, ed. by Jost Perfahl, Munich: Winkler, 383–384.

Heine, Heinrich (1973), 'Buch der Lieder: Die Heimkehr, 20', *Werke*, vol. 1, ed. by Stuart Atkins, Munich: Beck, 172–173.

Hoffmann, E. T. A. (1985), 'Der Sandmann', *Sämmtliche Werke*, vol. 3: *Nachtstücke, Klein Zaches, Prinzessin Brambilla, Werke 1816–1820*, ed. by Hartmut Steinecke and Wulf Segebrecht, Frankfurt a. M.: Deutscher Klassiker Verlag, 11–49.

Hoffmann, E. T. A. (2001), *Doge und Dogaresse, Sämmtliche Werke*, vol. 4: *Die Serapionsbrüder*, ed. by Hartmut Steinecke and Wulf Segebrecht, Frankfurt a. M.: Deutscher Klassiker Verlag, 429–483.

Hofmannsthal, Hugo von (1975), 'Das Märchen der 672. Nacht', *Sämtliche Werke*, vol. XXVIII: *Erzählungen 1*, ed. by Ellen Ritter, Frankfurt a. M.: Fischer, 13–30.

Lavater, Caspar David (1968–1969), *Physiognomische Fragmente zur Beförderung der Menschenkenntnis und Menschenliebe: Eine Auswahl mit 101 Abbildungen*, 4 vols. Zurich: Orell Fussli.

Mann, Thomas (1912/2013), *Der Tod in Venedig*, Frankfurt a. M.: Fischer.

Poe, Edgar Allen (1965), 'The Philosophy of Composition', *Literary Criticism of Edgar Allen Poe*, ed. by Robert L. Hough, Lincoln: University of Nebraska Press, 20–32.

Poe, Edgar Allen (1994), *The Narrative of Arthur Gordon Pym of Nantucket and Related Tales*, ed. by J. Gerald Kennedy, Oxford: Oxford University Press.

Roth, Joseph (1932), *Radetzkymarsch*, Berlin: G. Kiepenheuer.

Roth, Joseph (1976), 'Juden auf Wanderschaft', *Werke*, vol. 3, ed. by Hermann Kesten, Cologne: Kiepenheuer & Witsch.

Schlegel, Friedrich (1967), 'Athenäum: Fragmente', *Kritische Friedrich-Schlegel-Ausgabe: Zweiter Band*, ed. by Ernst Behler, Munich [et al.]: Verlag Ferdinand Schöningh.

Schreber, Daniel Paul (1995), *Denkwürdigkeiten eines Nervenkranken nebst Nachträgen*, Berlin: Kadmos.

Simmel, Georg (1995), 'Die Großstädte und das Geistesleben', *Gesamtausgabe*, ed. by Otthein Rammstedt, vol. 7: *Aufsätze und Abhandlungen 1901–1908*, vol. 1, ed. by Rüdiger Kramme, Angela Rammstedt and Otthein Rammstedt, Frankfurt a. M.: Suhrkamp, 116–131.

Simmel, Georg (1999), 'Lebensanschauung: IV Das individuelle Gesetz', *Gesamtausgabe*, ed. by Ottheim Rammstedt, vol. 16: *Der Krieg und die geistigen Entscheidungen, Grundfragen der Soziologie, Vom Wesen des historischen Verstehens, Der Konflikt der modernen Kultur, Lebensanschauung*, ed. by Gregor Fitzi and Otthein Rammstedt, Frankfurt a. M.: Suhrkamp, 346–425.

Stoker, Bram (1897/2011), *Dracula*, ed. by Roger Luckhurst, Oxford: Oxford University Press.

Secondary Literature on Schnitzler

Allen, Julie K. (2009), 'Dreaming of Denmark: Orientalism and Otherness in Schnitzler's *Traumnovelle*', *Modern Austrian Literature* 42 (2): 41–59.

Allerdissen, Rolf (1985), *Arthur Schnitzler: Impressionistisches Rollenspiel und skeptischer Moralismus in seinen Erzählungen*, Bonn: Bouvier.

Anderson, Susan C. (2003), 'The Power of the Gaze: Visual Metaphors in Schnitzler's Prose Works and Dramas', *A Companion to the Works of Arthur Schnitzler*, ed. by Dagmar C. G. Lorenz, Rochester, NY: Camden House, 303–324.

Arens, Detlev (1981), *Untersuchungen zu Arthur Schnitzlers Roman 'Der Weg ins Freie'*, Frankfurt a. M.: Peter Lang.

Aspetsberger, Friedbert (1966), '"Drei Akte in einem": Zum Formtyp in Schnitzlers Drama', *Zeitschrift für deutsche Philologie* 85: 285–308.

Aurnhammer, Achim (2013), *Arthur Schnitzlers intertextuelles Erzählen*, Berlin, Boston, MA: De Gruyter.

Beier, Nicolaj (2008), *Vor allem bin ich ich: Judentum, Akkulturation und Antisemitismus in Arthur Schnitzlers Leben und Werk*, Göttingen: Wallstein.

Biese, Alfred (1913), *Deutsche Literaturgeschichte. Dritter Band: Von Hebbel bis zur Gegenwart*, Munich: C. H. Becksche Verlagsbuchhandlung Oskar Beck.

Boehringer, Michael (2011), 'Fantasies of *White Masculinity* in Arthur Schnitzler's *Andreas Thameyers letzter Brief* (1900)', *The German Quarterly* 84 (1): 80–96.

Boetticher, Dirk von (1999), '*Meine Werke sind lauter Diagnosen': Über die ärztliche Dimension im Werk Arthur Schnitzlers*, Heidelberg: Winter.

Bronfen, Elisabeth (1993), 'Weibliches Sterben an der Kultur: Arthur Schnitzlers "Fräulein Else"', *Die Wiener Jahrhundertwende: Einflüsse, Umwelt, Wirkungen*, Vienna, Cologne, Graz: Böhlau.

Brucke, Martin (2002), *Magnetiseure: Die windige Karriere einer literarischen Figur*, Freiburg im Breisgau: Rombach.

Dangel, Elsbeth (1985), *Wiederholung als Schicksal: Arthur Schnitzlers Roman 'Therese. Chronik eines Frauenlebens'*, Munich: Fink.

Dieterle, Bernhard (1997), '"Keinesfalls kann ich weiterleben": Figurationen des Schreibens bei Arthur Schnitzler', *Modern Austrian Literature* 30 (1): 20–38.

Fliedl, Konstanze (1997), *Arthur Schnitzler. Poetik der Erinnerung*, Vienna, Cologne, Weimar: Böhlau.

Fliedl, Konstanze (2005), *Arthur Schnitzler*, Stuttgart: Reclam.

Freytag, Julia (2007), *Verhüllte Schaulust: Die Maske in Schnitzlers Traumnovelle und in Kubrick's Eyes Wide Shut*, Bielefeld: transcript.

Gay, Peter (2001), *Schnitzler's Century: The Making of Middle-Class Culture, 1815–1914*, New York: Norton.

Gerrekens, Louis (2011), '*Die Weissagung* oder wie aus schlecht erzähltem Theater eine spannende Novelle wird', *Theatralisches Erzählen um 1900: Narrative Inszenierungsweisen der Jahrhundertwende*, ed. by Achim Küpper, Heidelberg: Universitätsverlag Winter, 89–102.

Gidion, Heidi (1998), 'Haupt- und Nebensache in "Der Weg ins Freie"', *Text + Kritik, Zeitschrift für Literatur* 138/139: 47–60.

Gillman, Abigail (2004), 'Failed Bildung and the Aesthetics of Detachment: Schnitzler's *Der Weg ins Freie*', *Confrontations/Accommodations: German-Jewish Literary and Cultural History from Heine to Wassermann*, ed. by Mark Gelber, Tübingen: Niemeyer, 209–236.

Gillman, Abigail (2009), *Viennese Jewish Modernism: Freud, Hofmannsthal, Beer-Hofmann and Schnitzler*, University Park: Penn State University Press.

Gutt, Barbara (1978), *Emanzipation bei Arthur Schnitzler*, Berlin: Spiess.

Haberich, Max (2013), '"daß ich ja nicht im entferntesten daran gedacht habe, irgendeine Frage lösen zu wollen": The Development of Arthur Schnitzler's Position on the "Jewish Question" from *Der Weg ins Freie* to *Professor Bernhardi*', *Journal of Austrian Studies* 46 (2): 81–102.

Hawes, J. M. (1995a), 'The Secret Life of Georg von Wergenthin: Nietzschean Analysis and Narrative Authority in Arthur Schnitzler's *DerWeg ins Freie*', *Modern Language Review* 90 (2): 377–387.

Hawes, J. M. (1995b), '"Als käme er von einer weiten Reise heim." Fremderfahrung als Erfahrung des eigenen entfremdeten Ichs in Arthur Schnitzlers Roman *Der Weg ins Freie*', *Reisen im Diskurs: Modelle der Fremderfahrung von den Pilgerberichten bis zur Postmoderne; Tagunsgakten des internationalen Symposiums zur Reiseliteratur University College Dublin vom 10 –12. März 1994*, ed. by Anne Fuchs and Theo Harden, Heidelberg: Universitätsverlag C. Winter.

Heinzmann, Bertold (2006), *Arthur Schnitzler: Traumnovelle: Erläuterungen und Dokumente*, Stuttgart: Reclam.

Herzog, Hillary Hope (2003), '"Medizin ist eine Weltanschauung": On Schnitzler's Medical Writings.' *A Companion to the Works of Arthur Schnitzler*, ed. by Dagmar C. G. Lorenz, Rochester, NY: Camden House, 227–241.

Imboden, Michael (1971), *Die surreale Komponente im erzählenden Werk Arthur Schnitzlers*, Bern: H. Lang.

Janz, Rolf-Peter and Klaus Laermann (1977), *Arthur Schnitzler: Zur Diagnose des Wiener Bürgertums im Fin de siècle*, Stuttgart: Metzler.

Just, Gottfried (1968), *Ironie und Sentimentalität in den erzählenden Dichtungen Arthur Schnitzlers*, Berlin: E. Schmidt.

Katan, M. (1969), 'Schnitzlers *Das Schicksal des Freiherrn von Leisenbohg*', *Journal of the American Psychoanalytic Association* 17 (3): 904–926.

Kolkenbrock, Marie (2017), 'Der "graziöse" Autor und *Die Dame*: Arthur Schnitzlers implizite Autorschaft im Fortsetzungsroman *Traumnovelle*', *Poetologien des Posturalen: Inszenierungen von Autorschaft in der Zwischenkriegszeit*, ed. by Clemens Peck and Norbert Christian Wolf, Paderborn: Fink, 49–65.

Kolkenbrock, Marie (2018), 'Gothic Infections: Arthur Schnitzler and the Haunted Culture of Modernism', *MLR* 113 (1): 150–170.

Kollek, Caren (2011), *Literarische Selbstfindungsprozesse um 1900: Personen-, Erotik- und Moralkonzeption in Erzähltexten von Arthur Schnitzler, Eduard von Keyserling und Hermann Sudermann*, Kiel: Ludwig.

Körner, Josef (1921), *Arthur Schnitzlers Gestalten und Probleme*, Zurich, Leipzig, Vienna: Amalthea.

Krobb, Florian (2000), *Selbstdarstellungen: Untersuchungen zur deutsch-jüdischen Erzählliteratur im neunzehnten Jahrhundert*, Würzburg: Königshausen und Neumann.

Krotkoff, Helga (1973), 'Zur geheimen Gesellschaft in Arthur Schnitzlers *Traumnovelle*', *German Quarterly* 46: 202–209.

Lange-Kirchheim, Astrid (2003), '*Déjà-vue* einer Jahrhunderwende: Psychoanalyse als Traumatheorie: Zu Arthur Schnitzlers *Traumnovelle*', *Geschlechterforschung und Literaturwissenschaft*, ed. by P. Wiesinger, Bern [et al.]: Lang, 269–274.

Lawson, Richard H. (1963), 'An Interpretation of "Die Weissagung"', *Studies in Arthur Schnitzler*, ed. by Herbert Reichert and Herman Salinger, Chapel Hill: The University of North Carolina Press, 71–78.

Lin, Angela H. (2006), 'Resisting "Bad Taste": Sentimentality, "Jewishness", and Modernity in Arthur Schnitzler's *Der Weg ins Freie*', *The German Quarterly* 79 (3): 366–380.

Loewenberg, Peter (2006), 'Freud, Schnitzler, and *Eyes Wide Shut*', *Depth of Field: Stanley Kubrick, Film, and the Uses of History*, ed. by James Diedrick and Glenn Perusek, Madison: The University of Wisconsin Press, 255–279.

Lönker, Fred (2006), '"Flucht in die Finsternis": Wahnsinn – psychopathologisches Fatum oder metaphysische Logik?' *Interpretationen: Arthur Schnitzler: Dramen und Erzählungen*, ed. by Hee-Ju Kim and Günter Saße, Stuttgart: Reclam, 240–251.

Lorenz, Dagmar (2003), 'The Self as Process in an Era of Transition: Competing Paradigms of Personality and Character in Schnitzler's Works', *A Companion to the Works of Arthur Schnitzler*, ed. by Dagmar C. G. Lorenz, Rochester, NY: Camden House.

Low, D. S. (1986), 'Questions of Form in Schnitzler's *Der Weg ins Freie*', *Modern Austrian Literature* 19 (3/4): 22–27.

Lukas, Wolfgang (1996), *Das Selbst und das Fremde: Epochale Lebenskrisen und ihre Lösung im Werk Arthur Schnitzlers*, Munich: Fink.

Luprecht, Mark (1991), *What People Call Pessimism: Sigmund Freud, Arthur Schnitzler, and the Nineteenth Century Controversy at the University of Vienna Medical School*, Riverside, CA: Ariadne Press.

Malsch, Katja (2007), *Literatur und Selbsttopfer: Historisch-systematische Studien zu Gryphius, Lessing, Gotthelf, Storm, Kaiser und Schnitzler*, Würzburg: Königshausen und Neumann.

Meyer, Imke (2010), *Männlichkeit und Melodram: Arthur Schnitzlers erzählende Schriften*, Würzburg: Königshausen & Neumann.

Müller-Funk, Wolfgang (2006), 'Der gewohnte Bezirk seines Daseins: Räumlichkeit und Topografie Wiens in Schnitzlers *Der Weg ins Freie*: Mit einem Vergleich der Filmversion von Karin Brandauer', *Die Tatsachen der Seele: Arthur Schnitzler und der Film*, ed. by T. Ballhausen et al., Wien: Filmarchiv Austria.

Müller-Seidel, Walter (1997), *Arztbilder im Wandel. Zum literarischen Werk Arthur Schnitzlers*, Munich: Verlag der Bayerischen Akademie der Wissenschaften.

Neubauer, John (2003), 'The Overaged Adolescents of Schnitzler's *Der Weg ins Freie*', *A Companion to the Works of Arthur Schnitzler*, ed. by Dagmar C. G. Lorenz, Rochester, NY: Camden House.

Neumann, Annja (2016), 'Schnitzler's Anatomy Lesson: Medical Topographies in Professor Bernhardi', *Jahrbuch Literatur und Medizin*, Bd. 8, ed. by Christa Janson and Florian Steger, Heidelberg: Winter, 31–60.

Neymeyr, Barbara (2006), 'Nachwort', Arthur Schnitzler: *Flucht in die Finsternis*, ed. by Barbara Neymeyr, Stuttgart: Reclam.

Oosterhoff, Jenneke A. (2000), *Die Männer sind infam, solang sie Männer sind: Konstruktionen der Männlichkeit in den Werken Arthur Schnitzlers*, Tübingen: Stauffenberg.

Perlmann, Michaela L. (1987a), *Der Traum in der literarischen Moderne: Untersuchungen zum Werk Arthur Schnitzlers*, Munich: Fink.

Perlmann, Michaela L. (1987b), *Arthur Schnitzler*, Stuttgart: Metzler.

Rabelhofer, Bettina (2006), *Symptom, Sexualität, Trauma: Kohärenzlinien des Ästhetischen um 1900*, Würzburg: Königshausen und Neumann.

Rohrwasser, Michael (1999), 'Arthur Schnitzlers Erzählung "Die Weissagung": Ästhetizismus, Antisemitismus und Psychoanalyse', *Zeitschrift für deutsche Philologie* 118: 60–79 (Sonderheft: *Zur deutschen Literatur im ersten Drittel des 20. Jahrhunderts*, ed. by Norbert Oelers and Hartmut Steinecke).

Santner, Eric (1986), 'Of Masters, Slaves, and Other Seducers: Arthur Schnitzler's "Traumnovelle"', *Modern Austrian Literature* 19 (3/4): 33–45.

Saxer, Sibylle (2010), *Die Sprache der Blicke verstehen: Arthur Schnitzlers Poetik des Augen-Blicks als Poetik der Scham*, Freiburg i. Br., Berlin, Vienna: Rombach.

Scheible, Hartmut (1977), *Arthur Schnitzler und die Aufklärung*, Munich: W. Fink.

Schmidt, Harald (2000), 'Grenzfall und Grenzverlust: Die poetische Konstruktion des Wahns in Arthur Schnitzlers *Flucht in die Finsternis*', *Literatur als Geschichte des Ich*, ed. by Eduard Beutner and Ulrike Tanzer, Würzburg: Königshausen & Neumann, 185–204.

Schneider, Gert K. (2014), *Grenzüberschreitungen: Energie, Wunder und Gesetze: Das Okkulte als Weltanschauung und seine Manifestationen im Werk Arthur Schnitzlers*, Vienna: Praesens.

Schnyder, Peter (2002), 'Im Netz der Behausung: Arthur Schnitzlers Erzählung *Andreas Thameyers letzter Brief* in kulturwissenschaftlicher Perspektive', *Akten des X. Internationalen Germanistenkongresses Wien 2000: 'Zeitenwende: Die Germanistik auf dem Weg vom 20. ins 21. Jahrhundert'*, vol. 6: *Epochenbegriffe: Grenzen und Möglichkeiten; Aufklärung – Klassik – Romantik; Die Wiener Moderne*, ed. by Peter Wiesinger, et al., Bern: Peter Lang, 419–425.

Schön, Tiziane (2004), 'Nervenschwache Generation – begabte Neurastheniker: Georg Hermanns *Der kleine Gast* als Berliner Pendant zu Arthur Schnitzlers', *Der Weg ins Freie, Georg Hermann: Deutsch-jüdischer Schriftsteller und Journalist, 1871–1943*, ed. by Godela Weiss-Sussex, Tübingen: Niemeyer.

Schrimpf, Hans Joachim (1963), 'Arthur Schnitzlers *Traumnovelle*', *Zeitschrift für deutsche Philologie* 82: 172–192.

Schumacher, Katrin (2011), 'Wieder. Einmal. Wieder: Arthur Schnitzlers Akte der Wiederholung', *Contested Passions: Sexuality, Eroticism, and Gender in Modern Austrian Literature and Culture*, ed. by Clemens Ruthner and Ralleigh Whitinger, New York [et. al.]: Peter Lang, 197–208.

Sebald, W. G. (1985), *Die Beschreibung des Unglücks: Zur Österreichischen Literatur von Stifter bis Handke*, Salzburg: Residenz.

Segar, Kenneth (1973), 'Determinism and Character: Arthur Schnitzler's *Traumnovelle* and his Unpublished Critique of Psychoanalyis', *Oxford German Studies* 8: 114–127.

Segar, Kenneth (1988), 'The Death of Reason: Narrative Strategy and Resonance in Schnitzler's *Flucht in die Finsternis*', *Oxford German Studies* 17: 97–117.

Segar, Kenneth (1992), 'Aesthetic Coherence in Arthur Schnitzler's Novel *Der Weg ins Freie*', *Modern Austrian Literature* 25 (3/4): 95–111.

Swales, Martin (1971), *Arthur Schnitzler: A Critical Study*, Oxford: Oxford University Press.

Tarnowski-Seidel, Heide (1983), *Arthur Schnitzler, 'Flucht in die Finsternis': Eine produktionsästhetische Untersuchung*, Munich: Fink.

Thomé, Horst (1984), 'Kernlosigkeit und Pose: Zur Rekonstruktion von Schnitzlers Psychologie', *Fin de Siècle: Zur Naturwissenschaft und Literatur der Jahrhundertwende im deutsch-skandinavischen Kontext*, ed. by Klaus Bohnen, Uffe Hansen, and Friedrich Schmöe, Kopenhagen and Munich: Fink, 62–87.

Thomé, Horst (1993), *Autonomes Ich und 'Inneres Ausland': Studien über Realismus, Tiefenpsychologie und Psychiatrie in deutschen Erzähltexten (1848–1914)*, Tübingen: Niemeyer.

Webber, Andrew (2011), 'Threshold Conditions: Benjamin, Schnitzler, and the Sleeping Disorders of Modernism', *Die Halbschlafbilder in der Literatur, den Künsten und den Wissenschaften*, ed. by Roger Paulin and Helmut Pfotenhauer, Würzburg: Königshausen & Neumann, 275–290.

Weigel, Robert (1996), 'Schnitzlers Schicksalserzählungen *Die Weissagung* und *Die dreifache Warnung*', *Die Seele … ist ein weites Land: Kritische Beiträge zum Werk Arthur Schnitzlers*, ed. by Joseph P. Strelka, Bern [et al.]: Peter Lang, 149–162.

Weigel, Robert (1997): 'Schnitzlers Schicksalserzählungen "Die Weissagung" und "Die dreifache Warnung"', *Die Seele ... ist ein weites Land. Kritische Beiträge zum Werk Arthur Schnitzlers*, ed. by Joseph P. Strelka, Bern [et al.] Peter Lang, 149–162.

Weinberger. G. J. (2005), 'Cowardice and Paralysis: A Brief Glance at Some of Arthur Schnitzler's Male Characters', *Neophilologus* 89: 277–285.

Weinhold, Ulrike (1987), 'Arthur Schnitzler und der weibliche Diskurs: Zur Problematik des Frauenbildes in der Jahrhundertwende', *Jahrbuch für Internationale Germanistik* 19 (1), 110–145.

Wisely, Andrew C. (2004), *Arthur Schnitzler and Twentieth-century Criticism*, Rochester: Camden House.

Wunberg, Gotthart (2003), 'Arthur Schnitzler – oder über Kulturwissenschaften und Literaturwissenschaft', *Arthur Schnitzler im zwanzigsten Jahrhundert*, ed. by Konstanze Fliedl, Wien: Picus Verlag.

Wünsch, Marianne (2004), 'Logische Argumentation und erkenntnistheoretische Probleme am Beispiel von Arthur Schnitzlers *Flucht in die Finsternis*', *Littérature et théorie de la connaissance 1890–1935*, ed. by Christine Maillard, Strasbourg: Presses universitaires de Strasbourg, 302–317.

Xiaoli, Lü (2006), 'Die Raumdarstellung in Arthur Schnitzlers Roman *Der Weg ins Freie*', *Literaturstraße* 7: 249–279.

Other Secondary Literature and Theoretical Works Cited

Althusser, Louis (1971), 'Ideology and Ideological State Apparatuses', *Lenin and Philosophy and Other Essays*, London: New Left Books, 127–188.

Althusser, Louis (1990a), 'Theory, Theoretical Practice and Theoretical Formation: Ideology and Ideological Struggle', *Philosophy and the Spontaneous Philosophy of the Scientists and Other Essays*, London, New York: Verso, 1–42.

Althusser, Louis (1990b), 'Philosophy and the Spontaneous Philosophy of the Scientists', *Philosophy and the Spontaneous Philosophy of the Scientists & Other Essays*, London, New York: Verso, 69–166.

Anderson, George K. (1965), *The Legend of the Wandering Jew*, Providence: Brown University Press.

Barthes, Roland (1972), *Mythologies*, London: Vintage.

Battafarano, Italo Michele (1996), *Deutsche Romantik-Sehnsucht nach Italien: Wackenroders Auffassung der Kunst der italienischen Renaissance in den 'Herzensergießungen eines kunstliebenden Klosterbruders'*, *'Italien in Germanien': Deutsche Italienrezeption 1750–1850*, ed. by Frank-Rutger Hausmann, Tübingen: Narr, 351–371.

Beauvoir, Simone de (2009), *The Second Sex*, London: Jonathan Cape.

Benjamin, Walter (1986), 'Critique of Violence', *Reflections: Essays, Aphorisms, Autobiographical Writings*, ed. by Peter Demetz, New York: Schocken Books.

Bertschik, Julia (2005), *Mode und Moderne: Kleidung als Spiegel des Zeitgeistes in der deutschsprachigen Literatur (1770–1945)*, Köln: Böhlau.

Bourdieu, Pierre (1977), *Outline of a Theory of Practice*, Cambridge: Cambridge University Press.

Bourdieu, Pierre (1992), *Language and Symbolic Power: The Economy of Linguistic Exchanges*, ed. by John B. Thompson, Cambridge: Polity Press.

Bourdieu, Pierre (1996), *The Rules of Art: Genesis and Structure of the Literary Field*, Stanford, CA: Stanford UP.

Bourdieu, Pierre (2017), 'The Biographical Illusion (1986)', *Biography in Theory: Key Texts and Commentaries*, ed. by Wilhelm Hemecker and Edward Saunders, Berlin: de Gruyter, 210–216.

Brittnacher, Richard (2000), 'Welt ohne Väter: Söhne um 1900: Von der Revolte zum Opfer', *Kursbuch* 140: 19–31.

Broch, Hermann (1975), *Schriften zur Literatur 1: Kommentierte Werkausgabe*, vol. 9/1, ed. by Paul Michael Lützeler, Frankfurt a. M.: Suhrkamp.

Bronfen, Elisabeth (1992), *Over Her Dead Body: Death, Femininity and the Aesthetic*, Manchester: Manchester University Press.

Butler, Judith (1993), *Bodies That Matter: On the Discursive Limits of "Sex"*, London, New York: Routledge.

Butler, Judith (1997a), *Excitable Speech: A Politics of the Performative*, New York, London: Routledge.

Butler, Judith (1997b), *The Psychic Life of Power: Theories in Subjection*, Stanford, CA: Stanford University Press.

Butler, Judith (2000), *Antigone's Claim: Kinship between Life and Death*, New York, Chichester: Columbia University Press.

Cave, Terence (1988), *Recognitions: A Study in Poetics*, Oxford: Oxford University Press.

Crenshaw, Kimberlé Williams (2001), 'Twenty Years of Critical Race Theory: Looking Back To Move Forward', *Connecticut Law Review* 43 (5), 1253–1352.

Cusack, Andrew (2012), 'Introduction', *Popular Revenants: The German Gothic and Its International Reception, 1800–2000*, ed. by Andrew Cusack and Barry Murnane, Rochester, New York: Camden House, 1–9.

Dolar, Mladen (2006), *A Voice and Nothing More*, Cambridge, MA: MIT Press.

Dyer, Richard (2002), *The Matter of Images: Essays on Representation*, London: Routledge.

Fioretos, Artis (2004), 'Eine Studie in Blau (Novalis)', *Bilder-Denken. Bildlichkeit und Argumentation*, ed. by Barbara Naumann and Edgar Pankow, Munich: Fink, 139–152.

Földényi, Lásló F. (2004), 'Das zwiespältige Erbe der Romantik', *Das Jahrhundert der Avantgarden*, ed. by Cornelia Klinger and Wolfgang Müller-Funk, Munich: Fink, 53–61.

Foucault, Michel (1969), *Wahnsinn und Gesellschaft: Eine Geschichte des Wahns im Zeitalter der Vernunft*, Frankfurt a. M.: Suhrkamp.

Foucault, Michel (1989), *Madness and Civilization: A History of Insanity in the Age of Reason*, London, New York: Routledge.

Foucault, Michel (1991), *Discipline and Punish: The Birth of the Prison*, London: Penguin.

Freud, Sigmund (1941), 'Der Dichter und das Phantasieren', *Gesammelte Werke*, vol. 7: *Werke aus den Jahren 1906–1909*, ed. by Anna Freud et al., London: Imago Publishing, 211–223.

Freud, Sigmund (1942), 'Die Traumdeutung', in *Gesammelte Werke*, vols 2 and 3: *Die Traumdeutung/Über den Traum*, ed. by Anna Freud, Edward Bibring, Willi Hoffer, Ernst Kris, and Otto Isakower, London: Imago, 1–642.

Freud, Sigmund (1943), 'Über einen autobiographisch beschriebenen Fall von Paranoia (Dementia Paranoides)', *Gesammelte Werke*, vol. 8: *Werke aus den Jahren 1909–1913*, ed. by Anna Freud, Edward Bibring, Willi Hoffer, Ernst Kris, and Otto Isakower, London: Imago, 239–320.

Freud, Sigmund (1947a), 'Das Tabu der Virginität', in *Gesammelte Werke*, vol. 12: *Werke aus den Jahren 1917–1920*, ed. by Anna Freud, Edward Bibring, Willi Hoffer, Ernst Kris, and Otto Isakower, London: Imago, 161–180.

Freud, Sigmund (1947b), 'Das Unheimliche', *Gesammelte Werke*, vol. 12: *Werke aus den Jahren 1917–1920*, ed. by Anna Freud, Edward Bibring, Willi Hoffer, Ernst Kris, and Otto Isakower, London: Imago, 227–268.

Freud, Sigmund (2001), 'Creative Writers and Daydreaming', *Standard Edition*, vol. IX, ed. by James Strachey, Alan Tyson, Alix Strachey, Anna Freud, and Angela Richards, London: Vintage.

Gelder, Ken (1994), *Reading the Vampire*, London, New York: Routledge.

Giddens, Anthony (1992), *The Transformation of Intimacy: Sexuality, Love, and Eroticism in Modern Societies*, Oxford: Polity Press.

Gilman, Sander L. (1985), *Difference and Pathology: Stereotypes of Sexuality, Race, and Madness*, Ithaca, London: Cornell University Press.

Gilman, Sander L. (1995), *Freud, Race, and Gender*, Princeton, NJ: Princeton University Press.

Ginsberg, Elaine (1996), *Passing and the Fictions of Identity*, Durham, NC and London: Duke University Press.

Glenn, Cerise L. and Landra J. Cunningham (2009), 'The Magical Negro and White Salvation in Film', *Journal of Black Studies* 40 (2): 132–152.

Gockel, Heinz (1979), 'Friedrich Schlegels Theorie des Fragments', *Romantik: Ein literaturwissenschaftliches Studienbuch*, Ernst Ribbat, Königstein/Ts.: Athenäum, 22–37.

Goltschnigg, Dietmar (2009), *'Fröhliche Apokalypse' und nostalgische Utopie: 'Österreich als besonderer Fall der modernen Welt'*, ed. by Charlotte Grolleg-Edler Vienna, Berlin: Lit Verlag.

Gray, Richard T. (2004), *About Face: German Physiognomic Thought from Lavater to Auschwitz*, Detroit: Wayne State University Press.

Halberstam, Judith (1995), *Skin Shows: Gothic Horrors and the Technology of Monsters*, Durham and London: Duke University Press.

Haraway, Donna (1991), *Simions, Cyborgs, and Women: The Reinvention of Nature*, New York: Routledge.

Hegel, G. F. W. (1988), *Phänomenologie des Geistes*, ed. by H.-F. Wessels and H. Clairmont, Hamburg: Meiner.

Hilmes, Carola (1990), *Die Femme Fatale: Ein Weiblichkeitstypus in der nachromantischen Literatur*, Stuttgart: Metzler.

Hughey, Matthew (2009), 'Cinethetic Racism: White Redemption and Black Stereotypes in "Magical Negro" Films', *Social Problems* 56 (3): 543–577.

Janz, Marlies (1986), *Marmorbilder: Weiblichkeit und Tod bei Clemens Brentano und Hugo von Hofmannsthal*, Königsstein/Ts.: Athenaeum.

Kant, Immanuel (1972), 'Philosophische Religionslehre nach Pölitz', *Kants gesammelte Schriften*, vol. 5, ed. by Akademie der Wissenschaften zu Göttingen, Berlin: de Gruyter.

King, Martina (2009), *Pilger und Prophet: Heilige Autorschaft bei Rainer Maria Rilke*, Göttingen: Vandenhoeck & Ruprecht.

Kittler, Friedrich A. (1993), *Draculas Vermächtnis: Technische Schriften*, Leipzig: Reclam.

Kohns, Oliver (2007), *Die Verrücktheit des Sinns: Wahnsinn und Zeichen bei Kant, E.T.A. Hoffmann und Thomas Carlyle*, Bielefeld: transcript.

Kos, Wolfgang (2013), 'Einleitung', *Wiener Typen: Klischees und Wirklichkeit*, ed. by Wolfgang Kos, Vienna: Christian Brandstätter (= Exhibition Catalogue of *Wiener Typen: Klischees und Wirklichkeit – 387. Sonderausstellung des Wien Museums*, Wien Museum Karlsplatz, 25 April–6 October 2013), 14–23.

Kremer, Detlef (2007), *Romantik: Lehrbuch der Germanistik*, Stuttgart: Metzler.

Lafferty, Sean D. W. (2013), *Law and Society in the Age of Theoderic the Great: A Study of the Edictum Theoderici*, Cambridge: Cambridge University Press.

Lahmann, Heinrich (1987), *Die diätetische Blutentmischung (Dysämie) als Grundursache der Krankheiten: Ein Beitrag zur Lehre von der Krankheitsanlage und Krankheitsverhütung*, St. Goar: Reichl.

Le Rider, Jacques (1993), *Modernity and the Crises of Identity: Culture and Society in Fin-de-siècle Vienna*, New York: Continuum.

Lethen, Helmut (2002), *Cool Conduct: The Culture of Distance in Weimar Germany*, Berkeley: University of California Press.

Lipphardt, Veronika (2008), *Biologie der Juden: Jüdische Wissenschaftler über 'Rasse' und Vererbung 1900–1935*, Göttingen: Vandenhoeck & Ruprecht.

Luhmann, Niklas (1995), *Liebe als Passion*, Frankfurt a. M.: Suhrkamp.

MacKinnon, Catharine A. (1982), 'Feminism, Marxism, Method, and the State: An Agenda for Theory', *Signs* 7 (3), *Feminist Theory*, 515–544.

Magris, Claudio (2000), *Der Habsburgische Mythos in der österreichischen Literatur*, Vienna: Zsolnay.

Matt, Peter von (1989), *... fertig ist das Angesicht: Zur Literaturgeschichte des menschlichen Gesichts*, Frankfurt a. M.: Suhrkamp.

Moi, Toril (1991), 'Appropriating Bourdieu: Feminist Theory and Pierre Bourdieu's Sociology of Culture', *New Literary History* 22: 1017–1049.

Murnane, Barry (2012), 'Haunting (Literary) History: An Introduction to German Gothic', *Popular Revenants: The German Gothic and Its International Reception, 1800–2000*, ed. by Andrew Cusack and Barry Murnane, Rochester, New York: Camden House, 10–43.

Neumann, Gerhard (1999), 'Narration und Bildlichkeit: Zur Inszenierung eines romantischen Schicksalsmusters in E.T.A. Hoffmanns "Doge und Dogaresse"', *Bild und Schrift in der Romantik*, ed. by Gerhard Neumann and Günter Oesterle, Würzburg: Königshausen und Neumann, 107–142.

Otis, Laura (1999), *Membranes: Metaphors of Invasion in Nineteenth Century Literature, Science, and Politics*, Baltimore, MD and London: The Johns Hopkins University Press.

Perkins, T. E. (1979), 'Rethinking Stereotypes', *Ideology and Cultural Production*, ed. by Michèle Barrett, Philip Corrigan, Annette Kuhn, and Janet Wolf, London: Croom Helm, 133–159.

Pohle, Bettina (1998), *Kunstwerk Frau: Inszenierungen von Weiblichkeit in der Moderne*, Frankfurt a. M.: Fischer.

Ponstingl, Michael (2013), 'Otto Schmidts Spektakel der Wiener Typen', *Wiener Typen: Klischees und Wirklichkeit*, ed. by Wolfgang Kos, Vienna: Christian Brandstätter (= Exhibition Catalogue of *Wiener Typen: Klischees und Wirklichkeit – 387. Sonderausstellung des Wien Museums*, Wien Museum Karlsplatz, 25 April–6 October 2013), 192–201.

Pulzer, Peter (1997), 'Die Wiederkehr des alten Hasses', *Deutsch-jüdische Geschichte der Neuzeit 1871–1918*, ed. by Michael A. Meyer, Munich: Beck, 193–248.

Rabin, Nathan (2007), 'The Bataan Death March of Whimsy Case File #1: Elizabethtown', http://www.avclub.com/article/the-bataan-death-march-of-whimsy-case-file-1-emeli-15577 (accessed on 1 June 2017).

Santner, Eric L. (1996), *My Own Private Germany*, Princeton, NJ: Princeton University Press.

Santner, Eric L. (2011), *The Royal Remains: The People's Two Bodies and the Endgames of Sovereignty*, Chicago: University of Chicago Press.

Sarasin, Phillip (2007), 'Die Visualisierung des Feindes: Über metaphorische Technologien der frühen Bakteriologie', *Bakteriologie und Moderne: Studien zur Biopolitik des Unsichtbaren 1870–1920*, ed. by Philipp Sarasin, Silvia Berger, Marianne Hänseler, and Myriam Spörri, Frankfurt a. M.: Suhrkamp, 427–61.

Sarasin, Philipp, Silvia Berger, Marianne Hänseler, and Myriam Spörri (eds.) (2007), *Bakteriologie und Moderne: Studien zur Biopolitik des Unsichtbaren 1870– 1920*, Frankfurt a. M.: Suhrkamp.

Schlaffer, Hannelore (1993), *Poetik der Novelle*, Stuttgart: Metzler.

Schneider, Manfred (1999), 'Das Grauen der Beobachter: Schriften und Bilder des Wahnsinns', *Bild und Schrift in der Romantik*, ed. by Gerhard Neumann and Günter Oesterle, Würzburg: Königshausen und Neumann, 237–253.

Sedgwick, Eve Kosofsky (1985), *Between Men: English Literature and Male Homosocial Desire*, New York: Columbia University Press, 97.

Sledzik, Paul and Nicholas Bellantoni (1994), 'Bioarcheological and Biocultural Evidence for the New England Vampire Folk Belief', *American Journal of Physical Anthropology* 94 (2): 269–274.

Sontag, Susan (1991), *Illness as Metaphor & AIDS and Its Metaphors*, London: Penguin.

Strowick, Elisabeth (2009), *Sprechende Körper, Poetik der Ansteckung: Performativa in Literatur und Rhetorik*, Munich: Fink.

Volkov, Shulamit (2006), *Germans, Jews, and Antisemites: Trials in Emancipation*, New York: Cambridge University Press.

Webber, Andrew J. (1996), *The Doppelgänger: Double Visions in German Literature*, Oxford: Oxford University Press.

Webber, Andrew J. (2005), 'The Afterlife of Romanticism', *German Literature of the Nineteenth Century 1832–1899*, ed. by Clayton Koelb and Eric Downing, Rocherster, NY: Camden House, 23–43.

Webber, Andrew J. (2012), 'About Face: E. T. A. Hoffmann, Weimar Film, and the Technological Afterlife of Gothic Physiognomy', *Popular Revenants: The German Gothic and Its International Reception, 1800–2000*, ed. by Andrew Cusack and Barry Murnane, Rochester, NY: Camden House, 161–180.

Weininger, Otto (1903), *Geschlecht und Charakter: Eine prinzipielle Untersuchung*, Vienna and Leipzig: Wilhelm Braunmüller.

Wietschorke, Jens (2013), 'Die Stadt als Tableau: Zur kulturellen Konstruktion der "Wiener Typen"', *Wiener Typen: Klischees und Wirklichkeit*, ed. by Wolfgang Kos, Vienna: Christian Brandstätter (= Exhibition Catalogue of *Wiener Typen: Klischees und Wirklichkeit – 387. Sonderausstellung des Wien Museums*, Wien Museum Karlsplatz, 25 April–6 October 2013), 26–31.

Zijderveld, Anton C. (1987), 'On the Nature and Function of Clichés', *Erstarrtes Denken: Studien zu Klischee, Stereotyp und Vorurteil in englischsprachiger Literatur*, ed. by Günther Blaicher, Tübingen: G. Narr, 26–40.

Žižek, Slavoj (1994), *The Metastases of Enjoyment: On Women and Causality*, London, New York: Verso.

Index

www.ingramcontent.com/pod-product-compliance
Lightning Source LLC
Chambersburg PA
CBHW071500110726
47908CB00003B/681